*Indicates title now out of print.

The series *Making Contemporary Britain* is essential reading for students, as well as providing masterly overviews for the general reader. Each book in the series puts the central themes and problems of the specific topic into clear focus. The studies are written by leading authorities in their field, who integrate the latest research into the text but at the same time present the material in a clear, ordered fashion which can be read with value by those with no prior knowledge of the subject.

THE INSTITUTE OF CONTEMPORARY BRITISH HISTORY

50 Gordon Square, London WC1H 0PQ

British Politics since

St Helens College

Making Contemporary Britain Series

General Editor: Anthony Seldon
Consultant Editor: Peter Hennessy

British Politics since 1945

Peter Dorey

BLACKWELL
Oxford UK & Cambridge USA

The right of Peter Dorey to be identified as author of this work has been asserted in accordance with the Copyright, Designs and Patents Act 1988.

First published 1995

Blackwell Publishers Ltd
108 Cowley Road
Oxford OX4 1JF

Blackwell Publishers Inc.
238 Main Street
Cambridge, Massachusetts 02142
USA

British Library Cataloguing in Publication Data
A CIP catalogue record for this book is available from the British Library.

Library of Congress Cataloging-in-Publication Data
Library of Congress data for this book has been applied for.
ISBN 0 631 19074 0; ISBN 0 631 19075 9 (pbk)

Printed and bound in Great Britain by
Hartnolls Limited, Bodmin, Cornwall
This book is printed on acid-free paper

For Hannah and Rachael

Contents

General Editor's Preface

The Institute of Contemporary British History's series *Making Contemporary Britain* is aimed directly at students and at others interested in learning more about topics in post-war British history. In the series, authors are less attempting to break new ground than presenting clear and balanced overviews of the state of knowledge on each of the topics.

The ICBH was founded in October 1986 with the objective of promoting the study of British history since 1945 at every level. To that end, it publishes books and a quarterly journal, *Contemporary Record*; it organizes seminars and conferences for school students, undergraduates, researchers and teachers of post-war history; and it runs a number of research programmes and other activities.

A central theme of the ICBH's work is that post-war history is too often neglected in British schools, institutes of higher education and beyond. The ICBH acknowledges the validity of the arguments against the study of recent history, notably the problems of bias, of overly subjective teaching and writing and the difficulties of perspective. But it believes that the values of studying post-war history outweigh the drawbacks, and that the health and future of a liberal democracy require that its citizens know more about the most recent past of their country than the limited knowledge possessed by British citizens, young and old, today. Indeed, the ICBH believes that the dangers of political indoctrination are higher where the young are *not* informed of the recent past.

The book series has lacked until now a clear political history, written for students at an introductory level. Peter Dorey has now filled this gap and has done so in a sharply written text which is fully cognizant, unlike many of the other student texts, of the academic debates.

It is a masterly overview, which should meet the needs of all who want to know what the major political parties stood for and enacted when in government after 1945. It will also serve, I hope, as an excellent introduction to other books in the series, which explore the themes discussed in this book in greater depth.

Anthony Seldon

Preface

British politics since 1945 has been a relatively neglected topic amongst political scientists. Although there have been numerous books on specific Governments, and on particular periods, the tacit view appears to have been that a general overview of post-war British politics is best left to historians, thereby enabling political scientists to concentrate on more contemporary issues or theoretical considerations. Certainly, politics as an academic discipline in Britain seems particularly concerned with an 'institutional' approach, with most textbooks, for example, providing a chapter-by-chapter account of the workings of Parliament, the powers of the Prime Minister, the operation of the electoral system, and so on.

Clearly, these are of vital importance in providing an understanding of the British political system, but this 'institutional' approach provides only a partial picture of politics in Britain. Alongside an appreciation of how the various political institutions function and interact, the student of politics also needs a historical perspective, one which examines and explains the key events and developments which have taken place since 1945. Such a perspective is crucial in providing a fuller understanding of how British politics has evolved into its current situation, and how contemporary concerns have emerged.

Furthermore, an understanding of post-war British political history will indicate that many of the issues and problems which politicians are grappling with today are, to some extent, actually recurrences of earlier or previous debates and dilemmas. The notion of 'political cycles' manifests itself, whereby particular issues move to the top of the political agenda at particular junctures, are – apparently – dealt with and resolved, but then re-emerge in some guise at a later stage.

For example, the Labour Party's attempts at modernizing its policies and image during the late 1980s and 1990s, in an attempt at broadening its electoral appeal to the middle classes, echoed the debates and processes which took place inside the party during the late 1950s and early 1960s, when characters such as Anthony Crosland and Hugh Gaitskell sought to make the same kind of changes that Neil Kinnock and Tony Blair pursued three decades later.

A further reason for adopting a historical approach is that for most of the period since 1945, certainly until 1979, British politics was largely 'non-ideological'. Governments tended to govern pragmatically, responding to circumstances and crises as and when they arose, and seeking to implement solutions which were deemed practicable or technical, rather than based on ideological principles or partisan objectives. The corollary of this is that British politics since 1945 has evolved in a gradual, often subtle, manner, which thus requires that the student of politics correspondingly adopts a broader, historical perspective. It may be a cliché, but it none the less remains true that one cannot fully understand the present without some understanding of the past.

This book seeks to provide the basis of such an understanding. It seeks to combine historical narrative with political analysis, examining and explaining the *how* and *why* of what happened, thereby providing the reader with an appreciation of the pressures and processes which have determined post-war British politics, alongside the key events and personalities.

We have tried, as far as possible, to avoid simply basing each chapter on a particular government, opting instead, where appropriate, to focus on decades, in which particular trends or themes were discernible, and which thus provided the context within which Governments sought to govern. Chapter 1 is an exception to this approach, focusing as it does on the 1945–51 Labour Governments led by Clement Attlee, although even here, it is emphasized that the Second World War itself had a major impact and influence on many of the policies introduced during the years of Attlee's premiership. It is emphasized, for example, that some of the policies which have become associated almost exclusively with Attlee and his Governments were in fact formulated during the war iself, and enjoyed considerable cross-party support. Recognition of this vital fact also raises doubts about whether the Attlee Governments were really as radical or as 'socialist' as has often been assumed by both supporters and critics alike.

Chapter 2 focuses on British politics during the 1950s, an era in which the Conservative Party enjoyed three consecutive election victories, thereby raising questions about the future – if any – of the Labour Party. The Conservative Party reaped the electoral benefits of a decade of unprecedented economic prosperity for most British people, leading to Harold Macmillan's famous 'You've never had it so good' speech. Yet even during the course of the 1950s, there was a growing concern that Britain's economic and international position were not as secure or assured as had previously been assumed. The latter half of the decade witnessed the humiliating Suez episode, which raised serious doubts about Britain's role and status as a superpower, whilst at home, politicians became concerned at increasing economic problems, not least of these being inflation. None the less, there was still considerable confidence that Britain remained a society characterized by a very high degree of social and political stability, certainly much greater than that which existed anywhere else in Europe.

Chapter 3 focuses on the 1960s, during which time the concerns that first emerged towards the end of the 1950s become a major preoccupation of British politics, particularly the economic problems. The confidence which many had felt throughout much of the 1950s concerning Britain's economic performance and the efficacy of the country's social and political institutions was replaced by a growing sense of concern and consternation. There was a widespread recognition that things were going wrong, particularly – but not exclusively – in the economic sphere. Indeed, as Britain's economic problems became more extensive and more serious, so attention was increasingly turned towards the alleged deficiencies of certain institutions, such as the trade unions, Parliament, the Civil Service, etc. The premise was that many of Britain's problems stemmed from the outdated manner in which these institutions operated, hence the assumption that institutional reform – to secure 'modernization' – would somehow restore Britain's economic competence and competitiveness, and thereby reverse the process of accelerating decline which had become increasingly apparent. Chapter 3 also illustrates, however, that the 1960s witnessed the emergence of various other problems in British politics, not least of these being the flaring up of conflict in Northern Ireland, and growing concern over (coloured) immigration.

In chapter 4, we note how a sense of crisis often pervaded Britain during the 1970s, as the problems already referred to become deeper and more widespread, whilst being compounded by new developments. Continuing (and worsening) economic problems, growing industrial strife, the escalation of conflict in Northern Ireland, the rise of the far Right, increasing crime and disorder, and demands for devolution or independence for Scotland and Wales, all combined to create a climate of crisis, in which serious questions were raised about the political stability and future of Great Britain/the United Kingdom. There was concern amongst a number of politicians and political scientists alike that Britain was becoming 'ungovernable'.

At the same time, such concerns both reflected and reinforced a popular view – articulated particularly forcefully by certain sections of the tabloid press and individuals on the right of the Conservative Party – that Britain's problems were in large part a consequence of moral decline. It was argued by many that traditional values and lifestyles had been undermined or subverted by 'progressive' ideas and new social movements which had emerged during the 1960s. These, it was maintained, had encouraged the excessive questioning of authority and long-established social practices (such as marriage, sexual fidelity, etc), particularly by the young, to the extent that law and morality were effectively being undermined and challenged. The outcome, it was claimed, was evident in the increase in social unrest, civil disorder, political violence and direct action, divorce, illegitimacy, single parenthood, football hooliganism, drug addiction, and 'welfare dependency'. In short, Britain was deemed to be suffering from a 'surfeit' of permissiveness. What was needed, therefore, according to the proponents of this view, was the 'smack of firm government' which would restore order and authority, and replace 'trendy ideas' by the 'traditional values' which had been so disastrously discarded. It was this critique which constituted much of the basis of what was to become known as 'Thatcherism'.

Chapter 5 deals with the 1980s, the decade of Margaret Thatcher's premiership. This was a decade in which a number of radical policy initiatives were pursued, such as privatization, comprehensive curbs on trade unions, reform of local government, the Anglo-Irish Agreement, and anti-inflationary economic policies which disregarded the ensuing high levels of unemployment. Meanwhile, the decade witnessed events whose outcome served to boost further Margaret Thatcher's image as a tough, conviction leader, most notably the Falklands War in 1982 and the miners' strike of 1984–5. Margaret Thatcher's 'iron lady' image was reinforced by her strongly nationalistic stance towards Britain's partners in the European Community.

Meanwhile, the decade yielded important developments amongst the Opposition parties, with a new political party being formed by a group of MPs breaking away from the Labour Party in response to its swing to the left. This new party, the Social Democratic Party, eventually underwent a further split, when a majority of its membership amalgamated with the Liberal Party to form the Liberal Democrats, whereupon a small 'rump' of anti-merger SDP members tried in vain to keep their party going as separate entity.

The Labour Party, meanwhile, ended the decade seeking to modernize its image and policies by jettisoning the left-wing programme with which it had forlornly fought the 1983 and 1987 general elections. With Labour abandoning its left-wing policies, and Margaret Thatcher's replacement as Conservative leader and Prime Minister at the end of 1990 by the more emollient John Major, speculation grew that British politics was about to move back to the ideological centre.

Chapter 6 subjects this speculation to closer examination, focusing as it does on the 'pursuit of post-Thatcherism' from 1990 to 1994 under John Major's premiership. The policies pursued by John Major, the manner in which they have been pursued, and the problems he has encountered with some of his own colleagues in the Conservative Party, are all delineated.

The chapter also highlights the Labour Party's continued process of modernization, noting in particular the changing character of the relationship with the trade unions, and Tony Blair's commitment to revising Labour's constitution with a view to amending or even abolishing Clause IV. The chapter concludes with a consideration of the claim that British politics in the 1990s is characterized by a new consensus.

Chapter 7 provides an outline of three perspectives of British politics since 1945, namely the critiques advanced by those on the Right, those on the Left, and those who can be deemed to occupy a 'Centrist' (to some extent, Liberal Democratic) position. The chapter illustrates the extent to which post-war British politics is subject to vastly different interpretations and explanations. In so doing, it indicates that 'the facts' do not speak for themselves, as is so often claimed, but that political scientists and historians have to make judgements about them, however much they might profess or plead objectivity and impartiality.

The final chapter of the book, chapter 8, seeks to identify some broader themes and trends concerning British politics since 1945. In particular, it notes the extent to which post-war British politics has been characterized by pragmatism, and an 'incremental' approach to policy-making and problem-solving. This in turn reflects and reinforces the degree of importance which has been attached to consultation and consent in British politics. When Governments have sought to impose policies without having first consulted 'affected parties' and obtained their acquiescence, the policies have often proved less successful, and required significant amendment at the implementation stage, or occasionally been abandoned altogether. In many respects, even the Thatcher Governments proved rather more incremental and pragmatic than both their supporters and critics would acknowledge. The implication is that, to a certain extent, it does not necessarily matter too much which political party is in office, for Governments tend to face a similar repertoire or range of problems, and invariably find their room for manoeuvre impinged upon by a variety of constraints and circumstances.

It is intended that this text will provide the reader with a clearer understanding of the events which have defined and determined British politics since 1945, and the issues thereby raised. This in turn will hopefully highlight the problems of governing modern Britain, whilst simultaneously placing contemporary concerns and conundrums in a broader historical context.

In writing this book, I have received invaluable assistance and advice from a number of people. In particular, I would like to thank Anthony Seldon for providing me with the opportunity of writing this book, and for the encouragement which he offered throughout. I would also like to thank the members of the editorial team at Blackwell – Tessa Harvey, Jill Landeryou and Simon Prosser – for their enthusiasm and support whilst this book was being written. Heartfelt thanks are also due to Karen Owen for her help in typing parts of the original manuscript – as the Politics Secretary at Cardiff University, she really is irreplaceable and indispensable, so important is the role she plays, and the cheerful, unflappable manner in which she performs it. Last, but by no means least, I would like publicly to thank colleagues here at Cardiff with whom this book has been discussed at various stages. In particular, I am grateful for the comments and criticisms (always constructive!) of: David Broughton, Gordon Cumming, Mark Donovan, Chris Ealham,

David Hanley, J. Barry Jones, Stephen Mew, Duncan Mitchell, and Nick Parsons. Needless to say, I accept full responsibility for any faults or errors which remain.

Peter Dorey
March 1995
The West Country

Acknowledgement

The author and publishers are grateful to the Estate of Robert Frost and Jonathan Cape publishers for their kind permission to quote from Robert Frost's poem 'The Road Not Taken' at the beginning of chapter 1.

1 Achievements to Atrophy under Attlee (1945–51)

> Two roads diverged in a wood, and I – I took the one less travelled by, and that has made all the difference.
>
> Robert Frost, 'The Road Not Taken'

Labour's Surprise Election Victory

The victory of the Labour Party in the 1945 general election cannot be fully understood without first considering briefly Labour's role in the Wartime Coalition Government which was formed in 1940. It was participation in this administration which provided the Labour Party with invaluable experience and credibility, and which thus enabled it to appear as a serious and worthy contender for governmental office once the war was over. The war itself had also served to foster a framework of attitudes and aspirations amongst millions of people which, broadly speaking, prompted an unprecedented degree of support for 'collectivist' policies and government intervention in economic and social affairs. To an extent which no-one could have foreseen when the Second World War broke out in 1939, the ethos engendered during the next six years was one very much in tune with that of the Labour Party. According to one labour historian, Attlee and his colleagues:

> were especially fortunate, in that they came to power at the end of a long war, during which they had experienced office as members of a coalition government, and with many controls of the type that they might have wished to impose already in force as a result of wartime conditions. (Pelling 1983: 255)

Labour had experienced political office on two occasions prior to the Coalition Government of the Second World War, but on both occasions it had constituted a minority government. On the first occasion, following the 1923 election, Labour held office for only one year, whilst on the second occasion, from 1929 to 1931, the minority Labour Government fell when three of its Ministers – including its leader and Prime Minister, Ramsay Macdonald – incurred the undying wrath of the labour movement by joining a 'National' (Coalition) Government dominated by the Conservative Party.

It proved to be something of an irony, therefore, that the Labour Party's credibility was eventually restored through participation in another National Coalition Government again dominated by Conservatives. Labour entered the Wartime Coalition Government in May 1940, when Neville Chamberlain was replaced as Conservative Party leader and Prime Minister by Winston Churchill. Indeed, one commentator has suggested that 'May 1940 was in some ways more crucial for the Party than July 1945' (Howell 1976: 107). The Labour leader Clement Attlee was eventually (in 1942) appointed Deputy Prime Minister, whilst Herbert Morrison – who thought that he, rather than Attlee, ought to be Labour leader and Prime Minister – was to spend much of his time at the Home Office. Meanwhile, Ernest Bevin, the leader of Britain's then largest trade union, the Transport and General Workers, was appointed Minister of Labour, which ensured that the trade unions, as well as the Labour Party, were involved at the very heart of government, and thus similarly in a position to acquire greater credibility and public respect. As Kenneth Morgan, author of the seminal text on the 1945–51 Labour Governments, remarks: 'The government, the labour movement, the very mood of the nation were henceforth transformed' (Morgan 1984: 19). The extent of this transformation became most apparent once the war was over.

Almost immediately after Germany's surrender in May 1945, Winston Churchill sought the Labour Party's opinion on when a general election should be held. Two options were canvassed by Churchill, namely an immediate election, or an election after the war with Japan had been concluded (with the Coalition Government continuing in the meantime). After consulting his colleagues, Clement Attlee suggested that the Coalition should continue until the autumn, with the election being held then, partly because a new, up-to-date electoral register would be published during this time, and partly because an autumn election would be fairer to candidates who had been serving in the armed forces, ensuring that they enjoyed sufficient time to make themselves known to the voters. The Labour Party leadership was also understandably concerned that an immediate general election would allow Churchill to be swept to power on a wave of post-war euphoria. Ironically, in the letter which he sent to Churchill explaining Labour's decision to opt for an autumn election, Attlee warned the Conservative leader and Prime Minister: 'Should you, however, decide on an election in July despite all the disadvantages to the electors set out in this letter, with which you are familiar, the responsibility must and will, of course, be yours' (quoted in Attlee 1954: 138). So it proved to be. Churchill, urged on by a number of Conservative colleagues (and by Lord Beaverbrook, the right-wing owner of the *Daily Express*), did opt for an early election, and therefore visited Buckingham Palace to request a dissolution of Parliament on 23 May. The election was set for 5 July, thereby allowing a generous six weeks for campaigning and canvassing.

The Labour Party's programme placed strong emphasis on the attainment of full employment, the manifesto *Let Us Face the Future* insisting that:

> if we need to keep a firm public hand on industry in order to get jobs for all, very well. No more dole queues, in order to let the Czars of Big Business remain kings in their own castles. The price of so-called 'economic freedom' for the few is too high if it is bought at the cost of idleness and misery for millions.

Let Us Face the Future also emphasized Labour's commitment to: nationalization ('There are basic industries ripe and over-ripe for public ownership and management in the service of the nation'); a house-building programme which would ensure that 'every family in this land has a good standard of accommodation'; the extension of education, through raising the school leaving age, and ensuring the availability to all children and young people of free secondary schools and further education institutions; the creation of a National Health Service; and a proper system of social security – 'social provision against rainy days, coupled with economic policies calculated to keep rainy days to a minimum'. It was with policy pledges such as these that the Labour Party promised to provide 'a great programme of modernisation and re-equipment of its homes, its factories and machinery, its schools, its social services' in order to build 'a New Britain'.

The Conservative Party, meanwhile, accepted 'as one of its primary aims and responsibilities the maintenance of a high and stable level of employment', whilst acknowledging that this might entail 'mutual co-operation between industry and the State'. The Conservatives' manifesto – entitled *Mr Churchill's Declaration of Policy to the Electors* – also placed the utmost importance on housing, to the extent that the need for price controls on building materials was acknowledged, as was the necessity of providing subsidies to both local authorities and private builders alike. The party even stipulated a target for the number of homes which it sought to build, namely 220,000 completed during the first two years in office, with a further 80,000 under construction.

Mr Churchill's Declaration of Policy to the Electors also promised the establishment of 'a nation-wide and compulsory scheme of National Insurance' which would provide a system of social security benefits linked to each citizen's national insurance contributions paid via their wages whilst in employment, although special provision would be made for those sections of society not in paid employment, and not therefore directly paying such contributions, such as housewives, the sick and the disabled.

Meanwhile, there was also a pledge to establish 'a comprehensive health service', but one which eschewed the nationalization of hospitals (envisaged by Labour) in favour of leaving voluntary hospitals free, whilst functioning 'in friendly partnership with local authority hospitals'.

The Conservatives' manifesto serves to endorse the view that had the Party won the 1945 election, it would have pursued a number of policies not dissimilar to those implemented by the Attlee Government, although clearly a Conservative Government would not have created quite the same kind of health service as Bevan was to embark upon, nor would a Churchill administration have gone as far as the Attlee Government in nationalizing key industries and natural monopolies or public utilities. Yet even whilst acknowledging these caveats, it is apparent from a perusal of their respective manifestos that the Labour and Conservative Parties were thinking along broadly similar lines in 1945 in many areas of policy. How far a Conservative Government would actually have gone in implementing these policies if it had won in 1945 must forever remain a matter of speculation. The fact that the Conservatives retained most of the policies inherited from Labour when they won the 1951 general election does not itself prove that they would have pursued all of those policies themselves had they won in 1945.

Polling day was officially 5 July, but the results were not announced until 26 July. This was partly because in certain northern towns, polling day clashed with annual summer holidays, and hence the towns concerned – comprising nineteen constituencies, mainly in Lancashire – conducted their polls a week or two later. A further important source of delay was the time required to collect and collate the votes of Britain's armed forces still abroad.

When the results were announced, they came as a complete shock to the Conservative and Labour Parties alike. Many Conservatives expected that Churchill's leadership during the war itself would stand him and their party in good stead with the voters, whilst the Labour Party envisaged a hung parliament in which it would be the single largest party.

Instead, the 1945 election yielded an overwhelming victory for the Labour Party, led by Clement Attlee. Having held 166 seats in the previous Parliament, Labour won 393 seats in 1945, whilst the Conservative Party (and its allies) slumped from 397 to 213 seats. The Liberal Party saw its parliamentary representation decline from 20 seats to just 12, confirming its relegation to third-party status. In terms of actual votes, Labour received the support of just under 12 million people, whilst the Conservatives were supported by almost 10 million voters. The Liberal Party won just under 2.25 million votes.

The scale and scope of Labour's parliamentary majority in 1945 was deemed by the Party to represent an emphatic mandate from the British electorate to embark on a new course. According to Attlee: 'it was clear that there could be no return to past conditions. The old pattern was worn out and it was for us to weave the new . . . We had not been elected to try to patch up an old system but to make something new' (Attlee 1954: 163). Certainly, the election result was widely deemed to reflect and represent a leftward shift in public opinion. As we shall note during the course of this chapter, part of the reason for this apparent move to the left was the degree of state intervention in social and economic affairs which the war effort had engendered. Whereas the termination of the war might have been expected to have resulted in a backlash against the 'activist' state, the opposite seems to have occurred to a significant extent. This was because many voters, impressed by the success of state intervention during the war, wondered optimistically what might be achieved by the maintenance of an active state in peacetime. The war had served to raise the expectations of millions of British people about what government could achieve, and as such, many voters were not willing to tolerate a return to *laissez-faire*.

It should also be noted that Labour's role and conduct as a partner in the Coalition Government during the war had served to illustrate the Party's responsibilty and patriotism. This enabled it to secure the trust and confidence of many voters who might not otherwise have contemplated or risked voting Labour. Even though Labour campaigned on what was widely perceived to be a radical manifesto, the Party had none the less acquired an aura of respectability hitherto unattainable. By the same token, Labour's participation in the Wartime Coalition Government meant that, by the 1945 election, only two Ministers in Attlee's Cabinet had not previously held governmental office.

In view of Labour's new-found respectability, coupled with the Party's responsibility in the Coalition Government, Churchill's speech during the election campaign warning that a Labour victory would lead to totalitarianism in Britain, on the grounds that 'no socialist system could be established without a political police, a Gestapo', seemed singularly ill-judged and jejune.

Meanwhile, in the wake of their Party's emphatic electoral defeat, the bitter disappointment of some Conservatives manifested itself in a form of churlish petulance and irascible rancour (Kilmuir 1964: 136–47). In view of the Conservative Party's long-standing belief that it is 'the natural Party of government', the defeat in 1945 was clearly a particularly traumatic one.

The new Labour Government was characterized by a particularly noteworthy blend of youth and experience. Of course, given the number of seats won by the Labour Party in 1945, it was inevitable that the majority of its MPs – 250 out of 393 – would be sitting in the House of Commons for the first time because Labour had never previously secured such strong parliamentary representation. Yet at the same time, Attlee's first Cabinet contained many Ministers who had established their reputations and competence in the Wartime Coalition Government. For example, Hugh Dalton was appointed Chancellor of the Exchequer, Ernest Bevin became Foreign Secretary, Stafford Cripps took up the post of President of the Board of Trade, and Aneurin Bevan became Minister of Health. Meanwhile, Herbert Morrison became Lord President of the Council (with special responsibilities for co-ordinating domestic policies), whilst Harold Greenwood was appointed Lord Privy Seal. In view of the programme which this administration was about to implement, it is interesting to note that within Attlee's first Cabinet 'the Left was under-represented', its only standard-bearer being Bevan (Eatwell 1979: 47), although this is perhaps to overlook Emmanuel Shinwell, who served in the Cabinet as Minister of Fuel and Power.

Nationalization

For many in the Labour Party, both during the years of the Attlee Governments and ever since, the pursuit of nationalization was and is a litmus test of the Party's commitment to socialism. If capitalism was predicated upon private ownership of industry, then it logically followed that the creation of socialism required this ownership to be taken out of private hands and placed in the public domain on behalf of 'the people'. During the late 1950s, and then in the mid-1990s, this premise was seriously challenged by many in the Labour Party who considered the importance attached to nationalization (as enshrined in Clause IV of the Party's constitution) both simplistic and outdated. It was also deemed unpopular with the electorate, and thus a source of lost votes for the Labour Party, especially amongst the burgeoning middle class.

Yet upon election to governmental office in 1945, the Labour Party under Attlee's leadership appeared to be fully committed to a programme of extensive nationalization (it was partly the degree of state control that such a programme would entail which led to Churchill's alarmist warning during the election campaign about a Labour 'gestapo' being established in Britain). A couple of years before the outbreak of the Second World War, Clement Attlee had declared that under a Labour Government: 'All the major industries will be owned and controlled by the community . . .' (Attlee 1937: 152–3).

Apart from the general premise that nationalization was a defining feature or criterion of socialism, a number of other arguments were variously advanced in its favour by Labour Party members and supporters at the time of the 1945–50 Attlee Government. Some viewed nationalization of industry as a prerequisite or essential component of economic planning and regulation of the economy, to which Labour was also ideologically committed. Others considered it morally wrong that certain utilities essential to everyone, and which were, in any case, a natural, God-given, part of the world around us – such as water, gas, coal, etc. – should be owned by, and provide a source of wealth for, a small number of businessmen. Such utilities, it was believed, ought to be considered part of the community, which thus rendered their private ownership unacceptable.

Another reason why some in the Labour Party during this time were keen on nationalization was the belief (difficult to understand today) that public ownership would prove more efficient than private ownership and the 'anarchy' of the free market. This perspective enjoyed considerable credence at the time partly because of the experiences of some of the industries whilst under private ownership. For example, the coal industry was notorious for its lack of investment, and the poor industrial relations within it. Meanwhile, there was a recognition that a national and rational transport system could not be guaranteed unless transport itself was taken into public ownership.

Finally, there was the expectation (how naive it sounds in hindsight!) that nationalization would usher in a new era of harmonious industrial relations, as workers felt for the first time that they were working for the good of the community and their society, rather than being exploited by a ruthless employer or a handful of faceless shareholders who reaped the profits which the workers themselves ultimately produced through the product of their labour. For all these reasons, members and supporters of the Attlee Governments considered nationalization to be a core component of a fairer, more efficient, more harmonious Britain. According to Attlee, 'the creation of a society based on social justice ... could only be attained by bringing under public ownership and control the main factors in the economic system' (Attlee 1954: 162–3). Such faith in the alleged virtues of nationalization were, of course, partly due to the success engendered by state intervention and regulation during the war itself.

The first industry to be nationalized by the 1945–50 Attlee Government was the Bank of England, in 1946. The following year witnessed the nationalization of the coal industry, along with Cable and Wireless, whilst in 1948 the railways, electricity, gas and road transport were taken into public ownership. Finally, in 1949, legislation to nationalize iron and steel was passed, although actual nationalization was deferred until after the 1950 general election.

The particular form which most of these nationalizations took was the creation of a board or similar body – formally appointed by a government minister – which would be responsible for day-to-day management of the industries, but which would operate according to guidelines stipulated by the appropriate minister, to whom the chairman would be accountable. In practice, the lines of responsibilty were not always as clear-cut, and there existed a tension between the day-to-day degree of autonomy which the nationalized industries required in order to operate in a predominantly 'market economy' in which they too had to consider commercial factors, and, at the same time, the constitutional position concerning the degree of political direction and ministerial responsibility (to Parliament) entailed. The establishment of the semi-independent 'boards' to run the nationalized industries was always something of a messy compromise, representing a half-way house between autonomy and accountability.

The dilemma of the nationalized industries was compounded by the fact that they were expected to operate as far as possible on commercial lines, covering their operating costs through the revenues charged for their services or products, yet they were simultaneously required to consider the public interest, which ultimately meant that economic criteria had to be counterbalanced by social considerations. For example, British Rail might have felt that a particular rural route or service was not commercially viable, yet at the same time would be expected to bear in mind the importance of that route or service to the people living in the area concerned. Put starkly, the nationalized industries were sometimes put in a position whereby they were simultaneously expected to act both as a commercial enterprise and as a social or public service.

Full Employment

Prior to the Second World War, mass unemployment was widely considered to be an unfortunate, but unavoidable fact of economic life. Indeed, there were many who blamed the unemployed themselves for their plight, accusing them of being lazy, workshy, and feckless (one still hears these expressions of ignorance and insensitivity today).

However, the Second World War itself heralded a change in attitudes amongst the public and politicians alike, so that long before the end of the war, the goal of full employment had moved to the top of the political agenda. Three particular factors prompted this widespread rejection of the erstwhile acceptability or inevitability of mass unemployment.

Firstly, the war effort itself served to indicate the extent to which jobs could be created through the concerted action and intervention of the state in the economy. Indeed, the main employment problem during the war was that of labour shortages, for with so many men engaged in military service, domestic industry faced a number of labour shortages and recruitment problems. So serious was the situation that the Wartime Coalition Government effectively suspended patriarchal ideology and positively encouraged women to leave the kitchen and enter the factories, to the extent of providing child-care facilities. (Of course, once the war was over, women were expected to return quietly to their domestic role and responsibilities, the state no longer accepted responsibility for the provision of child-care for working mothers, and mothers who did go out to work were often frowned upon, the implication being that their children would suffer psychologically and emotionally from the lack of 'maternal bonding'.)

The degree – and success – of government intervention in the economy during the war (including the direction of labour) served to destroy much of the hitherto *laissez-faire* orthodoxy which had insisted that 'there is no alternative' to 'the market'. What the war effort illustrated, however, was not only that government intervention could work for the common good and the national interest, but, *pari passu*, that market forces alone were incapable of meeting the needs of the nation at a time of crisis. Even before the end of the war, therefore, many Conservatives themselves were insisting that their Party was not – and had never been – an advocate of the unfettered free market or untrammelled market forces. The history of British Conservatism was effectively rewritten to emphasize the Party's apparent long-standing commitment to social reform and willingness to use the state to assist those most in need in society.

Following on from the previous point, there was considerable concern that unless the state took a greater responsibility for employment (and economic management generally) once the war was over, then many of the soldiers risking life and limb for their country would merely return home to a life back on the dole, from where some of them had been recruited in the first place. There was a widespread acceptance, amongst both politicians and the public, that those fighting for Britain and for freedom deserved rather more than to return home to the dole queue.

The third reason why the war precipitated a public and political rejection of mass unemployment was that the economic theories of John Maynard Keynes finally became much more widely accepted by political leaders and Treasury mandarins. At its simplest, Keynesianism insisted that governments had it in their power to regulate the level of employment by virtue of regulating other economic variables, such as levels of demand in the economy, investment, interest rates, taxation, and so on. By adjusting these economic variables, Keynes argued, governments could increase demand in the economy (this demand manifesting itself in terms of greater consumer spending and purchasing power), which would therefore lead to the expansion of jobs as employers recruited more workers to cope with this increased demand.

At the same time, government expenditure itself would also stimulate demand in the economy. All of this would establish a virtuous circle, whereby higher levels of employment would mean more people spending money buying goods and services, which in turn would yield more employment opportunities as employers recruited more workers to cope with this increased demand.

Once the war was over, other factors emerged to underpin the commitment to full employment (actually meaning that not more than 3 per cent of the male workforce was unemployed), not least of these being that full employment was necessary to finance the welfare state (discussed below). It was recognized that a return to high unemployment would mean not only intolerable sums of money being paid out through the welfare state in the form of social security, but also a substantial loss of revenue – via income tax and national insurance contributions – which was needed to finance the welfare state in the first place.

It was also recognized by 1945 that a commitment to full employment was good electoral politics. Public expectations had been raised by the war effort and the success of government intervention which it had engendered. It would have been political suicide for a party to have entered the 1945 election campaign pledging a return to mass unemployment. There thus emerged a bipartisan commitment to the pursuit of full employment, and whilst the Conservative Party baulked at the degree of state intervention and regulation which Labour countenanced, it did not demur from a commitment to securing full employment.

The Welfare State

Although it is often taken for granted that the 1945–50 Attlee Government was the creator of Britain's welfare state, it ought not to be overlooked that several social reforms had been introduced by various governments previously. For example, a number of legislative measures to improve the living conditions of the masses had been introduced by the Conservative administration of Benjamin Disraeli back in the 1870s, whilst Lloyd George, as Chancellor in the 1906–11 Liberal Government led by Herbert Asquith, introduced his 'people's budget', which amongst other things provided a number of social security benefits pertaining to old age, sickness and unemployment. However, pensions were means-tested, whilst benefit payments for those who were sick or out of work depended upon their having paid national insurance contributions during employment.

As with state intervention in the economy, and the goal of full employment, the Second World War proved to be the catalyst which prompted widespread political acceptance of the need for a comprehensive system of welfare provision. Indeed, one social historian insists that even before the outbreak of the war, there had emerged amongst Britain's party leaders 'a private political consensus' that the state needed to ensure a national system of welfare provision for the most vulnerable sections of society (Gilbert 1970: vii).

Major moves in this direction were made during the war, with William Beveridge's *Report on Social Insurance and Allied Services*, published in November 1942, effectively providing the blueprint for the welfare state which would be established by the Attlee Government after the war. Beveridge declared his objective of eliminating the five 'giants' of 'Want, Disease, Ignorance, Squalor and Idleness'. To this end, Beveridge urged that the existing schemes for pensions, sickness and unemployment be consolidated and combined into a universal scheme of national insurance, with entitlement to be based on national insurance contributions, rather than the widely hated means test. At the same time, Beveridge recommended that those not eligible for these 'contributory' benefits and pensions (because they had not paid national insurance, for example) should be covered by a parallel system of means-tested benefits, whereby need, not national insurance contributions, would be the determinant of eligibility for assistance.

However, Beveridge believed that as far as possible, welfare provision should be linked to national insurance contributions, partly in order to help finance the social security system, of course, but also to maintain a semblance of individual responsibility, to prevent the idea that people were getting something for nothing. Entitlement would therefore be determined at least in part by what people had themselves paid in whilst working. At the same time, Beveridge envisaged that by linking eligibility to contributions, people receiving social security payments would no longer feel that they were recipients of charity, with all the humiliation and stigma that this often entailed. Instead, they would recognize that their welfare benefits were not hand-outs, but entitlements.

The publication of the Beveridge Report and the recommendations contained therein received widespread political support, with many Conservatives echoing Labour's endorsement of the proposals, although some, including Churchill himself, were concerned at the costs that implementation of the Beveridge Report would entail. However, Churchill's consternation at the financial implications of implementing Beveridge's proposals was ultimately subordinated to recognition of the political and electoral costs of *not* accepting them (Kavanagh and Morris 1989: 73). A flavour of the type of acclaim which the Beveridge Report attracted even amongst non-socialists was evident in *The Economist* at the time, which described it as 'one of the most remarkable state documents ever drafted', before proceeding to suggest that:

> The true test of the Beveridge Plan is whether or not it will inspire, regardless of vested interests, a nation-wide determination to set right what is so plainly wrong and a series of prompt decisions by the Government to ensure that whatever else this war may bring, social security and economic progress shall march together. (*The Economist*, 5 December 1942)

Analytically, the welfare state implemented by the 1945 Attlee Government can best be understood in terms of its four main spheres of policy, namely social security, the National Health Service, housing and education.

Social security

The consolidation of existing contributory benefit and pension schemes was brought about by the 1946 National Insurance Act. This constructed a comprehensive, universal system of benefits and pensions covering unemployment, sickness, motherhood and retirement. Payment of such benefits was funded by the national insurance contributions paid out of the wages of those in employment (usually full-time).

At the same time, a series of means-tested social security benefits were introduced for citizens who either lacked the requisite national insurance contributions, or whose benefits (based on their contributions) were inadequate to meet their basic day-to-day needs. These two categories of social security benefits, contributory and means-tested, were intended to ensure that all citizens were effectively guaranteed a minimum income, whatever their circumstances, from 'cradle to grave'.

National Health Service

For many, the National Health Service has been the jewel in the crown of the welfare state. The National Health Service was formally established in 1948, although the appropriate legislation had been passed two years previously. However, not only did such a major institution require time to be established, it was also necessary for the Attlee Government – particularly the Minister of Health, Aneurin Bevan – to overcome the opposition of sections of the medical profession.

The overall objective of the National Health Service was an equality of access to health care and medical treatment, irrespective of economic wealth or social status. No longer would medical care be dependent upon ability to pay, or require a family to wipe out their life savings in order to cover the cost of health care for one of its members suffering from illness or disease. Health care was to be free at the point of access (i.e. use), but paid for (like other components of the welfare state) by citizens through their taxes and national insurance contributions. On this point, Bevan was emphatic that: 'To call it something for nothing is absurd because everything has to be paid for in some way or another' (Bevan 1978: 106).

The 1946 National Health Service Act nationalized Britain's hospitals, whereupon they were placed under the control of regional boards, rather than leaving them to be run by local authorities as had previously been the case. A major reason for nationalizing them was to ensure uniformity of treatment throughout the country; the alternative, it was feared, was to maintain a plethora of hospitals (approximately 1,500) and health services run by local authorities, in which case regional disparities in resources and treatment would militate against *equal* access to, and standards of, health care and provision – what citizens received would depend in large part on where they lived, rather than on what they needed. It is interesting to note, incidentally, that Bevan's insistence on taking hospitals out of local authority control caused some friction with a few ministerial colleagues, not least Herbert Morrison, who wanted local authorities to retain a significant role in the provision of health care. A tension was thus evident between the drive towards standardization and equality insisted upon by Bevan, and the defence of accountability and responsiveness to local needs called for by Morrison.

Bevan faced greater opposition, however, from sections of the medical profession itself. In particular, the doctors' main pressure group, the British Medical Association, objected to state control of health care, not least because of the threat this posed to their professional status and autonomy. Eventually, in 1948, the BMA backed down, partly because of concessions offered by Bevan (such as permitting doctors in NHS hospitals to maintain a system of 'pay beds' for private patients), and partly because some of the concessions offered served to split the BMA membership, with increasing numbers of doctors and GPs supporting the implementation of the NHS. The BMA therefore recognized that it could no longer sustain united opposition to Bevan amongst the medical profession, and thus abandoned – rather reluctantly – its boycott of the NHS.

Housing

Although he had been appointed Minister of Health, Bevan was also charged with responsibilty for Labour's housing policy, and hence its manifesto commitment to pursue an ambitious programme of house-building. Not surprisingly perhaps, in view of the damage done to hundreds of thousands of dwellings by enemy bombing during the war, housing had been 'the issue which concerned voters the most during the 1945 election' (Eatwell 1979: 64–5). Bevan was keen to ensure that the vast majority of new houses would be in the public sector, rented out to those on low incomes and thus unable to afford to buy a home of their own. However, the Government's commitment to a massive house-building programme was seriously hampered by shortages of labour and building materials, compounded by the fact that these elements were also needed for other construction projects such as hospitals, schools and factories.

The Attlee Government had entered office apparently committed to the building of one million houses, yet by the end of January 1946, six months after coming to power, only 20,000 new houses had been completed. The situation did improve during the course of the year, to the extent that by the end of 1946, 188,000 new homes were under construction. Indeed, by the end of its six years in office in 1951, Labour could claim, with a reasonable degree of pride, that it had presided over the construction of just over one million new houses. This effectively 'prevented housing becoming an electoral albatross in the 1950 and 1951 general elections as had at one time seemed very probable' (Morgan 1984: 169).

Education

There was limited innovation by the Attlee Government in the realm of education because the 1944 Education Act, passed by the Coalition Government, had already introduced a significant change in this area. The Attlee Government was left largely to implement and oversee the 1944 Act, which established secondary schooling for all children, but involved a process of selection at the age of 11. This entailed the 11–plus exam, which was used to determine which type of school a pupil would proceed to, namely grammar, secondary modern or technical. In practice, there were few technical schools, and hence the majority of pupils were placed in either grammar or secondary modern schools. This served to institutionalize a class divide in education, for the vast majority of pupils in grammar schools came from middle-class families, whilst those who attended secondary modern schools were invariably of working-class origin. At the time, many assumed that this indicated the inherently higher intelligence of middle-class pupils. Only later did sociological explanations, focusing on environmental and cultural factors, become more widely accepted in accounting for the relatively poor educational performance of working-class pupils.

Labour's main innovation in the sphere of education was to raise the school leaving age, in 1947, from 14 to 15. Education was to become a much more important and prominent policy issue for the Labour Party in future years, but having come to power in 1945 just a year after the passage of a major piece of reforming legislation in this sphere, the Attlee Government evidently felt that there was little scope for further radicalism or innovation. Indeed, it is perhaps significant that in his political memoirs, Clement Attlee devoted just six lines to education in the chapter entitled 'Work of the Labour Government'.

The Role of the Trade Unions

The trade unions had acquired an unprecedented degree of responsibility and authority during the Second World War. The need for their co-operation in the war effort had resulted in Ernest Bevin, leader of the Transport and General Workers Union, being appointed Minister of Labour, whilst trade union representatives sat on a number of Whitehall committees.

Labour's victory in the 1945 general election ensured that the trade unions would continue to enjoy a significant degree of influence and involvement. This continuation and consolidation of the trade unions' wartime role was ensured by three particular factors:

1 The trade unions had close organizational and financial links with the Labour Party. For example, trade unions were represented at Labour's annual conference, where their delegates could predominate by virtue of the block vote. Trade unions also enjoyed representation on Labour's National Executive Committee. Furthermore, of the 393

Labour MPs elected in 1945, 120 were sponsored by trade unions, with 29 of these being appointed to ministerial posts, six of them being in the Cabinet itself. Bevin's successor at the Ministry of Labour, for example, was George Isaacs, the leader of the Trades Union Congress (TUC) (Pelling 1963: 221–2).

2   Trade union representatives continued to sit on a variety of governmental committees after the war, addressing a whole range of economic, industrial and social issues, and helping to formulate policies in these areas. Whereas in 1939, the trade unions had enjoyed representation on only 12 governmental committees, by 1949, union representatives sat on no fewer than 60 such bodies (Allen 1960: 34).

3   The Labour Party and the trade unions shared a great many policy objectives and political goals, and consequently found it desirable, even necessary, to work together. Only through close co-operation would their shared objectives effectively be realized. In this respect, the Attlee Government and the trade unions were, to a considerable extent, reliant upon each other. For example, the trade unions looked to the Attlee Government to repeal the despised 1927 Trades Disputes Act (passed by Stanley Baldwin's Conservative Government in the aftermath of the General Strike, and placing serious curbs on the rights and activities of trade unions), whilst the Attlee Government looked to the trade unions to exercise wage restraint and to practise 'responsible' collective bargaining, in order to ensure the economic conditions necessary for the creation and maintenance of full employment (a policy objective fully supported by the trade unions anyway).

One of the first legislative initiatives taken by the Attlee Government was indeed the repeal of the aforementioned Trades Disputes Act, so that 'contracting-in' to the political levy, whereby trade unionists wishing to contribute to their union's political fund had explicitly to state this wish, was replaced by 'contracting-out'. This served to increase immediately Labour's income from 'the members of unions with political funds who had not previously taken steps to contract-in, and who now, with equal passivity, failed to contract-out' (Pelling 1963: 222). It has been estimated that between 1945 and 1947, 'the number of trade unionists paying the political levy rose by approximately two million' (Kavanagh and Morris 1989: 53).

However, it was not long before tensions became discernible in the relationship between the Labour Government and the trade unions, tensions which have recurred ever since. In the face of serious economic difficulties, the Attlee Government elected in 1945 was eager to ensure that the trade unions practised wage restraint, yet at the same time it sought to avoid introducing an incomes policy, not least because of the trade unions' firm belief in free collective bargaining – that is, collective bargaining between unions and employers *free* from intervention by the state. Indeed, the Attlee Government itself professed its support for free collective bargaining, yet was simultaneously pursuing a broader policy which entailed considerable intervention in, and regulation of, the economy. The dilemma of seeking to exercise greater control over economic activity without also exercising greater control over wages soon became evident, particularly when nationalization and the expansion of the public services sector made government itself the employer. The problem facing the Attlee Government was clearly illustrated at Labour's 1947 annual conference, when the general secretary of the Transport Workers Union, Arthur Deakin, warned that 'Under no circumstances will we accept the position that the responsibility for the determination of wages . . . is one for Government.'

What further compounded the problem for the Attlee Government (and successive governments until 1979) was that whilst the pursuit of full employment required the trade unions to practise wage restraint, it actually served to strengthen their bargaining power, making it easier for them to press for higher wages. In other words, full employment meant providing trade unions with greater power whilst simultaneously demanding that they did not exercise it.

By 1948, however, concern over the state of the British economy was such that the Attlee Government was able to secure TUC support for a voluntary wage freeze, although trade union agreement was largely based on the assumption that this was a short-term measure, a temporary pause to help the Government through what they saw as its transient economic problems (Taylor 1993: 53). None the less, the following year, the TUC overwhelmingly voted to accept a further twelve-month pay freeze.

However, by early 1950, there was increasing opposition within the trade unions – particularly amongst the rank-and-file members on the factory floor – to any continuation of the wage freeze. This opposition was derived to a large extent from the fact that September 1949 had witnessed a devaluation of the pound, which thus had a detrimental impact on the cost of living by virtue of making imports more expensive.

Autumn 1950, therefore, saw the TUC reject a further, third year of frozen wages. It became apparent that the type of economic conditions which lead a Labour Government to seek trade union acceptance of a wage freeze are precisely the type of economic conditions which make it difficult to ensure the unions' continued compliance with pay restraint, because it entails a reduction in living standards for millions of union members.

Foreign Policy

The expectation or anxiety that the election of a Labour Government in 1945 would herald the pursuit of a 'socialist foreign policy', as favoured by the Left of the Party, was soon quashed. It rapidly became clear that the Attlee Government was not willing to adopt a 'fraternal' stance towards the Soviet Union, but was, instead, concerned to maintain and develop Britain's political and military links with the United States, even though many on the Party's Left were anti-American. As such, it has been suggested that 'Labour's [foreign] policy was in many spheres undoubtedly similar to that which would have been pursued by a Conservative government' (Eatwell 1979: 74). Indeed, an American Secretary of State during this time, James F. Byrnes, remarked that with regard to policy towards the Soviet Union: 'Britain's stand . . . was not altered in the slightest, so far as we could discern, by the replacement of Mr Churchill and Mr Eden by Mr Attlee and Mr Bevin. This continuity of Britain's foreign policy impressed me' (quoted in Howell 1976: 145). Hence many commentators, when talking about the existence of a 'post-war consensus' between the two main political parties in Britain, cite foreign policy as one of the defining features of this bipartisanship (see, for example, Kavanagh and Morris 1989).

Of course, the links established between the Attlee Government and the United States were not unrelated to the vital financial assistance which had been provided from across the Atlantic. Even the Labour Party's pragmatism did not extend to relying financially on the United States whilst aligning itself politically with the Soviet Union – and had it sought to do so, of course, then American money would not have been forthcoming in the first place.

It was westwards towards Washington, rather than eastwards towards Moscow, that the Attlee Government looked in terms of British foreign policy and Britain's (perceived) world role. Comradeship and fraternity did not, after all, extend beyond Berlin or the Baltic. As Denis Healey informed the Left: 'The class struggle does not alter geography. It is still the case that a ship travelling from the Aegean to the Black Sea must pass through the Dardanelles' (quoted in Pelling 1983: 262).

In any case, the fact that Britain had emerged victorious from the Second World War, and had successfully resisted Nazi invasion or occupation (the Channel Islands apart), reinforced British perceptions and assumptions that the country was a world power, a bulwark against Fascism, and a beacon of democracy and political moderation. This self-perception was further underpinned by Britain's continued possession of the Empire and close ties with the Commonwealth. For all these reasons, therefore: 'British foreign policy . . . rested on the assumption that Britain was a world power' (Kavanagh and Morris 1989: 93).

The surprising appointment of Ernest Bevin as Foreign Secretary in 1945 (it had been widely expected that Attlee would appoint Dalton to the post) actually served to strengthen Britain's 'Atlanticism' and its concomitant antipathy towards the Soviet Union. Bevin himself was profoundly distrustful of Communists generally, and of the Soviet Union in particular. Indeed, it is widely acknowledged that Bevin himself did much in the early post-war years to persuade the United States of the alleged risk to the West which was posed by the Soviet Union's apparent expansionist policy and ultimate goal of world Communism.

Bevin's stance, whilst often antagonistic to sections of the Left in the Labour Party, earned him considerable respect from the Conservative Opposition (a fact which merely irked the Left even more). Hence the claim by Anthony Eden, the previous (Conservative) Foreign Secretary, that: 'I would publicly have agreed with him more if I had not been anxious to embarrass him less' (Eden 1960: 5). In similar vein, Rab Butler noted that 'on the major public issues arising from the cold war there was rarely much between us save a difference of emphasis or detail' (R. Butler 1971: 131).

Bevin played a pivotal role in bringing about the creation of the North

Atlantic Treaty Organization (NATO), for example, a feat which was 'one of the great moments in Bevin's life' (F. Williams 1952: 267). Western concern over Soviet attitudes and activities was greatly compounded by the Communist coup in Czechoslovakia in February 1948, which extended Soviet hegemony in Eastern Europe. The following month therefore witnessed the signing of the Brussels Pact, whereby Belgium, Britain, France, the Netherlands and Luxembourg agreed to work together politically and militarily to defend the West from further Soviet expansion and aggression.

However, Britain – and Bevin in particular – was eager to involve the United States more closely in the defence of 'the West', and eventually, after considerable diplomatic effort by Bevin and his Foreign Office officials, the United States was persuaded of the efficacy of working more closely with the signatories of the Brussels Pact, whereupon, in April 1949, the North Atlantic Treaty Organization was formally established.

Yet whilst the Attlee Government was perceiving and presenting Britain as a world power, it was simultaneously presiding over the beginning of the end of the British Empire, and of Britain's political and military presence in other parts of the world, such as the Middle East. Particularly notable in signifying Britain's 'retreat from Empire' was the granting of independence to India in August 1947, with the last battalions of British soldiers departing in February 1948.

The issue of India's independence was not in itself new; back in 1818, the Marquess of Hastings had declared that: 'A time, not very remote, will arrive when England will, on sound principles of policy, wish to relinquish the domination which she has gradually and unintentionally assumed over this country' (quoted in Collins and Lapierre 1975: 12). A not dissimilar assertion had emanated from Lord Chelmsford, the Viceroy of India, in 1915. Certainly the early decades of the twentieth century witnessed the emergence of an increasingly confident nationalist movement in India which demanded independence from British rule. Hence, by the mid-1940s, Dalton recalled, the Attlee Government's attitude appeared to be: 'If you are in a place where you are not wanted, and where you have not got the force, or perhaps the will, to squash those who don't want you, the only thing to do is to come out . . . ' (Dalton 1962: 211).

Britain's relinquishing of parts of her Empire led the Foreign Secretary, Ernest Bevin, to complain to Attlee 'about the constant retreats and withdrawals that were being insisted upon at the time' (Pelling 1983: 263). Yet as Pelling points out, Britain's retreat from Empire owed less to ideological objectives or a commitment to self-determination and independence, but more to the search for economies and financial savings by the Treasury. Thus, when the Cabinet decided in September 1947 that British troops would be withdrawn from Palestine, the Chancellor, Hugh Dalton, explained that 'the maintenance of British forces in it merely led to a heavy drain on our financial resources . . . ' (quoted in Pelling 1983: 267).

There were certainly financial and political repercussions for the Attlee Government in the summer of 1950 when South Korea was invaded by the Communist North. Galvanized by the United States, the members of the United Nations – including Britain – mobilized to assist the South Koreans in defending themselves. This in turn led to a doubling of the defence budget. However, in order to raise the required revenue, the new Chancellor, Hugh Gaitskell, sought savings in the budget of the National Health Service, proposing to introduce charges for dentures and spectacles. In protest at this alleged attack on Britain's 'free' health service, the Health Minister, Aneurin Bevan, resigned, accompanied by Harold Wilson, who had been President of the Board of Trade. However, it ought to be noted that Bevan's resignation partly reflected personality and political differences with Gaitskell, for Bevan had resented the apparent speed with which Gaitskell had ascended to such an important Cabinet position; Bevan had not sought the Chancellorship himself, but still felt aggrieved at the way in which Gaitskell had been promoted before him. It was this resentment which underpinned much of the tension which developed as the Treasury looked increasingly closely at the National Health Service in the search for public expenditure cuts.

This last point also highlighted what was to become a recurring feature of British politics since 1945 generally, namely the tendency for the welfare state to be seen as a 'soft' target whenever the Treasury sought public expenditure cutbacks. Britain rightly condemned the Soviet Union for putting 'guns before butter', but Britain itself seems sometimes to have put weaponry before welfare. It was deemed possible to spend too much on social security, but apparently the country could never spend too much on defence.

The Conservative Opposition's Response

The shock of losing the 1945 general election, coupled with the magnitude of the defeat, had a profound impact on the Conservative Party. Whilst remaining fully committed to a capitalist economy and society, the Conservative Party none the less modified its stance whilst in Opposition, to the extent that it accepted the case for some degree of government regulation of economic activity – including a limited degree of nationalization – along with the pursuit of full employment. In so doing, some Conservatives insisted that the Party had long since abandoned a *laissez-faire* stance, and that it 'has never been frightened of using the power of the State to improve social conditions, to organize economic effort and to provide collective services such as defence, education and health' (Alport 1946: 14). Indeed, in 1944, Lord Hinchingbrooke had declared:

> True Conservative opinion is horrified at the damage done to this country since the last war by 'individualist' business-men, financiers, and speculators ranging freely in a laissez-faire economy and creeping unnoticed into the fold of Conservatism to insult the Party with their votes at elections . . . and to injure the character of our people.
>
> It would wish nothing better than that these men should collect their baggage and depart. True Conservatism has nothing whatever to do with them and their obnoxious policies. (Hinchingbrooke 1944: 21)

This claim was forcefully reiterated three years later by Anthony Eden, during a speech at the Conservative Party's 1947 annual conference, when he declared that: 'We are not a Party of unbridled, brutal capitalism, and never have been. Although we believe in personal responsibility and personal initiative in business, we are not the political children of the *laissez-faire* school. We opposed them decade after decade.' Even before the end of the Second World War, Quintin Hogg (later Lord Hailsham) was warning his Conservative colleagues that 'If you do not give the people social reform, they are going to give you social revolution' (quoted in Addison 1977: 232).

It was the publication, in May 1947, of *The Industrial Charter* which formally confirmed the Conservative Party's general acceptance of much of the state intervention which had been instigated by the Attlee Government (which itself had inherited the interventionist and regulatory framework laid down by the Wartime Coalition Government led by

Churchill himself). *The Industrial Charter* had emerged from the delib-
erations of a Conservative committee on industrial policy, established by
Churchill in response to calls from delegates at the Party's 1946 annual
conference for a clarification of Party principles and policies, and an
affirmation that Conservatism could provide a modern alternative to
the *laissez-faire* liberalism of the nineteenth century and the 'state
socialism' apparently threatening to dominate in the twentieth century.
This committee had comprised five members of the Shadow Cabinet
(including Rab Butler and Harold Macmillan) and four Conservative
back-benchers. It was itself part of the wider attempt by the Conservative
Party 'to wrest from the Left much of the middle ground in the battle of
ideas' (R. Butler 1971: 135).

Although *The Industrial Charter* reiterated the Conservative Party's
adherence to private enterprise and individual liberty, it also acknowledged a much greater role for the state in managing and regulating the
economy. Indeed, there was an acknowledgement that:

> much as we dislike nationalization . . . there might still be an argument
> for leaving certain industries – particularly those in the nature of
> public utilities – nationalized rather than have them for ever being the
> shuttlecock of every change of the party in power. (Kilmuir 1964: 163)

The Industrial Charter therefore called for an approach which 'reconciles
the need for central direction with the encouragement of individual
effort', whilst acknowledging that it was 'impossible for us to revert to
a policy of "go as you please"'. Instead, *The Industrial Charter* insisted
that 'there must be a partnership between the Government, Industry
and the Individual' (Conservative and Unionist Central Office 1947: 10).
Butler emphasized that: 'Our first purpose was to counter the charge
and the fear that we were the party of industrial go-as-you-please and
devil-take-the-hindmost, that full employment and the Welfare State
were not safe in our hands' (R. Butler 1971: 146).

One particularly notable aspect of *The Industrial Charter* was the conciliatory tone adopted towards the trade unions, and industrial relations
generally. Eager to shake off it reputation as a Party hostile towards
trade unions and the concerns of ordinary working people, *The Industrial
Charter* pledged a new-found commitment to seeking co-operation with
the trade unions, coupled with a commitment to improving the status
and security of workers in their place of employment. There was

an acknowledgement that many industrial disputes were ultimately a manifestation of the alienation and anxieties experienced by employees who were unable to appreciate the worth or value of their contribution to the manufacturing process in an era of mass production (Fordism). In such a context, relatively minor grievances and discontents were liable to flare up into more serious disputes.

Following on from this analysis of Britain's industrial relations problems, *The Industrial Charter* – and subsequent Conservative policy documents such as *The Right Road for Britain*, published in 1949 – sought to steer the Party away from 'Reds under the bed' explanations of industrial disruption and strike action and, instead, suggested that the key to improved industrial relations lay not in anti-trade union legislation, but in improving channels of communication and consultation between management and workers. This would foster a new climate of trust in industry, break down 'them-and-us' attitudes, and ultimately result in a sense of partnership between capital and labour, who would work together for the common good.

The Conservative Opposition's new conciliatory and constructive policy towards trade unionism was almost immediately put to the test by the Attlee Government's repeal of the 1927 Trades Disputes Act (which, as we saw earlier, had been passed by Stanley Baldwin's Conservative Government in the wake of the 1926 General Strike, and placed serious curbs on the rights and activities of trade unions). Initially, the Conservative Party favoured legislation to restore 'contracting-in' to the trade union political levy, and to prohibit the operation of the closed shop in public sector employment. However, the Conservatives' 1950 election manifesto confined itself to 'consult with the trade unions upon a friendly and final settlement of the questions of contracting out and compulsory unionism', whilst the Party's manifesto in the following year's general election made no reference to trade union reform at all. Indeed, just a few days before the 1951 election, the Conservative leader, Winston Churchill, was emphatic that his party had no intention of introducing legislation against the trade unions, but, instead, would (if elected) consult and co-operate with them on a friendly, non-partisan basis (*The Times*, 10 October 1951).

Another change in the Conservative Party prompted by the shock of the 1945 election defeat was an organizational one. In 1946 Lord Woolton was appointed Conservative Party chairman, having previously served in the Coalition Government as Minister of Food (although it was not until the day that Labour's election victory was confirmed that he had actually joined the Conservatives, so concerned was he about the future which awaited Britain under Labour rule).

Having reviewed the Conservative Party's organizational structure and financial arrangements, Lord Woolton proposed a number of closely related reforms, two of the most notable being:

1   A major recruitment drive to attract new members and constituency party activists.
2   Higher priority to be given to fund-raising at local level by the constituency parties. Not only would this relieve the pressure on Conservative Central Office to underwrite the activities and expenses of the Party at local constituency level, it might also yield income *from* constituency parties to Conservative head-quarters. Lord Woolton therefore proposed that Conservative constitueny associations should set an annual fund-raising target of £2,000–3,000, which was considered a large sum of money for local activists to raise in those days, to the extent that the target 'appears to have left some constituency officers gasping' (Hoffman 1964: 88).

As part of this review of Conservative Party organization and finance, a committee was also established, under the chairmanship of David Maxwell-Fyfe, to examine the financial arrangements of and for election candidates (and prospective parliamentary candidates). This committee operated in the context of the Conservative Party's professed desire to recruit a wider, more socially representative range of parliamentary candidates. Hitherto, it was suggested, the expectation that Conservative candidates and MPs would make significant contributions both to their constituency associations and towards the costs of their own election campaigns served to deter or debar good candidates who lacked con-siderable wealth and resources. This was deemed to be one of the reasons for the fact that so many Conservative MPs were drawn from a rather narrow and exclusive social milieu. In order that 'means should be found to remove financial obstacles which prevent suitable candidates from putting their names forward and constituency associations from selecting the best men and women available', the Maxwell-Fyfe Report (published in two stages, the first in October 1948 and the second in

July 1949) recommended that:

1   Constituency associations themselves should be responsible for the election expenses of Conservative candidates.
2   Candidates should be permitted to make voluntary contributions to their constituency association each year, but the amount tendered was to be limited to £25 per annum, although Conservative MPs could donate £50.
3   The question of financial contributions by the candidate was not to be raised by any Conservative selection committee until after a candidate had been adopted.

The imposition of strict limits on how much a Conservative candidate could contribute to their constituency association was intended not only to make it easier for less affluent candidates to seek adoption by the Party, but also to compel local parties to give more attention to fund-raising; no longer could they rely on the largesse of a wealthy aristocratic candidate, for example. Of course, it was fully recognized that one of the most effective means by which Conservative constituency associations could increase their revenue was by recruiting more members. In other words, the financial restrictions placed on Conservative constituency associations as a consequence of the Maxwell-Fyfe Report were intended simultaneously to increase both the number of Party members and the range of candidates. As such, in declaring these changes to be 'revolutionary', Lord Woolton claimed that they 'did more than any single factor to save the Conservative Party' (quoted in Hoffman 1964: 96).

Lord Woolton's view, of course, may be considered somewhat partial. It may also be a case of hyperbole, for not only has Conservative Party membership (along with that of Labour) declined significantly since 1945, it also remained socially exclusive, to the extent that almost twenty years later – following election defeats in 1964 and 1966 – Conservative Central Office was urging constituency associations to make a concerted effort to select younger, more socially varied and representative prospective parliamentary candidates.

To this extent, it could be suggested that the Conservative Party was returned to office in 1951 (and thereafter in 1955 and 1959) in spite of the changes recommended by Lord Woolton and David Maxwell-Fyfe, rather than because of them. According to Hoffman, for example: 'In a great number of cases the candidates in 1951 were the same as those chosen for the 1950 election and would therefore have been selected by the constituency associations before the new ruling.' As such, in terms of 'class-occupation backgrounds of successful candidates . . . there was very little change in the type of Conservative candidates chosen to contest seats in which the Conservative Party had the slightest chance of winning' (Hoffman 1964: 96–7; see also Criddle 1994: 156). Hence the perceived need for another attempt at 'modernization' during the mid-1960s.

Meanwhile, Lord Woolton was also among a number of Conservatives during the late 1940s who favoured a change of name for the Conservative Party, believing that in the climate of reform which characterized post-war Britain, '"conserving" seemed to be out of joint with this new world that was demanding adventure . . . ' (Woolton 1959: 334). Woolton was inclined to adopt the appellation 'the Union Party', signifying 'the unity of the Empire, the essential unity between the Crown, the Government, and the people . . . ' (*ibid.*: 335). In the event, however, Woolton decided that the time was not then ripe for such a significant change; the name remained the same.

Labour Runs Out of Steam

Towards the end of the decade, the radicalism hitherto associated with the Attlee Government appeared to have dissipated. To some extent, it had become a victim of its own success, for having introduced a major programme of economic and social reforms, there was an assumption among many Labour ministers that the Party's objectives had, to a large degree, been achieved. As a consequence of the 1945 Labour Government's 'peaceful revolution', Attlee claimed, 'there has been a great levelling-up of conditions. The great mass of abject poverty has disappeared' (Attlee 1954: 166). Meanwhile, Sam Watson, the leader of the Durham miners, proudly proclaimed at Labour's 1950 annual conference that: 'Poverty has been abolished. Hunger is unknown. The sick are tended. The old folks are cherished, our children are growing up in a land of opportunity' (quoted in Clarke 1991: 208).

What was thus required, some believed, was a period of consolidation. Consequently, whereas the early years of the 1945 Attlee Government had constituted 'a period of unprecedented legislative activity' during which 'the bills rolled in and the acts rolled out as if on a parliamentary production line' (Hennessy 1987: 35–6), the latter half of the Attlee premiership was characterized by a greater emphasis on routine administration and managerialism by the Government, although the controversial nationalization of the iron and steel industry did occur during 1949–50 to enliven matters somewhat.

Apart from the fact that Labour had successfully enacted the legislative programme on which it had fought the 1945 election, another crucial factor accounting for the Attlee Government's lack of radicalism at the end of the 1940s and the beginning of the 1950s was the state of the economy. Indeed, throughout its period in office, the Attlee Government had been beset by recurring economic crises.

The first of these occurred almost immediately after Labour's election victory, and placed the new Government in a potentially perilous position. Due to the economic consequences of the war, Britain had become heavily dependent on financial support from the United States, via a system known as lend-lease, financial aid and assistance provided by the United States during the war. However, as soon as the war with Japan was over, the United States announced that lend-lease was to be terminated forthwith. Given the parlous state of the British economy, and the Attlee Government's ambitious programme for establishing a comprehensive welfare state and achieving full employment, the American decision was profoundly disturbing. Lord (John Maynard) Keynes was thus despatched to Washington to negotiate a new loan from the United States in order to stave off Britain's virtual bankruptcy, or at the very least, far greater austerity and privation than had been endured during the war itself. The result was a loan of nearly four billion dollars – less than the Attlee Government had hoped for – to be repaid over fifty years. A condition of the loan, however, was that the pound sterling would become convertible to dollars in one year's time. The Attlee Government was not happy about such conditions, but felt that it had little choice but to accept them, so urgently did Britain need the loan from America.

The next financial crisis occurred early in 1947, prompted by a severe winter. In view of the shortages of fuel which still existed at this time, the Attlee Government was compelled to impose restrictions on the use of electricity. This in turn contributed to a 25 per cent loss of industrial output at a time when the Government's attempt at reviving the British economy relied heavily on boosting exports. Yet this drastic drop in factory production caused by the fuel shortages and restrictions resulted in the loss of £200 million worth of exports.

The summer of 1947 witnessed further serious economic problems for the Attlee Government. When the time came for the pound sterling to become fully convertible on the foreign exchanges, Britain's weak economic position – not least its poor balance of payments situation – resulted in the pound coming under such strong pressure that the Chancellor, Hugh Dalton, felt obliged to take the humiliating step of suspending convertibility. To compound his discomfort, Dalton then deemed it necessary to introduce a tough budget in order to help 'balance the books'.

Yet another economic crisis faced the Attlee Government in 1949, this time resulting in a 30 per cent devaluation of the pound in September, coupled with further pruning of welfare expenditure by the Treasury. Yet in effectively pushing up the cost of imports, devaluation helped to fuel inflation, which simultaneously threatened to damage further the Government's diminishing popularity, whilst also making it more difficult to secure continued wage restraint by the trade unions and their members.

Ultimately, the Attlee Government was only able to survive until 1950, and pursue its policies for full employment, welfare provision, and so on, by virtue of Marshall Aid. Named after General George Marshall, who in 1947 pledged American financial assistance for the reconstruction of Europe in the wake of the war, this was a massive programme of economic assistance provided to Western Europe by the United States, the objective being to help rebuild and regenerate the economies and infrastructures of the countries of Western Europe, which would, in turn, reduce their susceptibilty to Communist influence or appeal. This latter consideration was itself a reflection of the increasing concern over the apparent threat of Soviet expansionism. Whilst military defence could obviously be developed in order to protect the West physically, it was widely acknowledged that unless the countries of Western Europe could provide their citizens with material benefits in terms of jobs, higher living standards, housing, welfare protection, etc., then there would be a risk that Communism might gain an ideological victory over capitalism. Marshall Aid was a major part of the strategy to prevent such an occurrence.

Britain, and in particular Ernest Bevin, played a major role in work-ing with the Americans in developing the Marshall Aid programme. Although it applied to a number of Western European countries, with a total of 12 billion dollars having been disbursed by the beginning of 1951, Britain was the primary beneficiary. Indeed, the economic recovery that Britain had experienced by this time led Gaitskell, the Chancellor, to declare that the Government did not require any further Marshall Aid. For the Attlee Government, Marshall Aid had been a resounding success, for 'it is inconceivable that the economic and social policies of the Attlee government could have survived without this massive platform . . . ' (Morgan 1984: 272).

Yet in spite of this apparent success, Labour was returned in the 1950 general election with a greatly reduced parliamentary majority, although the number of actual votes won increased. Indeed, the economy was the main factor influencing Attlee's decision in January 1950 that a general election would be held the following month (Eatwell 1979: 119). In the wake of the previous September's devaluation, speculation had been rife about the date of the next election, and Attlee thus decided that continued uncertainty would be detrimental to Britain's trade and industry, as well as placing further pressure on the pound in the currency markets.

Deciding what to include in Labour's election manifesto proved to be somewhat problematic. The Party could either pledge further radical reforms, seeking to extend further the programme implemented since 1945, or it could offer an essentially cautious, consolidationist strategy. The problem with the former approach was deemed to be twofold. Firstly, the reforms introduced by the 1945 Attlee Government were considered by many in the labour movement to have secured most of what the Labour Party had originally set out to achieve. Furthermore, as we have previously noted, many in the senior echelons of the Labour Party believed that as a consequence of the Attlee Government's reforms, the problems of poverty, unemployment, deprivation, etc. had largely been eradicated. What need was there for further major reforms, and what could these possibly be anyway?

The second reason why further radicalism was deemed problematic was that it might well serve to forfeit any trust hitherto placed in the Labour Party by sections of the middle class, some of whom had voted for it for the first time in 1945. The question was whether they would continue to be attracted by a forthright promise of a further five years of radical reform and greater state intervention. The answer, a number of Labour ministers suspected, would be in the negative. Hence their inclination towards an essentially modest and moderate manifesto in 1950.

This was certainly the perspective subscribed to by Herbert Morrison, who was chairperson of Labour's Policy (and Publicity) sub-committee. However, his preference for a consolidationist approach was shared by a number of other senior Labour ministers, not least by Attlee himself. Consequently, Labour's campaign for the 1950 election placed great emphasis on achievements such as full employment and welfare policies, whilst nationalization was accorded rather less attention. Indeed, to a significant extent, the emphasis of Labour's campaign was on the alleged risks to the Attlee Government's achievements which the return of a Conservative administration would pose, rather than a forthright commitment to a new programme of radical reform. As Hugh Dalton later acknowledged, the Attlee Government by this time was 'suffering from an acute exhaustion of ideas' (Dalton 1962: 370).

Dalton's claim seemed to be vindicated by the contents and the general tenor of Labour's manifesto for the 1950 election. The confidence of the 1945 manifesto was replaced by a marked sense of caution. Indeed, in many respects, the manifesto seemed to be as much about summarizing Labour's achievements as about its plans for another term of office. Labour was almost presenting itself as a conservative party, emphasizing the extent to which the electorate ought to vote Labour in order to defend the status quo from alleged Conservative attack.

Particularly notable was the toning down of the commitment to nationalization. Pragmatism, rather than socialist principle, was to be the primary rationale for future public ownership of industries. Nowhere was this cautious, empirical approach more evident than in the manifesto's assertion that 'where private enterprise fails to meet the public interest, the Government will be empowered to start new competitive public enterprises in appropriate circumstances'.

Also of significance was the fact that the section dealing with the nationalization which had already taken place was actually entitled 'the socialized industries', a tacit acknowledgement that the very word 'nationalization' had begun to acquire negative connotations, associated as it increasingly was with bureaucratic inefficiency, massive government (taxpayers') subsidies, lack of innovation, and continued poor industrial relations.

In the event, the Labour Party was returned with an increased number of votes, but with far fewer seats in the House of Commons. Labour received the support of over 13 million voters (compared to just under 12 million in 1945), but its parliamentary representation fell from 393 seats to 315. Meanwhile, the Conservative Party increased its share of seats from 213 (in 1945) to 298. When the seats of the other parties were taken into consideration, the Labour Party was left with a majority of just six seats. Such a small Commons majority effectively ensured that Labour would be unable to achieve much by way of radical reform, even if it had wanted, and this merely compounded the image of a Government which had run out of steam, and was thus primarily concerned about day-to-day administration – and survival. It was clear that another general election would not be too far away.

The Attlee Governments: Just How Radical?

At the time, the Attlee Governments – more particularly the first one from 1945 to 1950 – were widely seen as radical and innovative, heralding a silent revolution in British politics. Many supporters at the time confidently anticipated the arrival of socialism, believing that the policies of the Attlee Governments represented the transcendence of capitalism. These policies certainly seemed, at the time, more far-reaching and fundamental than those of any previous British government. Attlee himself proudly declared that: 'The legislative programme on which the 1945 Labour Government embarked was much more extensive than that launched by any peace-time Government . . . It would certainly have astonished Members of Parliament of the days before the First World War' (Attlee 1954: 164–5). As such, in view of the fact that Attlee had, as a younger man, lived and worked in the East End of London for fourteen years, Addison suggests that: 'To a man with Attlee's frame of reference, any substantial increase in the welfare of the working class was in itself a revolution' (Addison 1977: 272).

Yet as is so often the case, hindsight puts a rather different gloss on the past, and leads us to re-evaluate or even reject erstwhile orthodoxies. To this extent, the decades since the Attlee Governments have seen many commentators downplay the alleged radicalism of the 1945–51 Labour administrations, although Hennessy insists: 'It is misleading to suggest that Labour's social programme after 1945 was merely a continuation of coalition policies with a red tinge' (Hennessy 1987: 33).

Three particular approaches would lend credence to the claim that the Attlee Governments were by no means as radical as originally thought. Firstly, as already intimated, many of the reforms pursued under Attlee's premiership had already been agreed or instigated during – and by – the Wartime Coalition Government led by Winston Churchill. The Beveridge Report which laid the basis for the welfare state was originally published in 1942, whilst the White Paper *Full Employment in a Free Society* was printed in November 1944. To this extent, it can be said that the 1945–50 Labour Government took the credit for the pursuit of major policies which had actually received cross-party support during the war. The 1945 election result conferred upon the Labour Party the opportunity to implement these policies, and thus take the credit, even though many of them 'were extensions and rationalisations of existing policies' (Howell 1976: 150).

Furthermore, it has been suggested that the election of the Attlee Government in 1945 merely confirmed a trend towards collectivism and a more active state which had been gathering pace long before the outbreak of the Second World War. Middlemas, for example, traces the development of 'corporate bias' back to 1911, since when 'central government . . . moved from a position of facilitating to one of supporting economic change, and finally to direction – but only with agreement of the governing institutions', such as trade unions and employers' associations (Middlemas 1979: 379).

Meanwhile, 1927 had witnessed the publication of a booklet entitled *Industry and the State* by four Conservative MPs, including Harold Macmillan (who was later to become Conservative Party leader and Prime Minister). In this publication, Macmillan and his co-authors set about:

> devising some coherent system lying between unadulterated private enterprise and collectivism . . . a policy . . . which I would later call 'The Middle Way'; an industrial structure with the broad strategic control in the hands of the State and the tactical operation in the hands of private management, with public and private ownership operating side by side. (Macmillan 1966: 223–4)

Such a system, Macmillan explained, was intended to provide 'a constructive alternative to Socialism'. Whilst the Right of the Conservative Party was highly critical of *Industry and the State*, as was much of the press, Macmillan recalled the favourable response it elicited from senior figures such as Neville Chamberlain, who claimed: 'I see nothing to be shocked at in your suggestions, and a good deal that is, or ought to be, stimulating to Members of the Conservative Party' (quoted in Macmillan 1966: 173). Indeed, one writer has suggested that:

> The Labour Party's strategy in 1945 was essentially a conservative one. Had they gone to the country in 1939 with the programme of 1945, they would have been issuing a strongly radical challenge. But in 1945, they had only to consolidate and extend the consensus achieved under the Coalition, and build upon the new foundations of popular opinion. (Addison 1977: 261)

Meanwhile, writing in the midst of the Second World War, George Orwell declared that:

> The English revolution started several years ago, and it began to gather momentum when the troops came back from Dunkirk. Like all else in England, it happens in a sleepy, unwilling way, but it is happening. The war has speeded it up, but it has also increased, and desperately, the necessity for speed . . . Progress and reaction are ceasing to have anything to do with party labels . . . The war and the revolution are inseparable. (Orwell 1982: 95)

Secondly, and following directly on from the above observations, many of the reforms introduced by the 1945–50 Attlee Government were broadly supported by the Conservative Party; they were a product of *cross-party* endeavour during the war. Consequently, we can plausibly suggest that had the Conservative Party won the 1945 election, many of the policies and reforms implemented under Attlee instead would have been introduced anyway. Hence Addison's claim that: 'The consensus developed in the 1940s represented a dilution of Conservative rather than Labour politics' (Addison 1977: 271). Admittedly, a Conservative Government would not have been quite so enthusiastic, but none the less, the broad framework would probably have still been established.

For example, although the Conservative Opposition remained publicly critical of the Attlee Government's nationalization programme, and continued – as we noted above – to espouse the principles and virtues of private enterprise, Quintin Hogg (later Lord Hailsham) acknowledged that 'Conservatives felt no particularly violent objection to the nationalization of the Bank of England or of Cable and Wireless Ltd . . . ' (Hogg 1947: 111–12). Meanwhile, in 1946, Winston Churchill informed the House of Commons that: 'I am not going to pretend I see anything immoral in the nationalization of the railways provided fair compensation is paid to the present owners' (House of Commons Debates, 5th series, vol. 430, col. 30). As such, 'the Conservatives put up only a token opposition' to much of the Attlee Government's nationalization programme' (Addison 1977: 273), although they did bitterly oppose the nationalization of iron and steel, as well as road haulage, both of which they subsequently denationalized when they were returned to office. None the less, one labour historian has noted that: 'The legislative programme of nationalization went through Parliament with remarkable smoothness' (Pelling 1961: 96).

Furthermore, it became increasingly apparent that Labour's plans for nationalization were not as ambitious as many had first hoped or feared. As we noted above, the Labour Government elected in 1945 seemed, by the end of the decade, largely to have exhausted its programme of reform, including the policy of nationalization. A situation thus emerged between the two parties whereby:

> . . . Conservatives . . . did not propose to denationalize most of [what] had already been taken into public ownership. Rather, they tacitly accepted the deed while reviling those responsible for it. Labour, on the other hand, while defending the principle and so far as possible the practice of nationalization, nonetheless went slow on the idea of bringing additional industries into public ownership. From their different doctrinal standpoints, and behind smokescreens of contrasting rhetoric, both parties largely accepted the status quo. (Smith and Polsby 1981: 94)

Thirdly, a number of left-wing commentators have argued that the most noteworthy feature of the Attlee Governments was not their radicalism, but on the contrary, their moderation and timidity. Far from ushering in socialism, it is argued that the reforms of the Attlee Governments merely constituted adjustments within, and adaptation to, capitalism. A predominantly capitalist system continued intact, but was given a more human face and humane demeanour. According to Marxist writers in particular, nationalization itself did not herald a socialist transformation of the British economy or society. Not only did 80 per cent of the economy remain under private ownership, but the former owners of the industries which were nationalized were generously compensated, even though the industries in question were often unprofitable anyway, so that the owners were more than willing to relinquish them in return for reasonable recompense. In any case, left-wing critics of the Attlee Government's nationalization programme point out, the formal change of ownership did not mark any significant transfer of power or control to ordinary workers, not even those employed in the newly nationalized industries. Employees did not acquire any say in the operation of or decisions concerning their industries. Instead, power and decision-making resided in the Boards established by the Government. Furthermore, according to David Coates, 'the men chosen to head these new public corporations were, with a few notable exceptions, members of the managerial and ownership class of the former private industries' (Coates 1975: 48). Trade unionists and ordinary workers from the nationalized industries were largely conspicuous by their absence on the boards established to run them. This paucity of workers' representatives clearly reflected the view held by many Labour ministers, particularly Stafford Cripps, that:

> There is not yet a very large number of workers in Britain capable of taking over large enterprises. I have on many occasions tried to get representatives of the workers on all sorts of bodies and working parties. It has always been extremely difficult to get enough people who are qualified to do that sort of job, and, until there has been more experience by the workers of the managerial side of industry, I think it would be almost impossible to have worker-controlled industry in Britain, even if it were on the whole desirable. (quoted in Coates 1975: 49–50)

How workers were supposed to acquire the requisite experience in the first place was not explained.

The alleged modesty of the changes introduced by the Attlee Governments thus led writers such as David Coates to declare that:

> ... power had not shifted between classes. Qualitative social transfor-

mation had not come. Nor was it any nearer for six years of office. In essence, the Labour Government of 1945–51 had not created a socialist commonwealth, nor even taken a step in that direction. It had simply created a mixed economy in which the bulk of industry still lay in private hands, and the six years of its rule had only marginally altered the distribution of social power, privilege, wealth, income, opportunity and security. (Coates 1975: 47)

Similar criticisms have been expressed in reference to the Attlee Governments' social policies, with Morgan claiming that:

The welfare measures of the Labour Government did not, in themselves, produce a more egalitarian or open society. The profile of the class structure, or even simply of the distribution of wealth, showed relatively little change between 1945 and 1951 . . . many of the new social reforms were financed by transfers of income within lower-income groups themselves, rather than by transfers from the rich to the poor. (Morgan 1984: 184, 185)

None the less, it is widely, but not universally (see, for example, Pimlott 1988), claimed that the 1945 Attlee Government laid down the basis of what has become known as the 'post-war consensus', establishing the framework of policies which were broadly accepted by subsequent governments – Labour *and* Conservative – until the 1970s. Certainly the Conservative Government elected in 1951 displayed a remarkable willingness to uphold many of the policies and reforms implemented by the 1945 Attlee Government, as the next chapter illustrates.

2 Peace and Prosperity (1951–60)

> In political activity . . . men sail a boundless and bottomless sea; there is neither harbour for shelter nor floor for anchorage, neither starting-place nor appointed destination. The enterprise is to keep afloat on an even keel . . .
>
> Michael Oakeshott, *Political Education*

The Conservatives Back in Office

The Conservative Party's jubilation at winning the 1951 general election was tempered somewhat both by the narrowness of the victory, and by the limited room for manoeuvre with which it seemed to be faced. With regard to the former point, the Conservatives were returned with 321 seats compared to Labour's 295, giving the new Conservative Government an overall parliamentary majority of 17 *vis-à-vis* all the other parties. However, the Conservatives actually won the 1951 election with fewer votes than the Labour Party (13,717,538 vs. 13,948,605).

It was partly the relative narrowness of the Conservatives' parliamentary majority, coupled with the fact that Labour polled more votes, that rather limited the new Conservative Government's room for manoeuvre, for it could hardly claim convincingly to have been given a mandate by the British people to pursue radically different policies from its Labour predecessor. Nor did it seriously attempt to do so. On the contrary, with one or two notable exceptions, the Conservative Government elected in 1951 was remarkable for the extent to which it maintained much of the policy framework and objectives inherited from the Attlee Governments (although this might be interpreted merely as further evidence that the Attlee Governments had not been as radical as originally thought). Seldon has remarked that 'one of the most remarkable features of the Government was the extent that Conservative policy followed on logically from Labour policy in the preceding six years' (Seldon 1981: 421).

In some respects, the overall continuity with most of the policies laid down by the Attlee Government ought not to have been such a surprise in view of the *Industrial Charter*. As the previous chapter pointed out, the 1947 publication of this major Conservative policy document had indicated the extent to which the Party was willing to accept a mixed economy and a greater role for the state in economic and social affairs. Furthermore, as we also observed, a number of the policies introduced by the 1945 Attlee Government had been approved or even partially drafted by Conservatives in the Wartime Coalition Government anyway.

Another reason why the 1951 Conservative Government was generally willing to accept most of the measures introduced by the 1945 Attlee Government concerns the background and character of many of Churchill's Cabinet colleagues. Two points are worth noting here. Firstly, there was the intellectual outlook of senior Conservatives such as Rab Butler and Harold Macmillan (Chancellor of the Exchequer and Housing Minister respectively in the first Churchill Cabinet), one which was undoubtedly on the left of the Conservative Party. Such Conservatives strongly reflected and represented the progressive, 'one nation' strand of British Conservatism originally articulated in the latter half of the nineteenth century by Conservatives such as Benjamin Disraeli and Randolph Churchill (although from the 1970s onwards, this brand of Conservatism was blamed by Thatcherites for constituting a betrayal of Conservative principles, and of representing a capitulation to socialism). Rab Butler, for example, had been closely involved in writing the *Industrial Charter*, whilst back in 1927, Harold Macmillan had co-written a pamphlet entitled *Industry and the State* calling for the development of a 'middle way' between unrestrained private enterprise and total socialist collectivism, whereby broad strategic control of industry would reside with the state, whilst day-to-day operations would remain the responsibility of private managers. This would enable a private sector and a public sector to function side by side; in short, a mixed economy. Macmillan also advocated a partnership between government, employers and trade union leaders to discuss and develop economic policies (Macmillan 1966: 223–4). However, during the 1920s, these ideas were rather out of line with mainstream Conservative policies and economic orthodoxies (it required the Second World War to give such ideas – along with Keynesianism – credibility and legitimacy).

The second point to note about the background and character of some of Churchill's Cabinet colleagues was that they had been profoundly influenced by experiences and memories of events which occurred some time before the Second World War. One of these events was actually the First World War, in which a number of Conservatives had fought as officers alongside working-class recruits. Writing about Anthony Eden, for example, Robert Rhodes James suggested that 'his brand of humane, liberal and progressive Conservatism' was 'born in the trenches on the Western Front in 1916' (James 1986: xi; see also Greenleaf 1983: 246).

The other event which exerted a crucial influence on some of the ministers in Churchill's 1951 Cabinet was the 'Great Depression' and accompanying mass unemployment of the 1930s. Macmillan in particular was inclined to cite his memories as an MP for Stockton-on-Tees during this time, recalling the social deprivation and personal misery he witnessed. Macmillan was therefore determined to do all he could to prevent a return to such circumstances, hence Reginald Maudling's subsequent reference to 'his experience in Stockton which so moulded his subsequent approach to economic affairs' (Maudling 1978: 103). Similarly, Macmillan's official biographer commented that: 'The haunting ghosts of Stockton in the 1930s were never to leave Macmillan, and undoubtedly if there were to have been a choice between modest inflation and the threat of a return to chronic unemployment, he would not have hesitated for many seconds' (Horne 1989: 65).

Policy Continuities

Although the Conservative Party had fought the 1951 election with the slogan 'Set the People Free', and the Labour Party had issued dire warnings about the threat posed to the mixed economy, full employment and the welfare state by a Conservative government, the Churchill Government – and its successors in 1955 and 1959 – retained much of the policy framework inherited from the Attlee Government, largely for the reasons given above. Indeed, one commentary on this period talks of 'Conservative Governments with Labour policies', for 'the administration's policies could just as easily have come from a

Labour government as a Tory one' (Pearce and Stewart 1992: 462 and 464).

With the exception of iron and steel, and road transport, the new Conservative Government – still led by Winston Churchill – retained the nationalized industries inherited from Attlee's Governments, although there was much greater emphasis on the need to make them more efficient and cost-effective, as well as on reducing political interference and bureaucratic centralization. Indeed, the retention of most of the nationalized industries was a defining feature of the Conservatives' acceptance of the mixed economy, whereby the public sector and the private sector ostensibly worked side by side in a mutually beneficial relationship.

Economic policy in general remained broadly similar to that pursued by the Attlee Government's, with Keynesian techniques of demand management being retained, along with the commitment to full employment. Again, there was much rhetoric about encouraging enterprise and competition in the economy, but overall, the similarity of Conservative economic policies and priorities to those of the previous Labour administrations led to the term 'Butskellism', a hybrid of Butler, the Chancellor in the 1951 Government, and Gaitskell, who had briefly been a Chancellor of the Exchequer under Attlee. However, Butler himself later claimed that although he and Gaitskell 'spoke the language of Keynesianism . . . we spoke it with different accents and a differing emphasis' (R. Butler 1971: 160).

Social policy was also characterized by considerable continuity, particularly the commitment to full employment. The Conservative Governments of the 1950s were also broadly in favour of maintaining the welfare state. Hence, in 1953, 327,000 houses were built, whilst the following year this figure was increased to 354,000, thereby easily exceeding the 1951 manifesto pledge to build 300,000 new homes. However, whilst the Conservative Governments of the 1950s were generally supportive of the welfare state, they were inclined to speak the language of priorities and targetting. One particular reason why the Conservative Party was able broadly to accept the mixed economy and the welfare state was precisely because the system seemed to be working extremely well. Prior to Thatcherism, British Conservatism emphasized the importance of governing according to circumstances, and only seeking to change institutions if and when they were patently not functioning properly.

The social democratic framework, and its constituent institutions, which the Conservatives inherited from Labour in 1951, appeared to be working very well; as such, apart from a few critics on the right of the Party who saw 'the middle way' as a dangerous drift towards socialism, most Conservatives, particularly the parliamentary leadership, were quite happy to continue with seemingly successful policies (Gamble 1974: 63). For them, maintaining the status quo as far as possible, whilst adapting to changes as and when necessary, perfectly accorded with the tradition and philosophy of British Conservatism.

Limited Denationalization

The Conservative Party's recent conversion to acceptance of a mixed economy and greater state regulation of the economy meant that their return to office in 1951 was followed by only a limited amount of denationalization, much to the evident disappointment of some MPs on the right of the Party. Indeed, just as the reforms introduced by the 1945 Attlee Government had constituted the very least which the Party needed to introduce in order to satisfy its supporters and members, so too was the limited reversal of these measures by the Churchill Government the very least which Conservatives expected when they were returned to office. In both cases, the more ideological 'wings' of the two parties were actually disappointed that their Party leaderships did not go rather further.

The Conservatives' 1951 election manifesto had not pledged the Party to wholesale denationalization; instead, apart from the commitment to denationalize the iron and steel industry, along with road haulage, the manifesto merely claimed that those industries remaining nationalized would 'come within the purview of the Monopolies' Commission and there will also be strict Parliamentary review of their activities'. These measures aside, however, 'the main thing to stress is how little was done by the Conservatives either to change the existing structures or to clarify the relationship between the government and the state-owned corporations' (Gourvish 1991: 121).

The denationalization of the iron and steel industry took place in 1953, almost a year and a half after the election victory. This apparent lack of urgency caused growing impatience on the Conservative back-benches, and considerable annoyance amongst industrialists and employers in the iron and steel industry itself. Even when the Churchill Government did announce its plans for denationalization of the industry, there was unhappiness over the fact that, due to the industry's vital economic and strategic importance, it would remain subject to supervision via an Iron and Steel Board, a body which would oversee investment and encourage co-ordination in the industry. Meanwhile, the road haulage industry was denationalized the following year (1954),

Even if the Churchill Government had been keen on further denationalization, it may have faced difficulties in attracting sufficient private sector funds. Many potential investors were concerned at the prospect that the next general election might result in the return of a Labour Government; certainly the commercial interest in taking over iron and steel, and road haulage, was not as great as the Churchill Government had expected (Bartlett 1977: 100). This reticence on the part of the private sector was perhaps not so surprising, given that most of the industries had been making a financial loss, or required massive new investment, at the time that they were taken into public ownership anyway. In the event, the Conservative leadership was not committed to large-scale denationalization, in spite of their rhetoric in favour of private enterprise and against state control of rthe economy. As Lord Kilmuir acknowledged:

> We had to face up to the problem that, much as we dislike nationalization and its top-heavy monopolies and inefficient consequences, there might still be an argument for leaving certain industries – particularly those in the nature of public utilities – nationalized rather than have them for ever being the shuttlecock of every change of the party in power. (Kilmuir 1964: 163)

With the exception of the denationalization of iron and steel, and road haulage, therefore, the Conservative Governments of the 1950s pragmatically accepted the bulk of the state ownership introduced by the 1945–50 Attlee Government.

Conciliation Towards the Trade Unions

With regard to the Conservative Governments' attitude and approach towards the trade unions, the 1950s were characterized by an unprecedented degree of conciliation and contrition. Most senior Conservatives were eager to make something of a fresh start with the trade unions, and to put the bitterness engendered by the 1926 General Strike, the subsequent 1927 Trades Disputes Act and the mass unemployment of the 1930s behind them. In any case, there was much admiration in the Conservative Party for the way in which the trade unions had contributed to the war effort, as well as recognition that the 'arrival' of the Labour Party as a serious and viable contender for governmental office meant that Conservatives could not afford to appear too hostile towards trade unions or the working class; there were too many votes at stake.

As noted in the previous chapter, the publication of the *Industrial Charter* had indicated the emergence of a more constructive approach towards industrial relations by the Conservative Party, and this was borne out when the Conservatives were returned to power in 1951. In fact, shortly before the election, Churchill warned fellow Conservatives that it would be the most reckless 'unwisdom' for a Conservative government to rouse the resistance of the trade union movement at a time when the British economy was in urgent need of industrial peace and increased productivity (*The Times*, 15 October 1951). In the wake of the election victory, Churchill appointed Walter Monckton as Minister of Labour, the latter recalling that: 'Winston's riding orders to me were . . . to do my best to preserve industrial peace' (quoted in Birkenhead 1969: 276). The same objective was entrusted to Monckton's successor, Ian Macleod, in December 1955.

Apart from the desire to establish a new rapport with the trade unions, and the electoral considerations previously referred to, there was also considerable support for the 'human relations' explanation of industrial conflict, whereby many strikes were deemed to be a reflection of other, underlying problems, such as the sense of anomie or worthlessness which workers often experienced. These largely derived from modern, Fordist techniques of mass production, which entailed each worker performing one specific task repeatedly. At the same time, this meant that workers were unable to appreciate the value or significance of their own contribution and effort to the overall product and output. If industrial conflict was often a manifestation of the frustration felt by employees on the factory floor, then it was deemed unlikely that legislation would prove particularly effective. Indeed, many Conservatives feared that legislation to tackle the problem of strikes, particularly 'wild-cat' (instant, unofficial) strikes, would merely compound the problem, creating even more frustration and resentment amongst the workforce.

Instead, the solution was deemed to lie in greater communication and closer co-operation between management and labour. Instead of invoking legislation, the Conservative leadership was strongly inclined to exhort managers and workers to overcome the divisive 'them and us' mentality which bedevilled industrial relations, and realize that they shared a common interest in improving productivity and profitability, and thus the overall competitiveness of their enterprise or industry. What was needed, it was claimed, was to increase the scope and frequency of contact and consultation between employers and employees, thereby breaking down distrust, and fostering a sense of partnership in the workplace.

Such developments, senior Conservatives maintained, could not be secured through legislation. It was deemed a nonsense to seek to compel people to trust each other through statutory measures. Instead, as Robert Carr (a future Employment Secretary) emphasized, 'it is upon voluntary agreement in industry that we must depend for good industrial relations . . . good relations cannot be enforced by laws' (HC Debates, 5th series, vol. 568, col. 2127). On the contrary, it was maintained that legislative intervention, particularly by a Conservative government, would be entirely counter-productive, serving to fuel distrust and disruption in industry. This underpinned the Conservative Government's reliance on encouragement and exhortation, rather than compulsion and coercion. Needless to say, not all Conservative back-benchers were sympathetic to this approach, suspecting their party leadership of cowardice and appeasement towards the trade unions. These back-benchers would doubtless have concurred with Enoch Powell's wry remark, years later, that: 'The Party came to power without any specific policy on trade union law and practice, and it faithfully carried that non-commitment out for thirteen years' (Powell 1968: 5).

However, concern over the trade unions did increase and spread within the Conservative Party during the 1950s, due mainly to the mounting economic problems with which the Government was trying to grapple. Whilst continuing to reject legislative measures, the Conservative Governments increasingly found themselves imploring the trade unions to exercise wage restraint, due to growing concern over inflationary pressures and the maintenance of full employment. The

latter policy objective had served to increase the bargaining power of
trade unions and their members, partly by eradicating the pool of
unemployment which employers might otherwise have recruited from,
and partly by increasing the actual number of trade union members. As
such, Harold Macmillan admitted that:

> What is beginning to worry some of us is 'Is it too good to be true?', or
> perhaps I should say 'Is it too good to last?' For amidst all this prosperity,
> there is one problem which has troubled us – in one way or another –
> ever since the war. It's the problem of rising prices. Our constant concern
> today is – can prices be steadied while at the same time we maintain full
> employment in an expanding economy? Can we control inflation? This
> is the problem of our time. (quoted in Kavanagh and Morris 1989: 40)

As the 1950s progressed, therefore, Conservative ministers found themselves faced with a number of unpalatable or unpopular options. Firstly,
they could abandon the commitment to full employment, and establish a
link between wage and unemployment levels, thereby placing the onus
on trade unions to exercise restraint and moderation in order to protect
their members' jobs. However, during this time, a conscious decision or
deliberate policy to allow unemployment to rise was deemed politically
and electorally unacceptable. Furthermore, as we have already noted,
senior Conservatives such as Macmillan were determined to prevent a
return to high unemployment.

Secondly, ministers could abandon their 'voluntarist' policy towards
industrial relations and trade unionism, and instead place statutory
regulations and restrictions on the trade unions in order to compel
them to exercise greater responsibility. Yet this was an approach which
most senior Conservatives were not yet ready or willing to contemplate,
partly because of their subscription to the 'human relations' approach,
and partly because many of them, including Ian Macleod whilst Minister
of Labour from December 1955 to October 1959, doubted whether
legislation would prove effective anyway, particularly in dealing with
problems such as unofficial or 'wild-cat' strikes (HC Debates, 5th series,
vol. 568, col. 1285).

Thirdly, Conservatives could resort to incomes policies, thereby
stipulating – with or without the agreement of the trade unions – the
amount by which wages could be increased each year. However, this
clashes with the traditional Conservative belief that wage levels ought

to be determined by the (labour) market, rather than by the state. In any case, there was always the question of how an incomes policy would actually be enforced in the absence of trade union agreement or compliance. Compulsion or coercion might be resorted to, but this would inevitably destroy any semblance of trust between the Conservative Party and the trade unions which had been fostered since the war. Furthermore, there would always be the problem of how to respond if trade unions defied the Government's pay guidelines. What then?

Throughout the 1950s, therefore, the Conservative Governments avoided the need to make such choices by reiterating – albeit with ever more urgency – the need for trade unions to exercise greater 'moderation' and 'responsibility' in wage bargaining, and warning of the dangers posed by 'excessive' pay awards. Indeed, in March 1956, the Government – now with Anthony Eden as Prime Minister – published a White Paper entitled *The Economic Implications of Full Employment*, which sought to demonstrate to the country the need for wage restraint. This was followed by a series of meetings between ministers, senior civil servants, TUC leaders and representatives from the main employers' organizations, in which the state of the economy was discussed, and the need to restrain price and wage increases was reiterated. However, as Anthony Eden himself explained, the meetings were entirely informal, and thus refrained from making formal arrangements or binding agreements (HC Debates, 5th series, vol. 550, col. 1968–72).

The following year witnessed the Chancellor of the Exchequer establish a Council on Prices, Productivity and Incomes, comprising Lord Cohen (a judge) and two economists. The Council's remit was: '. . . having regard to the desirability of full employment and increased standards of living, based on expanding production and reasonable stability of prices, to keep under review changes in prices, productivity, and the level of incomes (including wages, salaries, and profits), and to report thereon from time to time.' However, the Council lacked any power to ensure that its findings were acted upon, and as such, 'turned out to be harmless, producing a number of hand-wringing and ineffectual reports that exhorted trade unions and workers to restrain their wage demands and ensure any increases in earnings were more closely related to productivity improvements' (Taylor 1993: 104–5).

The establishment of the Council was therefore not enough to prevent the resignation, in January 1958, of the Chancellor, Peter Thorneycroft (and his two Treasury Ministers, Nigel Birch and Enoch Powell) over Macmillan's refusal to reduce public expenditure. Thorneycroft was deeply concerned about the level of government spending and inflation, and was of the view that these urgently needed to be curbed, even if it would result in higher unemployment. As already noted, this was anathema to Macmillan. Indeed, he once enquired of Thorneycroft's successor at the Treasury, Derek Heathcoat-Amory: 'What is wrong with inflation, Derry?', from whom the reply was 'You're thinking of your constituency in the 1930s?' (quoted in Horne 1989: 140).

The Government's 'policy' therefore remained that of relying on exhortation and educating trade unionists as to the economic facts of life. 'We do not', Macleod insisted at the Conservatives' 1958 annual conference, 'believe in a national wages policy. Nor do we believe in a wage freeze.' Whilst ministers had a duty to point out the economic consequences of 'excessive' wage increases, they could not compel trade unions and their members to behave more responsibly, nor should they seek to do so. Instead, Macleod insisted, 'only in a partnership independent of politics between the three great partners – government, trade unions and employers – was there any real lasting hope for good, sound industrial relations'. This approach was sustained through to the beginning of the 1960s.

Labour's Revisionist Debates

In some respects, Labour lost the 1951 general election because the Party had become a victim of its own success, for 'its programme for transforming British society had been completed . . . Labour had exhausted itself, in ideas as much as energy. It had succeeded only too well in implementing its policies, and was in real danger of becoming a rudderless conservative party' (Foote 1985: 206). Two further, consecutive, election defeats, in 1955 and 1959, clearly added to Labour's anguish, and lent the utmost urgency to the debates about the future – if any – of the Labour Party, particularly as the 1959 election witnessed the Conservatives win 400,000 more votes and 20 more parliamentary seats than in 1955, whilst Labour lost over 180,000 votes and 19 seats compared to 1955. The same period also saw the Liberal Party more than double its vote, although Britain's electoral system ensured that they did not win any extra seats. The overall outcome was that the Conservative Government increased its Commons' majority from 60 to 100.

The 1950s therefore witnessed much debate, both within the Labour Party and among sympathetic academics, over the direction in which the Party ought to move. Such debates, in turn, engendered a serious reappraisal over what, exactly, Labour stood for in terms of principles, and thus who it purported to represent. In short, what kind of socialism – if any – was the Labour Party committed to?

These debates took place within the context, not only of three successive Conservative election victories, but also amidst an apparent move towards a classless society in Britain. Indeed, it was widely recognized that a major explanation for the electoral success of the Conservative Party throughout the 1950s was that British people had 'never had it so good' (to invoke the legendary phrase which posterity has attributed to Macmillan). Economic prosperity and social mobility, both of which were seen as a manifestation of the Keynesian, welfarist policies laid down by the Attlee Governments in the first place, were deemed to be eradicating poverty and class divisions in post-war Britain.

These developments and changes were thought to be having a particularly profound impact on the British working class, which in turn raised serious questions about the future of the Labour Party, which had been officially launched in 1906 with the express purpose of providing parliamentary representation for the industrial working class, and then to secure for them improved working conditions and better living standards. If these objectives had largely been achieved – as many commentators believed they had by the 1950s – then it was reasonable to ask whether there was any future for the Labour Party. Had not its historic mission on behalf of the working class been successfully accomplished? (It is interesting to note that this reflected a wider problem for 'social democratic' parties, namely that they can become victims of their own success; if they succeed in tackling excessive inequality and poverty, and improving the opportunities and living standards of the working class, then those who benefit from these policies may well begin to see themselves as more prosperous and affluent, and thus become more conservative – with both a small and a large 'c' – in their political beliefs and behaviour. The left-of-centre party whose policies have helped to provide them with their improved position and living standards can thus lose their support as a consequence.)

During the latter half of the 1950s, the term 'embourgeoisement' was increasingly being used by sociologists (who else would use such a term!) to characterize the apparent changes taking place amongst the British working class. It was suggested that as a consequence of the type of policies and prosperity already referred to, the working class was increasingly adopting middle class lifestyles and values. The class structure of Britain was becoming looser generally, and to the extent that it still existed, it was often claimed that it was changing from its hitherto pyramid shape, with a large working-class base, to a diamond shape, entailing a narrowing working-class base and a correspondingly widening middle class.

These professed changes in Britain's socio-economic structure were also deemed to reflect the emergence of new 'white collar' jobs and professions, particularly in the recently established welfare state, and the burgeoning 'service sector' of the economy. These occupations, along with the expansion of education (between 1951 and 1955, the number of children staying on at school or college until the age of 17 doubled), were widely thought to offer unprecedented opportunities to those from working class backgrounds to become upwardly and socially mobile.

Much of the embourgeoisement debate, and the concomitant talk about the disappearance of poverty, inequality and class division, proved with hindsight to have exaggerated the changes which were occurring. Optimism had overtaken objectivity perhaps. Yet irrespective of whether the analysis being proffered by so many during the latter half of the 1950s was accurate or not, the important point here is that many in the Labour Party responded as if the analysis was accurate, and this thus had important implications for the direction in which they sought to steer the party.

Those who subscribed to the above type of analysis, and who therefore wished to modernize the Labour Party's principles and public image, became known as 'revisionists' – they wished to revise Labour's version of socialism (indeed, their critics on the Left accused them of seeking to cleanse the Labour Party of socialism altogether). The person who more than anybody else became associated with this 'revisionist' approach was Anthony Crosland, later to be a Cabinet Minister in the Wilson Governments. Crosland's *The Future of Socialism* was first published in 1956, and was soon to become the Bible of the 'revisionist' bloc in the Labour Party and among like-minded intellectuals.

The main tenets of Crosland's revisionist thesis were as follows.

1   Britain was no longer a capitalist society. Instead, the economic, political and social changes which had occurred during the twentieth century, but particularly since 1945, had drawn Britain beyond capitalism, and into a post-capitalist epoch. Instrumental to this fundamental change were the Keynesian, social democratic policies pursued by post-war governments in Britain. According to Crosland:

> the state and the political authority have removed a wide, and strategically decisive, segment of economic decisions out of the sphere of purely market influences, and made them subject to deliberate political control. Through fiscal policy, and a variety of physical, legislative and financial controls, the state now consciously regulates (or seeks to regulate) the level of employment, the distribution of income, the rate of accumulation and the balance of payments . . . the political authority has emerged as the final arbiter of economic life; the brief, and historically exceptional, era of unfettered market relations is over. (Crosland 1956: 29–30)

2   Ownership of the means of production was no longer particularly important. This obviously followed directly on from the previous point, for if the state could now determine economic activity and variables through fiscal and legislative means, then it did not matter particularly whether a firm or an industry was privately or publicly owned.

At the same time, revisionists such as Crosland pointed out that the character of ownership had changed markedly since the middle of the nineteenth century, due to the rise of joint-stock companies and wider share ownership. Ownership and control of 'the means of production' were increasingly separated; managers of enterprises were themselves usually salaried employees: 'The growth of the managerial joint-stock corporation has transferred the function of decision-making to a largely non-owning class of salaried executives . . . the classical capitalist class of entrepreneurs has largely disappeared' (Crosland 1956: 30).

One further factor which Crosland believed served to reduce the importance of industrial ownership in post-war Britain was the power of the trade unions. A combination of legal privileges and full employment imbued the trade unions with unprecedented economic power, it was suggested, to the extent that they could largely match that traditionally enjoyed by capitalists and entrepreneurs. To this extent, revisionists such as Crosland were endorsing the perspective enunciated by pluralists, namely that the strength of the trade unions enabled labour to act as 'countervailing power' against Capital, so that an equilibrium was ensured between 'the two sides of industry'.

This revisionist critique had profound implications for the Labour Party's commitment to nationalization of the 'commanding heights' of the British economy, and as such, fuelled a heated debate in the party over the continued relevance of such a policy commitment. The clear implication of Crosland's analysis of the economic and industrial structure of post-war Britain was that nationalization was no longer really necessary because, as we have already noted, it was believed that governments could achieve their economic goals through fiscal and legislative measures. It was no longer deemed necessary for the state to own firms and industries directly. The economy could be left predominantly in private hands, yet still regulated so as to function in accordance with the government's overall economic and social objectives. Private ownership – public control. According to the Croslandite perspective, 'ownership is not now an important determinant of economic power. The Government has all the economic power it needs . . . ' (Crosland 1956: 318).

Such an analysis, and its inevitable conclusion concerning nationalization, was to cause a furore in the Labour Party during the latter half of the 1950s, because Clause IV of the party's own constitution committed it to

> secure for the workers by hand or by brain the full fruits of their industry and the most equitable distribution thereof that may be possible, upon the basis of the common ownership of the means of production, distribution and exchange, and the best obtainable system of popular administration and control of each industry or service.

The clear conclusion of the revisionist analysis was that little, if any, further nationalization was necessary, and that the Labour Party ought to concentrate on achieving the effective and efficient management of the existing mixed economy. Further nationalization was not ruled out entirely, but it was emphasized that any further public ownership would have to be justified on pragmatic or economic grounds, derived from necessity, rather than being sought merely in accordance with socialist principles or ideology. For the most part, the revisionists suggested that the balance achieved by the Attlee Government between the public and the private sector was about right.

To this effect, in the wake of the Labour Party's 1959 election defeat – its third in succession – Hugh Gaitskell sought to have Clause IV removed from the party's constitution at that year's annual conference, arguing not only that nationalization was now largely an irrelevance or an anachronism in an era of Keynesian demand management, but that Labour was suffering electorally from its association with such a policy objective. Gaitskell sought to persuade delegates that 'our object must be to broaden our base, to be in touch always with ordinary people, and to avoid becoming small cliques of isolated doctrine-ridden fanatics, out of touch with the mainstream of social life in our time'. Clause IV would thus have to be abandoned if the Labour Party was to reverse its electoral decline and win the trust of an increasingly middle-class electorate for whom nationalization was either unpopular, or simply irrelevant. Dropping Clause IV was envisaged as a vital means of modernizing the Labour Party, and making it relevant again to voters on the eve of the 1960s.

In the event, Gaitskell and his fellow revisionists were compelled to back down in their attempts at getting Clause IV abandoned. Too many in the Labour Party, particularly amongst the constituency delegates and the trade unions, still adhered to the objective and sentiments enshrined in Clause IV. To abandon it, they claimed, would be to abandon any commitment whatsoever to socialism by the Labour Party. It would be rendered bereft of any real sense of principle or purpose, and end up seeking to do little more than pragmatically reform the status quo. Even many of Gaitskell's closest adherents in the Labour Party, whilst sharing his 'revisionist' views, believed that his attempt at removing Clause IV was ill-judged, and that he 'underestimated both the force of the idea of public ownership as the dominant idea within Labour's socialist myth and the appeal of Clause Four as the formal expression of that myth' (Jones 1991: 443). As such, those of Gaitskell's colleagues who had warned him that he would 'start a battle in the Party that will cause far more trouble than the thing is worth' were vindicated by his enforced climbdown (Crosland 1982: 93).

3   Britain had achieved an unprecedented degree of equality. This, of course, was inextricably related to the increased affluence and prosperity already referred to, and to the role of the welfare state in eradicating 'primary' or 'absolute' poverty. As a consequence of such developments, Crosland argued that Britain was becoming a more egalitarian society,

in which the gap between rich and poor was narrowing, and in which opportunities for social mobility were increasing all the time. Such a trend was cited as further evidence of the irrelevance of Marxism, for Marx had prophesied the increasing 'immiseration' of the working class under capitalism. Yet according to Crosland's critique, the opposite was happening in post-war Britain, thereby rendering Marxism redundant, and reaffirming the view that Britain was no longer a capitalist society.

4   To the extent that inequality still existed, it was mainly in terms of social status and outdated attitudes reflecting snobbery. According to Crosland, the way to eradicate remaining inequality or poverty was not by further appropriating and redistributing wealth from the better off in society – the poor could no longer be made less poor simply by making the rich less rich – but by further improving opportunities for the working class, such as investing more in education, and widening access, so that more people from humble backgrounds could obtain the qualifications necessary to become socially and occupationally mobile.

The conclusion to be drawn from the above premises was that Labour's traditional socialist goals had mostly been, or were well on the way to being, achieved. It was therefore deemed necessary for the party to revise its policies in order to take into account the social and economic changes which it had itself played a major part in bringing about. The emphasis needed to shift away from the pursuit of radical change, to the need to make the existing system work more efficiently, effectively and fairly. The priorities of sustained economic growth and greater social justice would not be achieved by further nationalization or higher taxes being imposed on the rich. As we shall see in the next chapter, this critique led to a serious questioning of the efficacy or desirability of retaining Clause IV of Labour's constitution, the clause which formally committed the Labour Party to nationalization as part of the pursuit of equality.

The Suez Crisis

Back in 1875, the King of Egypt was compelled to sell his 177,000 shares in the Suez Canal Company, in order to raise sufficient capital to pay off certain debts. These shares constituted 44 per cent of the total, the remainder belonging to France. Although a French consortium intended to purchase the other 44 per cent, thereby ensuring that sole ownership of the Suez Canal Company resided in France, Disraeli ignored the doubts of some of his Cabinet colleagues and bought the King of Egypt's shares for £4 million, although, because Parliament was in recess, Disraeli was unable to obtain formal approval to raise or spend such a sum of public money. He therefore borrowed the money from Lord Rothschild, who understandably enquired what security he was being offered: 'the British Government' was the reply (Pearce and Stewart 1992: 149–50).

In 1955, Anthony Eden replaced Winston Churchill as Conservative Party leader and Prime Minister, and then comfortably won the general election the following month. His campaign slogan 'Working for Peace' was soon to be rendered a tragic irony. In 1954, whilst serving as Churchill's Foreign Secretary, Eden had persuaded the Prime Minister to withdraw Britain's troops from the Canal Zone, although Churchill had done so with reluctance, not least because Britain was the largest user of the Suez Canal, with 25 per cent of British exports and imports being shipped through it.

Meanwhile, the new Egyptian leader, Colonel Nasser, was keen to rid Egypt of its colonial status and and achieve independence. At the same time, he was acquiring weaponry from Czechoslovakia and the Soviet Union, which itself was a major cause of concern to Britain and the United States in the context of the Cold War, and fears of Soviet expansionism, coupled with the rise of Arab nationalism in the Middle East.

Initially, Britain and the United States responded by promising Nasser financial aid to build the Aswan Dam, a pledge intended to lure Nasser away from Soviet influence, and to encourage a more conciliatory stance towards the West, particularly Britain. However, relations between Britain and Egypt continued to deteriorate, particularly when Eden suspected that Nasser was implicated in the sacking of Sir John Glubb, the (British) Chief of Staff to King Hussein of Jordan. Consequently, the promise to provide a loan for the building of the Aswan Dam was withdrawn.

Nasser's response, in July 1956, was to nationalize the Suez Canal. This was widely seen as deliberate and extreme provocation of the British Government by Nasser. Quite apart from the fact that Britain and France jointly owned the Suez Canal, it was also a vital transport link for British trade and commerce, 'the Clapham Junction of the Commonwealth' as Julian Amery had characterized it at the Conservatives' 1953 annual conference.

There was thus widespread support in the Conservative Party for a decisive response to Nasser's policy, namely military action against Egypt. As Peter Walker (a future Conservative Minister) put it in a speech at the party's 1956 conference:

> Suez is basic and vital to the economic survival of our nation . . . It would surely be unthinkable for a Tory Government to take any other action than a resolute stand against a dictator threatening the very life line of British trade and commerce.

Britain and France, as the joint owners of the Suez Canal, hatched a plan whereby Israel would invade Egypt, whereupon Britain and France would then intervene militarily under the pretext of separating the two sides, although the real objective, of course, would be to regain control of the Canal.

The United States, however, put pressure on Britain to desist from such action, partly because General Eisenhower wished to campaign for re-election in November's presidential elections on a ticket which emphasized the maintenance of peace in the Middle East, and partly because of concern that military action by the West against Egypt would serve to encourage the Arab world to shift its allegiance further towards the Soviet Union. Indeed, in September 1956, Eisenhower wrote to Eden, warning that:

> The use of military force against Egypt under present circumstances might have consequences even more serious than causing the Arabs to support Nasser. It might cause a serious misunderstanding between our two countries because I must say frankly that there is as yet no public opinion in this country which is prepared to support such a move, and the most significant public opinion that there is seems to think that the United Nations was formed to prevent this very thing . . . (quoted in Carlton 1981: 419)

Britain, in partnership with France, proceeded with their military venture regardless. Israel launched its attack against Egypt on 28 October, with British and French troops beginning their intervention on 31 October. However, a week later, Israel and Egypt accepted a United Nations call for a ceasefire. This had important implications for Britain, of course, because, as Eden himself explained:

> We had intervened to divide and, above all, to contain the conflict. The
> occasion for our intervention was over, the fire was out. Once the fighting
> had ceased, justification for further intervention ceased with it. (quoted
> in R. Butler 1971: 193)

At the same time, the episode was accompanied by a run on the pound,
the losses representing about 15 per cent of Britain's gold and dollar
reserves. Such a serious financial situation required immediate action,
but in this respect, Britain was dependent upon assistance from the
United States. Having opposed the military venture from the outset,
the response from the American Secretary to the Treasury was perhaps
not surprising: '. . . the President cannot help you unless you conform
to the United Nations resolution about withdrawal. If you do that, we
here will help you save the pound' (quoted in R. Butler 1971: 195). In the
words of Rab Butler: 'This was blackmail, but we were in no position to
argue' (*ibid.*: 195).

The whole episode was profoundly damaging to Britain economically,
politically and militarily. Along with the financial implications already
referred to, the affair cast serious doubts on Britain's 'special relationship' with the United States (although when he became Prime Minister
the following year, Harold Macmillan made a concerted effort to heal the
rift). The Suez episode also grievously weakened Britain's claim to be a
military superpower and a major force in world politics. As Pearce and
Stewart comment: 'Perhaps more than any other episode it symbolizes
Britain's decline' (Pearce and Stewart 1992: 567).

The End of Ideology?

The 1950s have been seen by many political scientists and historians as
a decade of unique tranquillity and harmony in domestic British politics.
Indeed, the decade has acquired the image of constituting the zenith of
the so-called 'post-war consensus', the foundations of which had been
laid during the 1940s, particularly under the Attlee Governments, but
which was to come under increasing strain during the 1960s, before
finally crumbling in the 1970s.

It was a decade during which, as previously noted, the Conservative
Party broadly accepted the policy framework established by the Attlee

Governments, so that apart from the denationalization of the iron and steel industries and road haulage, there was no serious attempt, or real desire, to reverse the type of policies, or repeal the legislation, introduced by the previous Labour Governments. In effect, therefore, the Conservative Party was committed to maintenance of the social democratic framework inherited from Labour, entailing a mixed economy, Keynesian demand management, full employment, a welfare state and partnership with the trade unions. With both Labour and the Conservative Parties accepting this 'middle way' between free market capitalism and state socialism, it seemed to many that the resultant consensus heralded 'the end of ideology'.

This term, which actually constituted the title of a book published in 1960 by the American scholar Daniel Bell, suggested that the traditional battle of political ideas between Left and Right was effectively over. The discrediting of both Fascism and Marxism in the West after 1945 (due in no small part to the atrocities committed by Hitler and Stalin) and the improvements wrought through a regulated, welfarist capitalism had 'meant an end to chiliastic hopes, to millenarianism, to apocalyptic thinking – and to ideology' (Bell 1960: 370). As such, the main political parties operated within a narrow framework of ideas and policies which eschewed ideological extremes or radicalism. Whilst public or parliamentary rhetoric gave the impression of fundamental differences and disagreements, the reality was that both of the main political parties shared a commitment to making the existing system function more effectively and fairly. The question was largely over means, not ends. 'In the Western world, therefore, there is today a rough consensus . . . on political issues: the acceptance of a Welfare state; a system of mixed economy . . . the ideological age has ended' (Bell, 1960: 373).

One further factor which accounts for the broadly similar policies supported by the Labour and Conservative Parties during the 1950s concerns electoral behaviour. During this time, it was widely assumed that general election results were largely determined by the preferences of a relatively small number of 'floating voters', which is the term traditionally used by psephologists to refer to voters who do not habitually vote for the same political party at each general election, but who instead are inclined to switch their support from one party to another on a pragmatic basis. It was widely assumed that 'floating voters' were politically moderate, and thus alienated by what they perceived as being too much ideology in party politics. Consequently, the Conservative and Labour Parties were compelled electorally to tone down their ideological commitment and rhetoric in order to 'capture' the middle ground, and hence woo the 'floating voters' deemed to be occupying that territory.

Britain: A Model 'Civic Culture'

During the 1950s, Britain's political system enjoyed an international reputation for its stability and moderation, an image reflected and reinforced by various studies and surveys of political attitudes and behaviour in Britain, but also endorsed by the country's immunity to fascism and communism during the twentieth century.

One of the most famous studies in this context was that conducted by Almond and Verba entitled *Civic Culture*. Using attitude and opinion surveys conducted during the latter half of the 1950s, Almond and Verba investigated the political values and beliefs of citizens in five countries, namely Germany, Italy, Mexico, the United Kingdom (UK) and the United States (USA).

One of the key features of British political culture during the 1950s was the widespread acceptance of the political rules of the game and the legitimacy of the political system. Indeed, in answer to the question about which aspects of their nation they felt most pride in, 46 per cent of UK respondents cited governmental and political institutions, compared to only 7 per cent in West Germany and 3 per cent in Italy (Almond and Verba 1965: 64). When asked about how they expected to be treated by governmental bureaucracy, 83 per cent of UK respondents replied that they expected 'equal treatment', whereas only 65 per cent of Germans and 53 per cent of Italians responded similarly (*ibid.*: 70). A slightly different question, about how people expected their point of view to be treated by government bureaucrats, showed that UK citizens had the greatest faith that their views would be considered seriously, with 59 per cent responding in this way, compared to 53 per cent in West Germany, 56 per cent in the USA, 35 per cent in Italy, and just 12 per cent in Mexico (*ibid.*: 72). Following on from this question, 50 per cent of UK respondents believed that they could influence local or national government, compared to 42 per cent of respondents in Germany, 31 per cent in the USA, 28 per cent in Italy, and only 9 per cent in Mexico (*ibid.*: 181). With regard to the effectiveness of government generally, UK respondents were the most satisfied of all, with 77 per cent answering in the affirmative when asked whether they thought 'the activities of the national government tend to improve conditions in this country'. In the USA, this question elicited a response of 76 per cent, whilst in Germany and Mexico, the figure was 61 per cent and 58 per cent respectively (*ibid.*: 48).

These findings meant that three particular characteristics were commonly ascribed to British politics and society during this time, namely deference, consensus and homogeneity. With regard to deference, Almond and Verba's study clearly indicated widespread respect and reverence among UK citizens towards political institutions and processes. This, in turn, implied a great deal of respect towards figures and officials in positions of authority. Indeed, this notion of deference was often cited as an explanation for the fact that up to one-third of the working class – defined as being manual workers – regularly voted Conservative, it being assumed that some sections of the working class considered Conservatives to be better suited to hold political office and govern the country by virtue of their 'breeding', background and education (McKenzie and Silver 1968).

Such was the degree of deference that Almond and Verba discerned in Britain that they were moved to suggest that 'It is possible that deference to political elites can go too far, and that the strongly hierarchical patterns in British politics . . . result from a balance weighted too heavily in favour of the direction of deferential roles' (Almond and Verba 1965: 361).

The second main characteristic which Almond and Verba ascribed to Britain as a consequence of their findings was that of 'consensus'. However, in this context, they were referring not so much to widespread agreement on actual policies as to common agreement and acceptance of the political 'rules of the game'. The British seemed particularly committed to the use of lawful, constitutional channels to achieve objectives or secure redress of grievances, rather than resorting to direct action, unlawful behaviour or political violence. By the same token, there existed a profound respect and reverence for the notion of parliamentary politics, whereby citizens sought changes or remedies by peacefully persuading elected representatives, either national or local, through such means as lobbying and letter-writing, for example. Almond and Verba's study revealed that in order to influence the government, 44 per cent of British people would seek to contact politicians, either in person or in writing, or write to a newspaper. None of the respondents said that they would 'just protest' or engage in violent activity. This widespread British belief in the sanctity of 'the law' and 'due political process' had once led George Orwell to speak of 'an all-important English trait: the respect for constitutionalism and legality, the belief in "the law" as something above the State and the individual, something which is cruel and stupid, but at any rate incorruptible' (Orwell 1982: 44). This faith in constitutionalism is entirely understandable given that so many people in Britain believed that their point of view would be taken seriously by politicians and bureaucrats; this provided the British political system with an aura of responsiveness and representativeness, and thereby enhanced its legitimacy.

The third and final characteristic confirmed by Almond and Verba's study was that of homogeneity, which meant that there existed a widespread sense of social unity and shared identity amongst British people. With the important exception of Northern Ireland, Britain was renowned for its absence of significant social or cultural cleavages along the lines of ethnicity, language, race, religion, etc., which was in stark contrast to the situation in many other European countries (Blondel 1963: 20–5). This led Birch to point out that:

> As the resolution of conflicts is one of the main functions of government, the nature of the divisions and cleavages in society has a major influence on the character of the political system . . . one of the most important lessons to be drawn from a study of politics is that conflicts deriving from linguistic, religious or racial cleavages are usually more difficult to resolve than conflicts deriving from economic cleavages . . . Britain can be counted as fortunate in that British society is relatively free from the most troublesome kinds of cleavage. (Birch 1993: 6)

Even the main cleavage in British society, the socio-economic one of class, did not pose a fundamental threat to social cohesion or political order. Inequalities of wealth and income did not lead to resentment or hostility amongst the working class, for example, partly because of the tendency of lower-income groups to adopt a narrow frame of reference, whereby they compared their socio-economic situation to those in similar circumstances, rather than to those much better off than themselves (Runciman 1966). To the eternal frustration of Marxists, the British working class has not been motivated by a serious desire to attack the rich or 'appropriate' their wealth and redistribute it.

In the absence of major divisions, therefore, Britain was deemed to be characterized by a remarkable degree of homogeneity. This is not to say that there was total uniformity or unanimity of political views and opinions, but that differences of opinion or belief were neither so wide nor so deep that they undermined the overall stability and cohesion of the existing governmental system. What a former Prime Minister, Arthur Balfour, had said back in 1927 seemed equally applicable to Britain in the 1950s, namely that: 'Our whole political machinery presupposes a people so fundamentally at one that they can safely afford to bicker, and so sure of their moderation that they are not dangerously disturbed by the never-ending din of political conflict' (Balfour 1927: xxiv). To a very considerable extent, this homogeneity both reflected and reinforced a strong sense of national identity and allegiance amongst English people (the Scots and the Welsh retained much of their own cultural identity to a significant degree, although not to the extent of posing a threat to the unity or homogeneity of Britain during the 1950s), and this invariably transcended other potential divisions such as class. Admittedly, the working class might occasionally grumble about a distinction between 'them and us', particularly in the context of industrial relations, but this never superseded national identity, and thus never posed a threat to national unity. As Orwell had observed in the 1940s:

Economically, England is certainly two nations, if not three or four. But at the same time the vast majority of the people feel themselves to be a single nation and are conscious of resembling one another more than they resemble foreigners. Patriotism is usually stronger than class-hatred, and always stronger than any kind of internationalism . . . In the working class, patriotism is profound, but it is unconscious. The working man's heart does not leap when he sees a Union Jack. But the famous 'insularity' and 'xenophobia' of the English is far stronger in the working class than in the bourgeoisie . . . the English working class are outstanding in their hatred of foreign habits. (Orwell 1982: 48–9)

By the 1950s, the gap between the rich and poor, between the working class and the 'bourgeoisie' might have narrowed somewhat, but there is little reason to suggest that Orwell's observation had diminished in accuracy or validity.

It is also important to recognize that a significant factor contributing to the degree of consensus and homogeneity which commentators such as Almond and Verba discerned in Britain during the 1950s was the fact that, economically amd politically, the 'system' seemed to be working remarkably well. The economy appeared to be operating effectively, providing full employment and rising living standards, whilst politically there was considerable trust in Britain's governmental institutions. After all, during times of economic growth and stability, politicians are better able to respond positively to the needs of the population, and thereby further imbue the political system with legitimacy. This was something which was to become increasingly difficult from the 1960s onwards.

3 1960–70: Decade of Doubt, Decade of Reform

When sorrows come, they come not single spies,
But in battalions . . .

William Shakespeare, *Hamlet*

The 1960s were a decade of doubt. They were also a decade of reform. The two aspects are inextricably related, for as politicians and opinion-formers became more aware of the deteriorating state of the British economy, so solutions were increasingly sought through the reform of institutions. The 1960s witnessed attempts at reforming the Civil Service, Parliament and the trade unions. They also saw the creation of new institutions, particularly in the economic sphere, such as the National Economic Development Council and the Department of Economic Affairs. The 1960s were a decade when it sometimes seemed that 'nothing was to escape the urge for institutional reform' (Walkland 1984: 41). There were also, it ought to be noted, important social reforms, such as the legalization or liberalization of abortion, divorce and homosexuality, whilst the death penalty was abolished. For many, the 1960s were also a decade of sexual and social revolution, nowhere more clearly evinced than in the rise of feminism. Yet whilst such changes, developments and reforms were seen by many people as 'progressive', traditionalists viewed them with a mixture of dismay and disgust, thereby adding to the sense of doubt which they felt about Britain's future. Indeed, during the 1990s Conservatives have sought to attribute many of Britain's problems such as crime, marital break-ups and single parenthood to the 'permissive revolution' of the 1960s.

In many respects, the 1960s were equally a decade of managerialism and technology. There was a widespread belief amongst Britain's political elites that problems could and should be solved through the application of expertise. The decade thus yielded a number of Royal Commissions and Committees of Inquiry, reflecting an assumption that investigation of a problem by 'a body of wise men' or 'the great and the good' would yield the appropriate solution. Even Harold Wilson, who had originally condemned Royal Commissions for 'taking minutes and wasting years', found himself establishing a number of such bodies during his premiership from 1964 to 1970.

Managerialism and modernization were the concepts which often underpinned the efforts of politicians to solve Britain's economic and political problems during the 1960s, particularly from 1964 onwards, when Harold Wilson had led the Labour Party to electoral victory talking of the 'white heat' of technological revolution. This era of 'technocratic reformism' (T. Smith 1986: 70) witnessed great faith being placed in rationalism, science and technology as the means of tackling the growing range of problems confronting political leaders and policy-makers, although this 'faith' seemed sometimes to be characterized by quiet desperation rather than quixotic optimism.

Much of the institutional reform and innovation which occurred during the 1960s reflected the search for greater efficiency in a number of spheres. As one commentator has pointed out: 'By far the overwhelming majority of the innovations have been introduced for administrative rather than democratic reasons. That is to say they have emphasised the need for efficiency as opposed to accountability . . . ' (T. Smith, 1986: 66). Whatever the rationale or primary purpose of these innovations, they can all, to a lesser or greater extent, be traced to the discernible feeling that things were 'not quite right' in Britain during the 1960s, either economically or politically. As Crick noted, 'we find ourselves at one of those times of crisis in the life of a nation when . . . great and sudden doubts have arisen about whether our whole machinery of government . . . is adequate to deal with modern problems' (Crick 1964: x). It is in this context that British politics during the 1960s has to be understood, although this in turn requires a brief consideration of economic circumstances and developments, for concern over the efficacy and efficiency of Britain's political institutions was inextricably linked to recognition of the relative decline and deteriorating condition of the British economy.

Problems with the Economy

During the 1960s it became apparent that the British economy was in relative decline, and beset by a number of difficulties. Whilst many commentators may argue that the origins for Britain's economic decline can be traced back to the late nineteenth century, it is widely acknowledged that the 1960s heralded a fundamental change in attitudes and assumptions regarding the strength and stability of the British economy; the genial confidence of the 1950s was replaced by genuine concern during the 1960s.

Whereas Britain had once been the world's largest exporter of manufactured goods (enjoying 33.2 per cent of the international market in 1899), its share had fallen from 25.5 per cent in 1950 to 16.5 per cent in 1960. By the end of the decade it had dwindled to barely 11 per cent. Throughout this period, Britain was being challenged and overtaken by a number of other advanced industrial countries, such as Japan and (West) Germany.

Similar cause for concern was prompted by the British economy's low rate of growth. By 1960 it had become evident that during the previous decade, Britain's economic rate of growth had been lower than that achieved by countries such as France, Italy, Sweden, the United States and (West) Germany. There was little improvement during the course of the 1960s. Indeed, during the latter half of the decade, Britain's average rate of economic growth was just 2 per cent, whilst during that time Japan's rate was 16.5 per cent, the EEC's was 6.5 per cent, and the United States achieved an economic growth rate of nearly 5 per cent.

Britain's declining share of the world market in manufactured exports, coupled with its low rates of economic growth, resulted in a concomitant deterioration in the country's balance of payments during the course of the 1960s. For example, during the 1960–4 period, Britain's overall current balance was in the red for three out of five years, whereas during the 1952–9 period it had consistently shown a surplus. What fuelled concern further was that the deficit on the 'visible' earnings account increased from an average of £377 million in the second half of the 1950s, to an average of £1,277 million during the first half of the 1960s. That Britain's overall balance of payments account was ever in credit was due entirely to the strength of her 'invisible' earnings (i.e. banking, financial services etc.). Such statistics served to indicate just how serious were the economic problems facing the nation which had spearheaded the Industrial Revolution, and had once been known admiringly as 'the workshop of the world'.

Yet other economic indicators also added to the growing sense of concern and consternation over the British economy during the 1960s. Inflation emerged as a serious problem during the decade due to an increase in the average rate of 3.5 per cent during the first half of the 1960s to 5.4 per cent in 1969. (In the same year, (West) Germany's inflation rate was just 1.9 per cent.) Meanwhile unemployment was also on the increase during the 1960s, and whilst its maximum of 2.5 per cent (or over 600,000) by the late 1960s seems negligible compared to the high levels of unemployment which Britain experienced throughout the 1980s and 1990s, it none the less gave cause for concern, largely because it raised doubts about the efficiency of Keynesian techniques for managing the economy and sustaining full employment.

All of these economic indicators served to fuel concern amongst Britain's political elites that the British economy was much less healthy and vigorous than had hitherto been assumed. Indeed, concern over Britain's apparently ailing economy was instrumental in causing a loss of confidence and increasing doubt during the 1960s, not only with regard to economic performance and prospects, but also with regard to the performance and machinery of government itself. Hence, the realization that Britain was experiencing relative economic decline was accompanied by the pursuit of institutional reform. Britain's political institutions, it was widely believed, needed to be modernized, and rendered more efficient. Indeed, in some cases, new institutions were to be created. Institutional innovation was – somehow – to provide the spur to economic regeneration.

Emergence of the Trade Union Problem

The economic problems just outlined understandably prompted suggestions as to their causes. It required little imagination or ingenuity to apportion at least some of the blame to the trade unions. From the early 1960s onwards, the trade unions were increasingly seen as a primary cause of Britain's deteriorating, declining economy. They thus became the 'scapegoats of economic decline' (Taylor 1993: 1–15).

A number of specific charges were levelled against the trade unions by politicians and press alike. Firstly, in the context of increasing inflation, there was concern over the level of wage increases. The orthodox view appeared to be that wage increases, unmatched by a corresponding increase in productivity and economic growth, fuelled inflation, either because employees raised the price of their products to cover increased wage costs, or because more money would be circulating in the economy, but chasing the same number of goods. In either case, therefore, the wage increases pursued by trade unions were deemed to be a major cause of the rising inflation which affected the British economy during the 1960s.

Secondly, trade unions were deemed to be an obstacle to increased productivity and greater efficiency, by virtue of 'restrictive practices'. The trade unions were accused of preventing management from introducing changes in working patterns and staffing levels, so as to improve efficiency and productivity, because of their obsession with defending their members' jobs. By opposing management proposals which might result in job losses, as firms sought to 'rationalize' themselves and become more cost-effective, competitive and profitable, the trade unions were variously accused of causing over-manning and exhibiting a Luddite mentality in opposing new working practices and technological innovations which might result in redundancies. Having long been accused of susceptibility to communist influences, the trade unions were doubtless intrigued to be berated for being too *conservative* and backward looking.

The third charge levelled against the trade unions by those seeking an easy scapegoat for Britain's economic decline was their propensity to engage in strike action. In particular, there emerged particular concern over the incidence of *unofficial* strikes – that is, strikes which are not called or endorsed by the union leadership. Indeed, such strikes might well be in blatant defiance of the advice or instructions of trade union leaders. In such instances, *unofficial* strike activity would be pursued by ordinary union members acting independently of their union leaders. The reason why concern emerged during the early 1960s over unofficial strikes was not actually a sudden increase in their frequency, but because it was only in 1961 that the Ministry of Labour began distinguishing between official and unofficial strikes when compiling its statistics on industrial stoppages. In so doing, it was discovered that approximately 95 per cent of strikes were unofficial. Thus unofficial strikes came to be seen by many as the key problem of British industrial relations and trade unionism.

However, opinions differed as to the precise cause of unofficial strikes, and their prevalence or preponderance. For many, they were merely a further manifestation of 'evil Marxists' and 'Communist sympathizers' at work inside Britain's trade unions, who were fomenting industrial disruption in order to undermine and destroy Britain's capitalist economy, and thereby pave the way for a socialist revolution. For more enlightened Conservatives, however (and in those days there were quite a few), the phenomenon of unofficial strikes was explicable in terms of the changing structure and organization of British industry – and, *inter alia*, the trade unions themselves. This perspective noted that as enterprises and industries became larger and more centralized, so the distance between management and workers, and between trade union leaders and their rank-and-file members, would become correspondingly greater. This, in turn, would result in problems concerning the maintenance of communication and cohesion. In such a context, workers were more likely to experience feelings of alienation and anomie, which in turn would be expressed in the form of an increased propensity to engage in strike action.

During the period 1960–4, this 'human relations' perspective continued to prevail in the Conservative Party, as it had done throughout the 1950s. However, it became evident that patience with the trade unions was wearing thin, even among many Conservatives who had hitherto been most committed to a 'voluntarist' approach. Even the arch-conciliator himself, Harold Macmillan, was moved to complain about the hopeless conservatism of labour in some of the old industries. With wild-cat strikes in the former, and restrictive practices in the latter, Macmillan pointed out, 'our poor economy suffers grievously' (Macmillan 1972: 375). The trade unions were increasingly warned that time was running out for them to put their house in order. If they didn't succeed in reforming themselves, and thereby deal effectively with the scale of unofficial strikes engaged in by their members, then legislative action by the Government would become inevitable.

In the meantime, the Macmillan Government sought to involve the trade unions far more closely in economic policy-making, by creating, at the end of 1961, the National Economic Development Council (NEDC). This was a 'tripartite' body comprising a number of Government ministers, trade union leaders and employee representatives. It was envisaged that the NEDC would provide a valuable forum through which economic issues and policies could be discussed, and views exchanged between the parties involved. The Government clearly hoped that the NEDC would serve to teach the trade unions the economic facts of life, 'would at least lead them to greater understanding of the real problems with which the nation was confronted' (Macmillan 1973: 51).

During this time, the Macmillan Government was also embracing incomes policies, seeing them as a vital means of restraining labour costs and inflation, and thereby helping to restore the competitiveness of British industry and the economy. Indeed, it became clear that far from seeing an incomes policy as a temporary, short-term expedient to tackle a particular economic problem or crisis, Macmillan and some of his ministerial colleagues were arriving at the view that 'an incomes policy is necessary as a permanent feature of our economic life' and 'an indispensable element in laying the foundations upon which to build a policy of sound economic growth' (Macmillan, HC Debates, 5th series, vol. 633, col. 1757).

The move to an incomes policy first came with the introduction in July 1961 of a 'pay pause' by the chancellor, Selwyn Lloyd. This was intended to provide the Government with a nine-month 'breathing space', during which time it would be able to formulate a more permanent incomes policy.

Whilst the NEDC was not in itself directly concerned to formulate an incomes policy, the Government undoubtedly envisaged that by participating in discussions concerning economic affairs, the trade unions would more readily be persuaded of the necessity for incomes policies. In fact, during 1963 and 1964, 'the NEDC became the major focus for wages policy largely because it was acknowledged that in the context of a planned economic expansion, there was a need for wage restraint' (Jones 1987: 61).

But this time, however, the Macmillan Government's patience with the trade unions was fast running out. The incorporation of trade union leaders into national level economic decision-making and wage determination merely widened the gulf between them and their rank-and-file membership, which compounded the problems of unofficial strikes and local-level industrial action. Pressure in the Conservative Party for legal curbs on the trade unions increased markedly, to the extent that the parliamentary leadership promised a review of trade union law after the forthcoming general election. However, the Conservative Party lost the 1964 general election, and thus had to conduct its own review in Opposition, as part of a wider review and revaluation of British Conservatism. Ironically, perhaps, it was the subsequent Labour Government which first sought to instigate statutory reform of the trade unions, as we shall note shortly.

Looking Towards Europe

The economic problems besetting the British economy during the 1960s led to an apparent change of attitude towards the European Communities.[1] When moves were instigated by Belgium, France, Holland, Italy, Luxembourg and West Germany during the 1950s to establish closer economic and political union in Europe, Britain had exhibited little desire or inclination to participate in such a venture. A number of reasons accounted for such reticence.

Firstly, Britain had not only emerged victorious from the Second World War, but had also been spared occupation and invasion (the Channel Islands notwithstanding). Britain had thus retained its long history of freedom from foreign conquest, and this buttressed a sense of independence and autonomy which militated against any desire or need to participate in a co-operative, collaborative venture with the country's continental neighbours.

Secondly, Britain was enjoying an unprecedented period of prosperity during the 1950s and thus saw little need to pursue closer, more formal or institutional economic links with other European countries. The affluence and prosperity which many British people enjoyed during much of the 1950s created a sense of confidence and contentment. Britain was, it seemed, capable of success and stability in its own right, an assumption underpinned by the widespread acceptance and application of Keynesian techniques of economic management. Such techniques fostered a belief that government regulation of economic activity could ensure constant growth and prosperity, along with the maintenance of full employment. Poverty and mass unemployment, many assumed, had been banished for ever. Furthermore, Britain's apparent economic strength was both reflected in, and reinforced by, both its perceived position in the world economy and its trading links with the Commonwealth countries in particular.

Thirdly, Britain's 'special relationship' with both the Commonwealth and the United States reinforced a sense of distinction from the rest of Europe, and the view that Britain's obligations and loyalties resided elsewhere. This 'special relationship' was partly cultural, in the sense that many of the inhabitants of countries such as Australia, Canada, New Zealand and the United States are ancestrally of British origin. As such, it was widely considered during the 1950s that the British people had much more in common with the inhabitants of the Commonwealth countries and the United States than they did with the people of continental Europe: a similar culture, a shared language, a faith in capitalism and the market economy, and support for the principles and institutions of liberal democracy. In addition, Britain perceived the United States to be a reliable military ally, upon whom the British people could depend to defend the Western world from the perceived threat posed by the Soviet Union and 'international Communism'.

A fourth factor underpinning Britain's reticence about being formally involved in the development of greater economic and political union was that of party politics. The Conservative Party has always been seen (and portrayed itself) as *the* party of nationalism and patriotism in Britain, for whom the national interest is always paramount. Furthermore, during the 1950s many Conservatives still thought of Britain's role and status in the world in terms of the Empire. Such images and self-perceptions militated against formal participation in a joint European venture which, it was feared, would ultimately result in the submergence or even loss of British identity and status.

The Labour Party, meanwhile, whilst ostensibly more likely to support a move to create a more united Europe – on the grounds of internationalism, fraternity, etc. – was characterized by ambivalence and division over the issue of whether Britain ought to become a member of the EC. Much of the opposition to EC membership emanated from the left of the Labour Party, where the EC was viewed suspiciously as a 'capitalist club', and thus one with which a self-proclaimed socialist party should have no truck. The Labour Left also believed that priority ought to be given to maintaining or even developing Britain's links with the Commonwealth.

On the right of the Labour Party, support for British membership was forthcoming, although considerable support also existed on this wing of the party for maintaining the 'special relationship' with the United States. Overall though, for most of the early 1960s, 'hostility tinged with indifference remained broadly the Party's official line for the next three or four years, and the Common Market was barely mentioned in the 1964 manifesto' (Stewart 1977: 77).

Yet during the 1960s, two particular factors contributed to a shift in the prevailing British position concerning Europe, to the extent that during the decade, Britain twice applied to join the European Community, once in 1961, and then in 1967, but was refused membership on both occasions (for reasons which will shortly become apparent).

Firstly, the economic indicators outlined earlier contrasted starkly with the economic success and prosperity being enjoyed by the six founder members of the EC. As noted previously, it became apparent during the 1960s that Britain's rate of economic growth was lower than that achieved by the member states of the EC (for example, Britain's growth rate was just 2 per cent during the latter half of the 1960s, compared to 6.5 per cent for the EC member states).

Secondly, Britain was seeking to come to terms with the loss of the Empire (having lost an Empire, Britain was yet to find a role, as Neal Ascherson remarked), for which the Commonwealth was no real substitute, particularly in view of South Africa's withdrawal in March 1961. In this context, Britain – or rather successive British governments – began to recognize that Europe *did* afford an opportunity and an arena in which the British could retain, or revive, an international role, and exert an influence on international affairs. The alternative, it was feared, would be an 'isolationist' stance for Britain, and whilst 'Little Englanders' in both main political parties might have looked favourably upon such a scenario, the *general* view of Britain's political elite was that Britain could no longer afford – economically or politically – *not* to seek membership of the EC.

Britain's first two applications for membership of the EC (in 1961 and 1967) were both vetoed by the French President, General Charles de Gaulle. He was not convinced about the sincerity of Britain's new found desire to join the EC. On the contrary, de Gaulle recognized that it was the factors just outlined which had led to Britain's belated desire to join the EC, not any genuine conversion to the ideal of European unity or union. In other words, it was circumstances, not commitment, which underpinned Britain's application, pragmatism rather than principle. In de Gaulle's view, this was not a particularly promising or propitious basis on which to become a member state. De Gaulle's doubts were reinforced by Britain's trade links with the Commonwealth, links which, it was made clear in the negotiations over entry to the EC, Britain wished to retain. Consequently, de Gaulle observed that: 'England in fact is insular, maritime, bound by her trade, her markets, her supplies to countries that are very diverse and often far away . . . How can England, as she lives, as she produces, as she trades, be incorporated in the common Market?' (quoted in Barker 1976: 79).

Britain's 'special relationship' with the United States only served to compound de Gaulle's suspicion of the British application for EC membership. Indeed one of the factors influencing Britain's application was pressure from the United States, and it was this wish which added to de Gaulle's antipathy, for he was deeply concerned that if admitted, Britain would act as a 'Trojan Horse' for American interests within the EC, and 'give a more Atlantic orientation to policy than he wished to see' (George 1990: 35; see also Werth 1965: 325–6). Of course, de Gaulle was also only too well aware that if Britain were to become a member of the EC, but retained a 'special relationship' with the United States, then France's own status and authority within Europe would be undermined.

Whilst the other five member states were amenable to admitting Britain to the EC, France, or rather the French President, de Gaulle, vetoed both of the applications tendered during the 1960s. In the context of Britain's loss of the Empire and relative economic decline, the failure to gain membership of the EC added insult to injury, compounding as it did the image of a once great nation and world power now in decline and on the wane.

Labour's 'Modernization' Plans

As was noted in the previous chapter, Labour's election defeats in the 1950s prompted a major debate, both within the Party and amongst sympathetic commentators, concerning the alleged socio-economic changes taking place in post-war Britain, and the implications of these changes for the future electoral success of the Labour Party. Indeed, some wondered whether Labour would ever get elected to office again, in view of the apparent embourgeoisement of the working class. The debates prompted amongst Labour MPs and supporters in the latter half of the 1950s, fuelled in no small part by Anthony Crosland's *The Future of Socialism*, were sustained by the 1959 election defeat and thus continued into the 1960s.

Certainly, the 'revisionists' viewed the 1959 election defeat as vindication of their case, and therefore deemed it even more vital that the Labour Party shake off its 'cloth cap', class-based image and eradicate the socialist rhetoric about further nationalization and expropriating the rich. Not only was it claimed that such rhetoric alienated many voters who assumed that Labour was not addressing them and their aspirations, it was also said to be frightening voters who were enjoying rising living standards and disposable incomes, and who thus feared that they too would be expropriated by a Labour Government. To win the trust and support of an allegedly more middle-class electorate, it was argued that Labour had to adopt more 'relevant' policies and a more modern image, more appropriate to a more democratic, technocratic society in which class divisions and antagonisms seemed to be disappearing. The 'revisionists' warned that: 'If the necessary changes are not made, the Labour vote will probably decline, unless some sudden crisis supervenes, by about 2% at each general election . . . and the pendulum, when it swings against the Tories, will swing it back to the Liberals' (Crosland 1960).

One particularly notable manifestation of the intra-party conflict engendered in the context of modernizing and revising Labour's policies and image occurred at the beginning of the decade, over the issue of nuclear disarmament. Three years after the formation of the Campaign for Nuclear Disarmament, Labour's 1960 annual conference voted in favour of a policy of unilateral nuclear disarmament, against the wishes of Hugh Gaitskell, the Labour leader, who was a committed multilateralist. As Labour's annual conference is – according to the party's constitution – its formal policy-determining body, the vote officially committed Labour to a unilateralist defence policy, even though the party leadership was fundamentally opposed to such a policy. In the wake of the 1960 annual conference rebuff, Gaitskell made his famous pledge to 'fight, fight and fight again to save the party we love', by seeking to reverse the unilateralist policy. This objective was achieved at the following year's annual conference, by which time Gaitskell had succeeded in mobilizing centre-right support in the Labour Party and the trade unions behind him on the issue of defence. The 1961 annual conference thus saw the unilateralist policy reversed, and Labour reverting back to its multilateralist stance.

With the issue of defence policy effectively resolved, Labour was able to give its full attention to domestic issues and policies with a view to winning the next election, which was due in 1964 at the latest. In fact, the 1960 annual conference had approved a policy document, drafted in the wake of the 1959 election defeat, simply entitled *Labour in the Sixties*, in which acknowledgement was made of the contraction of the traditional working class and industrial base (from where the party had traditionally drawn the bulk of its electoral support), and the concomitant expansion of the service sector and white-collar workers, supervisory staff, and the like. According to *Labour in the Sixties*,

> Many such people . . . are politically isolated. They are not in touch with Labour yet they are disgusted by the Tory view that status-seeking and ladder-climbing are the most important human activities . . . the aim is to broaden the base of the party, at present being eroded by social and occupational change. (quoted in Butler and King 1965: 59)

A subsequent policy document, *Signposts for the Sixties*, was published in July 1961, and formally approved as a statement of Labour policies and objectives at the annual conference in October. It effectively constituted a modified version of *Labour in the Sixties*, reiterating the need for the party to modify its image and policies, in order that it might broaden its electoral appeal in a Britain seemingly undergoing major socio-economic change. Policies such as more nationalization and higher taxation of the better-off were toned down in favour of measures intended to facilitate greater investment and faster economic growth. Greater public owner-ship was not generally necessary in order to achieve these objectives, and to the extent that nationalization might be implemented it would be according to specific circumstances or problems. In other words, any extension of public ownership by a Labour Government was to derive from pragmatism rather than principle. In any case, *Labour in the Sixties* and *Signposts for the Sixties* reflected much of the revisionists' view that Keynesian techniques for regulating the economy rendered further nationalization superfluous, on the grounds that governments could now achieve their objectives – social as well as economic – by fiscal and monetary policies, and planning which would ultimately determine levels of growth, investment, tax revenues and so on.

A discernible shift in emphasis occurred when Gaitskell's death early in 1963 resulted in Harold Wilson becoming leader of the Labour Party. Although Wilson was considered by many to have emanated from the left of the Party, his emphasis on 'modernization' and tackling Britain's problems partly through stronger economic growth appealed to Labour's 'revisionist' wing, and, in turn, enabled Wilson to imbue the party with greater unity.

One particular theme which Wilson propagated was that of using science and technology to modernize Britain and tackle the country's problems. Nowhere was this theme made more explicit than in Wilson's speech to the Labour Party's 1963 annual conference, in which he informed delegates that:

> If there is one theme running through this Conference this week . . . it is the theme of change, the over-due need for this country to adapt itself to different conditions . . . We are living perhaps in a more rapid revolution than some of us realise. The period of 15 years from . . . 1960 to the middle of the 1970s will embrace a period of technical change, particularly in industrial methods, greater than in the whole industrial revolution of the last 250 years . . . The problem is this . . . It is the choice between the blind imposition of technological advance, with all that means in terms of unemployment, and the conscious, planned, purposive use of scientific progress to provide undreamed of living standards and the possibility of leisure ultimately on an unbelievable scale . . . First, we must produce more scientists. Secondly, having produced them, we must be a great deal more successful in keeping them in this country. Thirdly, having trained them and kept them here, we must make more intelligent use of them when they are trained than we do with those we have got. Fourthly, we must organise British industry so that it applies the results of scientific research more purposively to our national production effort . . . Let us be clear, unless we can harness science to our economic planning, we are not going to get the expansion that we need . . . we are re-stating our Socialism in terms of the scientific revolution . . . The Britain that is going to be forged in the white heat of their technological revolution will be no place for restrictive practices or for out-dated methods on either side of industry. (quoted in Coates 1975: 98–9)

'White heat', maybe. Hot air, certainly. Wilson compounded this vacuous verbiage by declaring that: 'We must harness Socialism to science, and science to Socialism.' Certainly, 'Labour during this period increasingly made a virtue of consulting experts, many of them scientists, in the formulation of party policy' (Butler and King 1965: 73, n. 1). In so doing, not only was the Labour Party seeking to apply science and technology to Britain's economic, industrial and social problems, but also to win the electoral support of people such as scientists and technicians, which tacitly reflected the 'revisionist' view that Labour had to move far beyond the traditional, manual working class if it was to defeat the Conservatives at the polls. After all, a 1960 study had confirmed what most 'revisionists' already knew, namely that most people:

> ... see the Conservatives as exercising a much greater attraction for ambitious people, middle class people, young people, office workers, and scientists ... The image of the Labour Party, held by both its supporters and its non-supporters, is one which is increasingly obsolete in terms of contemporary Britain. (Abrams 1960: 23)

However, Wilson's approach merely seemed to confirm the suspicions of his critics in the Labour Party that 'he isn't a man of principle but a sheer, absolute careerist, out for himself alone' (Nye Bevan, quoted in Ponting 1989: 9). This suspicion was often reciprocated, with Wilson himself distrustful of some of his Cabinet colleagues. On one occasion, for example, Wilson rhetorically asked Richard Crossman: 'Do you really think there is anyone of them I can trust?', whilst on another occasion, Wilson said to Crossman: 'Has anyone else ever brought so many of his enemies into a Cabinet?' (Castle 1984: 379). This last lament was uttered just a couple of years after an 'enormously exhilarated' Wilson had boasted that, having completed a Cabinet reshuffle: 'What I have done this time is to surround myself with friends ... ' (Crossman 1979: 215).

The Conservatives' Policy Review

The loss of any general election is bound to be a profoundly depressing experience for a major political party, particularly if they have hitherto constituted the Government. For the Conservative Party, therefore, the loss of the October 1964 election, after thirteen consecutive years in office, was especially traumatic, not least because it cast doubt on its claim to be the 'natural party of Government' in Britain. Yet there was widespread feeling throughout the Conservative Party that, in terms of its policies, principles and parliamentary leadership, it had become out of touch with public opinion, and a new mood amongst the British people generally. This perception was largely prompted by the fact that the Labour Party had won the 1964 election not only espousing the language of modernization and meritocracy, but also by having a younger, more 'in touch' leader in Harold Wilson.

The Conservative Party's response was twofold. Firstly, it sought to rejuvenate itself, not merely by seeking a younger, more dynamic parliamentary leader who could more effectively challenge and compete with Harold Wilson, but also by seeking the selection of younger candidates at a constituency level. Secondly, but inextricably linked with, and following on from this aspect, the Conservative Party embarked on a major review of its principles and policies whilst in Opposition, in order to modernize itself and prove its continued relevance to the electorate. These two features warrant further examination and explanation.

In the wake of the 1964 general election defeat, many Conservatives concurred with the view that leaders such as Harold Macmillan, and his successor, Sir Alec Douglas-Home, had become an electoral liability, because of their aristocratic background or image. Whereas men of such origins or calibre would previously have been perceived as ideally suited to the task of winning support for the Conservative Party from a deeply deferential British people (including many deferential working class voters who respected such Conservative leaders, and considered them to be the best type of people to govern the country), it was felt by many Conservatives in the wake of the 1964 election defeat that older, patrician paternalists were now an electoral liability. Britain was widely perceived to be increasingly open, meritocratic and classless, and as such, many Conservatives themselves acknowledged the need for a new type of party leader. Yet at the same time, this entailed more than merely replacing the existing elderly leader with someone younger and more dynamic. It also involved a fundamental change in the method by which Conservative Party leaders were appointed in the first place.

Conservative leaders had traditionally 'emerged' by virtue of the most senior figures in the Party conferring together to decide upon a new leader (although when the party was in office, a new leader, because they would also be Prime Minister, would *formally* be appointed by the

Monarch, on the advice of a retiring leader): hence the notion that the new Conservative leaders materialized from smoke-filled rooms having been summoned by the 'men in grey suits'. It had once been claimed by a Conservative that: 'Great leaders of parties are not elected, they are evolved . . . I venture to hope that it will not be necessary – and I think it will be a bad day for this or any other Party – to have solemnly to meet to elect a leader' (Captain Pretyman MP, quoted in Fisher 1977: 6).

This assertion did not ring true, however, when Macmillan announced his imminent retirement on grounds of ill health, in the early autumn of 1963. Instead, the Conservatives' annual conference, which was taking place in Blackpool at the time of Macmillan's declaration, was effectively transformed into a campaign platform for senior Conservatives who publicly sought to parade their leadership credentials. Lord (Rab) Butler later lamented that the whole episode 'turned Blackpool into a sort of electoral convention *á l'Americaine*. After that there was no peace' (Butler 1971: 242).

One senior Conservative, Quintin Hogg (Lord Hailsham), was apparently Macmillan's preferred choice of successor, but in acting as if his appointment as Conservative leader was thus virtually assured, he had behaved in an ostentatious manner which proved counter-productive, merely serving to alienate sections of the party's opinion, including some which would otherwise have supported Hogg. His behaviour both raised questions about his political judgement and responsibility, and appeared distasteful to many Conservatives who felt that the tone of the annual conference had been lowered. Remembering that his own appointment as Conservative leader had caused some disquiet amongst sections of the party who felt that they ought to have had some say in the matter, Macmillan initiated a consultative exercise, so that the views of as many Conservatives as possible could be solicited concerning the choice of a new leader. The outcome was the appointment of Sir Alec Douglas-Home, who, by this time, was also Macmillan's choice of successor.

However, many Conservatives were unhappy at the appointment of Sir Alec as Conservative leader and Prime Minister. There were two objections. Firstly, it was considered by some Conservatives that Sir Alec's age (he was 60) and aristocratic social background would prove damaging to the party's electoral prospects. Secondly, there were questions among some Conservatives about just how much support in the party Sir Alec really enjoyed. Indeed, there were claims that the Cabinet itself had been seriously divided, with at least nine ministers favouring Rab Butler, six supporting Sir Alec, and five whose preferences were unknown. Such a division of opinion at the highest level of the Party, it was suggested, hardly indicated a convincing degree of support for Sir Alec (Fisher 1977: 107). Unease was exacerbated when the Chief Whip revealed that the opinions of some people had been ascribed greater weight 'since in every organisation there must be people whose opinion one would more strongly rely on than others' (Martin Redmayne MP, *The Listener*, 19/12/63: 1013).

The loss of the 1964 general election was instrumental in effecting a change in the Conservative Party's method of selecting its leaders. Those Conservatives who had warned that Sir Alec's age and social background would prove an electoral liability were deemed to have been vindicated. There was widespread recognition that a new – younger, less upper-class – leader and a new method of selection were needed. In February 1965, following a review of the Conservative Party's method of appointing its leaders, Sir Alec announced that a new procedure was to be adopted, whereby each Conservative MP would cast one vote by secret ballot. In order to secure a victory a leadership candidate would have to achieve a majority of votes cast *plus 15 per cent* over the candidate in second place. However, if no candidate secured the requisite majority, then a second ballot of Conservative MPs would be held, in which new candidates would be eligible to stand. In the second ballot, a simple majority would be sufficient to ensure victory. Lest this still failed to yield a victor, provision was made for a third ballot, contested by the three leading candidates from the second ballot, in which Conservative MPs would select two of the candidates in order of preference (by putting a '1' against the first choice and '2' against the second choice). The candidate with the fewest 'first preference' votes would subsequently be eliminated and the 'second preferences' on his/her paper distributed accordingly to the remaining candidates. This would ensure that one of the candidates would secure an overall majority and the Conservative Party would have a new leader – one who could confidently claim to enjoy considerable support among their parliamentary colleagues.

With a new leadership election procedure announced, it was inevitable that Sir Alec would face pressure to stand down as Conservative leader, thereby enabling a new leader to be appointed and established in time for the next general election. Sir Alec obliged by tendering his resignation in July 1965, thus paving the way for Edward Heath to become the beneficiary of the Conservative Party's first ever formal leadership election.

Meanwhile moves were also afoot to make the rest of the parliamentary Conservative Party younger, and thus more dynamic and 'in touch' with British society. In May 1965, the new Conservative Party chairperson, Edward Du Cann, announced that Central Office (the party's headquarters in Smith Square, London) was redrawing its list of prospective parliamentary candidates, with the objective of securing the selection of younger, more 'representative' candidates. At the same time, letters were sent to Conservative candidates defeated in the 1964 election, requesting them to reconsider their position, particularly if they were 'advanced in years'. Following this process half of the candidates who fought the 1966 general election for the Conservative Party were subsequently dropped or persuaded to stand down, in order to make way for a younger, more socially representative, selection of candidates for the next election.

The changes in the Conservative Party leadership selection procedure, coupled with the recruitment of younger, more representative parliamentary candidates and MPs, was a process which proceeded *pari passu* with a fundamental review of principles and policies. It was widely considered that after thirteen years in office, the Conservative Party had lost any real sense of direction or purpose, and had become bereft of ideas or vision. Towards the end of its thirteen years in Government, some Conservatives lamented, the party had merely drifted with the tide, rather than steering in any particular or predetermined direction. At the same time, there was a criticism that the parliamentary leadership had been so preoccupied with achieving consensus and common agreement on policies, that tough or controversial decisions had been avoided. Compromise had supplanted commitment; action on vital issues was tempered by appeasement of vested interests.

The years in Opposition, therefore, witnessed the Conservative Party engage in a comprehensive re-examination and review of its principles and policies. Such a review was warmly welcomed by many of the newer, younger Conservative MPs especially, for it was frequently these who were often most critical of the recent emphasis on compromise and consensus, rather than commitment and conviction. According to Timothy Raison MP, 'it is not the One Nation Spirit that we need today, but willingness to risk the tension that may arise from greater readiness to root out the weaknesses' (Raison 1965: 15).

Shortly after the loss of the 1964 election, Edward Heath launched a major policy review. This entailed the establishment of 21 advisory groups, each focusing on a particular area of policy, although it was not long before the number of groups had increased to 36. By July 1965, 248 Conservatives were directly involved in the work of these advisory groups: 120 MPs, 118 prospective parliamentary candidates and ten peers from the House of Lords. Support and assistance was also provided by Conservative sympathizers or supporters in industry, finance, commerce and academia. In addition 300 extra-parliamentary groups, involving 3,000 people, also contributed to the party's policy review, via the Conservative Political Centre's 'Two Way Movement of Ideas' network in the constituencies.

An early indication of the direction in which Heath was seeking to lead the Conservative Party was provided by the 1965 publication of a policy document of 'Conservative aims' entitled *Putting Britain Right Ahead*. Whilst acknowledging that the 'Party Policy Committees on whose studies it is based are still hard at work and will continue', Heath in his 'foreword' to the document emphasized the vital need for the British economy to be made 'more efficient, more productive, and more competitive' before proceeding to elaborate on how this would be achieved (whereupon it was interesting to note that 'modernization' was frequently cited as a key objective). *Putting Britain Right Ahead* signified a renewed Conservative commitment to such policies as lower direct taxes, less state interference in industry and the economy, curbs on irresponsible activity by trade unions, greater competition and individual enterprise in the economy, and greater powers for the police in order to tackle crime. These themes were to become more pronounced during the second half of the 1960s, as the policy groups continued their work, and the Conservative Party under Heath's leadership moved more discernibly to the right on many issues, leading eventually to the 'birth' of 'Selsdon Man' (to be discussed at the end of this chapter).

The Issue of Civil Service Reform

As noted at the outset of this chapter, the 1960s were, in many respects, a decade of reform (or attempted reform) which reflected, in large part, the modernizing managerialist ethos which seemed to prevail amongst many political leaders and opinion formers. At the same time, Harold Wilson's much-vaunted 'white heat of technological revolution' was also linked, at least indirectly, to the notion that Britain was becoming a more open, classless society, where wider educational opportunities and increased social mobility were creating a meritocracy – a society in which talent and ability were the means to success, not nepotism or the 'old school tie'. 'What you know' not 'Who you know' was supposed to become the basis of personal progress and social advancement.

In this context, coupled with Britain's increasingly apparent economic decline, it was perhaps not surprising that the Civil Service should become the focus of critical examination. The British Civil Service has long provided a target for politicians and political commentators wishing to inveigh against inefficiency, elitism and bureaucratic incompetence. The Civil Service has frequently been accused of all these vices and much more besides, such as obstructiveness, fear of change, and the most serious of all, presiding over Britain's decline in the post-war era. The British constitution might enunciate the doctrine of individual ministerial responsibility, whereby ministers, not their civil servants, are ultimately responsible for decisions and policies, but the reality is that politicians of both Left *and* Right have found it extremely useful to place much of the responsibility for many of Britain's post-war problems on the alleged failings of the Civil Service. According to this critique, it is civil servants, rather than the politicians themselves, who have let Britain down. Perhaps we should not be too surprised or shocked by this attempt at shifting the blame; the greatest gift possessed by many politicians is the ability to pass the buck.

The Fulton Committee on the Civil Service was established in 1966, with the objective of considering 'whether a civil service imbued with powerful generalist and conservative traditions was equal to the tasks expected of it by a technically advanced and increasingly complex society' (Drewry and Butcher 1991: 51). Few expected the conclusion to be in the affirmative. When the Fulton Report was published in 1968, nine particular criticisms were highlighted, namely:

1   'The Service is still essentially based on the philosophy of the amateur' which in a changed and changing world 'has most damaging consequences'. Civil servants were deemed to be recruited mainly from university graduates, who then received 'on the job' training. The Civil Service thus failed to recruit people with experience or expertise of life in 'the real world'.

2   Following on from the first point, too little scope was given to specialists. Instead, the assumption seemed too often to be that someone with a good degree from a good university would have the intellectual qualities and ability to tackle problems intelligently and effectively. To this extent, as well as being based on the 'philosophy of the amateur', the Civil Service was also criticized for its 'philosophy of the generalist'.

3   Not enough civil servants received training in management. The emphasis on policy formulation and implementation seemed to preclude much emphasis on managerial skills.

4   The management of civil servants was inadequate. For example, many civil servants were moved too frequently, from one post or department to another. This in turn prevented the acquisition of specialist knowledge and skills and, instead, reinforced the notion of the generalist, 'all-round' amateur.

5   The 'grading' of levels and 'classes' within the Civil Service was too rigid and complex. For example, there existed over 1,400 'classes' at the time.

6   Civil servants were too remote in terms of regular contact with the outside world. This was partly due to the narrow basis of recruitment and the emphasis accorded to 'on the job' training. This precluded the involvement of, or greater contact with, experts and professionals in the outside or 'real' world. Indeed, at a more general level, the Civil Service was susceptible to the charge of elitism, and of being closed off from the society which it was supposed to serve.

7   There was too much secrecy within, and by, the Civil Service.

8   The Civil Service was elitist, with its senior personnel drawn disproportionately from 'Oxbridge' (Oxford or Cambridge University). This, of course, is linked to '6' above.

9   The general organization of the Civil Service militated against the effective planning of policy, and also resulted in a lack of accountability.

In response to these alleged deficiencies, the Fulton Report made the following recommendations:

1   Consideration should be given to the 'relevance' of an applicant's degree when recruiting candidates.
2   Senior civil servants should specialize more in a particular sphere of administration thereby acquiring greater expertise.
3   A Civil Service college to be established, whereupon civil servants would receive training in management skills.
4   A Civil Service Department to be created, to take over the responsibilities of personnel management and pay hitherto determined by the Civil Service Commission and the Treasury.
5   A unified grading system to be introduced, whereby the Administrative, Executive and Clerical classes would all be subsumed into a single, albeit hierarchical, structure. It was hoped that this would facilitate greater scope and opportunities for promotion and career development within the Civil Service.
6   The development of secondments, whereby senior civil servants and industrialists, professionals, etc. could 'swap' places for short periods of time, thereby enabling each to understand the responsibilities and problems of the other, as well as breaking down the barrier between Whitehall and the world outside.
7   An inquiry to be launched into the provisions and operation of the Official Secrets Act.
8   An inquiry into recruitment methods.
9   The possible 'hiving off' of certain functions performed by government departments. It was also suggested that a policy unit should be established within each government department.

(Adapted from an outline provided by Drewry and Butcher, 1991: 52–3. For more on these – and other – recommendations (22 in total), see Hennessy 1990: 195–8.)

However, implementation of the recommendations suggested by the Fulton Report was partial and patchy, it subsequently being suggested in some quarters that 'only those bits of the Fulton report that the administrative elite in Whitehall liked were ever implemented' (Ponting 1989: 261–2). A Civil Service Department was established in November 1968, whilst June 1970 witnessed the official opening of a Civil Service College, based in Sunningdale, Berkshire. Meanwhile, there was some rationalization of the internal structure and grading system within the Civil Service; in 1971, the 1,400 'classes' were officially replaced by an Administration Group, including posts from clerks up to Assistant Secretary, above which was an 'open structure' comprising about 800 Under-Secretaries and other, higher grades – in fact, the highest positions within the Civil Service. At the same time, this new Administration Group was intended to facilitate the 'fast promotion' of suitably qualified and talented entrants.

Yet critics have since pointed out that not only did the Civil Service manage to block certain recommendations made by the Fulton Report, it also succeeded in undermining, or adapting to its own preferences, many of the reforms which were introduced. Not least of the criticisms was that the senior Civil Service remained overwhelmingly staffed by 'generalists', and that there continued to be a massive over-representation of Oxbridge graduates. According to one former civil servant: 'Cosmetic changes were introduced but the underlying structure remained and the amateur administrative elite was left in control.' A major reason for this failure to implement fully the recommendations of the Fulton Report was that 'much of the process, and all the key work, was left in the hands of the administrators and they were not prepared to commit suicide' (Ponting 1989: 262; see also Kellner and Crowther-Hunt 1980: chapters 3 and 4).

The Issue of Parliamentary Reform

In a decade of increasingly interventionist government and institutional reform, Parliament itself could hardly have been expected to be exempted from comment and criticism. For many, the ever greater complexity of modern British society, and the concomitant need for more efficiency, effectiveness, and expertise in managing it, served to highlight the archaic, amateurish manner in which Parliament conducted its affairs. Such criticisms were articulated against the backdrop of the accelerating economic decline, leading one academic expert on Parliament to note that 'cynical calls for parliamentary reform have accompanied cyclical downturns in the economy: the worse the economic crisis, the louder have been the demands for reform' (Judge 1983: 27–8). The 1960s yielded several critiques of Parliament and numerous recommendations for reform (see Conservative Political Centre (1963); Crick (1964); Grigg (1963); Hollis (1960); Ryle (1965); and the Study of Parliament Group (1965), for example).

Critics tended to focus on two inextricably related deficiencies. Firstly, at a general level, it was argued that the balance between Parliament and Government had tilted too far away from the former to the latter. According to one MP on the Opposition back-benches during the late 1960s: 'The Government can – almost – get away with murder' (Wright 1970: 167). Parliament, particularly the House of Commons, 'was viewed as a large, amateurish body, incapable of scrutinising effectively the increasingly complex work of government' (Norton 1981: 203). Britain seemed to be developing into what Lord Hailsham was later to term an 'elective dictatorship', hence the view of many critics that: 'The really urgent thing . . . is to strengthen the checks on the Executive itself' (Wright 1970: 169).

The second deficiency attributed to Parliament, and one which largely underpinned the first, was its internal workings and procedures. There was criticism of the manner in which the House of Commons especially conducted its business and arranged its activities. It was widely considered that Parliament was ill-equipped for the task of effectively scrutinizing the Executive, and that too many of its routines and rituals were relics from a bygone, pre-democratic age.

Tackling this second deficiency was deemed to be a prerequisite of ameliorating the first. If the House of Commons could be reformed from within, then it would more effectively and efficiently be able to scrutinize the activities of government and provide redress of grievances for citizens. This would itself serve to restore greater balance between Parliament and the Executive.

The most widely canvassed reform was the reorganization of the committee system in the House of Commons. In particular, many critics favoured extending the use of select committees to examine, on a systematic basis, the activities of particular government departments or policies. It was suggested that such investigative committees 'are far superior to question time as a probe and a curb on the government. We need more of them . . . we need to develop the Committee system far more thoroughly than we have done' (Wright 1970: 169–70).

A separate but not unrelated proposal emanating from some quarters was for back-bench MPs to be provided with improved research support and facilities. If more investigative committees were to be established, then MPs would need better resources and information in order to ask more intelligent questions. At the same time, without greater research assistance and administrative support, an extended committee would merely add to the already heavy workload of most MPs, with time spent reading and researching material in preparation for committee meetings impinging upon other duties and responsibilities.

However, the advocacy of better support and facilities for MPs did not pertain only to committee work. It was widely recognized that MPs needed more information to enable them to play a more effective role on the Floor of the House during Question Time, and during debates on legislation. In the absence of such information MPs would find it much more difficult seriously to challenge the actions of the government, for they would lack the requisite specialist knowledge or statistical evidence which might compel the ministers to reconsider or amend such policies and proposals. At the same time, the main Opposition might appear to be a more creditable, viable alternative in the eyes of the electorate if its scrutiny and criticism of the government was based on more accurate information and extensive research. This in turn would, it was undoubtedly envisaged, encourage more responsible, accountable government in Britain, thereby resulting in 'better' policies, whilst simultaneously imbuing Parliament itself with increased legitimacy in the eyes of the electorate.

Such demands and proposals were reflected in the Labour Party's 1966 election manifesto in which 'modernizing Parliament' was declared a commitment in order to 'improve procedure and the work of committees, and reform facilities for research and information' (see Craig 1975: 281). When Labour was re-elected in 1966, Richard Crossman was not only appointed Leader of the House, but also vested with the responsibility for introducing a package of parliamentary reforms. Of these, three in particular warrant mention here.

Firstly, a number of new specialist select committees were established, covering the areas of Science and Technology, Agriculture, Education and Science, Race Relations and Immigration, Scottish Affairs, and Overseas Aid. They were clearly intended to improve the ability of the House of Commons to scrutinize the policies of the government, although the actual choice of the 'policy areas' seemed rather idiosyncratic.

Secondly, a Parliamentary Commission for Administration (Ombudsman) was created, whose function was to investigate complaints made by members of the public, via their local MP, of maladministration by government departments. The Ombudsman was intended to help citizens secure the redress of grievances, whilst also helping to bridge the gulf which many felt existed between Parliament and the public.

Thirdly, an attempt was made to reform the House of Lords, via the 1969 Parliament (No. 2) Bill, which proposed that hereditary peers should no longer be permitted to vote, although they would still be allowed to speak and participate in debates. The right to vote in the House of Lords would be restricted to Life Peers along with the Bishops and Law Lords. Meanwhile, the upper chamber's power of delay would be reduced from one year to six months.

Yet these proposals lacked support on both sides of the House of Commons. The Left of the Labour Party tended to oppose the House of Lords on the grounds that it was essentially anachronistic, elitist and undemocratic. Nothing short of abolition or replacement by an elected upper House would suffice. The Left also feared that the Parliament (No. 2) Bill would actually serve to enhance its ability to block radical policies and legislation introduced by a Labour Government. Many Conservative MPs on the other hand, were anxious that the proposed reforms would seriously weaken the House of Lords, thereby preventing it from effectively blocking the 'extreme' measures introduced by a Labour Government. There was also concern that if only Life Peers were to be permitted to vote, then this would enhance, possibly to a dangerous degree, the power of patronage possessed by the Prime Minister. Conservatives were particularly fearful about the potential for a Labour Prime Minister to 'flood' the House of Lords with sympathetic peers in order to facilitate the passage of radical legislation.

Faced with such wide-ranging criticisms, spanning the Labour Left and the Conservative Right, the Parliament (No. 2 Bill) was eventually abandoned in April 1969. In any case, there had been considerable ambiguity as to whether the Bill was supposed to enhance or weaken the role of the House of Lords. Furthermore: 'Nowhere had the proposals generated real enthusiasm: the front benches of both parties offered support but only in a lukewarm manner' (Shell 1992: 23). In any case, Labour was in the process of attempting to reform both the Civil Service and the trade unions. Some reforms evidently had to be ascribed greater importance than others.

The Emergence of the Northern Ireland Problem

Northern Ireland was established during 1920–1, as a result of the 1920 Government of Ireland Act, and the 1921 Anglo-Irish Treaty. The British Government at the time hoped that these measures would provide a solution to the 'Irish problem' whose origins can be traced back to the twelfth century.[2] Faced with demands from the Nationalists for Home Rule (self-government as opposed to continued rule by Britain), and equally passionate demands from Unionists that they remain part of the United Kingdom, the Liberal Government of Lloyd George introduced the 1920 Act which partitioned Ireland, with the six north-eastern counties being geopolitically divided from the rest of the country, and declared a separate state. The rationale was that this was the part of Ireland in which the overwhelming majority of Unionists were concentrated. By partitioning Ireland in this manner, the British government hoped that 'both sides' would be pacified. It was not to be.

The Republic of Ireland (as it formally became in 1949) has never accepted the legitimacy or permanence of Northern Ireland, and has always maintained the long-term object of Irish reunification. To this extent, Northern Ireland has been perceived as a 'provisional state', one which will, sooner or later, be reunited with the Republic of Ireland. This perception has both angered the Unionists in Northern Ireland, and also fostered insecurity in them, due to their constant fear or suspicion that, sooner or later, they will be 'sold out' by the British Government and have reunification imposed upon them. Just as some Nationalists have been prepared to use violence in order to secure Irish reunification, so some Unionists have been prepared to use violence in order to oppose it.

However, although the partition of 1920–1 failed to satisfy either side, more particularly the Nationalists, British Governments up until the 1960s had reason to believe that the 'Irish Question' had largely been resolved. The Republic of Ireland had been granted independence, whilst Northern Ireland remained part of the United Kingdom, albeit with its own parliament, and thus a degree of autonomy: 'The British Government generally felt that the devolved arrangements that had been set in place meant that it could adopt a 'hands-off' approach to Northern Ireland' (Connolly 1990: 35).

Such a sanguine stance was to be severely shaken during the late 1960s. In 1968 the Northern Ireland Civil Rights Association (NICRA) was formed, an organization seeking an end to the discrimination in education, employment and housing which Catholics in Northern Ireland had regularly been exposed to at the hands of the Protestants, who outnumbered them by two to one, and thus enjoyed a permanent majority in the Northern Ireland parliament (Stormont). In seeking to pacify Catholic discontent, the Northern Ireland Prime Minister, Captain Terence O'Neill, was persuaded by the British Government in London to make some concessions to the Catholics, such as reforms in the criteria for allocating public housing and reorganization of local governments. As has so often been the case in Northern Ireland, however, an attempt at effecting a moderate reform or compromise merely antagonizes both sides, as was the case on this occasion, with the Catholics complaining that the reforms didn't go far enough and the Protestants complaining that they went too far. Indeed, such was the anger amongst Protestants in Northern Ireland that Captain O'Neill was replaced as leader of their Unionist Party by Major James Chichester-Clark. Thus it was that: 'The civil rights campaign, largely based on extra-parliamentary activity, produced a strong reaction from a section of the majority community which objected to what it considered a policy of appeasement orchestrated by an alien Labour Government in London and carried out by its O'Neillite puppets' (Arthur and Jeffery 1988: 8–9).

With the reforms satisfying neither Catholics nor Protestants in Northern Ireland, both communities became more active and militant. NICRA organized larger, more frequent public campaigns, marches and rallies whilst Loyalists (hard-line Unionists/Protestants) mobilized to form counter-marches and demonstrations. It was not long before marches and rallies ended in face-to-face conflict and confrontation, thereby setting in motion an escalation of violence. This, in turn, resulted in the rise of paramilitaries on both sides. For example the Provisional IRA (Irish Republican Army) was formed at the end of 1969, initially being seen by many Catholics as a 'vigilante' force which would protect their communities from Loyalist attacks. Needless to say, the rise of the Provisional IRA prompted many Unionists to join Loyalist security or paramilitary forces. Meanwhile, civil disturbance had become so common and violent that the Northern Ireland Prime Minister called upon the British Government to send in the army, to restore order. In agreeing to this request, it was universally believed that the presence of the British Army in Northern Ireland would be temporary, and that once order had been restored, the troops could be withdrawn. Twenty-five years later, the troops were still there.

For many Nationalists in Northern Ireland, the presence of the British Army was itself part of the problem, for it was seen by some as upholding or defending the status quo, namely a state in which Protestants/Unionists predominated and 'oppressed' the Catholic minority. Indeed for the Provisional IRA, and its political counterpart Sinn Fein, the British troops were viewed as a foreign army occupying Irish soil, and maintaining by force a state whose legitimacy Nationalists had never accepted. According to this perspective, military violence becomes justifiable and necessary to 'liberate' the Irish people from this 'occupation' of their territory by a 'foreign power' – Britain – and its army. Yet for the Unionists and the British Government, it was precisely the activities and atrocities perpetrated by the IRA which rendered necessary the presence of the British Army in Northern Ireland since 1969.

Anxiety over Immigration

For the first ten years or so after the end of the war, Britain operated an 'open door' policy *vis-à-vis* immigration from the countries of the Empire and Commonwealth. This partly reflected the need to overcome the labour shortages created by the rapid expansion of the British economy through post-war reconstruction and Keynesian techniques of economic management, but immigration also derived from the fact that citizens of the Empire and Commonwealth countries enjoyed the status of 'British subjects', and as such were entitled to take up residence in Britain, the 'mother country'. The first attempt at introducing legislation to place certain restrictions on the right of settlement came from a Labour Government, when the Attlee Administration passed the British Nationality Act in 1948, although at the time, the Conservative Party opposed restrictions on Empire/Commonwealth immigration, claiming that: 'There must be freedom of movement among its members with the British Empire and Commonwealth . . . The Mother Country . . . must be open to all citizens' (Conservative and Unionist Central Office 1949: 58).

By the mid-1950s, however, some Conservative MPs were expressing some concern over both the scale of immigration, and the rights accorded to immigrants, from the countries of the Empire and Commonwealth. Such Conservatives began demanding that the Government introduce legislation to curb the influx and the rights of immigrants, demands which Conservative Ministers refused to accede to. The demand for controls on immigration increased during the second half of the 1950s for three main reasons. Firstly, the number of immigrants was steadily increasing each year, as table 3.1 indicates.

Table 3.1   Immigration from the Commonwealth, 1953–1962

	West Indies	India	Pakistan	Others	Total
1953	2,000	—	—	—	2,000
1954	11,000	—	—	—	11,000
1955	27,500	5,800	1,850	7,500	42,650
1956	29,800	5,600	2,050	9,350	46,800
1957	23,000	6,600	5,200	7,600	42,400
1958	15,000	6,200	4,700	3,950	29,850
1959	16,400	2,950	850	1,400	21,600
1960	49,650	5,900	2,500	350	57,400
1961	66,300	23,750	25,100	21,250	136,400
1962	31,800	19,050	25,080	18,970	94,900

Source: Layton-Henry 1980: 53

Secondly, racial disturbances occurred in Nottingham and Notting Hill during the second half of 1958, thereby providing the issue of immigration with much greater prominence and poignancy. Indeed, during the autumn, Sir Alec Douglas-Home, the Minister for Commonwealth Relations, was suggesting that curbs might need to be placed on 'the unrestricted flow of immigrants from the West-Indies' (quoted in Layton-Henry 1980: 54). Meanwhile, the Conservatives' annual conference supported a motion calling for immigration controls, in spite of being urged to oppose it by the Home Secretary, Rab Butler.

The third reason why the demand within the Conservative Party for immigration controls increased during the second half of the 1950s was that the 1959 general election had resulted in a number of 'anti-immigration' Conservative MPs being elected for constituencies in the Birmingham area, where many Commonwealth immigrants were settling (Layton-Henry 1980: 55).

During 1960 and 1961, the number of immigrants entering Britain rose markedly, having fallen significantly in 1958 and 1959 in comparison to the mid-1950s. Thus whilst 21,600 immigrants had entered Britain in 1959, this figure increased to 57,700 the following year. Then, in 1961, it rose to 136,400. These figures, in the context of concern over Britain's deepening economic problems – including higher unemployment – served to push the issue of immigration up the political agenda. In May 1961, Macmillan wrote in his diary about 'a long discussion [in Cabinet] on West Indian immigration into the United Kingdom, which is now becoming rather a serious problem' (quoted in Horne 1989: 442). Indeed, such was the concern over the scale of immigration by the early 1960s that the 1962 Commonwealth Immigration Act was introduced, which established a voucher system to regulate the number of Commonwealth immigrants entitled to move to Britain.

However, this piece of legislation, far from allaying public concern over immigration, seemed actually to fuel it, and effectively legitimize it, by implying that people's concerns about the number of immigrants entering Britain were justified. This effect was compounded when the Labour Party itself – recognizing the danger of losing working class support to the Conservative Party on the 'race issue' – began to support tougher immigration controls, albeit with anti-discrimination legislation for those immigrants already settled in Britain.

However, the twin issues of race and immigration were catapulted to the top of the political agenda by a notorious speech from Enoch Powell in Birmingham in April 1968. According to Powell:

> Those who the Gods wish to destroy they first make mad. We must be mad, literally mad, as a nation to be permitting the annual influx of some 50,000 dependants who are, for the most part, the material of the future growth of the immigrant population. It is like watching a nation busily engaged in heaping up its own funeral pyre . . . As I look ahead, I am filled with foreboding. Like the Roman, I seem to see the 'River foaming with much blood'. (quoted in Blake 1985: 305)

Powell's graphic imagination and apocalyptic prophesies tapped into a deep reservoir of racism amongst much of the British public. Political leaders had hitherto been reluctant to make race and immigration a major political issue – although throughout the 1960s pressure was mounting in the Conservative Party for legislative curbs on 'coloured' immigration – recognizing, perhaps, that to do so would unleash an ugly tide of racial prejudice and bigotry. Yet, by largely avoiding the issue, they inadvertently allowed the public's frustration to fester, so that when Powell explicitly addressed the issue, he was widely greeted with a combination of reverence and relief. At last, many people seemed to say, here is a leading politician who has had the courage and conviction to express publicly what we have been saying privately for a great many years.

Whilst most educated people were appalled by Powell's speech and sentiments, the tabloid press applauded him, seeing him as a heroic figure and a true patriot merely concerned to save his people and their nation from invasion and take-over by 'alien forces'. Of the 110,000 letters which Powell received in response to his speech, the overwhelming majority were supportive, often congratulatory. The 'Alf Garnett' mentality of much of the British working class was clear for all to see when workers from the East End of London, such as dockers and meat-porters from Smithfield Market, staged a series of strikes, and marches to Downing Street in support of Powell, many of them calling for him to be made Prime Minister.

Instead, Powell's speech resulted in his dismissal from the Shadow Cabinet by Heath, even though Powell's views clearly enjoyed considerable support, both amongst the British public and amongst activists in Conservative associations (Layton-Henry 1980: 62). Many Conservatives and commentators subsequently viewed Powell as a rival to Heath as party leader.

Ironically, having dismissed Powell for his 'rivers of blood' speech, Heath himself spoke of the need for stricter controls on 'coloured' immigration, although this may owe something to the perceived need to counter any challenge by Powell for the Conservative leadership. It also represented an attempt by Heath at assuaging anti-immigrant feeling in the Conservative constituency associations and on the back-benches in Parliament. None the less, the Conservative Party still refrained from making immigration a key issue in the 1970 general election. Instead, the party's election manifesto pledged that existing Commonwealth immigrants would retain the right to be joined by their wives and children, but suggested that in future, immigrant workers and their families would not enjoy the right of permanent settlement in Britain – 'there will be no further large-scale permanent immigration'. With the Conservatives winning the election, these pledges were subsequently enshrined in the 1971 Immigration Act, although as the next chapter illustrates, the immigration issue was by no means resolved.

In Place of Strife

As mentioned earlier, it was the Labour Government, elected in 1964 and re-elected in 1966, which made the first post-war attempt at placing legislative curbs on the trade unions. Like the Conservative Party, Labour had also become deeply concerned about the incidence and impact of unofficial strikes, and consequently appointed, in 1965, a Royal Commission on Trade Unions and Employee Associations, chaired by Lord Donovan (hence it became known as the Donovan Commission).

However, the Donovan Report, published in 1968, merely recommended a strengthening of the voluntarist industrial relations system, rather than legislative reform of the trade unions and statutory curbs on their activities. It was claimed, in true voluntarist manner, that not only were industrial relations too complex to be subjected to statutory regulation, but that introducing the law into the workplace would exacerbate the distrust which often existed between management and workers, and in turn, compound Britain's industrial relations problems.

Harold Wilson, the Labour Prime Minister, was rather disappointed by the timidity evinced by the Donovan Report, and was emphatic that 'the confessed failure of the Commission to find any short term remedy for unofficial strikes could not be accepted' (Wilson 1971: 591). Wilson's response, in conjunction with his Employment Secretary, Barbara Castle, was to publish a White Paper, *In Place of Strife*, in which a comprehensive programme of industrial relations reform was proposed, including a number of statutory curbs on the trade unions.

In acknowledging the gap which had emerged between the trade union leaders at national level and the rank-and-file members at local or workplace level, a vacuum which was often filled by more visible active or militant shop stewards, *In Place of Strife* insisted on the need to restore 'responsible' trade unionism by reasserting the authority of official, national union leaders. This would reduce the scope for unofficial or local-level industrial action in defiance of formal, official procedures and agreements, which in turn would encourage greater industrial stability and economic confidence. According to *In Place of Strife*, it was no longer a case of *whether* the state should intervene in industrial relations, but the manner in which it would do so.

In Place of Strife pointed out that the two sides of industry had been given plenty of opportunities and encouragement, throughout the post-war period, to improve Britain's industrial relations, whilst the trade unions in particular had been exhorted on countless occasions to put their own house in order. It was now deemed evident that 'the efforts of employers, unions and employees to reform collective bargaining need the active support and intervention of Government'.

A total of 25 measures were proposed by *In Place of Strife*, and whilst many were intended to be beneficial to trade unions and employees generally, three particular proposals incurred the wrath of the trade union movement, namely:

- The Secretary of State for Employment be empowered to order a 28-day 'cooling-off' period when an unofficial strike was considered potentially damaging to the British economy. This 'cooling-off' period would provide time for a solution to be sought.
- The Secretary of State for Employment be empowered to order a trade union to ballot its members if a strike was called which might prove detrimental to the economic well-being of the country.
- A Commission for Industrial Relations be set-up, and given a major role in investigating inter-union disputes.

The trade unions were strongly opposed to what they saw as the excessive powers which would be conferred upon the Employment Secretary, thereby enabling the minister to 'interfere' in trade union affairs. For similar reasons, the trade unions were hostile to the proposed Commission for Industrial Relations. Yet opposition was by no means confined solely to the trade unions; many Labour MPs and ministers were also deeply unhappy with these proposals. They argued that, firstly, the proposals were unworkable and impracticable, and secondly, that they would cause immense, possibly permanent, damage to the Labour

Party's close and historic links with the trade unions. Neither these MPs and ministers, nor the trade unions themselves, were convinced by Barbara Castle's insistence that *In Place of Strife* would strengthen 'responsible' trade unionism, or that the legal powers vested in the Employment Secretary would be invoked only as a last resort.

Such was the opposition among many Labour MPs, particularly those who were sponsored by trade unions, that in March 1969, following a parliamentary debate on *In Place of Strife*, over 50 of them voted against it, whilst 40 abstained. Yet Wilson and Castle were undeterred, and shortly afterwards, during the Budget, it was announced that a short Industrial Relations Bill would be introduced as a prelude to the main piece of legislation. This 'short' Bill would enshrine two main features. Firstly, in cases where the TUC could not settle an inter-union dispute, the Employment Secretary would be able to impose a settlement, based on recommendations from the proposed Commission on Industrial Relations. If the trade unions concerned refused to accept the Employment Secretary's settlement, they were liable to be fined. Secondly, the 'short' Bill was to empower the Employment Secretary to order a 28-day 'cooling off' period in the case of unofficial strikes, with fines again liable to be imposed on trade unions who defied such orders.

Trade union opposition was as vehement as it was for *In Place of Strife* itself, as was that of Labour MPs and ministers. Consequently, from the middle of April through to the latter half of June, 'the TUC and the Government waged the most intense negotiations that any government ever had with a producing group since government first took up peacetime management of the economy in 1945' (Dorfman 1979: 35). However, no agreement appeared attainable. Wilson and Castle were only prepared to contemplate abandoning their proposed legislative reforms in return for a guarantee from the trade unions that they themselves could deal firmly with inter-union disputes and unofficial strikes. The TUC were unable to provide such a guarantee, particularly with regard to unofficial strikes. Wilson thus insisted that the reforms had to be pursued, declaring that 'the passage of this Bill is essential to the Government's continuance in office . . . ' (quoted in Jenkins 1970: 134).

Yet the importance that Wilson attached to the Bill's passage through Parliament failed to elicit the wholehearted support of Labour MPs. As with *In Place of Strife*, many back-benchers, especially trade union sponsored MPs, were opposed to the Wilson–Castle proposals. Indeed, such was the scale of opposition in the parliamentary Labour Party that the Chief Whip, Bob Mellish, warned the Cabinet that the 'short' Industrial Relations Bill was unlikely to gain sufficient support in the House of Commons. In fact, by June, many Cabinet ministers were also harbouring grave doubts about the wisdom of the Bill, in addition to those who had opposed it right from the outset.

Eventually, acknowledging his isolation on this issue, Wilson was compelled to make a humiliating climbdown, abandoning the legislative proposals in return for a 'solemn and binding undertaking' by the TUC's General Council that it would itself 'intervene in serious unconstitutional stoppages' (HC Debates, 19 June 1969, col. 700). The episode was grist to the Conservative Party's mill, for it was portrayed as a clear example of the growing power of the trade unions, and Labour's alleged subservience to them. As such, the Conservative Opposition believed that its own proposals for trade union and industrial relations reform, enshrined in *Fair Deal at Work*, had been proved more relevant and necessary than ever. With Labour vanquished, the Conservatives felt vindicated. The trade unions had to be tackled.

The Politics of 'Permissiveness'

As well as being a decade of institutional reform, the 1960s were also a decade of social reform. Among informed opinion, the 1960s were characterized by an unprecedented climate of social liberalism in which traditional attitudes on a range of 'moral' issues were challenged. Some of these changes, however, were – and still are – highly controversial, for it is arguable that public opinion was never in favour of them. Furthermore, the Conservative Governments of the 1980s and early 1990s were inclined to blame many of Britain's contemporary social and 'moral' problems on the alleged permissiveness and 'excessive' liberalism of the 1960s. For some Conservatives, present-day phenomena such as lack of respect for authority, crime, juvenile delinquency, drug abuse, divorce and single parenthood, AIDS, etc., are consequences of changes and reforms 'imposed' on British society by 'progressives' during the 1960s.

Abolition of the death penalty

Nowhere is the gulf between elite and public opinion so wide as it is concerning the death penalty. Ever since capital punishment was abolished in 1965, the House of Commons has repeatedly voted against its reintroduction, even though countless opinion polls have illustrated that between 80 and 90 per cent of British people are in favour of the death penalty, at least for particular crimes and offences (such as the murder of police officers, and terrorism). Those who supported abolition, however, inclined to the view that Parliament had a duty to try to lead or 'educate' public opinion, rather than slavishly follow it. MPs were to use their own judgement and make their own decisions, not act merely as delegates of their constituents (a version of parliamentary democracy most famously enunciated by Edmund Burke).

The Murder (Abolition of the Death Penalty) Bill was introduced by a Private Member (i.e. a back-bench MP) following Labour's 1964 election victory. The Bill then received its second reading in December 1964, when the House of Commons voted by 355 votes to 170 in favour. MPs were allowed a 'free vote', meaning that there was no official party line to follow. Instead, they were free to vote how they wished, according to their own personal views and their conscience.

The committee stage of the Bill witnessed numerous amendments being proposed to retain capital punishment for particular offences, such as the murder of a police officer, murder of a prison officer, murder in connection with theft, etc. All of these proposed amendments were defeated by significant margins (Richards 1970: 53).

One notable amendment which was accepted by the House was that the Bill would only remain in force for five years, and would thereafter need to be reaffirmed by further votes in Parliament. This proviso having been attached, the Bill was given its third reading in July 1965, when it received 200 votes in favour, and 98 against. The Bill then received comfortable majorities during the second and third readings in the House of Lords, before becoming law in November 1965.

Legalization of homosexuality

In a country as homophobic as Britain, homosexuality has long been viewed with much greater disgust and hostility than in many other

Western European countries, where attitudes to sexual matters have usually been – and remain – much more tolerant and enlightened. For all its proclamations of 'freedom', Britain remains a sexually repressed society, with attitudes towards sexuality and erotica widely afflicted by puritanism and prudery. The ghost of Queen Victoria haunts us yet.

Homosexual relations and acts between consenting men aged 21 or over were legalized in 1967 as a result of the Sexual Offences (No. 2) Bill introduced by a Labour back-bencher, Leo Abse. However, the antecedents of this legislation can be seen in the recommendations of the Wolfenden Committee, which had been established back in 1954, in order to consider 'the law and practice' with regard to homosexual offences and prostitution. In addition to government departments, and various individuals, 35 organizations submitted evidence to the Committee, and most of these either favoured reform of the existing law (which made sexual relations between men an imprisonable offence) or were at least neutral. Few expressed outright opposition to reform. Even the Church of England and Moral Welfare Council exuded a sympathetic tone, and found no justification for the existing legislation. After all, it pointed out, whilst homosexuals were liable to imprisonment, there was no punishment of adulterers or lesbians, even though their activities might be deemed just as immoral or inimical to the moral and social fabric of society. Indeed, not only did the Council call for homosexual acts conducted in private to be legalized, it also suggested that the age of male homosexual consent should be 17 (Richards 1970: 69). Other bodies which articulated a pro-reform line included the Catholic Church, and the Boy Scouts' Association.

When the Wolfenden Committee published its report in the summer of 1957, it was perhaps not surprising that it too recommended legalization of sexual relations between men provided that these were conducted in private, based on consent, and that those partaking in homosexual acts were not below the age of 21. However, the first parliamentary vote on the issue did not take place until June 1960, when a Private Member's motion was introduced by a Labour MP, urging the Macmillan Government to act soon in accordance with the Wolfenden Committee's recommendations. However, the motion was defeated by 213 votes to 99.

Various other attempts at legislative reform were instigated in subsequent years, but none reached the Statute Book (Richards 1970: 76–7).

When Leo Abse introduced his Sexual Offences (No. 2) Bill in 1967, it was shortly after Labour had won the 1966 general election, with an increased majority *vis-à-vis* its 1964 result. What was instrumental in helping to secure the Bill's success was the time made available by the Cabinet, for although it was a Private Member's Bill, it enjoyed considerable ministerial support. The Government was thus able to ensure that through its control of the parliamentary and legislative timetable, sufficient time and opportunity were provided to get the Bill through Parliament. Also crucial to the Bill's success was the favourable attitude of the Home Secretary at this time, Roy Jenkins, who was establishing himself as a man of 'liberal' attitudes with regard to social reform and 'moral' issues. Indeed, the Sexual Offences (No. 2) Bill greatly enhanced Jenkins's reputation as a 'liberal reformer'.

Liberalization of abortion law

Between the general elections of 1964 and 1966, no fewer than three Private Member's Bills were introduced concerning abortion, two in the House of Commons (one by a Labour MP, and one by a Conservative) and one in the Lords. None of these Bills were successful due in large part to insufficient parliamentary time – a problem common to many Private Member's Bills.

Shortly after the 1966 general election, however, another Private Member's Bill was introduced, this time by a Liberal MP, David Steel. Its second reading was secured by 223 votes to 29, and although the Labour Government's stance was officially one of neutrality, all but one of its ministers voted in support of Steel's Bill. However, lengthy debates during the committee stage, often over specific details and exemptions, meant that the Bill did not return to the floor of the House until June, by which time it was in danger of running out of time (legislation cannot be carried over from one parliamentary session to the next; it must pass through all its stages, or be reintroduced at the start of the following parliamentary session in November).

Once again, the sympathy of the Government, and particularly of the Home Secretary, Roy Jenkins, led to parliamentary time being made available to enable the Bill to pass through report stage and onto its third reading prior to a relatively smooth passage through the House of

Lords. As Richards remarked: 'There can be no doubt that the success of the Abortion Bill was due in great measure to the benevolence of Ministers. Their assistance was especially valuable in preserving the measure from shipwreck in the dangerous seas of the parliamentary timetable' (Richards 1970: 111). Yet of all the pieces of 'permissive' legislation introduced during the 1960s, it is the liberalization of abortion law which has been most frequently subjected to attempted amendments, either to reduce the number of weeks into a pregnancy during which an abortion can lawfully be performed, or to tighten up the grounds on which a woman can be granted an abortion. At the beginning of each Session of Parliament, when the ballot of MPs is conducted in order to determine who will be granted time to introduce a Private Member's Bill, anti-abortion campaigners lobby the successful MPs in order to persuade them to introduce a Bill to repeal or amend the existing legislation concerning abortion. Indeed, it has become a perennial feature of parliamentary politics in Britain.

Divorce law reform

Until the middle of the nineteenth century, divorce was only obtainable through a private Act of Parliament. Then, in 1857, a Matrimonial Causes Act was introduced, which enabled men to divorce their wives if the latter had committed adultery. Women, however, could not divorce adulterous husbands, unless other offences had been committed against a wife, such as desertion, cruelty or violent acts of a sexual nature. Obviously, the latter were exceptionally difficult for a woman to prove in a court of law, even assuming that she had the financial resources to instigate divorce proceedings in the first place. Needless to say, the 1857 Act was only really of benefit to wealthy men. Not until 1923 were women able to divorce their husbands solely on the grounds of adultery.

A major reform of the law on divorce was introduced in 1969, in accordance with the climate of social liberalism which apparently characterized the latter half of the 1960s (more particularly amongst political elites, perhaps, rather than amongst ordinary people). The 1969 Divorce Reform Act (actually implemented in 1971) stipulated that 'irretrievable breakdown of marriage' was to be legitimate grounds for divorce, provided that a couple had been married for at least three years. However, the Act also specified that the marriage needed to have 'irretrievably' broken down for at least two years in cases where divorce was sought by the mutual consent of both husband *and* wife. If the divorce was 'contested' (i.e. opposed by one partner), then a five-year period of breakdown or separation would have to elapse before a divorce could be granted.

Divorce law reform proved particularly controversial because in addition to its 'moral' aspect – challenging the sanctity of marriage, and acknowledging that marriage need not be 'until death us do part' as the marriage vows declared – there was some concern that women, once they had been divorced, might be left financially destitute, whilst the former husband was free to begin a new life, possibly with another woman. It was to meet this concern that the 1969 Act was not implemented until 1971, so as to enable further legislation to be introduced dealing with 'matrimonial property'.

Not surprisingly, perhaps, the introduction of the 1969 Divorce Reform Act was followed by a sharp increase in the number of divorces; whilst the divorce rate (rate of divorces per thousand married couples) in 1966 had been 3.2, by 1972 it had increased to 9.5. Indeed, whereas 47,000 divorces were granted in 1966, some 170,000 were granted in 1977. This, of course, served to confirm the fears of the opponents of divorce law liberalization, who had warned that it would encourage marital breakdown and divorce. The alternative view, however, is that, as with all statistics, great care should be exercised in interpretation; divorce liberalization may simply have enabled 'empty' marriages to be legally terminated (and in so doing, made it possible for the unhappy couple to find new marriage partners – most divorcees do get married again sooner or later). In other words, the 1969 Divorce Reform Act has not *caused* more broken marriages; it has merely enabled such marriages to be legally terminated once they have already broken down (for a fuller discussion of the debates surrounding the 1969 Divorce Reform Act, see Richards 1970: ch. 7).

Other examples and indications of greater social liberalism – or permissiveness – during the second half of the 1960s include liberalization of the laws governing sport, recreation and other forms of public or commercial leisure on Sundays (many of which had been either prohibited or subject to heavy restrictions, due to the fact that Sunday was the 'day of the Sabbath'). Also freed from legislative curbs and censorship were theatre performances and other forms of live entertainment. A whole series of factors had traditionally been cited as justification for theatre and performance censorship, namely the need to protect public and moral standards, and prevent blasphemy, defamation of character, indecency or the propagation of subversive ideas. As in other policy areas, however, the 1960s were characterized by increasing liberalism and tolerance amongst many sections of informed opinion, so that the Theatres Bill could be passed in 1968, which freed the theatre from most of its repressive restrictions.

In all of these areas, the issues were highly 'moral' in tone, in so far as they concerned ethical considerations of what constituted right or wrong, decent or depraved, acceptable or abominable, and so on. Those in favour of reforms in these areas saw them as a vital extension of individual freedom and liberty, providing people with the right to make their own choices and decisions. They were seen as hallmarks of a tolerant, enlightened society, one which was at last emerging blinking into the light of the latter twentieth century after decades of living shrouded in the dark shadow of Victorian repressiveness and prudery.

Yet to opponents of many of these reforms, they signified the degeneration of Britain into an increasingly decadent, depraved society, in which morals and standards of decency were being ditched in favour of immorality and indecency. What was being promoted was not so much liberalism as licentiousness, some feared. Certainly, from the late 1960s onwards, 'traditionalists' and many Conservatives have insisted that many of the social problems that Britain has increasingly suffered from can be ascribed to the 'liberal' reforms of the 1960s. These reforms are apportioned much of the blame for the apparent decline in morality in British society, and the concomitant increase in crime, marital breakdown and single parenthood. For proponents of this perspective, reference to the 'permissiveness' of the 1960s is pejorative in tone.

The Birth of 'Selsdon Man'

The Conservative Opposition's fundamental review of principles and policies discussed earlier provided a clear indication of a rightward shift by the party during the second half of the 1960s. This move was confirmed in late January 1970, when the Shadow Cabinet held a weekend meeting at the Selsdon Park Hotel in Surrey, in order to finalize the package of policies upon which the Conservative Party would be campaigning in the imminent general election. Some have also suggested that the Selsdon Park meeting was 'as much about public relations as about policy' (Ramsden 1980: 276), but this interpretation is rejected by other commentators, who have claimed: 'Publicity was not the object of the exercise' (Butler and Pinto-Duschinsky 1971: 129).

Whether or not a major purpose of the Selsdon Park conference was to garner publicity, the meeting provided a valuable forum for the Conservative Party to bring together the recommendations and proposals of the various policy review groups, and finally weave them into a cogent, coherent package of proposals, which could subsequently form the basis of the Conservatives' election manifesto.

These proposals included a reaffirmation of the Conservative Party's commitment to restoring 'the market' by reducing state intervention in, and government regulation of, the economy. Unprofitable firms and loss-making industries – 'lame ducks' – were no longer to be rescued by government via public take-over or subsidy, but instead were to be permitted to go bankrupt. Not only would this remove 'dead wood' from the British economy, it was envisaged, it would also provide remaining firms with a spur to become more competitive and profitable. This in turn would serve to reinvigorate the British economy itself, thereby reversing Britain's economic decline.

However, whilst the Selsdon Park conference committed the next Conservative Government to greater freedom in the economic sphere, it simultaneously committed it to greater discipline in the social sphere: a freer economy, a stronger state. In particular, a much tougher stance was adopted *vis-à-vis* law and order, immigration and social policy, with the last of these to be subject to greater 'selectivity' in the allocation of welfare resources and entitlement for benefits.

Yet given the Conservative Party's apparently clear and unequivocal vision of the policies and political direction it wished to pursue, it was somewhat ironic that in his foreword to the Conservatives' 1970 manifesto, Heath offered a new style of government in contrast to the alleged short-termism of the Wilson administration, declaring that:

The Government should seek the best advice and listen carefully to it. It should not rush into decisions . . . it should be deliberate and thorough . . . its decision should be aimed at the long term . . . once a decision is made, once a policy is established the Prime Minister and his colleagues should have the courage to stick to it.

Within eighteen months of the Conservatives' June 1970 election victory, Heath's noble words were to come back to haunt him.

Notes

1   The plural is used in this instance because at the time there existed three distinct organizations: the European Coal and Steel Community (ECSC), formed in 1951; the European Economic Community (EEC), created in 1957, and the European Atomic Energy Community (Eurotom), also established in 1957. Although these three organizations remain legally distinct bodies they were officially merged in 1967 to form what we now refer to as the European Community (EC).

2   For a short succinct overview of the history of the 'Irish Problem', see Connolly 1990, ch. 2.

4 Careering towards Crisis (1970–9)

Things fall apart: the centre cannot hold;
Mere anarchy is loosed upon the world.
The blood-dimmed tide is loosed, and everywhere,
the ceremony of innocence is drowned.

W. B. Yeats, 'The Second Coming'

'Selsdon Man' in Action

The election, in June 1970, of a Conservative Government under Edward Heath's premiership appeared to herald a sharp break with the type of policies and consensual style of governance which had predominated for most of the previous 25 years. Heath himself proclaimed that: 'We were returned to office to change the course and the history of this nation, nothing else' (quoted in Butler and Kavanagh 1974: 10). As the policy review and public statements of the late 1960s had indicated, there was much emphasis on objectives such as increased competitiveness, greater efficiency and a more dynamic economy (and, no doubt, opposition to sin). Heath was apparently committed to reducing state intervention in the economy, lowering public expenditure and income tax, and to refraining from 'bailing out' inefficient or bankrupt firms with taxpayers' money – there was to be no help for 'lame ducks'. The British economy, and the firms within it, were deemed to need exposure to the chill winds of greater competition, which would provide the spur for improved efficiency and increased productivity. British industry was to be made leaner and fitter.

Much of the 'Selsdon Man' programme of 1970 appeared to fore-shadow what was to come at the end of the decade, when a Conservative Government was elected under Margaret Thatcher's leadership. Angus

Maude had claimed that the Conservatives' objective was:

> to free as many people as possible from the need to rely entirely (or even mainly) on public authorities, to restore a greater degree of family responsibility by expanding the amount of private provision. At the same time, by reducing the pointless redistribution of funds where no benefit is secured, it should be possible both to lower administrative costs and concentrate help where it is most needed. (Maude 1969: 187)

Exactly the same words could have been articulated by any Thatcher minister during, or after, 1979.

October 1970 witnessed a mini-Budget in which the Heath Government did indeed introduce cutbacks in public expenditure; free school milk and subsidies for council house rents were both cut, whilst prescription charges and the cost of dental treatment were both increased. The Government announced planned cuts in public expenditure of £330 million in the next (1971–2) financial year, rising to about £900 million by 1974–5. Whilst these sums might not seem too significant today, they represented quite major cuts in the early 1970s. Their psychological and political impact was also considerable because of the extent to which British people had by this time grown accustomed to rising public expenditure (in fact, the Government's projected cuts were intended to result in a slower increase in the overall level of public expenditure, rather than a net reduction). Also announced by the Heath Government in October 1970 were proposals to abolish a number of interventionist or regulatory bodies set up by the previous Labour administration, such as the Prices and Incomes Board, the Industrial Re-organization Corporation and the Land Commission.

Yet the most significant and controversial policy of the Heath Government (with the exception, perhaps, of taking Britain into the European Community – of which, more shortly) was the ill-fated 1971 Industrial Relations Act.[1] The Heath Government had entered office in June 1970 determined to reform British industrial relations, a commitment which had been openly declared throughout the Opposition years, particularly with the publication of *Fair Deal at Work*.

The Industrial Relations Act enshrined eight main principles and provisions:

1   The statutory right to belong, or not to belong, to a trade union (thereby eliminating the closed shop).

2   Registration of trade unions with a new Registrar of Trade Unions and Employers' Associations (failure or refusal to do so resulting in loss of legal immunities).
3   Legally enforceable collective agreements.
4   Selective enforcement of procedural agreements.
5   A reduction in the legal immunities enjoyed by trade unions.
6   The legal right of trade unions to be 'recognized'.
7   The establishment of organizational machinery to define 'bargaining units' in the workplace.
8   Emergency powers to be vested in the Secretary of State for Employment enabling him/her to apply to a new Industrial Court for a 60-day 'cooling-off' period to be imposed if and when an industrial dispute was deemed likely to damage the British economy, or result in serious public disorder. The Secretary of State for Employment would also be entitled to apply to the Court for a strike ballot on the same grounds.

The Employment Secretary responsible for introducing the Industrial Relations Bill, Robert Carr, asserted that it was intended to realize four main objectives:

1   The achievement of freely and responsibly conducted collective bargaining.
2   The development of orderly procedures to resolve industrial disputes.
3   The principle of freedom of association for employees, whereby they could choose whether or not they wished to belong to a trade union. Both employers and trade unions would be required to respect the wishes of workers in this matter.
4   The guarantee of greater freedom and job security for workers, through the provision of protection against 'unfair industrial practices'.

Furthermore, and at a more general level, the Heath Government was emphatic that, far from constituting a draconian attack on the long-established 'voluntarist' character of industrial relations in Britain, the Industrial Relations Bill would actually strengthen it. Not surprisingly, the trade unions did not see it this way. What was surprising was the fact that a number of Conservatives also harboured reservations about the likely effectiveness and efficacy of the legislation. Whilst concerned about trade union power and irresponsibility, they were also concerned that the Industrial Relations Bill was too 'legalistic', a consequence, they pointed out, of its having been drafted by those with little or no experience of the realities and nuances of life on the shop or factory-floor. Certainly there was to be criticism, once the Act had failed, that the Government's Solicitor-General, Geoffrey Howe – a barrister by profession – had perhaps played too great a role in framing the Industrial Relations Bill.

As already indicated, Britain's membership of the European Communities was another significant and controversial policy or event of the Heath administration. Indeed, according to one commentator: 'The objective to which the Heath Government attached most importance during its first two years of office was not cutting taxation and public expenditure, leaving lame ducks to their fate, or even reforming industrial relations; it was getting Britain into the EEC' (Stewart 1977: 153). Similarly, George asserts that 'The first year and a half of Heath's premiership were devoted to getting Britain into the EC' (George 1990: 42). Heath had been pro-European long before becoming Prime Minister. He saw British membership of the EC as a vital means of modernizing the British economy and compelling industry to become more competitive. To this extent membership of the EC was not unrelated to the other policies of the Heath Government already referred to, namely reducing public expenditure and state intervention, coupled with radical reform of industrial relations. All of these policies, in their respective ways, sought to render Britain a more dynamic society with a more dynamic economy. Thus the desire for EC membership reflected Heath's professed objective of instilling greater competitiveness and efficiency into Britain's industrial performance and economic activity.

The Conservatives' 1970 election manifesto had stated that: 'If we can negotiate the right terms, we believe that it would be in the long-term interest of the British people for Britain to join the European Economic Community, and that it would make a major contribution to both the prosperity and the security of our country. The opportunities are immense.' Within a fortnight of its election victory, the Conservative Government had officially opened negotiations over the terms and conditions which would need to be satisfied before Britain would formally apply for membership of the EC. These terms and conditions mainly revolved around three main aspects, namely agricultural policy, budgetary contributions, and Britain's trading links with the Commonwealth countries (George 1990: 50–4; Nicoll and Salmon 1990: 144).

A year later, in June 1971, with the bulk of the negotiations completed, the Heath Government published a White Paper entitled *The United Kingdom and the European Communities*, which explained the case for Britain seeking EC membership. The White Paper was then debated in the House of Commons during late July, whilst a parliamentary debate on actual entry to the EC took place towards the end of October, although political and media debate had continued throughout the summer while Parliament was in recess.

At the end of the parliamentary debate in October, MPs voted on a motion declaring support for the Government's decision to join the EC 'on the basis of the arrangements which have been negotiated'. The result was 356 MPs supporting the motion, and 244 voting against, thereby providing the Heath Government with a majority of 112. However, the vote also revealed the divisions *within* the main political parties over EC membership, with 69 Labour MPs defying a three-line whip by voting *for* the motion, whilst 39 Conservatives voted against. Meanwhile, whilst five Liberal MPs voted in favour, one Liberal voted against.

It was not surprising, therefore, that the European Communities Bill (formally ratifying the Treaty of Accession which Heath signed in January 1972) did not enjoy a particularly smooth passage through the House of Commons during the first half of 1972. Indeed, it received its second reading by only eight votes. Although the Bill eventually received the Royal Assent, thereby ensuring that Britain became a member of the EC on 1 January 1973, it did reveal – and reinforce – divisions within both of the main political parties, particularly the Labour Party (see Norton 1975).

Heath's 'U-Turn'

Edward Heath had expected the trade unions' opposition to the Industrial Relations Act to dissipate once it reached the Statute Book. It was envisaged that the trade union movement would be compelled to acknowledge that the Government had been given a mandate by the electorate, and that the weight of public opinion would provide further pressure on the unions to accept the legislation. Besides, ministers reasoned, trade unionists themselves seemed to approve of the Heath Government reforms. Yet in spite of these political calculations, the trade unions' capitulation and compliance did not materialize. Ultimately, it was the Heath Government which felt obliged to back down, although the opposition to the Industrial Relations Act was by no means the only issue involved.

The official trade union response to the Industrial Relations Act was one of 'passive non-cooperation', although this did not preclude extra-parliamentary action in the form of demonstrations, marches and rallies seeking to 'kill the Bill' whilst it was still wending its way through Parliament. Once the Bill had become law, most trade unions simply refused, *en masse*, to register with the new Registrar of Trade Unions and Employers' Associations, as they were required to do if they were to retain their legal immunities.

However, it was the judiciary – not normally known for its fraternal sympathy with the trade unions – which effectively dealt the fatal blows to the Industrial Relations Act. Indeed, some commentators have characterized the events leading to the failure of the Act as 'a farce' (Dorfman 1979: 58; Stewart 1977: 127; Taylor 1993: 199). In one legal case, dock workers who were members of the Transport and General Workers' Union (TGWU) refused to handle the containers of Heaton's, a firm on Merseyside, because it was employing non-dock labour at its terminals. The TGWU refused to obey an instruction by the National Industrial Relations Court to order the dockers to cease their 'blacking' of Heaton's containers. The union was thus fined £5,000 for contempt of court, this subsequently being increased to £50,000 when the action of the dockers continued. The TGWU then took the case to the Appeal Court, claiming that it could not be held responsible for the actions of individual members who acted without the union's authorization, and who rejected the union's request to desist. The TGWU's appeal was upheld, and although it was subsequently overturned by the House of Lords, it none the less exposed flaws in the Industrial Relations Act, particularly a tension between the freedom of individual trade union members and the authority of their leaders. The twin Conservative tenets of liberty and order could not always be easily reconciled.

Meanwhile, a similar case, involving industrial action by dock workers against a container firm in east London, resulted in the threat of imprisonment. This again implied that it was individual trade union members, not the union itself, who were legally responsible in cases of unauthorized or unofficial industrial action. The NIRC's threat of imprisonment against the dock workers involved was sufficient to prompt a 'sympathy strike by more than 30,000 dockers in several ports . . . and strong indications that there would be a total national strike to follow if the arrests were carried out' (Dorfman 1979: 60). An extremely tense, volatile situation was defused by the sudden intervention of the Solicitor-General, who actually offered a defence of the dockers concerned, and thus prevented both their imprisonment and a national dock strike.

One other similar case at the time, however, did result in five shop stewards being sent to prison for defying an order by the NIRC to cease their picketing of a firm employing non-dock labour. This time, there was a national dock strike, accompanied by sympathy action from other workers and trade unions. However, the House of Lords' verdict in the earlier Heaton's case, in which the Law Lords maintained that it was the trade union, not individual members, which was legally responsible for industrial action, served to absolve the 'Pentonville Five' dockers from liability, thereby ensuring their immediate acquittal, and release from prison, in August 1972. The lack of consistency in judicial decisions, coupled with the willingness of trade unions to rally support for those prosecuted under the Industrial Relations Act, served to destroy the credibility or authority of the legislation. Those Conservatives who had themselves warned that the Act would be unworkable, and would create martyrs to whose support the trade unions could rally, were vindicated. Edward Heath refused to countenance the outright repeal of the Industrial Relations Act – that would have constituted further humiliation – but it was widely and tacitly acknowledged that the Act was all but dead.

The débâcle of the Industrial Relations Act was not the only factor, however, which compelled Heath to perform a U-turn, and lay Selsdon Man to rest. Of immense importance also was the 1972 miners' strike. Although Heath had entered office in 1970 espousing a more free market philosophy and programme, which included, amongst other things, a rejection of incomes policy, this was not applicable to the public sector. Here all governments need to apply some form of incomes policy, particularly when seeking to hold back public expenditure.

The incomes policy adopted by the Heath Government was known as 'N-minus-1': each year's pay increase for public sector workers was to be 1 per cent less than the previous year's increase. The pursuit of such a pay policy was intended both to reduce inflation, and help to reign in public expenditure, although it received a major setback in the very first year, when electricity power workers took industrial action in support of a 25 per cent pay claim. Whilst declaring a State of Emergency – the first of several – Heath also set up an inquiry into the power workers' case, headed by Lord Wilberforce. The subsequent report recommended increases of 15–18 per cent, thereby seriously weakening the credibility of Heath's public sector pay policy.

Far more damaging to the Government, however, was the miners' strike which began in January 1972, in support of a 47 per cent pay claim (the miners' union, the NUM, argued that during the previous ten years or so, the pay of miners had declined in relation to that of other groups of workers).

The miners' strike, which had been endorsed by a ballot of the NUM's members, was particularly noteworthy for its accompaniment not only of mass picketing, but also of 'flying pickets' – workers and sympathizers who travelled to other parts of the country in order to picket firms or industries which were deemed to be assisting the firm or industry at the heart of the dispute, by virtue of supplying it with materials or purchasing its products. Thus did the 1972 miners' strike witness mass picketing, involving 'flying pickets', of various companies or industries which themselves used or transported coal.

The most notorious example of such picketing occurred at the Saltley coke depot in Birmingham, which was used by the West Midland Gas Board. When about 15,000 workers, led by the future NUM leader Arthur Scargill, turned up to picket the depot, the police felt it necessary to close Saltley in the interest of public order.

For the Left, Saltley symbolized the power and the potential of organized action by the working class, particularly with the miners as the 'vanguard of the proletariat'. Saltley has thus entered the annals of trade union folklore, an example of what could be achieved by working class solidarity. For the Right, however, Saltley came to symbolize 'mob rule', and the use of brute strength by trade unionists to achieve their ends, with a callous disregard for others, and for the country generally.

In mid-February, Lord Wilberforce was once again wheeled out to chair an inquiry, this time into the miners' case. Meanwhile, the Government introduced a three-day working week, in order to conserve rapidly diminishing energy supplies. Although the Wilberforce Inquiry recommended a 20 per cent pay increase for the miners, to be introduced over 16 months, the NUM rejected it. Instead further concessions were wrought from the Heath Government, leaving its 'N-minus-1' policy in tatters, and Selsdon Man fatally wounded.

Selsdon Man was also slain because of Heath's anxiety over rising unemployment. For example, during the winter of 1971–2, against the background of the miners' strike, unemployment had exceeded one million, which in those days was widely considered to be politically unacceptable. No governing party could seriously expect to contest the next general election presiding over this level of unemployment. Heath's anxiety over unemployment was reinforced by the plight of both Rolls Royce and Upper Clyde Shipbuilders. The former, a world-renowned British firm, faced bankruptcy in 1971. Unwilling to stand by and see a major British company go out of business, and unemployment escalate further, Heath saved Rolls Royce by having it nationalized. The consternation and concern which this caused on the right of the Conservative Party was compounded when the Heath Government stepped in to save the financially stricken Upper Clyde Shipbuilders, an intervention prompted in part by the fear of social and political unrest which might erupt on Clydeside – an area with a reputation for militancy – if its major employer was allowed to go out of business. For some of the Conservative Right, Heath's policies towards Rolls Royce and Upper Clyde Shipbuilders were a total betrayal of all that they had stood for in the 1970 election. Thus did some disaffected Conservative right-wingers, in 1973, form the Selsdon Group, named in memory of the Selsdon Park Hotel meeting which had originally helped to draft the Conservative Party's free market programme for the 1970 election. The Selsdon Group was therefore formed in order to oppose the drift away from free market principles by the Conservatives' parliamentary leadership.

Certainly, 1972 had seen Heath and his ministerial colleagues return-ing to a more corporatist and interventionist approach with regard to economic and industrial affairs. In the wake of trade union hostility towards the Industrial Relations Act, and the miners' strike, Heath sought a reconciliation with the TUC, claiming that there had to be 'a more sensible way' of dealing with Britain's economic and industrial relations problems. Recent events had apparently taught the Heath Government that the Conservative Party could not prosper by setting one class against another, however many war-like telegrams its supporters might send (Hurd 1979: 105). Consequently, the summer of 1972 witnessed Heath and his ministerial colleagues seeking agreements with the TUC and CBI (the employers' organization) concerning pay and prices. The Government wanted wage increases limited to £2 per week, and price rises kept to 5 per cent per annum. In return, it would commit itself to securing an economic growth rate of 5 per cent for the next two years. However, the trade unions wanted tougher action by the Government to control prices, something which it was not willing to accept without a corresponding acceptance by the unions of statutory control of wages, a proposal which they rejected. The Heath Government also refused to accede to the TUC's demand that the Industrial Relations Act be repealed.

With a voluntary pay and prices policy unattainable, the Heath Government imposed a statutory one instead, so that November witnessed the start of a 90-day freeze on wages, prices and rents. This was to be a short-term policy during which time the Government prepared a longer-term follow up – 'stage two' – involving statutory limits on pay, with maximum increases of 4 per cent plus £1 per week. Heath hoped that once 'stage two' was due to expire, the trade unions would be willing to enter voluntarily into a third stage of incomes policy. In the event, as we shall see later, 'stage three' actually heralded the death-knell for Heath's Government.

Direct Rule of Northern Ireland

Although, in 1969, the British Army had been sent – at the request of the Northern Ireland Prime Minister James Chichester-Clark – to restore order to the province, the violence which had erupted in 1968 continued to escalate. Indeed, the army itself inadvertently provided a new, additional target for the IRA, who viewed the presence of the British troops as a military means, by the British and Northern Ireland Governments, of maintaining the status quo – one in which Catholics were an oppressed minority. Furthermore, because Sinn Fein and the

IRA had always refused to acknowledge the legitimacy of the 'State' of Northern Ireland (which they insisted had been artificially created and arbitrarily imposed against the wishes of the vast majority of the Irish people), the presence of British troops was deemed to be that of an unwelcome 'occupying' army who were seeking to uphold an 'unjust' and 'undemocratic' political regime in a 'foreign' country. To Sinn Fein and the IRA, therefore, the British Army in Northern Ireland constituted a 'legitimate' target of military violence. This is one of the main reasons why the sending-in of British troops in 1969 was followed by an increase in the number of deaths attributable to 'the Troubles' in Northern Ireland, as table 4.1 illustrates.

Table 4.1   Deaths due to the conflict in Northern Ireland, 1969–1972

	RUC[a]	RUC 'R'[b]	Army	UDR[c]	Civilian	Total
1969	1	—	—	—	12	13
1970	2	—	—	—	23	25
1971	11	—	43	5	115	174
1972	14	3	103	26	321	467

Source: Royal Ulster Constabulary
[a] RUC–Royal Ulster Constabulary; the official police force of Northern Ireland, 90% of whose membership is Protestant.
[b] RUC 'R' – a 'reserve' police force, comprising part-time auxiliaries. Also known as the 'B-Specials'. Disbanded in 1970.
[c] UDR–Ulster Defence Regiment; formed in 1970 in order to replace the 'B-Specials'. An armed security force which works closely with the British Army.

Such was the escalation of violence that, in 1972, the British Government of Edward Heath suspended the Northern Ireland Parliament (Stormont) and imposed direct rule of the province from, and by, Westminster and Whitehall. This followed two particular developments or events which had exacerbated tension and hostility in Northern Ireland amongst the Nationalist (Catholic) community. Firstly, in August 1971, the British Government introduced the policy of 'internment', whereby those suspected of being actively involved in the 'terrorist' activities of the IRA could be – and were – imprisoned without a trial. This proved grist to Sinn Fein's mill, for they and their military wing, the IRA, could cite this as further evidence of state-sanctioned persecution, and denial of the rights of Catholics by the British Government and the

Protestant-dominated security forces in Northern Ireland. In making this claim, Sinn Fein could point to the fact that hardly any of those 'interned' for suspected terrorist activities were members of loyalist (Unionist) paramilitary organizations, such as the Ulster Defence Association (UDA) and the Ulster Volunteer Force (UVF). Therefore, it is no exaggeration to claim that: 'Internment . . . managed to unite the Catholic community against both the Unionist and the British governments' (Connolly 1990: 61). Indeed, as a former Secretary of State for Northern Ireland acknowledged, 'with the benefit of hindsight . . . internment did nothing to stem the deterioration in the situation. On the contrary, it remained a source of discontent and a spur to more violence' (Whitelaw 1989: 78).

The second event which fuelled hostility amongst the Nationalist community in Northern Ireland – and again provided ample propaganda and political capital for Sinn Fein and the IRA – was the fatal shooting of 13 unarmed Catholic demonstrators in (London)Derry in January 1972. The episode – known as 'Bloody Sunday' – prompted the burning down of the British Embassy in Dublin, such was the outrage amongst Catholics.

When 'direct rule' was imposed in 1972, it was intended to be a temporary measure by the British Government, which would be rescinded once 'the Troubles' calmed down again. Direct rule continues today. The imposition of direct rule greatly angered much of the Unionist (Protestant) community in Northern Ireland, for it meant that they no longer enjoyed control over their affairs. They were now to be governed from London, rather than by their own elected Parliament at Stormont.

Recognizing that some initiatives needed to be taken in the meantime, the British Government immediately began considering measures which might bring the two communities in Northern Ireland closer together, and thereby facilitate a transference of political power and sovereignty back to the province. With this objective in mind, the Secretary of State for Northern Ireland (a new ministry established when direct rule was imposed), William Whitelaw, sought to create a 'Power-sharing Executive', which it was hoped would 'square the circle of meeting nationalist aspirations without fatally alienating the unionists' (Arthur and Jeffery 1988: 12).

This 'Power-sharing Executive' was to comprise moderates elected from both communities in Northern Ireland, who would then seek to develop policies which enjoyed support from both sides of the politico-religious divide. This, it was envisaged, would simultaneously serve to bring the two communities closer together politically, and also enable the restoration of devolved government to Northern Ireland. However, many, if not most, Unionists were passionately opposed to the initiative, resenting the proposition or expectation that they, the majority community, should share their power with an allegedly disloyal, quarrelsome minority (the Nationalists/Catholics). Indeed, such was the depth of Unionist hostility that neither of their two parties – the Official Unionist Party (OUP) and the relatively recently formed Democratic Unionist Party (DUP) – would participate.

The 'Power-sharing Executive' was accompanied by another initiative from William Whitelaw and the British Government, namely the creation of a Council of Ireland. This was to provide the Irish government in Dublin with a consultative role in the affairs of Northern Ireland. This was also totally unacceptable to Unionists, among whom the only difference of opinion was whether the Council of Ireland was an irrelevance or an outrage. Many subscribed to the latter view, furious that the Republic of Ireland – an entirely separate, foreign country in Unionist eyes – should be accorded any voice at all in the affairs of Northern Ireland.

Such was the outrage of many Unionists concerning both the Council of Ireland and the Power-sharing Executive that in May 1974, the Ulster Workers' Council (which had been formed in late 1973) organized a strike of Protestant/Unionist workers in Northern Ireland. Many of these workers were employed in key sectors of the Northern Ireland economy, such as the power industry (electricity, etc.), and their involvement in the strike was instrumental in its success. The Ulster Workers' Council strike lasted for fourteen days, during which time Northern Ireland was virtually brought to a standstill. The strike was backed by the main Unionist paramilitary group, the Ulster Defence Association, who 'assisted the strike by intimidatory tactics' (Connolly 1990: 140–1). The end of the strike came after the resignation of the Unionist members of the Power-sharing Executive, which in turn heralded the end of this body. Direct rule had once again to be imposed, pending the finding of a more workable – acceptable – solution to the problems in Northern Ireland.

The 1973–4 Miners' Strike

In October 1973, the National Coal Board (NCB) offered Britain's miners a 13 per cent pay increase, including about 4.5 per cent for 'unsociable hours'. Such an offer was the maximum which the NCB could make under the terms of 'stage three' of Edward Heath's incomes policy. The NUM, however, was seeking a 40 per cent increase, thereby making a compromise difficult to reach. As such, in spite of a number of meetings between Heath and NUM leaders, the miners began an overtime ban in support of their pay claim, on 12 November.

The miners' position had been strengthened by the 1973 Yom Kippur war in the Middle East, which led to a fourfold increase in oil prices being introduced by the OPEC (Organization of Petroleum Exporting Countries) countries. With Britain's North Sea oil not yet fully flowing, an energy crisis appeared imminent, particularly when engineers in the electricity industry also commenced a work-to-rule in support of their pay claim. Meanwhile, November witnessed train drivers also taking industrial action in support of higher pay, a dispute which had an important impact on the transportation of Britain's diminishing coal supplies. Faced with the massive increase in oil prices (and a cutback in production by the OPEC countries), electricity power cuts and dwindling stocks of coal, Heath declared that at the beginning of 1974, Britain would once again be put on a three-day working week, in order to conserve energy supplies. Most serious of all for many British people was the announcement that television broadcasts would cease at 10.30 each night.

January 1974 witnessed two possible 'peace' initiatives rejected by the Heath Government. The first emanated from the TUC, which sought to convince ministers that if they treated the miners as a special case by permitting them a pay increase above and beyond the limits stipulated by 'stage three' of the Government's incomes policy, then other trade unions would *not* use such a settlement as a benchmark or target for their own pay claims The TUC's proposal was swiftly dismissed by the Government, partly because it was adamant that 'stage three' was inviolate, and also because it did not believe that other trade unions would refrain from pushing for wage increases in breach of 'stage three' if the miners were treated as an exception – how could the TUC guarantee that trade unionists would not seek to follow the miners if the latter were allowed to breach the Government's pay limits?

The second 'peace' initiative came via a report published by the Pay Board (which had been established in January 1973) recommending the establishment of a Relativities Board, which could then consider whether specific groups of workers were entitled to 'special treatment' on the basis of comparability and differentials with other employees. The Government was prepared to countenance this, with the miners obviously being the first group of workers to be considered, but only on condition that the NUM immediately call off the imminent strike and order its members to return to work. This was not a condition that the NUM was prepared to meet; indeed, a few days later, its members voted four to one in favour of an all-out strike in support of their pay claim.

Meanwhile, throughout January and February, the issue of whether Heath should – or would – call a general election had added to the concerns of Conservative ministers and back-bench MPs. Many certainly believed that Heath ought to hold a general election as soon as possible, in order to obtain a mandate from the electorate for its firm stance against the miners. A snap election, fought on the issue of 'Who governs Britain, democratically elected politicians or militant trade unionists?', would, its advocates in the party believed, result in the re-election of the Conservatives with a resounding endorsement from the country to stand firm against the NUM.

Others in the Conservative Party were opposed to the calling of a general election against the backdrop of the miners' strike. For one thing, it was argued, the Government already had a comfortable parliamentary majority, and up to eighteen months before it needed to go to the polls. How would winning a snap general election change anything, it was asked? The Heath government already had a sufficient majority in the House of Commons to enable it to stand firm and assert its political authority against the miners; what difference would a few more parliamentary seats make? However, some Conservative opponents of an early or snap election were actually fearful that the party would not be re-elected if it went to the country in such a context. Indeed, the Employment Secretary at this time was one of those opposed to a general election, on the grounds that he 'did not accept the view that our party would win an election at a time of industrial dispute which was inevitably causing economic problems and personal inconvenience' (Whitelaw 1989: 130). In the event, Heath did call a general election, the date set being 28 February. However, it was the pessimistic prophecy of those opposed to such an election, like William Whitelaw, which, tragically for Heath, was to prove most prescient.

The 1974 Elections

There were two general elections in 1974, one in February and the other in October. As the previous section indicated, the February election was called by the Prime Minister Edward Heath in response to the miners' strike, with the question being 'Who governs Britain?' The electorate's answer was ambiguous. The Labour Party won 301 seats with 11,646,391 votes, whilst 11,872,180 votes yielded the Conservative Party 297 seats. In other words, Labour won four more seats than the Conservatives, yet polled almost million fewer votes. Yet these were by no means the only remarkable features of the election result in February 1974.

Also noteworthy was the marked increase in electoral support for third parties throughout Britain. In England particularly, the Liberal party witnessed a surge in support which provided it with 6,058,744 votes (compared to 2,117,035 in 1970), representing 19.3 per cent of the total national poll. However, the absurdity which masquerades as Britain's electoral system translated this support and share of the vote into just 14 parliamentary seats. Meanwhile, the Nationalist parties in Scotland and Wales also experienced unprecedented electoral success, with the Scottish Nationalist Party securing 21.9 per cent of the vote and seven seats in Scotland, and Plaid Cymru winning 10.7 per cent of the vote and two seats in Wales. Support for 'third' parties was such that the Labour and Conservative Parties witnessed their combined share of the vote reduced to 75 per cent, whereas in 1964 it had stood at 87.5 per cent.

Although Labour had won four more seats than the Conservative Party, it lacked an overall parliamentary majority because of the 37 seats won by other, 'third' parties. Indeed, Heath initially sought to form a coalition government with the Liberal Party. However, this invitation was unanimously rejected by the 14 Liberal MPs, leaving Heath with no real alternative but to resign (the Ulster Unionists having themselves declined an invitation by Heath to take the Conservative whip in the

House of Commons). Yet even if the Liberal Party had accepted Heath's invitation, it is difficult to see what would have really been achieved, because even a Conservative–Liberal coalition would still have been eight seats short of an overall parliamentary majority.

It was thus Harold Wilson, the Labour leader, who formed the new administration, albeit a minority one which was 34 seats short of an overall majority in the House of Commons. Right from the outset, therefore, the question being asked was not *whether* another general election might be called in the foreseeable future, but *when?* No government could last the full five-year term of office when it was so far short of a parliamentary majority. Wilson would almost inevitably call another general election soon, in order to try and secure an overall majority for the Labour Party (indeed, Wilson privately made it clear to senior officials at Transport House – Labour's headquarters at the time – that there would be another election by the autumn of 1974 at the latest: see Butler and Kavanagh 1975: 19). The political situation engendered by the result of the February 1974 election, and the implicit imminence of another election, had important consequences for the behaviour and strategies of both the Labour and the Conservative Parties.

The Wilson Government swiftly sought simultaneously to introduce a number of popular policies and election pledges whilst avoiding the more controversial commitments and measures favoured by the Left. Although the Labour Chancellor, Denis Healey, both increased income tax and extended VAT in his Budget towards the end of March, he also significantly increased old age pensions, and raised social security benefits. Food subsidies were introduced, whilst stricter control of prices was promised. There was also a rent freeze for tenants, and the introduction of mortgage subsidies for owner-occupiers. Another Budget in July saw Healey cut VAT. Not only were most of these policies intended to be electorally popular in themselves, they were also designed to assist in restraining pay increases; subsidies and price control were intended to keep down the cost of living and inflation, which in turn would dissuade trade unions from pursuing 'excessive' wage claims. Indeed, this trade off between an improved 'social wage' and the concomitant exercise of voluntary pay restraint by the unions was the very basis of the Social Contract (to be discussed shortly). This, in turn, was supposed to prove to the electorate that only a Labour government could work constructively and co-operatively with the trade unions.

Meanwhile, Heath and his Conservative colleagues found themselves in a position which was even more frustrating than that usually experienced by the Opposition. Normally, having lost a general election, a political party would be fairly sure that it had four or five years in which to develop a new programme of policies, whilst also seeking to convince the electorate that it constituted a clear and viable alternative to the governing party. Such a situation did not pertain to February 1974. Instead, it was evident that the minority Labour government would feel obliged to call another general election imminently, in order to obtain a working majority in the Commons. This afforded the Conservative Party very little time in which to formulate a new set of policies to replace those on which they had fought *and lost* the February election. Had it attempted to present a new policy programme immediately, it would have appeared, to many voters, as a panic response, or as naked opportunism bereft of commitment and sincerity. An immediate switch to a new programme would also have necessitated Heath, and a few close colleagues, taking it upon themselves to determine the new policies without allowing such intra-party consultations and discussions to take place. Such a move would have further alienated those Conservative back-benchers who already disliked Heath's allegedly aloof, almost autocratic, style of party leadership (see Norton 1978: 221–55).

In any case, what sort of policies or programme could Heath have adopted? The economic liberal/social authoritarian approach upon which the 1970 election had been won had been ignominiously abandoned by 1972, yet the switch to a more conciliatory, consensual approach had itself failed to prove successful. In the immediate wake of the February 1974 election defeat, Heath's dilemma over where to turn next was an acute one.

Heath also faced one further problem in this context, namely how far he and the Conservative Party should go in attacking the new minority Labour Government. Should he seek to bring down the Wilson Government as soon as possible, or would that be too widely perceived as a purely destructive, negative tactic from an Opposition which itself was uncertain over its policy direction? On the other hand, Heath recognized that if he refrained from vigorously attacking the Labour Government, he would disappoint and demoralize many of his Conservative colleagues, and thereby weaken his position and authority as party leader even further. Heath himself publicly acknowledged this dilemma when he rhetorically asked:

> What is the point of giving the present government the opportunity of having a general election? Say we had been able to defeat them on a major item on the Finance Bill because the other parties had supported us, and a general election was called before the country itself realized the disastrous direction in which the Labour Party is leading us. What is the point of that? What is the sensible leadership in doing that? (quoted in Butler and Kavanagh, 1974: 42)

Similarly, in April 1974, Central Office explained to Conservative Party activists that:

> Whilst our supporters will often wish for all-out opposition to a Government proposal, tactically this might be unwise. For Labour's obvious interest is to have a snap election on some issue helpful to them which would return them with an overall majority . . . (quoted in *ibid*.: 42)

In the event, when the inevitable general election did take place, in October 1974, Labour only managed to obtain a majority of three seats. The Conservative Party ended up with 20 fewer seats than in February, and received its lowest share – 35.8 per cent – of the vote in any post-war general election. Heath's days as Conservative leader were now definitely numbered.

'The Social Contract'

Having experienced a deep and damaging rift over *In Place of Strife* in 1969, the Labour Party and the trade unions sought, during the period of Heath's Government (1970–4), to repair the damage, and develop a new working relationship. This process was assisted considerably by the introduction of the Industrial Relations Act, for it provided both the Labour Party and the trade unions with a clear focal point against which to campaign. However, it was recognized that something more constructive was needed between Labour and the unions; merely being united in opposition to a government measure was not sufficient to convince the electorate that a future Labour Government could work harmoniously with the trade unions, and thereby spare the British people yet more industrial strife and unrest.

The Labour Party was acutely aware that if it was returned to office, it would need the acquiescence of the trade unions in order to manage the economy successfully. This would inevitably require that the unions exercise wage restraint, yet the trade unions were strongly opposed to incomes policies (free collective bargaining being a cardinal principle of British trade unionism). For their part, the trade unions wanted the next Labour Government to repeal the Industrial Relations Act, and to improve the 'social wage' (full employment, social security benefits, measures for the low-paid, etc.). The means to achieve the objectives of both sides was to be the 'Social Contract', which emerged out of a series of meetings of the Labour Party–TUC Liaison Committee, a body that had been set up in January 1972 comprising senior members of the TUC's General Council, the Shadow Cabinet and Labour's National Executive Committee (NEC).

The Social Contract proclaimed that in return for a commitment by the trade unions to exercise voluntary wage restraint, and take into account the overall state of the economy when submitting pay claims, the next Labour government would pursue a number of measures to improve the social wage, such as increasing old age pensions, and introducing subsidies for transport fares, rents and some food items. At a wider level, Labour would seek to effect a fairer, more equal distribution of wealth in British society. The Social Contract also entailed a commitment by the Labour Party to repeal the Industrial Relations Act, improve employment protection, and introduce industrial democracy. The Labour leadership clearly hoped that improvements in the social wage would deter the trade unions from pursuing significant increases in 'real' wages. Indeed, the success or failure of the Social Contract would depend upon it.

The Social Contract was thus accorded considerable prominence by the Labour Party in the two general elections which took place in 1974. Indeed, the Labour manifesto for the October 1974 election declared that: 'At the heart of this manifesto and our programme to save the nation lies the Social Contract between the Labour party and the trade unions.'

The EC Referendum

The Wilson Government's decision to hold a referendum on Britain's continued membership of the European Communities was not born of a sudden passion for genuine democracy, or respect for the opinions of *vox populi*. Instead, it owed much to the wily Wilson's attempt at party management, and the need to prevent a deep and damaging split in the parliamentary Labour Party. In fact, the impetus for a referendum on the issue of Britain's continued EC membership had originally emanated from the left of the Party, where it had been envisaged that nationalist sentiment amongst the British people would produce a 'no' vote. The Labour Left had always opposed Britain's membership of the EC on the grounds that it was little more than a 'capitalist club' which would obstruct the implementation of a radical socialist programme by a Labour government. The Left clearly recognized that its favoured policies, such as economic planning and import controls, were incompatible with Britain remaining signatories to the Treaty of Rome (which sought the establishment of a free trade zone between member states).

Debate over Britain's membership of the EC, both in the referendum campaign and also at a more general, ongoing level, tended to focus on two particular issues, namely those of sovereignty, and the economic consequences of (continued) membership. The issue of sovereignty (which continues today, particularly in the wake of the 1991 Maastricht Treaty and its provisions for greater economic and monetary union between member states) has often been seized by both the Conservative Right and the Labour Left as an argument either against membership of the EC, or against further integration. During the 1975 referendum, it was the Left of the Labour Party which was most inclined to rehearse the sovereignty argument, claiming that if Britain remained a member of the EC, then Parliament, hitherto representative of, and accountable to, the British people, would cease to be able effectively to fulfil these functions. Laws and policies binding upon the British people would no longer emanate solely from Parliament, or even require parliamentary approval: they would increasingly emanate from the European Commission. No longer would Parliament be the highest legislative authority exercising jurisdiction over the British people. EC law would enjoy precedence over domestic law. Westminster would be subordinate to Brussels.

Against this perspective, it was argued that the extent to which Britain was in control of its own destiny was something of a myth anyway: in a complex, interdependent world, Britain could not take political decisions and pursue policies in isolation, or with a lack of regard for what was happening elsewhere. Even if Britain were to leave the EC, it was emphasized, it would still be deeply affected by what the remaining member states did.

In any case, proponents of continued EC membership insisted, Britain would still retain considerable parliamentary sovereignty, and would therefore continue to exercise a significant degree of independence and autonomy over domestic affairs. Furthermore, it was pointed out, British ministers could veto EC proposals which were deemed to be against Britain's interests. In short, those who opposed continued EC membership were accused of exaggerating the threat to British independence, and of peddling a sentimental myth about parliamentary sovereignty.

With regard to the economic arguments concerning Britain's continued membership of the EC, those favouring withdrawal (and thus seeking a 'no' vote in the referendum) asserted that the tariff-free access to Britain enjoyed by other EC states would enable them to 'flood' the domestic market with cheaper goods and produce, thereby further destroying British industry and jobs. Indeed, as British industry was destroyed by the importing of cheap(er) EC products, so Britain's balance of payments would correspondingly deteriorate, with the country increasingly importing more than it was exporting.

It was also pointed out that because Britain was not primarily an agricultural, farming nation, the nation would end up paying more into the EC, through budgetary contributions each year, than it would get back, due to the fact that two-thirds of the EC's budget went to predominantly agricultural countries via the Common Agricultural Policy.

Those favouring continued British membership of the EC (and thus seeking a 'yes' vote in the referendum) retorted that whilst the other member states did indeed enjoy tariff-free access to Britain, the converse was equally true, that British industry and manufacturers now enjoyed tariff-free access to eight other European countries, to whom goods could thus be exported more cheaply. This was presented as a marvellous opportunity to secure the revival of British industry – and the economy generally – and, *pari passu*, to safeguard existing jobs whilst also creating new ones. Were Britain to withdraw, it was warned, then British exports to Europe would be subject to tariffs on the grounds that they were no longer EC goods. This would obviously make them more expensive, and thus even less competitive, thereby resulting in the continued decline of British manufacturing industry, and an exacerbation of Britain's economic problems.

With regard to the issue of Britain's budgetary contributions and the operation of the Common Agricultural Policy, advocates of continued EC membership reasoned that the solution lay in continuing to renegotiate the amount that Britain paid in, whilst seeking to reform the Common Agricultural Policy.

As already indicated, the main advocates of EC withdrawal during the 1975 referendum campaign were to be found on the left of the Labour Party. During this period, only a handful of Conservatives, on the right of the party, publicly supported Britain's withdrawal from the EC. It was therefore the Labour Party which was most seriously divided over the issue on this occasion. Hence, when the Cabinet voted, on 18 March 1975, over acceptance of the terms of Britain's EC membership which Wilson had renegotiated, the outcome was 16 ministers in favour and seven against. However, the parliamentary Labour Party was rather more seriously split, so that in a House of Commons vote on the renegotiated terms, on 9 April, 137 Labour MPs voted in favour, 145 voted against and 33 abstained. It was only by virtue of the support of the Opposition parties that the Wilson Government secured Parliament's endorsement, by 396 votes to 172.

The result of the actual referendum, held on 5 June 1975, was 17,378,581 voting 'yes' (to continued EC membership) and 8,470,073 voting 'no'. This translated as 67.2 per cent in favour compared to 32.8 per cent against, on a turn-out of 64.6 per cent. However, whilst the result seemed to represent an emphatic 2-to-1 victory in favour of Britain retaining its membership of the EC, it has been suggested that 'the verdict of the referendum . . . was unequivocal, but it was also unenthusiastic. Support for membership was wide but it did not run deep' (Butler and Kitzinger 1976: 280). Furthermore, expectation that the result of the referendum would herald a new phase of membership, based on a more constructive and co-operative role by the British Government, was subsequently proved premature and unfounded. Britain had already acquired a reputation for being an 'awkward partner'; it apparently had no subsequent desire to shake off this image.

Thatcher Replaces Heath as Conservative Leader

Conservatives are intolerant of many things, but electoral failure is undoubtedly something which they particularly abhor. Obviously, no major political party is happy losing a general election, but for a Conservative Party which views itself as the 'natural party of government', electoral defeat incurs the leader particular displeasure. So it was when the Conservative Government of Edward Heath was defeated in the February 1974 election, then again eight months later. Having been leader of the Conservative Party when it had lost the 1966 general election as well, Heath was viewed by many of his critics in the Party as a three-times loser.

Many Conservatives had been angered by Heath's calling the February 1974 election in order to obtain a 'mandate' for his stance *vis-à-vis* the miners. With a comfortable majority already, many Conservatives were bewildered by Heath's desire to obtain electoral backing in his conflict with the NUM. His 'strategy' seemed to imply cowardice or vacillation. Indeed, Enoch Powell refused to stand as a Conservative candidate in February 1974, claiming that the election was a 'fraudulent' one and 'an act of gross irresponsibility' (Butler and Kavanagh 1974: 66).

Heath's unpopularity amongst many Conservatives in the wake of the 1974 election defeats was also derived from his 'U-turn' in 1972, when he had abandoned the 'Selsdon' programme upon which the Conservative Party had fought and won the 1970 election. Ever since 1972 many on the right of the party had viewed Heath as a traitor. The loss of the 1974 elections, therefore, meant that Heath's reservoir of sympathy and support in the Conservative party was dangerously low. Yet, in spite of his unpopularity – or perhaps because of it – Heath initially refused to relinquish his leadership, and seek re-election by his parliamentary colleagues. However, under pressure from the 1922 Committee of back-bench Conservative MPs, Heath reluctantly established a group to examine the rules governing the election of Conservative leaders.

This group met five times in just three weeks, and was able to submit a report to Heath on 11 December 1974, prior to its being made available to Conservative MPs six days later. Two main changes to the (1965) leadership election rules were proposed. Firstly, and most significantly, it was suggested that Conservative leadership elections ought to be held annually, unless there were no challengers, in which case the existing leader would be returned unopposed. Secondly, a candidate would be required to obtain a majority plus 15 per cent of all those eligible to vote (i.e. all Conservative MPs, not solely those who actually voted) in order to be elected leader of the Conservative Party. This proviso was intended to prevent a candidate emerging victorious by virtue of the apathy or abstentions of those MPs who did not vote.

Heath accepted these recommendations, and announced that the first ballot of a leadership contest would be held on 4 February 1975. However, there appeared to be 'a dearth of likely leaders' in the Conservative Party at this time, partly because of Heath's tendency to choose 'affable, like-minded and somewhat colourless men as colleagues . . . ' (Behrens 1980: 37). Some of those who had once been considered leadership material were no longer available, such as Enoch Powell, who by this time had left the Conservative Party and been elected as an Official Unionist MP in South Down, in Northern Ireland. Other potential candidates, such as William Whitelaw, felt disinclined to stand against Heath due to a deep sense of loyalty and continued support. In any case, those closest to Heath would have been unacceptable to the Right of the Conservative Party precisely of this proximity to the existing leader – they were deemed to share 'collective responsibility' for the 'U-turn' and other alleged policy failures of the first half of the 1970s.

It was Sir Keith Joseph who initially emerged as the most likely challenger to Heath, the former having announced that, since 1974, he had discovered 'true Conservatism', thereby seeking to downplay his collective responsibility for policies pursued by the Heath Government of which Sir Keith had been a member. These policies, he declared, had not been genuinely Conservative policies at all, although he had not realized it at the time. It was after the loss of the February 1974 election that Sir Keith 'discovered' economic neo-liberalism, a firm belief in the economic efficiency and moral superiority of the free market, and a private ownership, private enterprise economy in which the 'natural laws' of supply and demand, not state intervention or direction, effectively determined economic activity and variables, such as what was produced, by whom, at what price, etc. Having become thoroughly disillusioned with the direction of post-war British politics generally, and with that of the contemporary Conservative Party in particular, Sir Keith discovered Milton Friedman and Friedrich Hayek in 'the manner of a sudden vision on the road to Damascus' (Keegan 1984: 60). Yet Sir Keith raised serious doubts about his sense of political judgement and tact when he made a controversial speech in Birmingham, in October 1974, which expressed concern that: 'The balance of our population, our human stock is threatened', and which thus suggested that in the context of growing social problems such as crime and juvenile delinquency, stricter birth control ought to be applied to working-class women.

In the wake of Sir Keith's public dabbling with eugenics, it fell to Margaret Thatcher to don the mantle of leadership challenger. Although she had also been a member of the Heath Cabinet, her position of Education Minister had effectively distanced her from the controversy surrounding economic policies between 1970 and 1974. In any case, it was no secret that, even during this period, Edward Heath and Margaret Thatcher disliked each other. Margaret Thatcher was thus better placed to stand against Heath for the leadership of the Conservative Party than those of his ministerial colleagues who had either been more closely involved in economic policy, or who were close friends and supporters of Heath. The fact that Margaret Thatcher was a relatively unknown 'outsider' actually enhanced her potential, due to the fact that many Conservative MPs considered the time ripe for a fresh start under a new leader. That said, however, it ought to be emphasized that Margaret Thatcher's right-wing views and principles had by no means become fully developed or widely known at this stage – she was not yet a 'Thatcherite'. None the less, she appeared sufficiently distinctive in style and general philosophy to attract support from those who wanted Heath replaced. She also attracted respect and support within the Conservative Party due to her skilful performance at the Commons' Despatch Box during the parliamentary debates on the Labour Government's Finance Bill (the legislation which gives formal approval by Parliament for the Budget).

When the ballot for the Conservative Party leadership contest was finally held on 4 February 1975, Margaret Thatcher received 130 votes to Edward Heath's 119, with the rank outsider Hugh Fraser mustering just 16. This victory was, according to the Party's '15 per cent majority' rule, insufficient for Margaret Thatcher to be declared leader, but it was sufficient for Heath to acknowledge defeat and resign.

In the requisite second ballot (in which a simple majority would be sufficient for outright victory), four new candidates came forward to stand against Margaret Thatcher, namely Sir Geoffrey Howe, John

Peyton, James Prior and William Whitelaw. When the second ballot was held, one week later on 11 February, the result was:

Margaret Thatcher	146
William Whitelaw	79
James Prior	19
Sir Geoffrey Howe	19
John Peyton	11

This was sufficient to provide Margaret Thatcher with a majority of 18. Yet as we will now explain, it would be too simplistic to characterize Margaret Thatcher's election as evidence of a sudden and decisive swing to the right by the Conservative Party.

Ascendancy of the New Right in the Conservative Party

Although the Conservative Party moved to the right after the election of Margaret Thatcher as leader, it is important to note that this ideological shift did not occur immediately. Indeed, it would be claiming too much to say that Margaret Thatcher's election reflected a clear wish amongst Conservative MPs for a more right-wing brand of Conservatism. Not only did 119 Conservative MPs still vote for Heath in the first ballot, thereby forcing a second ballot (in which Heath stood down), it was also the case that in the latter ballot, the two candidates from the patrician 'one nation' wing of the Conservative Party, James Prior and William Whitelaw, polled a total of 98 votes. Although this was obviously rather less than Margaret Thatcher's 146 votes in the second ballot, it none the less indicated that the Conservative Party as a whole had not suddenly or universally become Thatcherite (indeed, even during the 1980s, when Margaret Thatcher was Prime Minister, only a minority of the Party's MPs could be labelled Thatcherites – see Norton 1990).

In any case, many of those Conservative MPs voting for Margaret Thatcher in 1975 had little real idea about what she actually believed in or stood for. For some Conservatives, the other candidates were too closely associated with Heath, and although Thatcher herself had served as Education Minister in Heath's administration, she enjoyed something of an advantage in not being seen as one of Heath's closest colleagues. She was thus spared the 'guilt by association' which tarnished the reputations – and leadership prospects – of candidates such as Prior and Whitelaw. To some extent, therefore, a number of the votes which went to Margaret Thatcher were not so much votes *for* her as votes *against* Heath and his adherents: 'She won because she was not Heath' (Blake 1985: 320; see also Keegan 1984: 63).

There was one other important reason why the election of Margaret Thatcher to the leadership of the Conservative Party in 1975 did not signify a clear or coherent shift to the Right, namely that she herself had not yet fully developed a distinct style or set of policies; 'she was not elected as a Thatcherite' (King 1985: 97). As another commentator has emphasized: 'she was something of an accidental leader, and it is a rewriting of history to see her election as a victory for monetarism' (Kavanagh 1987: 199; see also Blake 1985: 321).

With hindsight, one can see an indication of the imminent rightward drift in the establishment of the Centre for Policy Studies, which was set up in 1974 by Sir Keith Joseph. It was mooted as a think-tank which would undertake research and produce pamphlets in order to encourage support for a market economy. Sir Keith claimed that the experiences of being a minister in the Heath administration had made him realize the necessity and virtues of a private enterprise economy, free from state interference. To this end, Sir Keith envisaged that the Centre for Policy Studies would provide an intellectual forum for Conservatives who wished to challenge the social democratic, Keynesian orthodoxy which had enjoyed hegemony since 1945. Whilst Margaret Thatcher was appointed President of the Centre for Policy Studies by Sir Keith – with whom she developed a close ideological and intellectual affinity – it was only after her election to the Conservative leadership that the Centre seemed to exert a greater influence on Thatcher's political views, and *ipso facto*, party policies.

The more obvious manifestation of a rightward shift in the Conservative Party during the latter half of the 1970s was thus in the sphere of economic philosophy and policy. Margaret Thatcher herself followed Sir Keith down 'the road to Damascus' from the mid-1970s, discovering the alleged virtues of free market principles as expounded by Friedman and Hayek (although she was a little less forthright in her espousal of such ideas). Whilst Conservatives throughout the twentieth century had espoused the virtues of private enterprise, profit-making, wealth creation, competition, independence from the state, and so on, Margaret Thatcher began to do so with rather more vigour and verve than most previous Conservative leaders. A clear indication of the direction in which she wished to take the Conservative Party – and Britain – was provided in a 1976 speech to the Greater London Young Conservatives, when she spoke reverentially of the Victorian era as one which witnessed 'the burgeoning of free enterprise . . . the greatest expansions of voluntary philanthropic activity'; she also expressed her admiration for Adam Smith, and his notion that 'the self-interest of many can further the mutual interest of all . . . a major drive which can be a blessing to any society able to harness it', emphasizing that Smith 'showed how the market economy obliges and enables each producer to serve the consumers' interest by serving his own' (quoted in Russel 1978: 104–5). It is hard to imagine a previous Conservative leader, such as Harold Macmillan, making such a speech.

Although the Conservative Party thus discernibly moved to the right under Margaret Thatcher's leadership from 1975 onwards, the extent and uniformity of this ideological shift ought not to be exaggerated: 'the image of radicalism was not borne out by her early actions as a party leader' (Kavanagh 1987: 201). Not dissimilarly, Gamble emphasizes that 'The pace at which new policies were developed was . . . very slow. The Conservatives were not committed to a radical Thatcherite programme by the 1979 election' (Gamble 1988: 86). As the result of the leadership contest had indicated, there remained a significant segment of opinion within the Conservative Party which adhered to the traditional 'one nation' approach. Such Conservatives were thus rather anxious about the direction in which Margaret Thatcher was seeking to take the party. James Prior, for example, recalls that 'as she seemed to grow progressively more dedicated to the doctrine [monetarism], I became increasingly worried about the importance being attached to it at the expense of other measures . . . ' (Prior 1986: 109).

The self-proclaimed willingness of the neo-liberals or New Right to countenance higher levels of unemployment in order to reduce both inflation and trade union power was a cause of considerable consternation to 'one nation' Conservatives. Heath himself, having been severely chastened by his experiences as Prime Minister from 1970 to 1974, warned that: 'We will never be able to win popular support for an economic system which tolerates with general indifference a steady one or two million people, or more, out of work for any length of time. Nor will we deserve to do so' (quoted in Russel 1978: 55). Similarly, concerns were harboured by a number of other senior Conservatives on the 'one nation' wing of the party during this time. Ian Gilmour, for example, suggested that: 'A Tory would have to examine the political and economic consequences of a monetarist policy. He might, for instance, come to the conclusion that such a policy would produce an unacceptable level of unemployment, or he might think that the pursuit of such a policy would be likely to lead to civil disturbance' (quoted in Russel 1978: 44).

As a consequence of such doubts and disagreements in the Conservative Party whilst in Opposition, the extent of the rightward shift discernible after 1974 was tempered somewhat, due partly to the need to reflect the balance of opinion amongst MPs, but also because of the need to avoid frightening the electorate. Such factors ensured that many policies reflected something of an uneasy compromise between neo-liberals and 'one nation' Conservatives. For example, whilst it was no secret that Conservatives such as Keith Joseph and Margaret Thatcher despised the trade unions, this did not prevent the latter, upon becoming party leader, appointing the extremely conciliatory James Prior as Shadow Employment Minister. Indeed, it was doubtless intended that Prior would be able to soothe the electorate's fears about an all-out right-wing assault on the trade unions. In any case, Prior himself later acknowledged that with the Tory Right attacking him for being too soft on the unions, and left-wing trade union leaders accusing him of preparing to impose draconian curbs on the unions, he was able to present himself as a moderate (Prior 1986).

The related issues of incomes policies and economic management also provided an indication of the compromises which were being reached in the Conservative Party between the different 'wings'. Whilst neo-liberals on the right of the party were ideologically opposed to trade union involvement in economic policy-making, much of the Conservative leadership still mooted the notion of an 'economic forum' involving ministers and representatives of the 'two sides of industry', which would meet periodically to discuss economic circumstances and determine common objectives. This would, of course, entail some consideration of wages, and thus, almost inevitably, some form of incomes policy. Even

Sir Geoffrey Howe still adhered to the idea of an 'economic forum' as a tool of economic management, in spite of his own increasing commitment to monetarism.

A clear indication of the tensions and compromises manifesting themselves in the Conservative Party, and particularly within the Shadow Cabinet, during the mid to late 1970s was evident in the party's 1976 policy document *The Right Approach*, and the publication the following year of *The Right Approach to the Economy*. Whilst Prior wanted these documents to acknowledge the need for some form of incomes policy, Thatcher was strongly opposed. As a result, *The Right Approach to the Economy* – signed by Prior, Geoffrey Howe, Keith Joseph, David Howell and Angus Maude – contained a rather woolly reference to the need for the Government to 'come to *some* conclusions about the likely scope for pay increases if excess public expenditure or large-scale unemployment is to be avoided' (emphasis in original). Yet even this was too much for Margaret Thatcher, who 'absolutely refused to allow the document to be published as a Shadow Cabinet paper' (Prior 1986: 109).

By 1979, however, opinion in the Conservative Party against incomes policy had hardened considerably, not least because of the problems which the Labour Government had increasingly experienced in setting pay limits. There had also emerged a recognition amongst some leading Conservatives that many trade unionists might be attracted to the party electorally if it pledged to restore free collective bargaining.

English Nationalism – The Rise of the Far Right

Although the National Front was formed in February 1967, and might have been expected to benefit from Enoch Powell's 'rivers of blood' speech the following year when it pushed the twin issues of race and immigration high onto the political agenda, it was not until the mid-1970s that the party came to be seen as a serious electoral force in British politics.

Whilst the National Front was undoubtedly a political party rather than a pressure group, it was perceived by most people to be concerned almost exclusively with the issue of coloured (i.e. non-white) immigration and race. Indeed, it was formed from the amalgamation of three far-right organizations, namely the British National Party, League of Empire

Loyalists, and Racial Preservation Society, with a combined membership of about 4,000, although by early 1974 this had risen to 15,000.

The 'ideology' or programme of the National Front was largely based on the notion that British society, and the (white) British race, were being undermined by coloured immigration, much of it from countries which had hitherto belonged to the British Empire or Commonwealth. The National Front's vehement – and often violent – opposition to coloured immigrants and their dependants was articulated at two levels. Firstly, there was the notion of eugenics which National Front leaders and intellectuals (*sic*) espoused, entailing arguments about racial hierarchies and innate, biologically determined levels of intelligence, civilization, culture, etc. According to this 'theory', the white caucasian European race is the most advanced, and superior, race in the world (although white Americans, and also whites in the Commonwealth countries such as Australia, Canada and New Zealand are also included in this racial premier league). Needless to say, the National Front deemed the British to be the most advanced, superior race of all. Non-white races and civilizations are thus deemed inherently and innately inferior, intellectually deficient and socially backward. Following on from this perspective, the National Front warned – as Hitler had done in *Mein Kampf* – that the purity and superiority of a race was destroyed if its members began breeding with the members of another (inferior) race. Like mixing milk and water, the result would be a dilution and weakening of the strongest element. Hence the National Front insisted that the purity and superiority of the British race depended upon putting an end to mixed-race marriages and sexual relationships.

The second level of the National Front's total opposition to immigration was the electoral or populist one, whereby British people were warned of the threat that coloured immigrants posed to their everyday lives. Hitler and the Nazis had warned the people of Weimar Germany that the Jews would take their jobs, their homes, their money, etc.; the National Front issued the same kind of warning, but replaced the word 'Jews' with 'blacks'. To this extent the National Front played the numbers game, suggesting that many socio-economic problems in Britain – rising unemployment, slum housing, increasing crime, poverty, the escalating cost of maintaining the welfare state – were caused by 'too many immigrants'. If a 'black' person was in paid employment, the National Front claimed that they were denying a white person that job; if a 'black' person was unemployed, they were then accused of 'scrounging' off the welfare state, paid for by the taxes and national insurance contributions of British workers.

The development or intensification during the 1970s of the socio-economic problems just referred to, particularly unemployment in urban, inner-city areas, made it relatively easy for the National Front to scapegoat immigrants and ethnic minorities. The least intelligent, most uneducated in British society were always particularly susceptible to the National Front's claim that Britain's problems were the consequence of immigration, and that, *ergo*, the way to solve those problems was to repatriate all non-whites. Numerous socio-psychological and attitudinal surveys have consistently indicated that it is usually those in society who have had a minimal education, and are of low socio-economic status, who tend to have the most authoritarian attitudes, and are thus most intolerant and hostile towards people who are considered different from them.

Whilst race and immigration were undoubtedly the most widely recognized elements of the National Front's ideology, it should be noted that its concern to defend the 'supremacy' of the British nation-state and its indigenous population led logically to total opposition to Britain's membership of the European Communities. Not only was membership seen as a fatal loss of sovereignty and independence, the European Communities were also deemed to be the institutional manifestation of a conspiracy between international capitalism and Jews on the one hand, and Communism on the other, both of which allegedly sought the destruction of individual nation-states and their sovereignty, in order to achieve world domination.

The National Front's electoral 'breakthrough' came in the West Bromwich by-election in May 1973, when it polled over 4,700 votes (over 16 per cent of the total cast). The following year, in the two 1974 general elections (February and October), the National Front fielded 54 and 90 candidates respectively, polling 76,000 votes in February, and 113,579 in October. In fact, the October 1974 result 'confirmed its position as England's fourth party' (Butler and Kavanagh 1975: 351). In 1976, the May local elections saw two National Front councillors elected in Blackburn, whilst in Leicester, although the party did not win any seats, it did receive over 43,000 votes (18½ per cent of the poll). A year later, in elections to the Greater London Council (GLC), the National Front polled 119,000 votes, and won over ¼ million votes nationally.

However, it was not only the National Front's electoral performances which gave cause for concern. Alongside its strategy of constitutionally contesting elections like any other legitimate political party, the National Party was also engaged in direct action, usually in the form of physical assaults on 'non-white' individuals and criminal damage – including arson – to their property. Such racial attacks have long been particularly prevalent in the East End of London.

Whilst racist violence has continued (indeed, is on the increase), the electoral performance of the far Right has declined significantly since the late 1970s. Indeed, the electoral decline may well underpin, at least in part, the increase in racial attacks, for as the parties of the far Right see their chances of success through the ballot box dwindling, so they feel fewer qualms about relying almost exclusively on direct action and violence in order to 'drive out' ethnic minority sections of society. Many racial attacks are not solely the expression of a pathological hatred of 'foreigners' and 'immigrants', but are also intended to make life so unpleasant and intolerable for ethnic minorities that they will 'choose' to leave Britain and 'go home' (notwithstanding the fact that most of them were born here, so that Britain *is* their home).

The electoral decline of the far Right since the late 1970s can be explained by reference to two particular factors. Firstly, the Conservative Party, under Margaret Thatcher's leadership, contested the 1979 general election on a manifesto which promised much stricter immigration controls. Indeed, the previous year, Margaret Thatcher had herself said, in a television interview, that she understood the 'fears of our people' about being 'swamped' by 'alien cultures'. Within the next few weeks, the Conservative Party's opinion poll ratings increased 9 per cent, whilst one opinion poll showed that the proportion of the electorate who considered immigration to be an 'urgent issue facing the country' had increased from 9 to 21 per cent. Many of those who might have voted for the National Front could now consider it worthwhile voting Conservative. In the 1979 election, the National Front fielded 301 candidates, but secured just 0.6 per cent of votes cast nationally.

The second factor accounting for the electoral decline of the far Right in Britain since the late 1970s is the factionalism and fragmentation which has sporadically occurred, partly as a consequence of its diminishing electoral support. In 1982 a former senior figure in the National Front, John Tyndall, created the British National Party, taking many NF members with him, providing a membership of about 2,000–3,000. Since its formation, the British National Party has displaced the National Front as Britain's main party of the far Right, eventually securing the election of a councillor in a local by-election in Tower Hamlets, London, in 1993.

After the split in 1982, meanwhile, the National Front underwent further schisms and in-fighting concerning the type of party it ought to be, and the direction in which it ought to move – electoralism vs vanguardism, mass membership vs cadre party, working class or middle class appeal, and so on (Husbands 1988).

Celtic Nationalism – The Rise of Scottish and Welsh Nationalism

The marked increase in 'third' party electoral support which manifested itself in the 1974 general elections was by no means only an English phenomenon. In Scotland, the Scottish Nationalist Party (SNP) experienced a surge of its support in February and October 1974, the latter election providing it with its highest ever percentage of the vote in Scotland, and a record number – eleven – of MPs (see table 4.2).

Table 4.2 Scottish National Party vote 1955–1974

Year	Votes	% of Scottish vote	MPs
1955	12,112	0.5	0
1959	21,738	0.8	0
1964	64,044	2.4	0
1966	128,474	5.0	0
1970	306,802	11.4	1
1974 (F)	633,180	21.9	7
1974 (O)	839,628	30.4	11

In Wales, meanwhile, Plaid Cymru (the 'Party of Wales') also attained its best ever parliamentary representation in October 1974, when three of its candidates were elected, although the party's percentage share of the Welsh vote was actually less in 1974 than in 1970 – when no Plaid Cymru candidates were elected (see table 4.3).

Although the SNP and Plaid Cymru both sought greater independence and autonomy for their respective nations, in the form of devolution and their own elected assemblies, albeit within the framework of a federal Britain, the history and politics of Scotland and Wales were quite distinct.

Table 4.3   Plaid Cymru vote 1955–1974

Year	Votes	% of Welsh vote	MPs
1955	45,119	3.1	0
1959	77,571	5.2	0
1964	69,507	4.8	0
1966	61,071	4.3	0
1970	175,016	11.5	0
1974 (F)	171,364	10.7	2
1974 (O)	166,321	10.8	3

Scotland had been politically united with England through the 1707 Act of Union. However, it retained many of its own institutions, which thereby provided a strong source of national identity and independence:

> The Act of Union of 1707, which is the 'fundamental law' joining Scotland with England, laid down that Scotland would retain for all time certain key institutions such as the Scottish legal system, the Presbyterian Church of Scotland (the Established Church), the Scottish educational system, and the 'royal burghs' (local authorities). These became the transmitters of Scottish national identity from one generation to the next. (Kellas 1975: 2)

By the 1970s, however, dissatisfaction was increasing in Scotland, both over the way that political and economic power seemed to be concentrated more and more in London, and with regard to the manner in which this power was exercised *vis-à-vis* Scotland. With traditional industries in Scotland experiencing decline, and unemployment consequently increasing, there developed a growing sense that Scotland was suffering from continued neglect by governments at Westminster, a view reinforced by the concentration of many white collar, service sector jobs in and around London.

With the discovery of North Sea oil in the early 1970s, opinion against continued 'domination' by England hardened considerably. Arguments that Scotland was not economically strong enough to become self-governing were seriously discredited. The revenue envisaged from North Sea oil was deemed by Scottish nationalists to offer Scotland the potential for economic independence and prosperity. Indeed, this automatically prompted the question about 'ownership' of the oil. The Westminster-based government considered the North Sea to be British: many Scots insisted that it was – or ought to be – Scottish. Thus did the SNP publish a pamphlet entitled *England Expects . . . Scotland's Oil*, in which it was alleged that England expected Scottish oil in order to finance various English projects such as building a third London airport, Concorde, the Channel Tunnel, etc., all of which would 'damage the Scottish economy by concentrating even more jobs and prosperity in the South of England'. On the other hand, it was claimed, 'we could be the wealthiest nation in Europe if we controlled our own resources' (quoted in Birch 1977: 110–11).

Scotland's economic decline, coupled with the discovery of North Sea oil, therefore provided a major fillip for the SNP (Kellas 1975: 132–3). As the figures in table 4.2 illustrated, the SNP more than doubled its number of votes between 1966 and 1970, and again between 1970 and February 1974. Its electoral support soared from 64,044 in 1964 to 633,180 in the February 1974 election. Just eight months later, in the October 1974 poll, the SNP won a further 206,448 votes, taking its total to 839,628.

Meanwhile, whilst Plaid Cymru was also enjoying record levels of electoral support in the 1970s, Welsh politics and history was rather different from that of Scotland. Wales had been conquered by England under the reign of Edward I, but unification did not really occur until the 1536 Act of Union. Unlike Scotland, Wales did not retain its own social and political institutions. Instead, English laws applied equally to Wales, and the Church of England became the established religion.

English penetration of Wales was significantly reinforced during the Industrial Revolution and beyond, when much of the industry in South Wales was developed by virtue of English investment and expansion. The nineteenth and early twentieth century also witnessed considerable migration from England to Wales, as businessmen, managers, engineers, and the like moved to the newly industrialized regions of South Wales. Whilst the 1881 Census revealed that 15 per cent of people in Wales had been born in England, the 1911 Census indicated that by this time, 22 per cent of the Welsh population was English-born. As these are figures for Wales overall, it ought to be borne in mind that, proportionally the figures would be rather higher in South Wales, where most English émigrés settled during this time.

This process of 'Englishization' had an important impact on the Welsh language itself. For example, whilst in 1901 some 50 per cent of people in Wales could speak Welsh, only 8.2 per cent of those living in Cardiff were able to do so. By 1971, however, the number of Welsh-speakers in Wales had fallen to 21 per cent, most of these residing in the rural districts of North and West Wales.

The issues of Welsh language and culture have been integral to the politics and policies of Plaid Cymru. Formed in 1925, Plaid Cymru placed great emphasis on the need to defend the Welsh language and Welsh culture – entailing a strong sense of community and regular attendance at church. In other words, much of Plaid Cymru's philosophy reflected moral and social concerns, resulting in a conservative, traditionalist outlook: 'cultural domination by the English . . . is the mainspring of modern Welsh nationalism' (Birch 1977: 118). Morality was threatened by materialism, and community undermined by consumerism, some believed.

However, in a predominantly English-speaking, increasingly secular, Wales, Plaid Cymru's identification with, and promotion of, the Welsh language and traditional culture was a serious political limitation. It meant that its electoral appeal was largely confined to the rural, Welsh-speaking regions of the North and West of Wales. Elsewhere:

> the non-Welsh speaking areas are generally suspicious of Welsh nationalism, or perhaps more precisely Plaid Cymru, which they identify as seeking to impose the Welsh language on the non-Welsh speaking population. They are afraid that an independent Wales (or even a Wales with a devolved government) would be run largely by Welsh speakers, with non-Welsh speakers discriminated against. (Kellas 1990: 126; see also Birch 1977: 131)

In recognition of this problem, the 1960s had witnessed many in Plaid Cymru seeking to broaden its electoral appeal and increase its membership, by giving greater prominence to economic issues and policies. In particular, more attention was paid to the emergent problems facing the industries of South Wales. Whilst the relative electoral success of the 1970s suggests that Plaid Cymru benefited considerably from the greater emphasis placed on economic and industrial issues pertaining to South Wales, it still seemed to suffer overall from its image as a party primarily concerned with linguistic and cultural issues. The industrial working class in South Wales has tended, therefore, to remain loyal to the Labour Party in general elections, although Plaid Cymru has enjoyed sporadic victories in by-elections, and also in local elections, in parts of South Wales.

In response to the increased electoral support enjoyed by both Plaid Cymru and the SNP during the 1970s, the 1974–9 Labour Government granted the people of Wales and Scotland a referendum to gauge their support for devolution. The referendum was held on 1 March 1979, the Government having stipulated that a 40 per cent vote in favour would be required in order for devolution to be introduced. In Scotland, the vote was 1,230,937 (32.9 per cent) for, and 1,153,502 (30.8 per cent) against – a narrow victory in favour of devolution, but well short of the 40 per cent threshold required. Meanwhile, in Wales, the result was a resounding rejection of devolution, with 243,048 (11.9 per cent) voting in favour, and 956,330 (46.9 per cent) voting against.

One consequence of the referendum result was that the Scottish Nationalist Party subsequently tabled the motion of No Confidence which precipitated the downfall of the Callaghan Government. In the ensuing general election, the SNP saw its electoral support fall from 30.4 per cent of the votes and 11 MPs in October 1974 down to 17.3 per cent and two MPs in 1979. Plaid Cymru also experienced a decline in electoral support and parliamentary representation, although this was much less significant than the SNP's decline. In the 1979 election, Plaid Cymru saw its vote fall from 10.8 to 8.1 per cent, accompanied by a reduction in the number of its MPs from three to two. Yet to have concluded that the issue of 'Celtic nationalism' was redundant would have been premature.

The 'Winter of Discontent'

One of the Labour Party's self-professed advantages over the Conservative Party was its ability to work closely and more harmoniously with the trade unions. Whilst the events surrounding 1969's *In Place of Strife* seemed to cast some doubt over the reality of such a claim, the industrial conflicts which characterized the Heath Government's term of office certainly enabled the Labour Party to enter the 1974 elections emphasizing that only it could restore and maintain industrial peace, and establish a more constructive relationship between government and trade unions. By the winter of 1978–9, such a claim seemed to have lost all credibility. The notion that only Labour and the trade unions could guarantee harmonious industrial relations no longer appeared tenable. The widespread industrial action which gave rise to the *modern* use of the term 'winter of discontent', predominantly involving public sector workers, further diminished the public's already low opinion of trade unions (the belief that the trade unions were too powerful being widely and strongly held, even among many Labour voters), whilst causing immense damage to the Labour Party's own image and electoral standing. The 'winter of discontent' was a crucial factor in accounting for Labour's subsequent defeat in the 1979 general election. The close organizational and financial links between the Labour Party and the trade unions became an electoral liability, and remain so today. As such, neither the Labour Party nor the trade unions have ever recovered from the 'winter of discontent' and the public anger which it engendered. Even in 1992's general election, the Conservative was able to gain political mileage out of reminding voters about the 'winter of discontent', and suggesting that the election of a Labour Government would constitute a vote for a return to trade union tyranny and industrial anarchy.

The antecedents of the 'winter of discontent' lie in the incomes policies which the Labour Government began pursuing in 1975, in spite of entering office the previous year rejecting incomes policy, and proclaiming that the Social Contract obviated the need for one anyway. However, so parlous was the state of the British economy, with inflation in 1975 reaching 25 per cent, and unemployment inexorably rising also, that July heard the Labour Chancellor, Denis Healey, announce that during the next twelve months, pay increases would need to be limited to £6 per week, with a total pay freeze for those earning more than £8,500 per annum. This particular policy was supported by the TUC, not least because the invoking of a flat-rate, rather than a percentage, increase was more beneficial to the low paid (£6 per week making more difference to someone on a weekly wage of £60 than to someone on a wage of £160). Indeed, such a pay policy could be – and sometimes was – portrayed as one which neatly accorded with Labour's avowedly socialist, egalitarian principles.

The following year, in May 1976, by which time James Callaghan had been elected Labour leader, the Labour Government announced a 'stage two' of incomes policy, to commence in August. This time, there was to be a 'pay norm' of 4.5 per cent for twelve months, at the end of which a return to more normal forms of wage determination was envisaged. This last point was crucial in securing TUC support for a second successive year of incomes policy, for union leaders were convinced that their members would not be amenable to a further period of formal pay restraint in a year's time, especially as inflation remained in double figures, unemployment was still rising, and – as a condition of obtaining a loan from the International Monetary Fund – the Labour Government was cutting public expenditure, which had serious implications for the social wage, and the Government's ability to honour its side of the Social Contract. Indeed, whereas the Social Contract had originally been seen as obviating the need for a formal pay policy, the Labour Government found itself invoking incomes policies as a prerequisite of sustaining or salvaging the Social Contract.

By the autumn of 1976, the Labour Government was facing a serious dilemma: the very economic variables which would make the trade unions hostile to continued pay restraint – high inflation (which thus eroded workers' living standards), rising unemployment, cuts in public expenditure, etc. – also made incomes policy more necessary, at least for the Government itself. In the event, whilst the TUC refused to agree to a 'stage three' entailing a pay limit of 10 per cent, it was prepared to give the Government an assurance that the end of 'stage two' would not be accompanied by a wage explosion, and that the unions would allow for a twelve month gap between each pay settlement. Such a pledge was seen to constitute 'tacit TUC support' for a third stage of incomes policy (Coates 1980: 75).

However, trade union patience was sorely tried when, in July 1978, the Labour Government published a White Paper, *Winning the Battle Against Inflation*, which indicated that there would be a 'stage four' of incomes policy, with pay increases limited to just 5 per cent.

Furthermore, the Labour Government was clearly envisaging incomes policy becoming a permanent feature of economic and industrial life in Britain, rather than a short-term expedient as hitherto intended (Callaghan, 1987: 521). The TUC, on the other hand, warned that: 'The General Council do not see the future in terms of the continuation of restrictive policies on current lines'. Indeed, it intended 'to bring about the restoration of collective bargaining, in which negotiators themselves are able to deal in a responsible way with the specific circumstances and problems facing them' (TUC Annual Report, 1978: 291). With the Labour Government insisting that further wage restraint was unavoidable, and the TUC equally insistent that further wage restraint was unacceptable, conflict between Labour and the unions seemed inevitable.

Delegates at the TUC's annual conference in September 1978 supported a motion which stated that:

> Congress declared its opposition to Government policies of intervention and restraint in wage bargaining ... and to any form of restrictive Government incomes policy. Congress instructs the General Council to oppose any arbitrary pay limits and that there must now be a return to normal and responsible collective bargaining ... which is the only fair and practical method of setting remuneration levels.

The motion ended with the demand that: 'Instead of pay restraint, the Government concentrate on developing agreement with the trade union movement on ... economic strategy and social priorities'. One particularly poignant contribution to the debate on the motion was made by Ken Gill, leader of the engineering workers' union AUEW-TASS, who warned that:

> When a Labour Government disagrees with the trade union movement, then it is almost certain that the Government is wrong. History has always shown this to be the case, and when as a result of that disagreement clashes have occurred, Labour suffers and those clashes end in disaster. (quoted in Taylor 1987: 102)

In November 1978, a nine-week strike by Ford car workers was called off when the union accepted the management's 17 per cent pay offer. This immediately rendered it highly unlikely that other trade unions would readily accept wage increases within the Government's 5 per cent pay target. So it proved to be. The onset of winter was accompanied by a series of strikes in support of wage increases greater than 5 per cent. However, it was the start of 1979 which witnessed the most widespread, damaging strike action, much of it pursued by public sector workers. The impact of such action was compounded by the severe weather which Britain suffered during January.

The New Year opened with a strike by both petrol tanker and road haulage drivers, whilst train drivers held a number of one-day stoppages. The disruption caused was considerable. Commuters were unable to get to work some days, whilst firms found themselves unable to transport raw materials, supplies or finished products ready for sale or export. Supermarket shelves became emptier by the day, giving rise to concern that a food shortage was imminent. Meanwhile, strikes were conducted by over one million local authority manual workers, who constituted some of the lowest paid employees in Britain: to them a 5 per cent pay increase would make very little difference to their take-home pay. Indeed, with inflation at about 8 per cent, the Labour Government's pay limit would have meant an even lower standard of living for those doing some of the dirtiest or most physically demanding jobs. A particular consequence of the industrial action by local authority workers was that the ice- and snow-covered roads remained ungritted and unsalted. With roads treacherous, train services disrupted, and lorry drivers on strike, Britain was literally coming to a standstill.

However, whilst transport problems undoubtedly caused considerable inconvenience to many people, what really inflamed public opinion was the plight of the most vulnerable sections of society, who were most reliant upon the public services. Newspaper readers and television viewers were regularly regaled with graphic stories and images about those who were suffering as a consequence of the widespread strike activity. As one commentator recalls:

> Patients were refused admission to hospitals; vermin-infested refuse piled up on the streets; bodies were left unburied in the graveyards; and water supplies became contaminated. These different events happened at different times, and in different places, and most were of short duration. However, they received a great deal of publicity in the national press and on television.

Those participating in the industrial action were widely portrayed as totally selfish, callous and insensitive. The words 'trade union' acquired an even greater degree of opprobrium, and Keith Joseph wrote a pamphlet published by the Centre for Policy Studies, entitled *Solving the Union Problem is the Key to Britain's Economic Recovery*. Most British people saw little reason to demur from such a view, with one Labour minister acknowledging that 'the trade unions are now the most unpopular institutions for 100 years' (Barnett 1982: 172). This unpopularity rebounded on the Labour Party in the 1979 election, leaving it incapable of claiming – as it had in previous elections – that only it could work constructively and harmoniously with the trade unions, and that the election of a Conservative Government would herald industrial conflict or confrontation between Government and trade unions. The close relationship with the trade unions that had previously been seen by many Labour leaders as providing the party with an electoral advantage over the Conservatives was transformed by 1979 into a distinct disadvantage – and has remained so ever since.

Decade of Dealignment

We noted earlier in this chapter the unique result of the two 1974 general elections. Yet according to many political scientists, these two elections were reflective and representative of a more general process of dealignment which was already under way in Britain by the mid-1970s. What dealignment refers to is the changing character of political allegiance and electoral behaviour, particularly with regard to identification with, and regular support for, a specific political party. In fact, two forms of dealignment are invariably highlighted (although they are inextricably related), namely 'class' and 'partisan' dealignment.

Class dealignment

During the 1950s and 1960s, it was accepted wisdom in Britain that the working class predominantly voted Labour, whilst the middle class invariably cast its votes for the Conservative Party. Electoral studies (psephology) illustrated that approximately two-thirds of the working class (manual workers) regularly voted Labour, whilst four-fifths of the middle class (non-manual or white-collar workers) consistently voted Conservative. Hence Pulzer's oft-repeated assertion that: 'Class is the basis of British party politics; all else is embellishment and detail' (Pulzer 1967: 98).

During the 1970s, however, class ceased to be the 'basis of British party politics'. True, it remained an important factor, but the established link between social class and political allegiance became weaker. It became increasingly apparent that support for the Labour Party amongst the working class was discernibly declining, as was middle class electoral support for the Conservative Party. As table 4.4 illustrates, whereas 64 per cent of manual workers had voted for the Labour Party in the 1964 general election, only 57 per cent of them did so in the 1974 general elections. During the same ten-year period, the Conservative Party saw its electoral support amongst the middle class decline from 62 to 51 per cent (in October 1974), although there was a (temporary) revival in the 1979 general election. Labour, meanwhile, witnessed its working-class support fall to 50 per cent in 1979 (and to 42 per cent in 1983).

Table 4.4 Class dealignment 1964–79 (%)

	1964		1966		1970	
	Non-manual	Manual	Non-manual	Manual	Non-manual	Manual
Conservative	62	28	60	25	64	33
Labour	22	64	26	69	25	58
Liberal	1618	14	6	11	9	

	Feb 1974		Oct 1974		Oct 1979	
	Non-manual	Manual	Non-manual	Manual	Non-manual	Manual
Conservative	53	24	51	24	60	35
Labour	22	57	25	57	23	50
Liberal	25	19	24	20	17	15

Source: Denver (1989: 54)

Whilst class dealignment affected both main parties during the 1970s, it was the Labour Party which suffered the most. Admittedly, the figures in table 4.3 seem to suggest that in terms of loss of support from their 'natural' class base, the Labour and Conservative Parties fared equally badly between 1964 and 1974. Yet a closer look at other patterns discernible in table 4.3 places this trend in a wider context. In particular, it becomes apparent that during the 1970s, manual workers evinced a far greater propensity to switch their votes to the Conservative Party compared to non-manual workers transferring their electoral support to the Labour Party. Whereas in 1964, only 28 per cent of manual workers voted Conservative, this increased to 33 per cent in 1970, whilst by 1979, the figure stood at 35 per cent. During the same period, Labour's electoral support amongst non-manual workers rose from 22 per cent in 1964 to 25 per cent in 1970, but had fallen back to 23 per cent by 1979. Not only did the Labour Party find it more difficult to attract middle class support, it also found it more difficult to retain it.

What also proved particularly damaging to Labour electorally was the increasing share of the vote being garnered by the Liberal Party during the 1970s. In 1964, the Liberal Party was supported by 16 per cent of non-manual workers and 8 per cent of manual workers. By October 1974, this support had risen to 24 per cent and 20 per cent respectively. Two related points need noting here. Firstly, the increase in working class support for the Liberal Party during this period merely compounded the loss of votes to the Conservative Party which Labour was suffering from. Secondly, it was the Liberal Party, not Labour, which was the main beneficiary of middle-class disillusion with the Conservative Party. Whereas middle class support for the Labour Party was just 3 per cent higher in October 1974 than it had been in 1964, support for the Liberal Party amongst non-manual workers during the same period increased from 16 to 24 per cent.

A further vitally important factor explaining (and compounding) Labour's electoral problems during the 1970s – and ever since – was the contraction of the working class as a proportion of the population generally, due to the simultaneous decline of heavy/manufacturing industry and the continued expansion of the service sector. This change in socio-economic structure had profound implications for the Labour Party, for not only was it suffering from a decline in electoral support amongst the working class, but that working class was itself becoming smaller. Thus did the Labour Party face a problem even greater than the figures in table 4.3 indicated. It was suffering from diminishing electoral support amongst a diminishing section of the British population. Put another way, even if Labour had retained the same proportion of working class support that it enjoyed in 1964, its vote would still have declined – albeit more slowly – because the manual workers from whom it was receiving 64 per cent support would themselves have been diminishing in numbers.

The process of class dealignment thus became firmly established during the 1970s as more and more electors ceased to vote for their 'natural' class party. This both reflected and reinforced greater electoral volatility, which in turn seemed symptomatic and symbolic of a society which was itself beset by a profound sense of crisis, instability and uncertainty. Yet as noted above, class dealignment proved far more damaging (and continued to do so into the 1980s) to the Labour Party than to the Conservative Party.

Partisan dealignment

Partisan dealignment is inextricably linked to class dealignment; the two phenomena occur together. Partisan dealignment refers to the process by which voters become less strongly attached – electorally, ideologically or psychologically – to a particular political party. Their identification with one specific party diminishes, and may disappear altogether. This in turn fuels the trend towards increased electoral volatility, as voters become less inclined to vote habitually for the same political party at each election.

As with class alignment, the 'golden age' of partisan alignment had been from 1950 to 1970. For example, as table 4.5 indicates, in the 1964–70 period, 81 per cent of the electorate professed an identification with either Labour or the Conservative Party, with 40 per cent expressing 'very strong' identification. During the 1970s, however, this 'partisan alignment' declined markedly. By 1979, identification with one of the two main parties had fallen to 74 per cent, but far more notable was the decline of 'very strong' identifiers, down to 19 per cent – less than half the 1964–70 figure.

A number of explanations have been proffered to account for the phenomenon of partisan dealignment.

1 A more educated electorate – it is suggested that the British electorate is now more educated both in the sense of more people

having received a longer period of formal education, and also in a more general, indirect sense of being more aware of political affairs, due in large part to the emergence of a *mass* media. It is assumed that a more 'educated' electorate will be less likely to support or vote for a particular political party just because they have previously done so, or because their parents voted for it. Indeed, it has been noted that partisan dealignment has tended to be more pronounced amongst those citizens who have experienced higher education (Crewe, Sarlvik and Alt 1977: 166–7).

2   The performance of the parties – it is suggested that a significant source of weakening party identification is the apparent lack of success both major parties have had in office . . . the series of disappointments, policy failures and U-turns that have marked government performances, and the persistence of major problems facing the country, must surely have shaken any conviction voters might have had that 'their' party had all the answers (Denver 1989: 51).

Table 4.5   Partisan dealignment 1964–79 (%)

	With Con or Lab identification	'Very strong' Lab or Con identification
1964–70	81	40
Feb 1974	75	27
Oct 1974	74	23
1979	74	19

Extrapolated from Denver (1989: 47)

To this extent, partisan dealignment is part of a more general cynicism about politicians which has developed in Britain since the 1970s. It is reflective of a more general 'they're all pretty much as bad as each other' attitude on the part of increasing numbers of voters. During the 1950s, opinion polls revealed that on average, 46 per cent of people approved of the government's record; during the 1970s, only 33 per cent did so.

Two reasons probably account for this loss of confidence in politicians and governments. Firstly, since the 1950s, people's expectations have increased considerably, both in terms of what they expect or want for themselves and their families, and also – following on from this – what they expect from politicians and the government. Indeed, the expectations of many voters have increased far beyond government's ability to satisfy them. Secondly, and inextricably linked to the first point, the social and economic problems which have beset British government since the 1960s have induced a sense of despondency and despair in many people, with one of the manifestations of this being growing disillusionment with politicians and government. Obviously, increasing social and economic problems meant that the disjuncture between the electorate's expectations and 'reality' became ever wider.

3   Ideological disjuncture – this, according to Denver (1989: 52–3), has mainly affected the Labour Party. In this context 'ideological disjuncture' refers to the declining support for a political party's basic principles and policies amongst its own supporters. In particular, the Labour Party experienced an increasing loss of support for several of its ideological and policy commitments amongst Labour voters themselves. According to one study, derived from Gallup polling data between 1957 and 1980, there was a significant decline in the percentages of Labour voters who agreed with Labour's commitments to restrict dividends and profits, cut defence expenditure, and abolish the House of Lords (Harrop 1982). Such an 'ideological disjuncture' will clearly impact upon a party's electoral support amongst its traditional voters, for if those voters increasingly disagree with or disapprove of 'their' party's policies on certain issues, then their identification with, and allegiance to, that party will diminish accordingly. This is an important reason why the Labour Party in particular was affected by both class and partisan dealignment from the 1970s onwards.

Class and partisan dealignment both increased markedly during the 1970s, the two being inextricably and intimately linked. The 1970s were a decade in which many people's voting behaviour changed. More and more people became less and less inclined to vote consistently or habitually for the same political party, and to vote for a particular party simply because of their social class. In this decade of dealignment, electoral behaviour became more unpredictable, and volatile, and more voters than at any time since the war proffered their support to the Liberal Party, whilst Scotland and Wales, as we have already noted, witnessed a marked increase in electoral support for the SNP and Plaid Cymru respectively. Yet dealignment can also be interpreted as part of a wider phenomenon, namely the decline of civic culture.

The Decline of Civic Culture

We noted in chapter 2 how Britain was viewed by many political scientists and commentators during the 1950s as a 'model' civic culture. This accolade was rather less readily applied during the 1970s. Instead, this decade was one of deepening despair and despondency as a consequence of the economic, political and social developments and problems discussed in this chapter. One only has to glance at the titles of some of the books published about Britain in the 1970s to appreciate the pervasive pessimism which had emerged: : *Britain Against Itself* (Beer 1982), *Britain in Agony* (Clutterbuck 1978), *Britain in Decline* (Gamble 1981), *Drifting into a Law and Order Society* (Hall 1980), *Policing the Crisis* (Hall *et al.*, 1978), *The Break-up of Britain* (Nairn 1977), *The Collapse of Democracy* (Moss 1977), *What's Wrong with Britain?* (Hutber 1978), *Why is Britain Becoming Harder to Govern?* (King 1976), and so on.

This chapter has already highlighted many of the events and developments which seemed to signify a marked decline of Britain's 'model' civic culture – the use of industrial action by trade unions in order to defeat government policies; violence on picket lines and political marches, the (re)-emergence of Scottish and Welsh nationalism, the apparent disillusion with the two main political parties in the mid-1970s, class and partisan dealignment, the increasing demands placed upon governments by an increasing number of citizens, etc. Such trends reflected – and reinforced – a growing disillusionment with politicians generally, aligned to a growing belief that governing and political elites did not really reflect or represent the views of ordinary citizens. In an oft-cited study of political attitudes published in 1977, Alan Marsh revealed that 47 per cent of respondents believed that governments could be trusted to do what was right 'only some of the time', whilst 10 per cent replied 'almost never'. In other words over half of those questioned seriously lacked confidence in the inclination of central government to do what was right. The honesty of politicians was also seriously doubted, with 60 per cent of respondents believing that people in politics told the truth 'only some of the time'. Again, 10 per cent replied 'almost never'. Only 3 per cent believed that politicians 'just about always' told the truth. Meanwhile, 45 per cent of Marsh's respondents believed that governments could be trusted to place the needs of the country above the needs of their own party 'only some of the time', with 15 per cent believing that governments could 'almost never' be trusted in this manner. Finally, 48 per cent of respondents believed that the country was run by a few big, vested interests, with only 37 per cent confident that the country was run 'for the benefit of all the people' (Marsh 1977: 118).

The growing belief that politicians and bureaucrats tended to govern and legislate in favour of particular interests and sections of the community, rather than on behalf of society as a whole, was deemed by some commentators to be a significant factor in the apparent decline in respect for the law generally. It was suggested that as people came to see legislation favouring individuals or groups other than themselves, they would increasingly feel disinclined to obey or respect the law. This was particularly likely during a drift towards corporatism, when major interest groups were routinely involved in policy-making at the highest levels; those who were not members of these groups would be increasingly inclined to feel that their own views and interests were not being considered, and as such would question the legitimacy and impartiality of laws introduced in this manner. If individuals increasingly felt that legislation suffered from a lack of legitimacy and impartiality, then their inclination to respect and obey the law would diminish accordingly.

Certainly the 1970s evinced a trend amongst greater numbers of people to engage in, or condone, certain forms of 'direct', unlawful or violent political action. Some 13 per cent of those interviewed by Marsh approved of occupying buildings and/or blocking traffic by way of political protest, whilst 16 per cent approved or strongly approved of unofficial strikes. Meanwhile, 24 per cent approved or strongly approved of rent strikes, and 37 per cent approved or strongly approved of boycotts.

In terms of respondents' own previous or potential political behaviour, Marsh discovered that whilst only 1 per cent had actually blocked traffic, 7 per cent said that they would do so, whilst a further 15 per cent declared that they might do. Similar responses were forthcoming when respondents were asked about occupying buildings. With regard to rent strikes, whilst only 2 per cent of those questioned by Marsh had taken part in such action, nearly one-third admitted their actual or possible willingness to do so. Meanwhile, 4 per cent admitted that they might be prepared to resort to personal violence, even though only 2 per cent approved of such behaviour!

When Marsh asked whether it was ever justifiable 'to break the law to protest about something that is very unjust or harmful', 56 per cent of respondents said 'yes', whilst 36 per cent answered 'no, never'. In other words, over half of those questioned believed that breaking the law *was* justifiable in certain circumstances. When respondents were pressed to indicate what these circumstances might be, the most commonly cited scenarios were resisting threats to living standards (such as excessive rent or rate increases), industrial action/strikes (in support of wage claims or in defence of jobs, workers' rights, etc.), and protecting civil liberties and human rights in the face of unjust laws or tyrannical political leaders (Marsh 1977: 53).

Such evidence, combined with the instances of political instability and industrial action already discussed, led many commentators to sombre conclusions and predictions about the British body politic. Richard Rose noted that: 'Something has happened to government and to our belief in government in the past decade . . . people who have looked to government to resolve their problems no longer look with confidence' (Rose, quoted in Marsh 1977: 230).

However, political scientists disagreed over just how far Britain's civic culture really declined during the 1970s. Samuel Beer claimed that 'it is no exaggeration to speak of the decline in the civic culture as a "collapse"' (Beer 1982: 119), whilst Marsh himself suggested that: 'There appears to be a movement of British political life . . . towards a noisy and disrespectful participatory democracy' (Marsh 1977: 234). Similarly, Dennis Kavanagh believed that 'traditional bonds of social class, party, and common nationality are waning, and with them the old restraints of hierarchy and deference' (Kavanagh 1980: 170).

By contrast, other commentators believed that the overwhelming majority of citizens continued to exhibit and express predominantly law-abiding sentiments and generally disapproved of direct action or violence for political or industrial/economic purposes. Norton, for example, argued that 'the political culture has neither declined nor been threatened to the extent suggested by Beer . . . The civic culture may be weakened but it has not collapsed' (Norton 1984: 34). Birch, meanwhile, claimed that 'it is more helpful to think of the British political culture as being fragmented than it is to describe it either as having collapsed or as being substantially unchanged' (Birch 1993: 20). Yet if two of the defining features of Britain's political culture – as originally defined by Almond and Verba – were consensus and homogeneity, then 'fragmentation' would itself surely signify its decline?

Note

1　For an excellent detailed account of the Industrial Relations Act, see Michael Moran, *The Politics of Industrial Relations* (1977).

5 Renaissance of the Right (1979–90)

'What does it matter, after all, if by humiliating one's mind one succeeds in dominating everyone? I discovered in myself sweet dreams of oppression.'

Albert Camus, *The Fall*

The Election of the First Thatcher Government

The first Thatcher Government entered office on 3 May 1979, winning a majority of 43 seats. The full result was as shown in table 5.1.

Table 5.1   1979 general election results

	Seats	Votes	% of votes cast
Conservatives	339	13,697,923	43.9
Labour	269	11,532,218	37.0
Liberals	11	4,313,804	13.8
Ulster Unionists	5	254,578	36.6
			(of N.I. vote)
Democratic Unionists	3	70,975	10.2
(Other N.I.	4)		(of N.I. vote)
Scottish Nationalists	2	504,259	17.3
			(of Scottish vote)
Plaid Cymru	2	132,544	8.1
			(of Welsh vote)

Whilst this result appeared to mark a decisive shift to the right in British politics in terms of electoral attitudes and public opinion, two caveats ought to be borne in mind before arriving at such a conclusion. Firstly, it is difficult to evaluate the extent to which the result reflected the unpopularity of the Labour Party, particularly in the wake of the 'winter of discontent', rather than a ringing endorsement of Thatcherite Conservatism. To some extent it may have been testimony to the adage that 'oppositions don't win elections, governments lose them'. Secondly, it was not entirely clear in 1979 just how radical the Thatcher Governments would prove to be. Even some of the policies often cited as being distinctive and decisive in the 1979 election, such as the pledge to curb the trade unions, evinced a certain caution and ambiguity.

Yet having acknowledged these caveats, it remains true that the election of the first Thatcher Government did reflect public opinion on a number of issues – trade union reform, income tax cuts, law and order, curbs on (coloured) immigration, nuclear defence and a pruning of the welfare state, particularly with regard to eligibility for, and public expenditure on, social security benefits. Particularly important for the Conservative Party from 1979 onwards was the support it attracted from the skilled working class – the 'C2s'; in 1987, for example, the Conservatives enjoyed a 7 per cent lead over Labour amongst the skilled working class. Lenin's 'labour aristocracy' was alive and well and continuing, in ever greater numbers, to turn its back on socialism, social democracy, and all other points left of Centre. The Conservative Party not only appealed successfully to the material instincts of sections of the working class (tax cuts, council house sales, etc.) but also to 'moral' aspects, namely the deeply rooted authoritarianism with which the working class has long been afflicted – its xenophobia and racism, its 'lock 'em up' attitude towards law-breakers, and its virulent anti-intellectualism (which is replaced by prejudices and gut instincts masquerading as common sense). Only middle-class Marxists and Hampstead liberals, savouring their nut roast and bean curd, clung – and *still* cling – to the notion that the British working class is, in essence, a 'progressive' political force brimful of camaraderie and solidarity towards their fellow men and women. Margaret Thatcher's Conservative Party knew this to be nonsense and thus remained in office throughout the 1980s – and into the 1990s.

The Monetarist Experiment

The Thatcher Governments entered office determined to jettison the Keynesianism which had underpinned the economic element of the post-war consensus. Admittedly, this change in approach had already been instigated by the previous Labour Government, but whereas Denis

Healey and James Callaghan had adopted a monetarist approach due to circumstances, Margaret Thatcher and her closest colleagues set out to pursue monetarism as a fundamental principle, an article of faith. The Thatcherite embracing of monetarism was wholehearted, and sought to elevate it to the status of new economic orthodoxy. It was deemed 'time to proclaim the message: Mr Keynes is dead' (Joseph 1978).

Although there are various definitions or forms of monetarism, it has been suggested that in general 'a monetarist believes that excessive increases in the supply of money . . . cause inflation, a case of too much money chasing too few goods' (Kavanagh 1987: 9–10). Certainly, the Thatcher Governments constantly reiterated the vital importance of controlling the money supply and eliminating – as far as possible – inflation. Wider aspects of Thatcherite monetary policy included attempts at reducing, or at the very least restraining, public expenditure, and cutting rates of income tax. The belief has been 'that by curbing the growth in public spending they would create the headroom for tax reductions which in turn provide incentives and liberate the entrepreneurial energies of the British people. By strictly controlling money supply they would restore sound finance and squeeze inflation out of the system' (Kavanagh 1987: 225). By curbing public expenditure and cutting income tax, Thatcherites held out the promise of low inflation and low tax economy. It was envisaged that low inflation would restore business confidence, thereby leading to increased investment, whilst low taxation would provide citizens with more money in their pockets, thereby leading to increased consumer spending. The combined effect was supposed to be increased economic growth, and – eventually – a reduction in unemployment as firms began recruiting more workers in response to greater consumer demand and fuller order books.

Yet as is so often the case, the theory was more straightforward than the practice. Throughout its first term of office (1979–83) the Thatcher Government repeatedly exceeded its monetary targets – the targets it set itself regarding the amount of money in circulation. Although a Medium Term Financial Strategy was announced in the 1980 Budget, proclaiming that the Government was seeking an annual reduction (i.e. a tightening) in monetary targets, exercising such control proved far more difficult, to the extent that in the financial year 1980–1, the amount of notes and coins in circulation, coupled with deposits held by UK residents (known as M3), increased by 19 ½ per cent, even though the Government's target was 7–11 per cent. Meanwhile, whilst the target set for March 1980 to March 1984 was 46 per cent, the actual increase was 70 per cent. Perhaps not surprisingly, M3 was officially abandoned in 1985, although this certainly did not mean that the Thatcher Government was reneging on its commitment to reduce inflation, and cut public expenditure (at least as a proportion of Gross Domestic Product, or GDP).

Yet cutting public expenditure also proved to be a task fraught with practical difficulties, and characterized by failed targets. For example, the 1980 Medium Term Financial Strategy had envisaged a reduction in public expenditure of 5 per cent over the next four years; in fact, this period witnessed an increase of 8 per cent in real terms (i.e. over and above increases to cover inflation). Indeed, by 1990–1, public expenditure stood at £216.2 billion, whereas in 1979–80, it had been £196.4 billion (in real terms). Even so, this represented a 4 per cent reduction in public expenditure as a proportion of GDP.

Much of the increase in public expenditure was actually attributable to the priorities and policies of the Thatcher Governments. For example, the emphasis on law and order, and defence, engendered significant increases in expenditure on police, prisons, military personnel and nuclear weapons, so that during 1979–80 to 1989–90, government spending on law and order had increased by £5 billion, whilst expenditure on defence had risen by £4 billion.

Another important reason for the *increase* in public expenditure which occurred during the 1980s was the mass unemployment which characterized much of that decade. Conservative economic policy, high interest rates, world recession and the contraction of many traditional manufacturing industries (itself part of the establishment of a new international economic system and division of labour entailing relocation of firms to the 'Third' World) all contributed to the existence of 2–3 million unemployed during the 1980s, and into the 1990s. This necessitated a marked increase in the number of people to whom the Thatcher Governments were obliged to pay social security. At the same time, each person joining the dole queue represents one person less paying income tax and national insurance to the Exchequer. Along with the infrastructure and personnel needed to administer the social security system, *each* unemployed person effectively 'costs' the government £8,000 per annum (1994 figures). With three million unemployed, this means that unemployment alone costs the state £24 billion pounds per annum – virtually half of the 'public deficit' which the Major Government (since 1992) was so determined to reduce.

One other factor which contributed to the *increase* in public expenditure during the 1980s was Britain's ageing population. The increasing number of elderly people – living longer as a consequence of improved living standards, health care and advances in medical science – itself meant both more recipients of old age pensions (and other social security payments) and greater demand placed on the NHS. Hence, social security expenditure increased by £18 billion between 1979 and 1990, whilst health spending during the same period rose by £8 billion.

Thus it was that government political priorities, economic policies, industrial restructuring and relocation, and demographic trends combined to *increase* public expenditure. By 1990, the most that the Conservative Government could claim was that it had slowed down the increase in public expenditure since 1979 – a rather different matter from securing an actual reduction.

One area of economic policy where the Conservatives *have* experienced *some* success since 1979 has been in reducing inflation. Whilst he was Chancellor of the Exchequer, Nigel Lawson proclaimed that 'it is the conquest of inflation, not the pursuit of growth and employment, which is or should be *the* objective of macro-economic policy'. Thus, although inflation rose to 18 per cent in 1980 (more than twice its 1978 rate), it thereafter fell to 4.5 per cent in 1983. The inflation rate did increase again during the second half of the 1980s, rising from 3.4 per cent in 1986 to 7.8 per cent in 1989 (but then fell to 2.6 per cent in 1992). That inflation increased during the second half of the 1980s merely reaffirmed the Conservatives' commitment to tackling inflation at the expense of other economic objectives, such as reducing unemployment.

Doubts and Divisions in the First Cabinet

The first Thatcher Cabinet was characterized by considerable doubt and division, as ministers disagreed over the direction and consequences of the Government's policies. Indeed, one commentator has claimed that: 'At no time since the 1940 confidence vote which led to Neville Chamberlain's resignation had the Conservative Party been so divided' (Holmes 1985: 74) According to one ministerial member of the first

Thatcher administration: 'We must have been the most divided Conservative Cabinet ever. There was a deep division on economic and social policy' (Prior 1986: 134) The pursuit of monetarism, and the implications for unemployment levels, caused much anxiety and anguish to a number of ministers, particularly the 'one nation' Conservatives (labelled 'Wets' by Margaret Thatcher). These Tory 'Wets' were concerned that if unemployment was permitted to rise too far and too fast, and public expenditure was cut too drastically, then social cohesion and political stability might well be undermined, and the legitimacy of the system generally called into question.

There were a number of 'one nation' Conservatives or Tory 'Wets' included in the first Thatcher Government, reflecting the fact that the Thatcherites had by no means fully established their hegemony (political dominance and leadership) within the parliamentary Conservative Party. Indeed, as is usually the case when a political party wins power after a period of Opposition, the first Cabinet is virtually the same, in terms of membership and portfolios, as the shadow cabinet. During the period when the Conservatives had been in Opposition from 1974 to 1979, the Shadow Cabinet had itself comprised a mixture of Thatcherites and 'Wets', partly to ensure that the range of back-bench views were fully reflected and represented at the highest levels in the parliamentary Party, and also to allay fears which some potential Conservative voters might have had about the Conservative Party under Margaret Thatcher moving too far to the right.

The subsequent 'balanced' composition of the first Thatcher Cabinet meant that on a number of proposed policies, Margaret Thatcher and her 'supporters' were compelled to compromise, or even back down in the face of opposition from the 'Wets'. For example, the initial pace and scope of trade union reform, as enshrined in Jim Prior's 1980 Employment Act, was widely recognized to be too limited for Margaret Thatcher's liking – indeed, the Cabinet was split down the middle over the issue of whether tougher measures against the trade unions ought to have been invoked at that time (Prior 1986: 162–5).

Another issue on which Margaret Thatcher and her ministerial adherents were obliged to bow to the opposition and criticism of the Tory 'Wets' was that of public expenditure. The neo-liberal or 'New Right' bloc in the first Thatcher Cabinet was strongly in favour of significant cuts in public expenditure, on grounds of both ideological principle and economic necessity. Yet the 'Wets', whilst acknowledging the need to pursue *some* curbs on government spending, were deeply concerned at the scale of the cuts being sought by their ministerial colleagues on the Right of the Conservative Party. To cut public expenditure too much, the 'Wets' argued, would exacerbate the economic problems Britain was facing in the context of a deepening recession, not least by increasing unemployment even further and reducing demand in the economy (via lower consumer spending, etc.) This in turn would exacerbate social tensions and divisions in British society. The 'Wets' were 'haunted by the thought that in the future people would look back and wonder what on earth we were up to, cutting public spending with 2.4 million unemployed and our infrastructure and industrial base crying out for modernisation'. Such Conservatives 'did not think that we, as a Party, would be lightly forgiven, and . . . feared that it would take us as long to live down . . . as it had to recover from the errors which had been made in the 1930s' (Prior 1986: 131).

It was not until 1982 that 'Thatcherism' became rather more firmly ensconced in the Cabinet itself, partly because Margaret Thatcher's own authority was enormously enhanced by victory in the Falklands War, and also because her first major Cabinet reshuffle, in the autumn of 1981, had enabled her either to dismiss a number of 'Wets' entirely, or to reshuffle them to less influential or politically important positions in the ministerial hierarchy. For example, Jim Prior was cruelly made Secretary of State for Northern Ireland, based in Belfast, thereby keeping him away from Margaret Thatcher as much as possible. His place at the Department of Employment was taken by the distinctly Thatcherite Norman Tebbit (although in the event, his trade union reforms proved less draconian than had been hoped by the Tory Right, or feared by the 'Wets').

It would be a mistake, however, to assume that after 1982, the Thatcherites *entirely* dominated the Conservative Party, either on the back-benches or in the Cabinet. Their influence was certainly considerable and they undoubtedly set much of the policy agenda, but it is also remarkable to note that throughout the 1980s, those MPs and ministers who could be characterized as 'Thatcherites' (in the sense of fully sharing and supporting Margaret Thatcher's economic, political and social objectives and policies) continued to constitute a minority of the Conservative Party at parliamentary level (Norton 1990). This obviously begs the question as to how and why Thatcherism seemed to enjoy hegemony throughout most of the 1980s. A number of explanations can be advanced.

1   The majority of Conservative MPs were 'agnostic' about much of Thatcherism. They either agreed with *some* policies and objectives, whilst demurring from others, or were prepared to offer general, if unenthusiastic, support. For such MPs and ministers, it was loyalty to an electorally successful Conservative leader, rather than reverence for Margaret Thatcher *per se*, which ensured their broad support for the policies of the Thatcher Government. For such Conservatives, it was sufficient that Margaret Thatcher was leading the party to election victories. This was largely the basis of much of their support for 'her' policies, rather than fervent ideological commitment.

2   The 'Thatcherites', whilst numerically a minority in the parliamentary Conservative Party, enjoyed organizational strength and intellectual coherence. Thatcherism was a doctrine which drew upon the ideas of individuals such as Milton Friedman, Friedrich Hayek, Ludwig von Mises and Enoch Powell, and of think tanks such as the Institute of Economic Affairs and the Adam Smith Institute, among others. Whilst publicly appearing anti-intellectual, and emphasizing the 'common sense' basis of its principles and policies, Thatcherism was none the less very much derived from, and underpinned by, the theories and ideas espoused by right-wing economists, philosophers and political scientists. As such, Thatcherism drew upon intellectual theories to a much greater extent than any previous mode of Conservatism. Indeed, many 'one nation' Tories insisted that Thatcherism was not a form of Conservatism at all, precisely because it was based so heavily on intellectual theories and 'programmes'. This was deemed incompatible, and at variance, with the traditional Conservative eschewal of intellectual doctrines and ideological dogma in favour of pragmatism and moderation (Gilmour 1992: *passim*).

3   By contrast, the critics of Thatcherism in the Conservative Party, the Tory 'Wets', lacked organizational cohesion or ideological strength. Indeed, these 'one nation' Conservatives had always characterized British Conservatism as essentially non-ideological, so that they were ill-suited to coping adequately with an intellectual phenomenon such as Thatcherism. The 'Wets' were thus unable to provide a clear doctrine or programme with which to counter or challenge the Thatcherites. Instead, they found themselves re-emphasizing the traditional Conservative emphasis

on moderation, caution, pragmatism, balance, consent, harmony, and so on – values which were derided as euphemisms for cowardice and appeasement by Thatcherites. Furthermore, the 'Wets' still retained a faith in many of the policies which had constituted the post-war social democratic consensus, which in turn rendered them vulnerable to the charges of being 'the weaker willed, the craven-hearted and the embittered failures' amongst the Conservative Party (Tebbit 1988: 180), and of sharing responsibility (with Labour) for the type of policies that had economically and morally bankrupted Britain during the 1960s and 1970s. Throughout the 1980s, therefore, the 'Wets' were on the defensive in the Conservative Party, organizationally weak, and ideologically discredited in the eyes of many. To the extent that they were able to offer alternative policies to Thatcherism, these appeared to constitute little more than either a return to the 'middle way' consensus of the pre-Thatcher decades, or a toning down of Thatcherite policies – *less* drastic cuts in public expenditure, *less* hostility towards the trade unions, etc. Yet by urging a slower or more gentle application of Thatcherite principles and policies, the Tory Wets were, tacitly or unwittingly, giving credence to Thatcher's own views that 'There Is No Alternative' – they appeared to be advocating, not a distinctive set of different policies, but merely a more cautious application of Thatcherite ones. As such, the 'Wets':

> gave only a series of *ad hoc* responses . . . they did not disagree with the need for a change of direction of policy. Their concern was about the pace of change. So their criticisms and suggestions seemed limp in the face of the certainty and confidence of the Thatcherites. Moderation was not a strong rallying cry. (Riddell 1983: 45)

Thus although Thatcherite MPs and ministers constituted a minority of the parliamentary Conservative Party, they were able to predominate in terms of ideas, arguments and policies throughout most of the 1980s; they enjoyed, and exercised, *hegemony*.

4 The 'Wets' also underestimated Margaret Thatcher's determination and durability as Conservative leader and Prime Minister. Many of them expected (hoped!) that the anticipated consequences of 'her' monetarist policies – high unemployment, increased inequality and financial hardship, cuts in public services, social unrest, etc. – would result in her own downfall, whereupon she would then be replaced by a more traditional Conservative leader in the paternalist mould. Back in

1979, the 'Wets' were 'totally unprepared for . . . the extent and duration of Margaret Thatcher's hegemony of British politics in the ten years which followed . . . totally unprepared for . . . her continued dominance of British politics' (Hailsham 1990: 407). As Jim Prior, a leading 'Wet' in the Thatcher Cabinets up until the mid-1980s, recalled: 'Those of us in Cabinet who were out of sympathy with Margaret's views grossly under-estimated her absolute determination . . . to push through the new right wing policies'. The 'Wets' had 'assumed that quite a bit of what Margaret claimed we would do was Opposition rhetoric which would be moderated by the realities of Government' (Prior 1986: 118 and 112).

Tackling the Trade Unions

In one respect, the 1970s ended as they had begun, with the election of a Conservative government committed to a radical reform of Britain's trade unions and industrial relations. Yet that was the sum of the similarity, for whereas the Heath government had entered office in 1970 ready to introduce one major, all-embracing piece of legislation, and had subsequently performed a humiliating U-turn eighteen months later, the Thatcher Government elected in 1979 was much more cautious and circumspect, and partly as a consequence, was not compelled to renege on its policy in this field.

To talk of the Thatcher Government's 'programme' of trade union reform itself necessitates a certain care, for it would be wrong to suggest that the Conservative Party entered office in May 1979 with a detailed list of measures already drafted and ready to be introduced as and when it desired. On the contrary, it has been noted that whilst the Thatcher Government clearly entered office determined to do 'something' about the trade unions, and was particularly concerned about specific aspects of British trade unionism, this in no way amounted to a coherent pro-gramme of reform: instead, the Thatcher Government's reform of trade unions and industrial relations was highly pragmatic and incremental, with particular measures often being introduced only in response to particular concerns as and when they arose (Dorey 1993; Marsh 1992). In many respects, therefore, it is more in hindsight or retrospect that we can speak of the Thatcher Government's 'programme' of trade union reform.

Yet the cautious, piecemeal nature of the Conservatives' trade union reforms during the 1980s and into the 1990s accounts for much of their apparent success. The experience of the Heath Government's ill-fated Industrial Relations Act provided a salutary lesson to the Conservative Party under Margaret Thatcher's leadership, for it illustrated the dangers of attempting to do too much too soon. It was also widely recognized that both the comprehensive nature of Heath's Industrial Relations Act, and a number of its specific clauses, had provided the trade unions with a major target against which to mobilize a counter-attack; the scope of the Act, and the nature of some of its provisions, had made it easier for ordinary trade union members to be persuaded by their leaders that it constituted a draconian attack on the working class and their representative institutions by 'the most reactionary Conservative Government since the 1930s', etc. Armed with the benefit of hindsight, therefore, the Thatcher Governments proceeded to reform Britain's trade unions in a manner which would avoid the hostility and opposition engendered by the Heath Government's attempt. A brief outline of the trade union legislation introduced by the Thatcher Governments will indicate how this was achieved.

Employment Act 1980

- New closed shop agreements had to be supported by at least 80 per cent of the workforce voting in a secret ballot.
- Compensation payable to employees who lost their jobs as a consequence of refusing, as a matter of principle, to join a trade union.
- Government funds made available to enable trade unions to conduct postal ballots, both for the election of senior union officials, and to gauge support for proposed strike action.
- Strict curbs placed on picketing and secondary or 'sympathy' action.

Employment Act 1982

- Existing closed-shop agreements had to be supported by at least 80 per cent of the workforce voting in a secret ballot.

- *Increased* compensation payable to employees who lost their jobs as a consequence of refusing to join a trade union.
- Definition of a 'trade dispute' narrowed, thereby rendering 'sympathy' strikes, 'politically motivated' strikes, and industrial action against a non-union company, illegal.

Trade Union Act 1984

- Strikes only lawful (and thus immune from legal action) if they have been endorsed by a majority of the workforce voting in a secret ballot.
- Trade unions obliged to hold a ballot for the election of senior officials if their members request one.
- Trade unions to hold ballots, at least once every ten years, to gauge support for the maintenance of a 'political fund'.

Employment Act 1988

- Unlawful to dismiss an employee for refusing to join a trade union, even if at least 80 per cent of the workforce has voted in favour of a closed shop (in accordance with the 1980 and 1982 Acts).
- Unlawful for trade unions to pursue industrial action in support of a closed-shop agreement.
- Unlawful for a trade union to take disciplinary action against any members for refusing to participate in a strike (even though the strike may have been endorsed by an overwhelming majority of the union's members).

Employment Act 1990

- Unlawful for an employer to turn down job applicants on the grounds that they are not members of a trade union.
- All secondary or sympathy industrial action unlawful.

There are, perhaps, three main points worth noting about this programme of trade union reform:

1 The manner in which the legislation was introduced gradually

over a fairly lengthy period of time. As already noted, this reflects the pragmatic, incremental approach adopted by the Thatcher Governments, and the extent to which much of their trade union legislation was *ad hoc* in nature. However, the Thatcher Governments also calculated – correctly – that relatively small reforms, introduced one at a time (and with at least a couple of years elapsing since the previous piece of legislation) would render it extremely difficult for trade union members to be mobilized against them; trade union leaders would have a hard task in convincing their members that such modest, piecemeal, reforms constituted a draconian assault on them and their unions. In pursuing trade union reform in such a manner, the Thatcher Governments clearly recognized the merits of 'changing the law gradually, with as little resistance, and therefore as much by stealth, as possible' (Prior 1986: 158).

2   The content and presentation of the legislation was specifically designed to elicit maximum support from trade unionists themselves. This objective was pursued by characterizing the Thatcher Governments' reforms as being intended to 'democratize' Britain's trade unions, by transferring power to the trade union membership, and thus away from their leaders. The avowed objective of empowering ordinary trade union members *vis-à-vis* the leadership of the unions was clearly intended to endear the reforms to the rank-and-file membership itself. The discourse and rhetoric of the Conservative Governments portrayed a downtrodden, powerless trade union membership being exploited and intimidated, not by employers or the state, but by the union leaders themselves. According to this characterization, the vast majority of trade union members were decent, hard-working, politically moderate, patriotic people, who were all too often manipulated and misled by their allegedly extremist, politically motivated, power-hungry union leaders. To this extent, the union reforms introduced by the Conservatives during the 1980s and 1990s have been portrayed as measures to 'democratize' the unions, and 'liberate' ordinary trade union members from tyrannical union bosses and repressive regulations laid down in union rule books. Thus ballots prior to strike action, and for the election of union officials, provide for the 'democratization' of the trade unions, whilst the weakening, and eventual abolition, of the closed shop constituted the 'liberation' of trade union members from compulsory union membership. The Conservative Governments since 1979 clearly anticipated

that such reforms would prove highly popular amongst ordinary trade union members, thereby making it virtually impossible for their union leaders to mobilize them against such measures.

3   The Conservative Governments since 1979 have carefully sought to ensure that any breaches of their trade union legislation constitute civil, as opposed to criminal, offences. The significance of this is three-fold. Firstly, it has meant that if they act unlawfully, trade unions can be sued, and thus liable to pay compensation or damages. It was envisaged that many trade unions, quite literally, could not afford to break the law. Secondly, it has ensured that legal action against trade unions is instigated by aggrieved individuals or other corporate bodies, rather than by the Government itself. This was intended to avoid the risk of 'politicizing' legal action against recalcitrant trade unions, and of bringing the Government itself directly into conflict with a union in the context of a court case. The danger of the Government becoming embroiled in this manner, and of bringing the law into disrepute, was a valuable lesson learnt from the experience of Heath's Industrial Relations Act. Thirdly, by ensuring that breaches of its trade union laws were deemed to be civil, rather than criminal, offences the Thatcher Governments ensured that no trade unionists would be sent to prison, thereby creating 'martyrs' in whose support the Labour movement might be mobilized. To this end, when he was appointed Employment Secretary, Norman Tebbit informed his departmental staff that:

> If necessary I will surround every prison in the country with police – and if needs be the army. I am willing to seal them off with barbed-wire barricades. Under no circumstances will I allow any trades union activist – however hard he tries – to get himself *into* prison under my legislation.
> (Tebbit 1988: 182)

This was further evidence of the extent to which valuable lessons had been learnt from the débâcle of the Industrial Relations Act.

Rejection of Incomes Policies

The legislation just outlined was not the only manifestation of the Conservative Government's antipathy towards the trade unions. Also of immense importance was the Thatcher Government's rejection of *formal* incomes policies (although it is important to note that a *de facto* pay policy has been rigorously applied to the public sector since 1979). Economically, the eschewal of formal incomes policies is clearly derived from the Conservative Government's ideological commitment to the free market, in which wages, like the price of any other commodity, are deemed to be determined by supply and demand. Wages are also considered to be linked to both productivity and profitability. However, three other factors have underpinned the Conservative Government's rejection of incomes policies.

Firstly, the Conservative Party under the leadership of Margaret Thatcher rejected the premise upon which incomes policies had previously been pursued, namely that inflation was directly caused by excessive wage increases. This perspective had been subscribed to by Labour *and* Conservative governments during the 1960s and 1970s, and consequently meant that restraining pay increases was seen as the way to control inflation. Thus did incomes policies, in all their various guises, come to be the means by which successive governments sought to hold down inflation. However, the Thatcher–Major Governments rejected the premise that wage increases were themselves the cause of inflation, and thus rejected the corollary that incomes policies were the means by which to conquer inflation. Instead, it was argued that inflation was ultimately caused by excessive increases in the money supply (excessive by virtue of the fact that they were not matched by increased productivity or economic growth). Once this thesis was accepted, then the need for an incomes policy dissipated (although the 'Tory Wets' continued to believe that an incomes policy could play a useful role in encouraging pay restraint, and 'educating' trade unions about the 'economic facts of life').

Secondly, the Conservative Government's rejection of incomes policies was inextricably linked to their total lack of commitment to securing full employment. One of the reasons why previous post-war governments had been so keen to restrain wage increases *and* inflation was to maintain full employment, something which would be undermined if excessive wage increases or inflation eroded profit margins and competitiveness, with the result that firms went out of business, or laid off workers in order to stay in business. Either way, the outcome would be an increase in unemployment. Now whilst the Thatcher Governments fully accepted that excessive wage increases or inflation undermined the competitiveness of firms, thereby raising unemployment levels, they were not concerned to pursue incomes policies in order to protect jobs. Instead, it was claimed that if workers or trade unions demanded higher pay rises than their employers could really afford through increased profitability or productivity, then they would have to bear the responsibility for the increased unemployment which would inevitably ensue. This tied in perfectly with the Thatcherite espousal of 'individual responsibility' – that people ought to accept responsibility for the consequences of their actions. Thus, if workers 'price themselves out of work', they should recognize that they have only themselves to blame, and not look to the 'nanny state' to come running to their rescue. Indeed, the Conservative Governments since 1979 have believed that high unemployment itself ought to act as a restraint on wage increases, on the grounds that the fear of losing their jobs, and thus joining the dole queues, would induce workers to accept lower pay rises. Certainly, in times of high unemployment, the bargaining position of employers is strengthened, as is evinced by reports of pay *cuts* and increased working hours being imposed on many employees during the recession of the early 1990s.

Thirdly, the Thatcher Governments rejected incomes policies on the grounds that they merely serve to politicize the issue of pay, and transform wage determination into a political, rather than economic, matter. The downfall of the Heath Government in 1974, and the Callaghan Government in 1979, were largely attributable to their pursuit of incomes policies, which had the effect of bringing about major confrontations between Government and trade unions. The post-1979 Conservative Governments thus concluded that on grounds of both economic principle and political practice, direct determination of wages by the Government is doomed to failure.

The End of Corporatism

Given their antipathy towards trade unionism, and their rejection of incomes policies, it was only natural that the Conservative Governments since 1979 eschewed the corporatist approach to economic policy-making and industrial affairs. The previous trend towards corporatism in Britain was rapidly reversed, although the institutional symbol of British corporatism, the NEDC, was not actually abolished until shortly after the 1992 election victory. The only surprise was that it had not been abolished much earlier.

Certainly, the promulgation of market forces, coupled with the avowed objective of 'rolling back the state', and restoring 'management's right to manage', all served to render corporatism redundant. The notion that industrial decisions and economic policy should be determined through consultations between government, trade unions and employers was incompatible with the Conservative emphasis on the primacy of 'the market'. Hence Lord Young's boast that: 'We have rejected the TUC; we have rejected the CBI. We do not see them coming back again. We gave up the corporate State' (*Financial Times*, 9 November 1988).

Furthermore, it was held that corporatism had the pernicious effect of 'politicizing' what were – or ought to be – primarily economic decisions. Matters such as wages, price levels, investment, employment, and so on became subject to the political goals of governments and organized interests, rather than being determined according to 'market' criteria. The consequence was not merely that the economic sphere became 'politicized', but that it became subordinated to the political realm. Politics came to dominate economics, thereby destroying the distinction between the two as espoused by Conservative neo-liberals.

A further consequence of this 'politicization' was the tendency for the state itself to become besieged by the competing and conflicting demands of a plethora of pressure groups, as they increasingly looked to Government to satisfy their policy aspirations or protect their interests. Indeed, during the 1970s, there was considerable concern that Britain was experiencing an 'overload of government' (King 1976), so that the scope of demands made of Government rendered it virtually impossible for Government to fulfil its primary function – to govern.

To compound this problem, having become the focus of an infinite variety of demands, it was feared that Government and the state would subsequently become the focus of resentment from citizens and groups whose demands were not satisfied. Government and the state would face a 'crisis of legitimacy'.

The Thatcher Governments thus deemed it essential that the state should disengage as far as possible from economic decision-making with organizational interests, thereby further enhancing the role of 'the market'. Only by doing so, it was held, would Government once again enjoy the degree of autonomy required for effective government, whilst simultaneously enjoying a concomitant revival of its authority.

One final factor worth noting in explaining the Thatcher Governments' eschewal of corporatism was their emphasis on individualism. Corporatism enshrined the politics of collectivism because citizens, in order to be effectively represented in decision-making, needed to be members of organized interests, such as a trade union. Indeed, individuals were often compelled to join such groups, as in the case of the 'closed shop'. Not only did the Thatcher Governments deem this a fundamental negation of individual liberty, it was also claimed that millions of people who did not belong to an organized interest group – such as consumers – were not effectively represented in economic policy-making; their interests would not be effectively articulated or receive due consideration. According to one Conservative critic, 'corporatism is never concerned with the individual, but only with the collectivity; never with the consumer, but only the producer' (Raison 1979: 37). Given the Thatcherite emphasis on individualism – the primacy of the individual in social and economic affairs – the collectivism intrinsic to corporatism was clearly unacceptable.

For all these reasons, therefore, the Thatcher Governments assiduously downgraded corporatist structures and processes. Tripartite meetings between ministers, the TUC and CBI became fewer and farther between, whilst trade union representation on a wider variety of commissions and advisory bodies was greatly reduced.

The Formation of the Social Democratic Party

The Labour Party's shift to the left, in the wake of the 1979 election defeat, effectively created a vacuum in the ideological centre of British politics. With nature abhorring a vacuum, it was not long before it was filled. On 26 March 1981, the Social Democratic Party was launched, led by four former Labour ministers: Roy Jenkins, David Owen, William Rogers and Shirley Williams. The 'Gang of Four', as they became popularly known, were accompanied by thirteen Labour MPs, and one Conservative. By the end of the year further defections from the parliamentary Labour Party provided the Social Democratic Party with a total of 28 MPs.

Yet the formation of the Social Democratic Party was the culmination of decades of conflict and disagreement between the Left and Right of the Labour Party. As the 'revisionist' debate of the late 1950s had clearly indicated, the Labour Party had been characterized, throughout the post-war period at least, by a division between those on the left of the Party, who sought a fundamental and radical transformation from capitalism to socialism in Britain, and those on the right, who were more limited in their objectives, seeking instead to make capitalism fairer and more humane. This division, between 'fundamentalists' and 'revisionists', or 'social democrats', had become sharper during the 1970s, when the left appeared to become more influential in the Labour Party, at both constituency and parliamentary level. The concomitant disillusion amongst many on the right of the Labour Party fuelled speculation that a split might occur, with a new political party being formed through the desertion of despondent Labour MPs.

Such speculation was significantly strengthened by Roy Jenkins's Dimbleby Lecture broadcast live on BBC television in November 1979. Having been one of Britain's European Community Commissioners in Brussels since 1976, Jenkins entitled his talk 'Home Thoughts from Abroad', whereupon he depicted his view of developments in British politics at that time. In so doing, he expressed concern at the 'ossification' of the British political system, which was becoming too rigid to meet the demands and aspirations of the electorate. More specifically, Jenkins claimed that the leftward and rightward drift of the Labour and Conservative Parties respectively meant that the politically moderate British electorate was increasingly inadequately represented. If such a trend towards ideological extremes continued, Jenkins declared, the electorate might welcome the formation of a new political organization which provided a clear alternative to the two established parties. Jenkins was undoubtedly expressing publicly what a number of Labour MPs had been thinking privately, yet in the wake of his speech, some on the right of the Labour Party became more willing to express their concerns openly. Jenkins's Dimbleby Lecture has been described as 'the single most important event in placing on the agenda for serious discussion the idea of some new party or grouping in the middle ground of British politics' (Stephenson 1982: 20).

However, it was in the wake of the Labour Party's special Wembley Conference in May 1980 that senior figures in the party began publicly talking about the possibility of creating a new political organization. The adoption of the Left's 'Peace, Jobs, Freedom' programme, followed by an announcement (by John Silkin, Labour Shadow Industry spokesperson) that a motion calling for Britain's withdrawal from the European Community would be debated at Labour's annual conference in October, led to an open warning by David Owen, William Rogers and Shirley Williams that if withdrawal from Europe became official Labour policy, then they would resign from the party. Two days after this declaration, Roy Jenkins announced his imminent intention of forming a new 'centre' party.

Meanwhile, June and July witnessed further advances by the Left in the Labour Party, most notably endorsement of the principle of mandatory reselection of Labour MPs, and support for the creation of an electoral college to select the party leader. Such was the consequent concern of David Owen, William Rogers and Shirley Williams at these and other developments in the Labour Party already noted, that they wrote a 3,000 word 'open' letter to their Labour colleagues, which was published in *The Guardian* on 1 August 1980. They declared that whilst a centre party would lack roots, and a coherent philosophy, support for such a party would none the less increase if Labour continued with its drift to the left.

This drift to the left was confirmed at Labour's annual conference a couple of months later, when unilateral nuclear disarmament and withdrawal from the European Community were voted official Labour Party policies, along with proposals for further nationalization and the abolition of the House of Lords. There was also agreement on the proposal to establish an electoral college for the election of future Labour leaders, although in the meantime, in November, Michael Foot was elected leader under the existing system of election, namely one person-one vote, within the parliamentary Labour Party only.

On 24 January 1981, the Labour Party held a special conference at Wembley to determine the actual structure of the proposed electoral college for the election of future leaders. The resultant 'formula' was that 40 per cent of the vote would be allocated to affiliated trade unions, whilst 30 per cent each would be given to constituency parties and the parliamentary Labour Party (i.e. Labour MPs). Put another way, it meant that 70 per cent of the votes to elect a future Labour leader resided outside Parliament. The Labour MPs who would have to work with any leader elected via the electoral college possessed a minority share of the vote.

This decision represented the point of no return for people such as Roy Jenkins, David Owen, William Rogers and Shirley Williams. The day after the Wembley Conference they issued their 'Limehouse Declaration', in which the need for a new political approach in Britain was emphasized. This entailed the pursuit of an egalitarian, classless society, but one which avoided ideological extremes of Left or Right.

The final break with the Labour Party came on 26 March 1981, when the Social Democratic Party (SDP) was officially launched, after weeks of speculation, not so much about whether a new 'centre' party would be formed, but when. At the time of its launch, the SDP comprised thirteen Labour MPs (including the 'Gang of Four', of course) and one Conservative. By the end of the year, further defections by Labour MPs meant that there were now 28 SDP MPs in the House of Commons. Meanwhile, in November 1981, Shirley Williams became the first MP to be elected as an SDP candidate, winning the by-election in Crosby by turning an 18,000 Conservative majority into one of more than 5,000 for the SDP. Such a result certainly seemed to confirm the electoral support which had been ascribed to the SDP in numerous opinion polls throughout 1981. A poll by Gallup in December indicated that an Alliance (discussed below) between the SDP and the Liberal Party would attract 50 per cent of the vote, leaving both Labour and the Conservatives on 23 per cent each.

The launch of the SDP immediately raised the question of its relationship with the Liberal Party. Indeed, this was to become a major problem for a few members of the SDP throughout much of the 1980s, not least for David Owen. Initially, the SDP and the Liberal Party agreed to form an electoral 'Alliance', whereby both parties would work together in by-elections and general elections, and ensure that, among other things, the two parties did not compete against each other at constituency levels. Instead, they would agree to field only one candidate, either a Liberal or a Social Democrat, in each constituency, whilst campaigning jointly, at both local and national level. Whilst this strategy was not particularly vexatious, apart from occasional tensions over which party would contest particular constituencies – there were a few instances when Liberal activists in a constituency resented having a SDP candidate 'imposed' on them – it did raise the question of the longer-term relationship between the two parties. There was a widespread recognition that sooner or later, there ought to be a merger; it was not deemed feasible for the SDP and the Liberal Party indefinitely or permanently to work together electorally, but remain two distinct, separate political entities.

It was from within the SDP that the opposition to a merger with the Liberal Party mainly emanated, and much of this existed at elite level (i.e. among certain SDP MPs) rather than among the grass-roots membership. The leading opponent of a merger was David Owen, who feared a loss of identity for the SDP, and a dissipating of its values and principles. For Owen and his followers in the SDP, to support a merger effectively meant that they might just as well have joined the Liberal Party in the first place, and not bothered with the trials and tribulations of forming a new political party (Owen 1991: ch. 35).

Yet Owen and his closest colleagues were clearly in a minority. The disappointing result for the Alliance in the 1987 general election, in which it ended up with one seat less than in 1983, whilst simultaneously seeing its share of the vote fall by nearly 3 per cent, greatly increased the pressure for a merger to be completed with all due haste. A ballot of SDP members revealed that 57 per cent were in favour of starting formal talks with the Liberals about a merger of the two parties, whilst 43 per cent were opposed. The same question, when put to Liberal Party delegates at their 1987 annual conference, yielded a vote of 998 to 21 in favour. David Owen resigned as leader of the SDP, recognizing that the tide of opinion was clearly running against him, although a pro-Owen, anti-merger SDP 'rump' continued to field candidates against their former Alliance colleagues after the latter had merged to form the Social and Liberal Democrats (SLD) in March 1988. However, the SDP was by now in terminal decline, and by the end of 1988, whilst the SLD had over 77,000 members, the 'rump' SDP had barely 10,000. The 'rump' SDP also fared disastrously in local and by-elections. For example, in the May 1990 local government elections, the Liberal Democrats (as the SLD was now officially titled) won 669 seats, whereas the SDP won just five. During the same month, a by-election was held in the Merseyside constituency of Bootle, in which the SDP candidate received just 155 votes – 263 less than the Monster Raving Loony Party candidate! The final humiliation for the SDP was when their remaining two MPs lost their seats in the 1992 general election.

The SDP, the Alliance, the SLD, and now the Liberal Democrats, failed to 'break the mould' of British politics. The high expectations and optimism which accompanied the launch of the SDP was never translated into sufficient parliamentary seats.

These parties all suffered from the vagaries and vices of Britain's first-past-the-post electoral system, so that the votes they received nationally were not accurately or proportionally translated into seats in the House of Commons. Thus in the 1983 general election, the result was as shown in table 5.2.

Table 5.2   1983 general election result

	Votes won	Share of the vote (%)	Seats won
Conservative	13,012,315	42.4	397
Labour	8,456,934	27.6	209
Alliance	7,780,949	25.3	23

The unfairness endured by the Alliance is clear to see. The centre parties are in a catch-22 situation. They seek the introduction of electoral reform in Britain, but are unable to secure such change because of the manner in which the existing electoral system militates against them. The Liberal Democrats' only hope of securing the introduction of proportional representation is for a Hung Parliament leading to a coalition or pact with the Labour Party, in which the Liberal Democrats would hold the balance of power, and would thus offer to support Labour in the House of Commons only in return for pursuit of electoral reform.

Yet it is by no means certain that the Labour Party would accede to such a proposition, divided as it is over the issue of electoral reform. However, if a future general election were to result in a Hung Parliament, then this would prove the futility of the 'one last heave' stance adopted by many Labour MPs and shadow ministers (the belief that a mustering of all Labour's energy and strength into a final big 'push' would finally get rid of the Government), and thus possibly force a rapid and radical rethink, resulting in Labour's final conversion – for reasons of political expediency – to electoral reform.

The Falklands War

The failure of the Alliance to do as well in the 1983 general election as its initial levels of public support indicated can partially be attributed to the Falklands War, victory in which had a profound impact on the popularity of Margaret Thatcher and the Conservative Party. At the beginning of 1982, a Gallup poll gave the Alliance 39 per cent of the vote (which was itself 11 per cent down on the previous month) compared to the Conservative Party's 27 per cent. By July, in the wake of the Falklands victory, the Conservatives' support had risen to 46 per cent, whilst the Alliance saw its share fall to 24 per cent. Although the next general election was almost a year away, the Alliance never recovered the degree of support it had enjoyed in the opinion polls prior to Britain's victory in the Falklands War.

The Falklands War began when Argentina invaded the Falkland Islands, in the South Atlantic, in April 1982, seeking to repossess the islands to which it had long claimed possession. The invasion owed much, however, to Argentina's leader, President Galtieri, seeking to restore his flagging popularity at home by securing a military victory for his country. Ironically, it was Margaret Thatcher's popularity which was dramatically restored as a consequence of military victory, thereby proving instrumental in securing the Conservative Party success in the 1983 general election, although signs of economic recovery by this time also had an impact.

In the immediate aftermath of the invasion, the Foreign Secretary, Lord Carrington, and his two ministers at the Foreign Office, Richard Luce and Humphrey Atkins, resigned, ostensibly on the grounds of individual ministerial responsibility (claiming that they had failed to take sufficient heed of intelligence services warnings that Argentina might be contemplating seizure of the Falkland Islands). However, as with many instances of ministerial resignations in accordance with the convention of 'individual responsibility', there were deeper considerations involved, namely the desire and need to shield the rest of the Cabinet, and particularly the Prime Minister, from blame and criticism. After all, it has been argued: 'The responsibility for the misinterpretation of events seems to have been collective, not individual; it was a failure not simply on the part of a department, but on the part of a government'. As such, 'the doctrine of individual ministerial responsibility was utilised to obviate the need for any resort to collective responsibility' (Pyper 1984: 53). Certainly, Carrington was acutely aware that 'the same signals he saw at the Foreign Office went to the Prime Minister' (Dickie 1992: 194).

The political aftermath of the Falklands victory was a remarkable revival in the public popularity of both the Conservative Party *and* Margaret Thatcher. Certainly the Prime Minister simultaneously reflected and reinforced a widely held sense of national pride when she chided those who thought 'that Britain was no longer the nation that had built an Empire and ruled a quarter of the world . . . they were wrong'. Indeed, what the Falklands victory had proved, Margaret Thatcher declared, was that 'Britain has not changed . . . We have ceased to be a nation in retreat. We have instead a new-found confidence.' She therefore called for 'the spirit of the South Atlantic' to be invoked at home in order to defeat Britain's domestic problems and 'enemies within' – such as trade unions and strikers (quoted in Barnett 1982: 149–53).

It was no surprise, therefore, when Margaret Thatcher led the Conservative Party to victory in the 1983 general election, securing a phenomenal 144-seat majority. The election victory was not solely due to the 'Falklands Factor', because apparent signs of economic recovery had also restored or renewed support for the Conservative Party among many British voters. Furthermore, the Opposition was no real opposition at all. The Labour Party had undergone four years of in-fighting, and was patently lacking in unity, little more than a fractious farrago. At the same time, it fought the 1983 election on a notably left-wing (by British standards) programme, one which included a commitment to 'a non-nuclear defence policy', incomes policy, withdrawal from the EC and further nationalization and state 'regulation' of the economy. Labour's manifesto was subsequently described by a senior Labour Party figure as 'the longest suicide note in history'. To compound Labour's problems, the party was led by the rambling, shambling Michael Foot, who was disliked not only for his left-wing views, but even more for being an intellectual – a heinous crime in Britain. The masses would not vote for a man who read books – let alone wrote them. Indeed, Foot's Hampstead 'bookish' image merely served to enhance Margaret Thatcher's image as a 'doer', a woman of action, someone who actually sought to tackle problems rather than merely theorize about them. The salvation of Britain, and the renaissance of the nation, were not to be achieved by wielding a pen in one hand, and a biography in the other.

(Indeed, one of the reasons why the Right so often triumphs over the Left in politics is that the latter's tendency to 'theorize' about society's problems is no match for the Right's appeals to 'common sense' and 'gut instinct' about what needs to be done.)

The 1984–5 Miners' Strike

According to Margaret Thatcher, the Argentinians had constituted the 'enemy outside', whilst the miners, when they began a year-long strike against pit closures in 1984, represented 'the enemy within'. Certainly the Conservative Government displayed the same type of hatred and hostility towards the striking miners that it normally directed against 'foreigners'. The leader of the NUM, Arthur Scargill, was vilified by the Government and most of the press, presented as a modern day folk-devil, whilst the miners who continued to work in defiance of the strike were venerated by Conservatives in a manner usually reserved for war heroes. Yet whatever the merits of the miners' strike, and the manner in which it was conducted, the Government was entirely justified in claiming that the strike was 'politically motivated' – the Conservative Party had begun preparations for confrontation with the miners six years previously whilst still in Opposition.

In 1978, the 'Ridley Report' was leaked to *The Economist* (by no means a subversive left-wing publication), and its main recommendations published on 21 May 1978. The 'Ridley Report' – prepared by the then Shadow Energy Minister, Nicholas Ridley – suggested that in readiness for a likely confrontation with the miners, the next Conservative Government ought, immediately after being elected, to pursue a number of measures by way of preparation. The recommended measures included: building up coal reserves by encouraging overtime and productivity bonuses to miners; making contingency plans to import coal; recruiting non-union lorry drivers through road haulage companies, to guarantee the movement of coal during a strike; reducing social security payments to strikers; and ensuring that the police were well-organized and resourced, in order to tackle mass picketing.

Although Margaret Thatcher would like to have taken on the miners in 1981, she was persuaded by ministerial colleagues that this was too early; the ground had not sufficiently been prepared. Instead, the miners' strike began in March 1984, following the announcement by the National Coal Board that it was going to close down the Cortonwood colliery in South Yorkshire. However, the strike was certainly not solely, or primarily, about the closure of this particular pit. Instead, the National Union of Mineworkers, and particularly its President (elected in April 1982) Arthur Scargill, saw the strike as a means of opposing the wider programme of pit closures being sought by the Thatcher Government and the National Coal Board. Whilst the Government strenuously denied Scargill's claims that it was intending to close down the majority of Britain's coal mines as a prelude to privatizing the few which would be reprieved, with the consequent loss of 80,000 miners' jobs, it did insist that certain pits would have to be closed down because they were 'uneconomic'.

The year-long miners' strike was controversial for two particular reasons. Firstly, the NUM leadership refused to ballot the miners to gauge their support for strike action, claiming that to do so would enable miners in 'safe' areas, such as Nottinghamshire, to vote against strike action because their jobs were not primarily at risk, and thereby effectively consign their colleagues in other areas to the dole; no miner, it was insisted, had the right to vote another miner out of a job (Goodman 1985: 46). This refusal to conduct a ballot enabled the Government and the press to portray Scargill as a tyrant and dictator afraid of democracy. It also raised serious doubts about the legitimacy of the strike. In any case, the Thatcher Government repeatedly claimed that the primary purpose of the strike was nothing to do with preventing pit closures and defending miners' jobs, but about Scargill's political motives, namely to bring down a Conservative Government, as the miners had apparently done ten years previously. This perspective portrayed the bulk of the striking miners as unwilling dupes of Scargill's Marxist machinations and motives.

The second controversial aspect of the miners' strike was the violence which regularly occurred on picket lines. Graphic scenes of violence between pickets and police, coupled with the bitter hatred openly displayed by striking miners towards those of their colleagues continuing to work in defiance of the strike, shocked and alienated many British people, particularly as such scenes appeared regularly on their television screens during news broadcasts.

The violence enabled Government ministers to depict striking miners on picket lines as bully-boys and thugs, whilst the miners seeking to continue working were lauded as courageous heroes, men of virtue and valour.

The miners' strike was doomed to failure. Lacking support and legitimacy due to the NUM leadership's refusal to countenance a ballot, coupled with the methodical and meticulous manner in which the Thatcher Government had prepared for such a dispute, the striking miners were always at a strong disadvantage. They were also bereft of support from many other workers. There was little active sympathy or solidarity. Whilst middle-class Marxists harboured romantic delusions that the striking miners might act as a catalyst encouraging other sections of the working class to mobilize against the Thatcher Government, most workers remained resolutely indifferent. Many of them had other, more important, matters to concern them, such as fixing a shiny new carriage lamp next to the mock mahogany front door of their recently bought council house. As such, the miners' strike has been characterized as 'the last, almost primeval scream, of a dying proletariat' (Taylor 1993: 298).

Britain and Europe

It was during the 1980s that Britain's image of 'an awkward partner' *vis-à-vis* the European Community was fully confirmed. Margaret Thatcher's style of strong leadership, coupled with her fervent nationalism, rendered conflict with Britain's European partners inevitable. Yet such conflicts were grist to Thatcher's mill, for they enabled her to pander to the xenophobic instincts of the British people, and thereby reinforce her image as a strong leader, and courageous defender of British interests against 'foreigners'.

At the risk of over-simplification, the 1980s can be divided into two halves concerning the nature of Britain's – or rather the Thatcher Governments' – disputes with the EC. In the first half, the main source of conflict was primarily financial, with Thatcher disputing the amount Britain paid into the EC budget. In the second half of the 1980s the conflict was mainly institutional, as legislation was introduced, and plans unveiled, to facilitate closer European integration, both through economic and social policies, and through institutional reforms.

Concern over the size of Britain's budgetary contributions had actually been a feature of the Callaghan Government in the late 1970s, but it was during the first half of the 1980s, under Margaret Thatcher's premiership, that the issue acquired greater prominence. There were actually two main problems concerning Britain's contributions to the EC budget. The first derived from the fact that Britain still imported many products, particularly food, from outside the EC, partly due to remaining links with the Commonwealth countries. The EC's imposition of levies on industrial and agricultural commodities imported from non-EC countries meant that Britain's budgetary contributions were rather higher than those of most other member states. Furthermore, the cost of the levies was passed on to the consumer in the form of higher prices which, in turn, had implications for the Government's anti-inflation policy.

The problem of Britain's budgetary contributions was compounded by the fact that the amount to be paid was partly determined by national VAT receipts. As George explains, this would normally mean that when a nation was prospering, and its citizens were spending more, the government's VAT receipts, and hence the contribution to the EC budget, would be higher. Conversely, if a country's economy was in recession, consumer spending would normally be lower, thereby yielding less VAT for the government, and thus resulting in a reduction in that country's budgetary contributions (George 1990: 132). However, during the early 1980s, the Thatcher Government was effectively using the revenues from North Sea oil to reduce or hold down income tax. This had the effect of allowing higher consumer spending, of course, but it also meant that the Government's VAT receipts were higher, as was Britain's budgetary contribution. Indeed, in his first budget, the Chancellor of the Exchequer offset income tax cuts by increasing the rate of VAT from 8 to 15 per cent. To compound the problem from the Government's point of view, this higher consumer spending also sucked in more imports, thereby increasing Britain's budgetary contributions further still (whilst worsening the balance of payments situation generally).

However, it was not solely the size of Britain's budgetary contributions which was a bone of contention for the Thatcher Government, but also how much – or, rather, how little – Britain received in return from the EC. This problem derived from the fact that the British economy was primarily based on industrial manufacturing (although this was experiencing an accelerating decline) and an expanding service sector. Britain was not, in other words, an agricultural nation. Yet two-thirds of the EC's budget was disbursed through the Common Agricultural Policy, which meant that the main beneficiaries were precisely those member states whose main economic activity was agricultural. As such, the Thatcher Government (like the Callaghan Government before it) claimed that Britain was not only contributing too much to the EC budget, but was also receiving too little in return. Furthermore, there was deemed to be an element of wealth distribution involved, whereby richer nations (such as Britain) were being compelled to subsidize poorer nations, the very notion of which was anathema to Margaret Thatcher. So strained did relations between Britain and the other member states become that in the summer of 1982 the French President François Mitterrand caustically suggested that it might be in everyone's interests for Britain to leave the EC. Eventually, at a European Council meeting at Fontainebleau in 1984, Margaret Thatcher accepted a compromise solution to the issue of Britain's budgetary contributions, whereby Britain would receive a rebate of one billion ecu for that year, and then in future years, 66 per cent of the difference between Britain's VAT contributions and its receipts for the budget (George 1990: 156).

However, hopes that the resolution of the dispute over Britain's budgetary contributions would herald a more harmonious relationship with other member states during the second half of the 1980s were to prove premature and naive. Instead, with the dispute over the EC budget out of the way, attention turned to institutional developments and reforms, which themselves served to provoke Margaret Thatcher's ire and indignation. The issue of greater, closer, European integration moved up the EC's agenda, and hence up the domestic political agenda in Britain. A number of other member states wished to proceed with plans and proposals to create common policies, and also to create new institutions – as well as reforming (strengthening) existing ones – to facilitate such policies.

At a general level, it became clear that many, if not most, other member states were thinking in terms not only of greater economic integration, but social integration as well. The Thatcher Government was enthusiastic about *some* aspects of economic integration, but hostile towards others, whilst the proposals for social integration were opposed entirely by Thatcher.

What Margaret Thatcher did fully support was the development of a single market within the EC, which is what the 1957 Treaty of

Rome (originally establishing the European Economic Community) had envisaged when it called for the development of 'an area without internal frontiers in which the free movement of goods, persons, services and capital is ensured'. The 1986 Single European Act sought to give effect to this goal, although the Thatcher Government was unhappy about the provision or harmonization of VAT between member states, and the free movement of people and abolition of border controls. The latter two issues were opposed by the Thatcher Government on the grounds that they might facilitate illegal immigration, whilst also undermining the fight against terrorism and drug trafficking.

Margaret Thatcher was also unhappy about some of the associated institutional developments and reforms which were intended to facilitate economic integration between member states. For example, the issue of monetary union proved particularly vexatious. France and Germany were among those member states who argued that, sooner or later, a single European market would require a single European currency. This in turn would necessitate the establishment of a central European bank. This was anathema to Margaret Thatcher, who argued: 'A European central bank . . . means surrendering your economic policy to that banking system that is in charge of the maintenance of the value of the currency, and must therefore be in charge of the necessary economic policy to achieve that' (*The Independent*, 22 October 1988). Similar sentiments were expressed in the Conservative Party's manifesto for the 1989 Euro-elections, it being claimed that: 'full economic and monetary union would involve a fundamental transfer of sovereignty. It would require new European institutions to administer a common currency and decide interest rates, and a considerable degree of central control over budgetary policy. [This] implies nothing less than the creation of a federal Europe.'

Margaret Thatcher's antipathy to closer economic union and integration – beyond the removal of barriers to a free market within Europe – was further illustrated by the delay over Britain's entry into the Exchange Rate Mechanism (ERM). In fact, she only agreed to Britain's membership when the Chancellor, Nigel Lawson, and the Foreign Secretary, Sir Geoffrey Howe, confronted her at a European Council meeting in Madrid in 1989, and threatened their joint resignation if she did not agree to British membership of the ERM. Recognizing that her own authority as Conservative leader would be seriously – possibly fatally – undermined if both Lawson and Howe resigned, Thatcher reluctantly agreed, although by the time Britain actually joined, Nigel Lawson had long since resigned anyway, having clashed with Thatcher during the autumn of 1989 over her appointment of Sir Alan Walters as her personal economic adviser.

However, it remained the 'social dimension' of integration which attracted the most consistent and emphatic opposition from the Thatcher Government during the late 1980s. In a speech to the TUC's annual conference in 1988, the President of the EC Commission, Jacques Delors, insisted that:

> It is impossible to build Europe only on deregulation . . . 1992 is much more than the creation of an internal market abolishing barriers to the free movement of goods, services and investment . . . It is necessary to improve workers' living and working conditions, and to provide better protection for their health and safety at work.

The speech – indeed the fact that Jacques Delors had been invited to speak at the TUC in the first place – deeply angered Margaret Thatcher and other Tory 'Dry' ministers. They were strongly opposed to the 'social dimension', whereby the rights of employees would be enhanced and enshrined in EC law (thereby taking precedence over domestic law). Not only would this constitute a further undermining of national/parliamentary sovereignty, it would also impede the effective operation of the internal market, as well as impinge upon management's right to manage. The advocacy of a 'social dimension' to the EC prompted Margaret Thatcher's speech in Bruges (Belgium) in September 1988, which she elaborated upon in her speech to delegates at the Conservative Party's annual conference the following month. Here, she claimed that the economic liberty envisaged in the Treaty of Rome 'is under attack from those who see European unity as a vehicle for spreading socialism. We haven't worked all these years to free Britain from the paralysis of socialism only to see it creep through the back door of central control and bureaucracy in Brussels.'

It was this perspective which was eventually to result in Britain's 'opt-out' from the Social Chapter provisions of the Maastricht Treaty in 1992, although by this time Margaret Thatcher was no longer Conservative Party leader and Prime Minister. Indeed, as we will note later, her belligerent and bellicose attitude towards Europe was partly responsible for Thatcher's downfall, for whilst senior Conservatives such as Norman Tebbit and Nicholas Ridley fully shared her views, others in the party began to worry that Britain would find itself isolated and left behind if Thatcher's stance was maintained. It was not only her partners in the EC that Thatcher antagonized and alienated.

The Anglo-Irish Agreement

According to one writer: 'The elections of 1979 signified both the continuity and change in overall British policy' (Lyons, 1990: 220). Continuity was epitomized by the twin policies of Ulsterization (whereby the main responsibility for law and order was delegated to the Royal Ulster Constabulary and the Ulster Defence Regiment) and 'criminalization' (which meant that IRA prisoners lost their 'political prisoner' status and were deemed to be ordinary criminals). It was this policy of criminalization which prompted a series of hunger strikes by IRA prisoners during the early 1980s, resulting in the death of ten such inmates, including Bobby Sands, who had been elected as MP for the constituency of Fermanagh and South Tyrone.

Whilst the Thatcher Government was not moved by the IRA hunger strikes and consequent deaths, it was concerned at the increased support attained by Sinn Fein among sections of the Catholic community in Northern Ireland, for some of whom the dead hunger strikers were martyrs. As the newly appointed Northern Ireland Secretary James Prior recognized; 'The Government had to seize the initiative and try to wrest back the advantage' (Prior 1986: 189). It was here that the continuities in British policy were accompanied by changes – at least, according to Lyons – although some of these 'changes' were not dissimilar to initiatives introduced in the 1970s.

In order to 'build a bridge between the communities' and 'open a political dialogue', Jim Prior sought to initiate a policy of 'rolling devolution', which would entail an elected Northern Ireland Assembly scrutinizing policies and legislation in the Province. It was envisaged that over a period of time, moderate politicians from both sections of the community would develop sufficient trust and co-operation to forge a working relationship, which would, in turn, enable further powers to be devolved to Northern Ireland from London, so that eventually, Northern

Ireland would largely be self-governing, albeit still part of the United Kingdom for as long as a majority of its citizens wished it to be so.

Prior's programme of 'rolling devolution' made very little headway, however. The constitutional Nationalist/Catholic party, the Social Democratic and Labour Party, boycotted meetings of the Assembly, claiming that no long-term solution would be achieved without the inclusion or incorporation of an Irish dimension, entailing some involvement by the Republic of Ireland. This was anathema to the Unionists in Northern Ireland, and thus 'the Assembly lapsed into no more than an expensive and futile talking-shop' which was finally disbanded in June 1986 (Arthur and Jeffery 1988: 16).

The main initiative concerning Northern Ireland was the Anglo-Irish Agreement, signed at Hillsborough Castle, County Down, by Margaret Thatcher and Garret Fitzgerald, the Irish Taoiseach (Prime Minister), in November 1985, although its origins can be traced to meetings between Thatcher and the then Irish premier, Charles Haughey, which began back in 1980. These meetings continued in subsequent years, even though Charles Haughey was replaced by Garret Fitzgerald as Irish Taoiseach in June 1981.

The 1985 Anglo-Irish Agreement (occasionally referred to as the Hillsborough Accord or Agreement) laid down the following principles and proposals:

- Northern Ireland would remain part of the United Kingdom for as long as the majority of the population wished it to do so.
- There should be a devolved form of government in the province, involving power-sharing between the two communities.
- The Irish government to be given a consultative and advisory role over Northern Ireland affairs, via an inter-governmental conference involving regular meetings between political leaders from London and Dublin.
- Closer co-operation between Northern Ireland and the Republic over security, particularly along the border of the two countries. Also, the extradition of alleged or suspected terrorists from the Irish Republic to be made easier. It was also recommended that more Catholics be recruited by the overwhelmingly Protestant RUC.

Unionists were hostile to the Anglo-Irish Agreement, viewing it as a betrayal of Northern Ireland's Protestant community by the British Government, with the leader of the DUP, Ian Paisley, accusing Margaret Thatcher of being a 'traitor'. The Unionists had two major objections to the Anglo–Irish Agreement. Firstly, whilst it sought to allay their fears about the constitutional position of the province within the United Kingdom, Unionists were deeply suspicious of the reference to 'the current status of Northern Ireland', and the claim that the province would remain part of the UK for so long as a majority of its population wished it to do so. To the Unionists, these phrases implied that Northern Ireland's constitutional status was conditional, rather than permanent and guaranteed. They had long suspected that Britain was not fully committed to maintenance of the Union, and would sooner or later withdraw, politically as well as militarily, in order to bring about Irish unification, and certain phrases within the Anglo–Irish Agreement merely fuelled these fears and suspicions. Indeed, with regard to the provision that Northern Ireland would remain part of the UK so long as a majority of its population wished it to do so, Unionists were deeply concerned that the higher Catholic birthrate would eventually render Protestants the minority population in the province. 'What then?' they wondered in trepidation.

The other main Unionist objection to the Anglo–Irish Agreement was the role – albeit advisory and consultative – it gave to Dublin *vis-à-vis* Northern Ireland. To Unionists, this constituted a totally unwarranted interference in the internal political affairs of Northern Ireland by a foreign country and its government. It was deemed greatly to undermine the independence, autonomy and sovereignty of Northern Ireland, effectively placing it under the joint rule of London and Dublin.

Nationalists were divided in their response to the Anglo–Irish Agreement. The Social Democratic and Labour Party had itself urged an 'Irish dimension' with regard to seeking a solution to the Northern Ireland problem, and was therefore very favourably disposed towards the Agreement. Not only did it offer better representation and fairer treatment – economically, socially and politically – for the minority Catholic community in Northern Ireland, it also offered the possibility, if not likelihood, of marginalizing Sinn Fein and the IRA. Indeed, one of the motives of the Thatcher Governments in introducing the Anglo-Irish Agreement was to undermine the increasing support for Sinn Fein/IRA which occurred in Northern Ireland during the early 1980s. Furthermore, this factor implicitly acknowledged that the defeat of terrorism would not be achieved solely by military means and improved security measures; instead, there needed to be a political dimension as well.

Sinn Fein, meanwhile, were totally opposed to the Anglo-Irish Agreement, seeing it merely as a reaffirmation of the status quo, namely the maintenance of Northern Ireland as a state entirely independent of the Republic of Ireland. Given Sinn Fein's total commitment to a united Ireland, the Anglo-Irish Agreement was clearly unacceptable. Furthermore, as noted in chapter 3, Sinn Fein was emphatic that Northern Ireland was not a *legitimate* state, on the grounds that it had been artificially created, and then imposed, against the wishes of the majority of the Irish population. As such, the Anglo-Irish Agreement was rejected by Sinn Fein as representing nothing more than a policy initiative by the British Government designed simultaneously to reaffirm the continuities of an 'illegitimate' Northern Irish state *and* undermine Catholic support for Irish reunification.

Given such opposition, the 1985 Anglo-Irish Agreement enjoyed little tangible success. Indeed, subsequent relations between London and Dublin were occasionally strained due to the latter's reluctance to extradite certain suspected terrorists, arguing that they would not receive a fair trial in Britain and Northern Ireland. Needless to say, this also fuelled the anger of the Unionists. For the remainder of the decade, therefore, whilst committed to the Anglo-Irish Agreement and continuing to meet their Irish counterparts, the Thatcher Governments found themselves pursuing a more familiar strategy of 'containing' the problem, and countering terrorism. In other words, whilst committed to a longer-term political solution, in the shorter term, the approach to Northern Ireland primarily remained that of law and order and improving security against the IRA, as well as imposing a broadcasting ban on Sinn Fein in mainland Britain, so as to deprive them of the 'oxygen of publicity'. It would be nearly a decade later before a more significant breakthrough was made in the search for a solution to the Northern Ireland problem.

Privatization

As with trade union reform, privatization was a policy which evinced rather more pragmatism, at least initially, than is usually acknowledged. For all the talk of 'rolling back the state', the Thatcher Government originally ascribed little significance to privatization. The Conservatives' 1979 election manifesto made only passing reference to it, emphasizing instead that nationalized industries were to be run more efficiently and successfully, with less political interference, and within a stricter financial framework. Higher productivity was also deemed vital. Indeed, privatization only became an integral – defining – feature of Thatcherism after the second election victory in 1983.

During the first Thatcher Government, the avowed objective was 'a determination not to intervene in industry, and to subject the nationalised industries to strict financial limits' (Kavanagh 1987: 220). However, the financial losses incurred, and subsidies required, by many of the publicly owned industries resulted in a search for new solutions to this old problem. Having already proceeded with a few relatively moderate sales of shares, in firms such as British Petroleum, British Aerospace, Cable and Wireless, and the National Freight Company (among others) between 1979 and 1982, the Thatcher Governments soon realized the advantages to be accrued by developing a more coherent, systematic programme of privatization. The advantages can be categorized as economic and political, although there are clear, and close, overlaps.

Three main *economic* advantages accrued to the Thatcher Governments by the privatization of nationalized industries.

1   By having major state-owned firms and industries transferred to the private sector, the Government would be spared the need to spend billions of pounds each year subsidizing such enterprises. For a government committed to reducing public expenditure, this was a vitally important, and attractive, consideration. In any case, many Conservatives suggested, the former reliance on government subsidies had itself acted as a disincentive to nationalized industries to become more competitive and cost-effective.

2   The money saved through no longer having to subsidize nationalized industries, combined with the revenue raised from the sale of shares themselves, would enable the Government to fulfil another manifesto commitment, namely a reduction in (direct) taxation. To

this extent, privatization helped the Thatcher Governments finance the lowering of income tax rates, the revenue raised from share sales helping to offset the loss of revenue resulting from tax cuts.

3　Privatization relieved the Government of responsibility for wage determination. Once in the private sector, wages were to be determined by market forces and profit levels, not by the Government. Given the British experience of incomes policies during the 1960s and 1970s, and the extent to which these 'politicized' wage determination, thereby bringing large numbers of workers and their trade unions into direct conflict with successive Governments, the extent to which privatization was seen by the Thatcher Governments as a solution to this perennial problem should not be underestimated.

Apart from the reduced scope for such conflict between workers or trade unions and the Government over pay, privatization offered the Thatcher Governments two particular political benefits. Firstly, privatization was, during most of the 1980s, extremely popular with the British public, with many share sales being heavily over-subscribed as millions of people sought – most of them for the first time – to buy shares. Thus, whereas the Conservative Governments of the 1950s had promoted the concept of a 'property-owning democracy', the Thatcher Governments of the 1980s waxed lyrical about creating a 'share-owning democracy' as well. Indeed, with deliberate irony, some Conservatives suggested that privatization was actually achieving what Socialists and the Labour Party had always called for – a radical transfer and irreversible redistribution of wealth to ordinary working people!

Secondly, but following on from this last point, the Thatcher Government gleefully recognized that privatization would pose serious problems for the Labour Party, and thus provide the Conservative Party with a considerable political and electoral advantage. For with millions of voters possessing their own shares, and enjoying the concomitant tax cuts, how could the Labour Party fight an election pledging to renationalise the recently privatized industries, when such a policy would entail 'seizing' the newly acquired wealth of ordinary people, *and* reversing the recent tax cuts? In order to become electable the Labour Party would have to ditch its commitment to nationalization and public ownership, thereby ensuring the maintenance of a market economy, whichever party was in power. Labour would thus be compelled to engage in electoral battle on an ideological terrain staked out by the Conservative Party. As the section on Labour's 'policy review' will indicate, the Conservative Party's calculations that Labour would have to embrace the market economy, and thus renege on its commitment to (re)nationalization, were entirely vindicated.

Yet in other respects, the 'success' of the Thatcher Governments' privatization programme – even in terms of its own criteria and avowed objectives – has been more questionable. Although privatization has invariably been accompanied by the standard (New Right) Conservative rhetoric about ensuring competition and consumer choice, these have often both been notably lacking. What were formerly public monopolies have 'merely' become private monopolies in most cases. The much vaunted competition and consumer choice have largely been notable for their absence. To compensate for this deficiency, the privatization of many industries has been accompanied by the establishment of a plethora of regulatory bodies, intended to ensure 'fair practice' and protect consumer (customer) interests. Given the Thatcher Governments' declared objectives of *reducing* the regulation of industry, and of cutting a swathe through Quangos and bureaucracy, the establishment of a range of regulatory bodies to 'monitor' the activities of privatized industries is rather ironic.

Another question which has been raised by critics of the Thatcher Governments' privatization programme concerns the extent to which a widening of share ownership has actually been achieved. Whilst millions of people originally applied for shares in industries at the time of their privatization – four million people registered for shares with British Gas when it was privatized in 1986, for example – it has been suggested by many commentators that most of these investors soon sold their shares, seeing them merely as a means of making a quick and easy sum of money (understandable, given that many shares have been sold at rather less than their 'real' market value). Critics thus suggest that the apparent success of the Thatcher Governments' privatization programme, in terms of widening share ownership, merely reflected an economically rational decision by many ordinary people to buy shares which were being sold at an unrealistically low price – aided by 'payment by instalments' – in order to sell them at their 'real' market value almost immediately afterwards, thereby making a quick profit, to be spent on consumer durables or a holiday, for example. As such, it has variously been suggested that the number of people purchasing shares in industries being privatized is not a realistic measure of the scale of share ownership in Britain; one also needs to consider the proportion and value of shares owned by individuals, particularly after the initial sale. Many 'small investors' bought shares with the intention of selling them soon afterwards, thereby making a quick profit; the ability of ordinary individuals to do this was due to the Thatcher Governments' shrewd tactic of deliberately offering the shares at a price lower than their true marked value on the Stock Exchange (something which the Public Accounts Committee of the House of Commons was critical of).

The fact that so many individuals quickly sold their shares had serious implications for the Thatcher Governments' avowed objective of widening share ownership, and *inter alia*, redistributing wealth in favour of ordinary people. For example, within a year of the sale of Cable and Wireless during 1981–2, the number of shareholders fell from 150,000 to less than 26,000. Similarly, in the wake of the partial sale of British Aerospace in 1980–1, the number of people owning fewer than 100 shares – the Government's apparently revered 'small investors' – declined from 44,000 to 3,300 (Abromeit 1988: 78). Meanwhile, by 1990 the number of shareholders in British Airways, which was privatized during 1986–7, had fallen from over 1,000,000 to less than 350,000, whilst share ownership in British Gas reduced from 4,407,079 to 2,780,813. Share ownership in Rolls Royce also declined, falling from 2,000,000 to 924,970 (Treasury 1990: 7).

This contraction in post-privatization share ownership suggests that contrary to the Thatcher Governments' avowed objectives: 'A process of concentration of privatized shares in the key City institutions has taken place' (Richardson 1994: 75). In any case, even in companies where large numbers of employees bought shares, 'their total share in the firm's capital nevertheless stayed ridiculously small: it fluctuated between 0.1% and 4.3% . . . ' (Abromeit 1988: 78–9).

One other point noted by critics of the Conservative privatization programme is that the public popularity of privatizing state-owned industries waned from the late 1980s onwards, not least because people had come to realize that a private monopoly by no means provided a better, cheaper, or more efficient service after all. Furthermore, some of the industries which still remained in the public sector by the late 1980s were ones which seemed to arouse particular concern among the public with regard to the likely consequences of privatizing them. For example, according to opinion polls, most people were opposed to the 1990 privatization of the water industry, whilst the proposed privatization of British Rail proved even more unpopular than British Rail itself. For many people, it would seem that the privatization of an oil company or airline is qualitatively different from privatizing a major public utility such as water or the railway network.

Straddling the boundary between 'privatization' and reducing the role and powers of local government was the sale of council houses, which itself became a key policy of the Thatcher Governments during the 1980s. It was also a policy which perfectly accorded with the Thatcherite espousal of private property ownership, although this in itself was an integral part of a more general, long-standing Conservative commitment to increasing home ownership and establishing a 'property-owning democracy'.

The 1979 election manifesto had pledged that: 'In the first session of the next Parliament, we shall . . . give council and new town tenants the legal right to buy their homes'. Once elected, the policy was swiftly put into practice in the form of the 1980 Housing Act, which provided council tenants with the right to buy their homes from their local authority. Furthermore – as with most of the Thatcher Governments' privatization sales – the price at which council houses were sold was considerably lower than the actual market value, due to the discounts which tenants were entitled to, depending on length of residency. With such generous discounts available, it is hardly surprising that the sale of council houses proved highly popular among tenants. Furthermore, the policy freed them from the petty rules and regulations which had applied to local authority tenants. By 1990, about 20 per cent of (ex-) council houses had been sold.

Obviously, however, this represented a somewhat disappointing figure from the Government's point of view, for it meant that four-fifths of council houses remained under local authority control. Two additional measures were thus subsequently introduced to encourage a further reduction in local authority housing. Firstly, the financial reform of local government – discussed in the next section – which was pursued throughout the 1980s included a measure prohibiting local authorities from subsidizing council house rents out of the general rates: 'This policy has forced local authorities to dramatically increase rents for council houses, making it financially more expedient for all but the poorer tenants to buy their own homes' (Chandler 1991: 42).

Secondly, the 1988 Housing Act enabled tenants in the remaining council houses to vote on whether they wished to be transferred to the 'control' of a private landlord or housing association, rather than remain under local authority jurisdiction. Many tenants were not in favour of such a change, recognizing, perhaps, that however bad local authorities might be in terms of pushing up rents and being slow to carry out maintenance and repairs, private landlords were likely to prove even worse (Stoker 1991: 214–16). Certainly, many people in Britain who do live in the private rented sector are those who cannot afford to buy their own homes, yet the rents they actually pay each week or month are often similar to what a monthly mortgage repayment would be anyway. With a depletion of council house stock, and the exorbitant cost of renting privately, or buying – particularly in the wake of the mid-1980s property boom – a home, the result has been that alongside record levels of home ownership, there are now also record numbers of people homeless, either compelled to live in overcrowded bed-and-breakfast accommodation, or simply left to sleep in shop doorways. When asked about the plight of such people, one of Margaret Thatcher's housing ministers allegedly retorted: 'The homeless? Oh, they're the ones you have to step over when you come out of the theatre.'

Like the privatization of formerly nationalized industries, the Thatcher Governments' policy of selling council houses also enshrined a more subtle political objective: to undermine support for the Labour Party amongst council tenants. In this, the Conservatives have achieved considerable success.

In the 1987 general election, for example, 57 per cent of the working class were owner-occupiers (a 3 per cent increase since the 1983 election), of whom 44 per cent voted Conservative, compared to 32 per cent voting Labour and 24 per cent supporting the Liberal/SDP Alliance.

The sale of council houses was also part of the Thatcher Governments' attack on local government in general.

Local Government

Throughout the 1980s, relations between central and local governments became ever more conflictual and confrontational. Traditional assumptions that 'local government' was a rather boring, humdrum topic, of little interest or significance to ordinary people, politicians or academics, were rendered obsolete. The Thatcher Governments' commitment to 'rolling back the state' and extending market forces made conflict with local government virtually inevitable; what was, perhaps, surprising was the scope of the changes which ministers sought to introduce, and the scale of the ensuing confrontations between central government and particular local authorities. Indeed, one policy in this area, namely the poll tax, was to prove instrumental in the downfall of Margaret Thatcher herself, so much bitterness and hostility did it arouse.

The Thatcher Governments harboured five main objections to local government in Britain:

1   Economically, it was considered to be costly and inefficient. Labour-controlled local authorities in particular were accused of being extravagant and profligate in their spending of ratepayers' money. Local government generally was viewed as a major burden on public expenditure, for example, in 1978–9, 44 per cent of local government income was derived from grants from central government. Reducing the scope and scale of local government was thus perceived to be a vital means of achieving a reduction in public expenditure generally.

2   Politically, there was deep concern at the policies and activities of many Labour-controlled authorities, particularly those who, during the mid-1980s, were committed to tackling racism and sexism in their communities. The exaggerations of the Thatcher Governments, and the fabrications of the tabloid press, concerning the measures invoked by certain Labour councils in order to tackle discrimination and disadvantage led to coinage of the term 'loony Left'. The Government and its allies in the media ridiculed and reviled the principles and policies of such Labour councils, leading people to believe that one would not be allocated a job or house unless one was a disabled vegetarian single-parent lesbian from an 'ethnic minority' background. With many voters only too willing to accept at face value these depictions of life under 'loony Left' councils – and encouraged to believe that this was what life would be like generally under a Labour government – the Thatcher Governments were

able to pursue a radical approach to the reform and reduction of local government. The onslaught against 'municipal socialism' thus became an integral part of Margaret Thatcher's avowed objective of eliminating socialism from Britain altogether.

3   Local authorities enjoyed a monopoly of the provision of services, such as education, which thus allowed for no choice to the users (customers) of those services. Not only was this a basic denial of freedom of choice – a cardinal principle of Thatcherism – it also meant that there was little incentive to improve quality, because the local authorities did not face any competition in the provision of such services. Local government was largely immune to the market forces which shaped the functioning of the private sector.

4   Following on from this last point, the Thatcher Governments were inclined to view local government as inherently bureaucratic, and thus cumbersome, inefficient, and over-staffed, in much the same way as the Civil Service was deemed to be. Incorporating the 'public choice' school of political economy, the Thatcher Governments were inclined to see local authorities and their officials as self-serving 'empire builders', forever seeking to maximize their powers and budgets, with little regard for the communities and citizens they were supposed to serve: 'Local officials were seen as drones, placing their own career prospects before . . . their clients and the beleaguered taxpayers' (Kingdom 1991: 153).

5   There was concern that the nature of local authority finance and democracy was such that those who supported, or benefited from, the provision of costly services at local level were often not the same people who actually contributed the most towards them. In other words, the poor could vote for a high-spending (Labour) council safe in the knowledge that the high(er) rates necessary to finance local services would be paid mainly by the middle class, whose property was ascribed a higher rateable value, and who thus bore the brunt of rate increases, whilst also being ineligible for rate rebates themselves. For Thatcherites, therefore, local government could be criticized on similar grounds to progressive taxation generally – the rich and financially successful were 'penalized' in order to subsidize and support the less well off. Not only was this deemed grossly unfair on the well-to-do middle class, it was also considered to constitute a disincentive to the poor to become more responsible and self-reliant. Local government itself was helping to foster

a 'dependency culture'. For all of these reasons, therefore, the Thatcher Governments viewed local government with unconcealed contempt, thereby rendering confrontation inevitable.

This confrontation, however, was greatly compounded by the afore-mentioned pursuit of 'municipal socialism' by a number of left-wing Labour controlled councils during the mid-1980s, entailing the pursuit of policies and patterns of expenditure which were fundamentally at odds with Thatcherite principles and objectives. The multi-faceted nature of the problem which local government posed the Thatcher Governments was, not surprisingly, met by a multi-faceted response. A number of measures, therefore, were invoked to reduce the role and power of local government.

Competitive tendering

Legislation such as the 1980 Local Government Planning and Land Act, and the 1988 Local Government Act, compelled local authorities to put a range of services out to 'competitive tender'. This meant that private firms were to be allowed to apply to provide services such as road maintenance, refuse collection and street cleaning, with local authorities expected to 'tender' these services out to those firms offering the most cost-effective (i.e. cheapest) service.

The Thatcher Governments were emphatic that the private sector could provide local-level services much more efficiently and cheaply than the local authorities themselves, and to this extent, competitive tendering was envisaged as an important means of reducing the financial burden of local government, both for central government, and for ratepayers.

Deregulation

This particular policy was mainly carried out in the sphere of locally pro-vided public transport, most notably bus services. Prior to deregulation, bus services had been operated mainly by local authorities themselves, and often with cheap fares subsidized out of the rates. Deregulation, however, made it easier for private companies to provide passenger services either in competition with, or instead of, local authority transport provision. Furthermore, from 1985, local authorities which continued to operate their own public transport services were required to transform themselves into private companies operating on a commercial basis; they would no longer subsidize local public transport, such as bus services, with ratepayers' money. Once again, the Thatcher Governments' rationale was that deregulation would yield further savings in local government finance, whilst simultaneously providing passengers – now termed 'customers' – with a choice of services.

Opting-out

This policy applies mainly to schools, which had traditionally been the responsibility of local education authorities. The 1988 Education Reform Act endowed schools with the right to 'opt out' of local (education) authority control and be run 'independently', with funding received direct from central government. The decision on whether a school should 'opt out' was to be taken by parents through a secret ballot.

Encouraging 'Enabling Authorities'

The reforms just highlighted were not merely intended to reduce the political powers and economic costs of local government in Britain, important though those objectives were. They were also part of the Thatcherite objective of changing the very character and purpose of local government. Not only did the Thatcher Governments (and the Major Governments subsequently) seek to minimize the role, functions and powers of local government, it was also intended that they would become 'enablers' rather than direct providers of services. For example, in the case of social services, this meant that local authorities would be expected to arrange and 'buy in' services provided by the private and voluntary sectors, instead of actually providing these services themselves, 'replacing the idea that local government provided services with the idea that it merely co-ordinated their provision by others . . . Instead of providing services the local authority merely arranges for the job to be done by others' (Kingdom 1991: 44, 253–4). This was also part of the Thatcherite strategy of reducing dependency on the state – in this case, the *local* State.

However, the most controversial aspect of the local government reforms pursued by the Thatcher Governments during the 1980s proved to be the community charge, more commonly known as the poll tax. Indeed, so significant was it, in terms of both its rationale and its repercussions, that it undoubtedly warrants a section of its own.

The Community Charge (The 'Poll Tax')

Few issues or measures in post-war British politics have aroused such controversy or criticism as the community charge, or been associated so closely with one particular political figure. Indeed, the unpopularity and hostility engendered by the community charge was instrumental in bringing about Margaret Thatcher's downfall as Conservative Party leader and Prime Minister. The community charge subsequently earned the soubriquet 'the legendary débâcle of the Thatcherite administration' (King 1993: 196).

The community charge constituted a replacement of the traditional domestic rating system which had provided the basis of local government revenue-raising. The rates had been based on a formula which – among other things – calculated a notional or hypothetical rental value of a property; how much rent could be charged for such a property if it were to be let to private tenants. From this notional figure, and various others, the annual domestic rate for each household was calculated, and then paid to the local authority.

Whilst the domestic rates had never been popular, they were particularly disliked by the Thatcher Governments for three particular reasons. Firstly, wealthy home-owners invariably paid more in rates than those in more modest property. Thatcherite principles deemed this to constitute a financial penalty on the hard-working, successful, and wealthy, in a similar manner to the imposition of high rates of income tax on those earning large salaries. In any case, a 'tax' on property – particularly one which was higher on more expensive properties – was deemed ill at ease with the Conservative objective of encouraging a 'property-owning democracy'.

Secondly, the Thatcher Governments objected to the fact that whilst the less well-off paid lower rates – and often no rates at all if they were entitled to 100 per cent rebate by virtue of being on a low income – they tended to make greater use of public services, or, at least, enjoyed various concessions, again by virtue of being on low incomes. In Thatcherite eyes, those who paid least often received most in return. The wealthy were being compelled to subsidize the less well-off; once again, wealth was being redistributed from the rich to the poor – anathema to the Thatcher Governments.

Thirdly, it was alleged that because the less well-off paid little or nothing by way of the rates, they had no incentive to vote 'responsibly' in local elections – i.e. to vote for low-spending councils. Instead, it was argued, the poor could vote for high-spending local councils, secure in the knowledge that the higher rates necessary to finance 'their' public services would be borne mainly by the better off. The domestic rates system, therefore, was seen to undermine individual responsibility amongst the poorer sections of society, whilst penalizing the well-off and suburban home owners.

The poll tax was seen by the Thatcher Government as a solution to these 'problems'. Introduced in England and Wales in 1990 (having been implemented in Scotland a year earlier), the poll tax enshrined the principle that every adult in a district ought to pay exactly the same towards local government and the services that they provided or 'bought-in' from private contractors. Local authorities would calculate their financial requirements to cover expenditure for the next financial year, and then simply divide that amount by the number of adults living in the area served by that local authority. The figure arrived at would constitute the poll tax to be paid that year by each adult resident in the district.

With local government financed on this basis, the Thatcher Government reckoned, no longer would the rich be subsidizing the poor, and the less well-off themselves would become cognizant of the costs of local government and the services provided. This in turn, it was envisaged, would discourage the less well-off from voting for high-spending Labour councils in local elections, and instead, persuade them of the virtues of having a financially prudent Conservative council. As in so many other policy areas, therefore, political considerations and calculations were inextricably intertwined with the economic ones.

Yet the poll tax proved to be a major political blunder, and played a significant part in Margaret Thatcher's eventual downfall. People might have disliked the domestic rates, but many of them disliked the poll tax much more. The intellectual and political arguments advanced by the Thatcher Government in support of the poll tax fell on deaf ears.

The poll tax engendered widespread and passionate opposition, even amongst many Conservatives. As a leading 'one nation' Conservative critic commented, 'the community charge embodied every known feature of a bad tax. It was wholly unfair . . . it was expensive; it was difficult to collect.' Furthermore, the community charge 'would effectively destroy what remained of the independence of local government' (Gilmour 1992: 219, 263). It also effectively destroyed Margaret Thatcher's authority, so great was the widespread, cross-party opposition the 'poll tax' engendered among voters the length and breadth of Britain.

In addition to the political repercussions, there were also – as Gilmour intimated – the financial costs and administrative problems associated with implementing and collecting the community charge. The fact that the community charge was to be paid by 38 million people (compared to 14 million paying the domestic rates) itself more than doubled the administrative costs, whilst merely setting up the system cost about £270 million. However, it was non-payment which proved most problematic for local authorities, and ultimately the Government. During the 1990/91 financial year (the year in which the community charge was introduced in England and Wales), the non-payment rate in England was 7 per cent, whilst in Scotland it reached 16 per cent. Yet non-payment itself left local authorities with two possible solutions: either to increase the community charge for the majority who *were* paying it, thereby increasing its unfairness and unpopularity (as well as possibly leading to even further non-payment), or to instigate legal proceedings against non-payers, a process which was itself costly and cumbersome to go through. The latter remedy also meant adding further to the case-loads of the courts, who might therefore need to employ extra staff to cope – thus increasing administrative costs still further. Furthermore, the problem of non-payment was accompanied by the problem of keeping track of the movement of so many people, due to tenants moving to new addresses, for example, particularly in the larger cities (Stoker 1991: 189–99). According to one estimate, about 38 per cent of names on the community charge register would need to be changed during the first year of operation (*The Times*, 14 January 1991). For a variety of reasons, therefore, about £1 billion (10 per cent of the total due) remained unpaid by early 1991. By this time, the Conservative Government, now led by John Major, had already acknowledged the folly of the community charge.

Labour's Policy Review

In the wake of a third successive general election defeat in 1987, the Labour Party embarked upon a fundamental review of its principles and policies (just as the Conservatives had done two decades previously). The review raised certain questions which had first confronted the Labour Party thirty years earlier, in the late 1950s, concerning both its identity – socialist or social democratic? class-based or catch-all? – and apparent changes in the socio-economic structure of British society, which indicated that the traditional working class was dwindling, whilst a new working class was emerging, and the middle class was expanding. The old embourgeoisement thesis, so beloved of sociologists in the late 1950s, was dusted down and given a new airing.

Responding to the view that the 1983 and 1987 election defeats had been occasioned by the electorate's perception of the Labour Party as being 'out-of-date' in its attitudes, and 'too left-wing' in its policies and objectives, the Policy Review sought to provide Labour with more modern, popular policies and, *inter alia*, a more voter-friendly image. Seven review groups were established, comprising members of the Shadow Cabinet and the National Executive Committee (including a number of senior trade union officials).

The main proposals of the seven review groups were outlined in Labour's 1989 policy document, *Meet the Challenge, Make the Change*. The main subject headings, and the policy proposals made under them, were as follows.

1 A productive and competitive economy

There was a clear acceptance by Labour of a market economy, for this was deemed to provide the best means of creating wealth and distributing products. However, the need for government regulation was also emphasized, to ensure that social needs and the national interest were not neglected or jeopardized by predominantly private economic activity and monopolies. None the less, this section of *Meet the Challenge, Make the Change* evinced a definite toning down of Labour's former commitment – in principle – to nationalization and public ownership. Modernization and regulation, not outright ownership and control, were clearly deemed to be more important – and electorally viable, although *some* public ownership of key utilities was not ruled out.

2   People at work

The commitment to full employment was retained, to be achieved partly through improved and more extensive training. There was also a pledge to provide a comprehensive framework of employment rights, along with a commitment to the introduction of a statutory minimum wage. On the other hand, many of the Conservative Governments' trade union reforms would be retained, such as the prohibition of the closed shop, and the provisions on ballots *vis-à-vis* strike action and the election of union leaders. One area of industrial relations where a divergence from Conservative legislation was evident concerned Labour's proposal to permit some forms of 'secondary' or 'sympathy' action.

3   Economic equality

In addition to the introduction of a minimum wage, Labour's Policy Review proposed reform of tax levels, with the top rate being increased to 50 per cent for the higher paid, and some bands of less than 20 per cent for the lower paid. There was also a pledge to increase old age pensions (by £8 per week for a married couple) and child benefit. The proposals for a statutory minimum wage, and improved pensions and child benefit, were to constitute the building of 'pathways out of poverty', which in turn would lead to *less* reliance and dependency on the state.

4   Consumers and the community

A new Department of Consumer Affairs was proposed. It was also maintained that 'the market' offered little effective choice for those on low incomes, and thus the state would need to assume a major responsibility in certain policy areas, such as education and health, particularly as such areas were considered somewhat inappropriate for the operation of 'the market'. Meanwhile, a Quality Commission was mooted in order to monitor and improve standards in the provision of public sector services.

5   *The individual and the community*

Mainly focusing on constitutional matters, this section proposed that the House of Lords be replaced by an elected second chamber, with elections possibly being on a regional basis.

Also suggested was state funding of political parties, coupled with limits on the amount which they could spend during general election campaigns. Although Scotland was promised devolution, the decision on a Welsh Assembly was deferred.

The Policy Review also proposed the creation of ten new elected regional authorities in England. These would assume some of the functions hitherto performed by Whitehall.

6   *The physical and social environment*

On the basis that 'the environment' is an issue which cannot simply be left to market mechanisms, the Policy Review suggested that a Minister for Environmental Protection be appointed, coupled with an Environmental Protection Executive which would operate as a kind of 'Green Watchdog'. Reference was also made to 'green' tax incentives, which would be used to encourage consumers to buy environmentally friendly products.

7   *Britain in the world*

The commitment to unilateral nuclear disarmament was abandoned in favour of a multilateral policy, one which sought the attainment of a nuclear-free world by the year 2000. Meanwhile, it was pledged that a Labour Government would not proceed with the construction or completion of a fourth Trident submarine, although the existing three would be retained, but included in disarmament talks.

With regard to the European Community, *Meet the Challenge, Make the Change* was decidedly delphic, calling for 'a Community which promotes economic growth, creates jobs, and forces industrial and technological advance' whilst simultaneously giving a strong priority to social and regional concerns, and protection of the environment. Such objectives were to be attained through greater co-operation between the member states. Meanwhile, a new European Community Affairs

Grand Committee was proposed, which would provide the House of Commons with a more systematic and effective means of scrutinizing EC politics with regard to their application to Britain. Labour subsequently incorporated a call for a strengthening of the European Parliament.

Published in May 1989, *Meet the Challenge, Make the Change* was given final, formal approval at the Labour Party's annual conference in October. This approval was very much a formality, the policy documents a *fait accompli* (Garner 1990: 31). Not only had the proposals been widely publicized, and supported in speeches by the party leadership, throughout the period of the Policy Review, they were also supported by the overwhelming majority of delegates – most importantly, the trade union delegates – at the annual conference. In any case, delegates were only presented with the option of accepting or rejecting *Meet the Challenge, Make the Change* in its entirety. Not surprisingly, in the aftermath of three consecutive general election defeats and the evident electoral unpopularity of radical left-wing policies, Labour's annual conference overwhelmingly endorsed *Meet the Challenge, Make the Change*.

Conservatives and the Economy in Trouble

During 1987 and early 1988 there was widespread economic optimism, as Britain experienced a credit boom, fuelled by tax cuts in the 1987 budget, and financial deregulation, which served to make it easier for people to borrow money from banks and building societies This period also witnessed large and rapid increases in house prices, as the easy availability of finance, coupled with low interest rates (the base rate down to 7 ½ per cent in May 1988), encouraged many to make property purchases. Indeed, as property values initially rocketed, many first-time buyers feared that if they did not buy also, then house prices would soon be out of their reach for ever. Thus the boom in property prices was fuelled further by first-time buyers over-committing themselves financially in order to obtain mortgages and gain a foothold on the lower rungs of the housing ladder.

During the course of 1988, the economy went into rapid decline. The inevitable overheating of the economy engendered by tax cuts, easy credit and soaring property prices resulted in rising inflation, which in turn led to the Chancellor, Nigel Lawson, having to raise interest rates. This had a number of consequences. Firstly, as the economy degenerated into recession, so unemployment once again began rising, having fallen slightly during the mid-1980s. Moreover, much of this resurgent unemployment was affecting the white-collar middle class in the South of England. Once assured of jobs for life, those such as accountants, bank clerks and estate agents suddenly found that they too were being made redundant, as the term 'job shedding' entered the vocabulary of the financial services sector in 'the City'. Many of those who had been used to clasping a Pimms suddenly found themselves clutching a P45.

Secondly, the increase in interest rates (up to 15 per cent by October 1990) had a disastrous impact on the housing market. Previously rocketing property prices began to plummet. By the early 1990s another phrase had entered the English language, 'negative equity', whereby home-owners found that their properties were now worth less than they had paid for them. This phenomenon was particularly distressing for those who bought their property at the peak of the house price boom, for the subsequent slump in the market value of their homes meant that they carried the largest amount of 'negative equity'. This clearly had serious implications for those who wished to sell their property, for the amount they would receive from selling would, in many cases, be several thousand pounds less than the amount of their mortgage. Quite literally, many home-owners found that they could not afford to sell their homes.

A third consequence of the rise in interest rates was that many home-owners found their monthly mortgage payments escalating, thus causing them considerable financial hardship. Indeed, by the early 1990s, thousands of homes were being repossessed because of the inability of their purchasers to maintain the mortgage payments, or pay off the arrears which they had accrued.

The economic downturn, reflected in the factors just outlined, had serious political consequences. As the economic situation deteriorated, so too did the popularity of the Conservative Government. Having won the 1987 general election with 42.3 per cent of the vote, by the spring of 1990 – when the poll tax came into effect in England and Wales – Conservative support in opinion polls had slumped to 30 per cent. In the 1989 Euro-elections, the Conservative Party lost thirteen of its seats to the Labour Party, so that it held 32 seats to Labour's 45. The Green Party, meanwhile, received 15 per cent of the vote, although it won no seats. The Conservative defeats in the Euro-elections occurred just three months after Labour had won a by-election in mid-Staffordshire with a swing of 21 per cent, whilst in October 1990, a by-election in traditionally Tory Eastbourne witnessed a Conservative majority of over 17,000 transformed into a 4,550 majority for the Liberal Democrats. The impact of this result can hardly be exaggerated. 'Eastbourne . . . helped to convince a sizeable proportion of the party that Mrs Thatcher's style of leadership and the preservation of the poll tax were unlikely to give the Conservatives a realistic prospect of victory at the next election' (Stevenson 1993: 111).

Margaret Thatcher's Resignation

Margaret Thatcher had periodically suffered from unpopularity and rumours of imminent downfall throughout the 1980s, yet had always managed to restore her authority, if not her popularity. At the end of 1981, many senior Conservatives – particularly 'the Wets' – believed that her days were numbered, in the face of unpopular public expenditure cuts, inner-city riots, rapidly rising unemployment, and plummeting ratings in opinion polls, yet a few months later, the victory of British troops in the Falklands War transformed her into a highly popular leader, which, in turn, played a major role in helping to secure victory in the 1983 general election. Meanwhile, in 1986, the resignation of Defence Secretary Michael Heseltine, following disagreements with Cabinet colleagues over the future of the Westland helicopter company, and his allegations about her style of leadership and conduct in Cabinet, once again placed Margaret Thatcher's premiership in a precariously balanced position, although she managed to recover, and thus led the Conservatives to a third successive general election victory the following year. However: 'By November 1990, actions and circumstances were conspiring against Mrs Thatcher' (Wickham-Jones and Shell 1991: 337).

Many of these factors have already been acknowledged, most notably the rapid deterioration of the economy at the end of the 1980s (entailing rapidly rising interest rates and 'white-collar' unemployment), the deep unpopularity of the 'poll tax' and Labour's revival in popularity, as evinced in numerous opinion polls. However, what compounded Margaret Thatcher's unpopularity amongst many Conservatives was her antipathetical attitude towards closer political and institutional ties between Britain and the European Community, ties which went rather beyond the establishment of an internal (free) market for capital, goods and services.

In October 1989, Margaret Thatcher re-appointed Sir Alan Walters as her personal economic adviser. Sir Alan was known to be condemnatory of Nigel Lawson's positive policy towards the Exchange Rate Mechanism, but more importantly, Margaret Thatcher was widely thought to share Sir Alan's opinion. This clearly created tension between the Prime Minister and her Chancellor, with Lawson threatening to resign if Thatcher refused to dismiss Sir Alan. Thatcher did refuse, and so Lawson did resign, arguing that his position had become 'untenable'. Ironically, Sir Alan then resigned also, thereby further undermining Margaret Thatcher's authority and credibility. As with Heseltine's resignation in 1986, Thatcher's style of leadership was called into question, as was the tenability of her own position.

Indeed, December 1989 saw a 'stalking-horse' candidate, Sir Anthony Meyer, challenge Margaret Thatcher's leadership of the Conservative Party, and although he only received 33 votes (with a further 27 MPs abstaining or spoiling their ballot papers), it was considered by many commentators and Conservatives to have provided a distinct warning to Mrs Thatcher that she – and things generally – could not continue in the same way. Thatcherites themselves were inclined to emphasize the size of her majority over Sir Anthony as evidence of her popularity and security as Conservative leader, but other Conservatives took the view that if a 'no-hope' candidate such as Sir Anthony could deprive Mrs Thatcher of 60 votes, how many votes might accrue to a 'serious' leadership candidate – such as Michael Heseltine?

The answer was provided a year later. In November 1990, in the wake of the Eastbourne by-election defeat, Sir Geoffrey Howe – having already been publicly humiliated by Margaret Thatcher when she had removed him from the Foreign Office, and half-heartedly granted him the 'non-post' of Deputy Prime Minister in the summer of 1989 – resigned from the Cabinet, largely due to his disagreement with Thatcher's stance towards Europe. Thatcherites sought to downplay the significance of Sir Geoffrey's resignation, claiming that it was ultimately a disagreement over policy style, rather than substance. However, this merely served to antagonize Sir Geoffrey even further, to the extent that he made a devastating 'resignation speech' from the back-benches of the House of Commons, in which he made the most thinly veiled call for a leadership challenger to come forward when he declared that 'the time has come for others to consider their own response to the tragic conflict of loyalties with which I myself have wrestled for perhaps too long' (HC Debates, 13 November 1990). From this moment all eyes turned expectantly to Michael Heseltine, widely acknowledged to be 'the man most likely to'. Yet in fact, Heseltine was placed in something of an awkward situation. If he declared his candidature, he would be accused by many Conservatives, at both parliamentary and constituency level, of rank disloyalty and treachery against Margaret Thatcher. Yet if he declined to put his name forward for election, Heseltine would be accused – not least by Thatcherites themselves – of cowardice, and of lacking the courage of his convictions.

It was the former course of action which Heseltine opted for, declaring himself a leadership candidate the day after Sir Geoffrey's devastating resignation speech. One of Heseltine's advantages, it seemed, was that not having held ministerial office since 1986, he was free of the collective responsibility which Cabinet colleagues had to share for unpopular policies, such as the poll tax. Indeed, Heseltine shrewdly made the poll tax one of the central issues of his leadership campaign, pledging that if he were to be elected, he would fundamentally review the tax, presumably with a view to replacing it altogether. This was clearly intended to place ministers on the defensive, for as they were 'collectively' responsible for the introduction of the poll tax, they could hardly disavow it, and admit that it was misconceived.

In focusing on the unpopularity of the poll tax, Heseltine was also seeking to persuade Conservative back-benchers that if Margaret Thatcher and the poll tax were still in place at the next general election, then the accompanying unpopularity of both could have serious consequences for their own chances of re-election in their constituencies. In a skilful and subtle manner, Heseltine sought to convince Conservative MPs that their own self-interest would best be served by electing him as leader of the Conservative Party. Failure to do so, he intimated, would lead to many of them suffering from the imminent electoral backlash against Margaret Thatcher and the poll tax.

By contrast, once Heseltine had declared his candidature, it was Margaret Thatcher who was placed on the defensive, not least because she was so widely and publicly identified with the despised poll tax. However, what further compounded her vulnerability was the recognition, not least among some of her own supporters in the parliamentary Conservative Party, that anything other than an overwhelming victory would grievously undermine her own authority and credibility as leader; if her victory was a narrow one, then it would merely highlight the nature and depth of the division in the parliamentary party, and indicate that a very large minority of Conservative MPs did not support her continued leadership.

Indeed, the result of the first ballot revealed that Margaret Thatcher had received the support of 204 Conservative MPs, whilst Heseltine won 152 votes: 55 to 41 per cent. However, because the Conservative Party leadership election rules stipulate that a candidate requires a majority of 15 per cent in order to be elected, it was evident that Margaret Thatcher's lead over Heseltine was four votes short of outright victory. A second ballot would be necessary.

Margaret Thatcher's immediate decision to proceed to the second ballot caused considerable consternation amongst many of her own supporters and ministerial colleagues. There was a view that with the margin so close, and some Conservatives likely to switch their votes to Heseltine in the second ballot, Thatcher would better serve the party (and the country) by standing down, thereby permitting other candidates to come forward in an attempt to prevent Heseltine's election as Conservative leader and Prime Minister. According to this perspective (subscribed to by many Conservatives who had voted for her in the first ballot): 'Mrs Thatcher's continued participation in the contest could only prove disastrous for the party: she might either scrape a narrow victory and limp on, having lost the confidence of the party, or lose and allow Heseltine to become Prime Minister' (Alderman and Carter 1991).

On 21 November, Margaret Thatcher returned earlier than scheduled from a meeting which she had been attending in Paris, in order to elicit the opinions of ministerial colleagues, whom she interviewed individually. Whilst most of them pledged their personal support, they also advised her that she could not win, and that standing down would therefore be the best course of action in the circumstances, thereby enabling a ministerial colleague to stand against Heseltine.

At 9 a.m. on 22 November, Margaret Thatcher informed the Cabinet of her decision to stand down, thus freeing Douglas Hurd and John Major to enter the second ballot alongside Heseltine. The result of this ballot, held on 27 November, was John Major 185 votes, Michael Heseltine 131 and Douglas Hurd 56. Although technically John Major narrowly lacked the straightforward majority required in the second round ballot, Heseltine and Hurd stood down, thereby allowing him formally to become leader of the Conservative Party – and of the country.

The Pursuit of Post-
Thatcherism (1990–4)

> The creatures outside looked from pig to man, and from man to pig,
> and from pig to man again; but already it was impossible to say which
> was which.
>
> George Orwell, *Animal Farm*

Major – A New Style and Direction?

John Major was always going to have an extremely difficult task in
succeeding Margaret Thatcher as Conservative Party leader and Prime
Minister. Many of his colleagues had voted for him on the basis that he
was Thatcher's own choice to replace her, and as such, it was envisaged
that he would seek to continue the ideological objectives and policies
pursued by Thatcher. Once elected, therefore, he was highly likely to
attract criticism within the Conservative Party whatever he said or did. If
Major sought to implement 'Thatcherite' policies, he would alienate the
Left of the Conservative Party who would wonder why they had gone to
the trouble of ditching Thatcher in the first place. Yet, if Major sought
to don the mantle of 'one nation' Toryism, he would be castigated by the
Right of the Conservative Party for betrayal of their Thatcherite vision.
Of course, if Major sought a middle course between the two wings of the
Conservative Party, he was liable to be accused of all round dithering,
of lacking any real sense of leadership. In fact, Major has variously been
criticized on all three accounts and it is partly the degree and scope of
criticism he has attracted which reinforces the image of a weak indecisive
leader lacking in any definitive sense of purpose or principles.

As the above comments imply, John Major has evinced a number
of styles and strategies, some of them appearing rather contradictory
or at odds with each other, and this has compounded criticisms of a

lack of coherence or clear strategy. For example, in some respects, Major has sought to prove his Thatcherite credentials by preparing the privatization of British Coal and British Rail, pressing ahead with radical reforms of the Civil Service, introducing further trade union legislation, adopting a tough, nationalistic stance *vis-à-vis* Europe, and launching a 'back to basics' campaign which sought a return to traditional morality, respect for authority and the restoration of social discipline. Yet, in other respects, Major appeared to be seeking a more consensual mode of politics, one generally associated with the 'one nation' Toryism which had enjoyed hegemony in the parliamentary Conservative Party for most of the post-war era up until the mid 1970s. Thus, did Major preside over the replacement of the poll tax by the council tax, seek greater consultation with various bodies and interested parties over proposed reform of local government, and emphasize his 'social liberalism' – the 1992 Conservative manifesto contained a notable passage on 'responsibility for others'. Indeed, seekers of evidence that Major represented a change in ideology away from Thatcherism made much of his avowed goal of creating 'a nation at ease with itself'. This was widely perceived as indicative of Major's intention of pursuing gentler, more conciliatory policies than his predecessor. On the other hand, more cynical souls were inclined to recall Margaret Thatcher's speech in front of 10 Downing Street after her 1979 general election victory when she had quoted words (incorrectly) attributed to St Francis of Assisi: 'where there is discord, may we bring harmony'. This proclamation was later deemed by Jim Prior to be the 'most awful humbug' and critics would doubtless pass a similar verdict on John Major's plea to create 'a nation at ease with itself', particularly as the 1990s have witnessed not only the continuation of high unemployment, but its spread into the hitherto safe white-collar professional sections of British society, coupled with numerous reports and surveys showing that not only has the gap between rich and poor widened significantly in recent years, but that the poorest 10 per cent have actually experienced a reduction in their share of national wealth (*The Guardian*, 3 June 1994).

One other manifestation of John Major's alleged departure from Thatcherism concerns his style of political leadership: in particular, his manner in conducting Cabinet meetings and working relations with his ministerial colleagues. Once again, it has been widely noted that Major was not autocratic or hectoring in the manner that he chaired

Cabinet meetings, but, instead, that he sought to restore collegiality and genuine discussion to the Cabinet room at 10 Downing Street. Indeed, it has been suggested that 'When John Major became Prime Minister it was as though he had read the text books on constitutional theory, had observed very closely the circumstances of Margaret Thatcher's downfall, and had come to the conclusion that he was going to do things differently' (King 1993: 63). Yet John Major's style of leadership cannot be understood solely either as a manifestation of his own personality and innate humility, or as a reaction against Thatcher's premiership and the backlash which that eventually engendered in the parliamentary Conservative Party, important though both of these factors undoubtedly are. What must also be considered are the ideological divisions and power struggles within the Conservative Party itself, and the attitudes and behaviour of the British electorate.

The Conservative Party under Margaret Thatcher's premiership had also been subject to divisions, both over general ideological direction and on specific policies, yet for most of the 1980s, Thatcher's critics on the left of the party did little but grumble amongst themselves over a glass of sherry, or make 'coded' criticisms through public speeches. Yet with the ideas of 'one nation' Tories discredited by the economic and political events and experiences of the 1970s, coupled with the enormity of Thatcher's parliamentary majorities, critics of Thatcher were largely unable – or unwilling – to create too many problems for her.

John Major has presided over a rather different situation, not least because it is largely from the Thatcherite Right of the Conservative Party that most criticism and opposition has emanated. For those who still mourn the demise of Margaret Thatcher, John Major has proved a disappointing, unreliable replacement. Many of those seeking a continuation of the 'Thatcherite revolution' have viewed Major as too much of a 'consolidator', someone who would see their primary objective as strengthening the (new) status quo, rather than seeking to continue – and surpass – the radical reforms of the 1980s. The Thatcherites' fear has been that Major would prove too willing to backtrack, thereby allowing the momentum and achievements of Thatcherism to dissipate. Hence, the Thatcherite wing of the Conservative Party has deemed itself duty-bound to maintain a constant pressure on Major to uphold the principles and policies of Thatcherism lest he betray them, either by design or default. Unlike the 'one nation' critics of Thatcher in the 1980s, the Thatcherite critics of Major in the 1990s have been emboldened by great ideological coherence and sense of purpose or mission. They also continue to enjoy the intellectual strength provided by pressure groups and 'think tanks' such as the Adam Smith Institute.

What has also made it extremely difficult for John Major to ignore his critics on the Thatcherite Right of the Conservative Party, at least since 1992, is the narrow parliamentary majority held by the Government. The 21-seat majority with which the Conservative Party was re-elected in April 1992 was much smaller than the size of the electoral victories enjoyed by Margaret Thatcher during the 1980s, and this rather weakened John Major's authority in the eyes of his critics. At the same time, it meant that he would be much more vulnerable to dangerous back-bench rebellions by his Thatcherite critics – dangerous in that they were far more likely to result in defeat for the Government than back-bench revolts in the 1980s (the 1986 Shops Bill apart). Consequently, John Major has constantly found himself trying to set out his own agenda while having to respond to agendas set by the Thatcherite wing of the Conservative Party. Not only has this compounded Major's difficulties in establishing his authority and providing a sense of strong leadership, it has also added to the difficulty of discerning just what Major himself actually believes in; if John Major makes a speech critical of Europe, for example, it is difficult to determine whether it genuinely reflects his personal views and policy preferences, or is really intended to assuage and appease his critics in the Bruges group.

The fact that John Major's Conservative Government was re-elected with a parliamentary majority of 'only' 21 seats in April 1992 brings us to consider the attitudes and behaviour of the British electorate, and the concomitant implications for the premiership of John Major. Whilst the Conservative victory in April 1992 was a surprise to most people – a small Labour majority or a 'hung' Parliament having been widely predicted – it none the less represented a loss of 40 seats for the Conservative Party compared to the 1987 election victory, with Labour *gaining* 42 seats. With the Labour Party having ditched most of its radical or 'left-wing' policies in the wake of the policy review instigated by Neil Kinnock, who had replaced Michael Foot as party leader in October 1983, there was a feeling amongst some Conservatives that British politics might be moving back towards the centre ground, and that much of the electorate was weary of Thatcherite radicalism (even if they were not yet willing to elect a Labour Government). It was such an analysis which led Douglas Hurd to warn, in a speech to the Tory Reform Group (a grouping on the left of the party) during the party's 1993 annual conference, that Conservatives should not pursue a Thatcherite 'permanent cultural revolution', nor continue giving the impression that they were motivated by dogma and malice towards the public sector and its institutions. He claimed that: 'We do not want to break the mould of every public service afresh in every parliament. We must show that we are not driven by ideology to question every function of the state.' To those on the right of the Conservative Party seeking to carry forward the mantle of Thatcherism, Hurd pointed out that: 'I do not find in the 1990s many people impressed by the argument that the principle of a public service is wrong.' Hence the party should refrain from 'looking at the problems of the 1990s with the language and ideas of the 1980s' (*The Times*, 8 October 1993).

If Major was in any doubt over the electorate's antipathy to further Thatcherite radicalism (and, in any case, we ought to remember that attitude surveys conducted during the 1980s indicated that on many issues, the electorate was *not* predominantly Thatcherite, and actually became even less so as the decade progressed), then the public demonstrations in support of the miners which followed the November 1992 announcement of a further 31 pit closures, and widespread public opposition to the privatization of British Rail, provided just two examples of the shape of public opinion in the early 1990s. Indeed, public and professional opposition to various Government proposals and policies for further reforms in British society led some Conservatives to complain about the conservatism of the British people!

Yet the Thatcherite Right of the Conservative Party maintained that apparent public disillusion with the Major Government, and the narrowness of its parliamentary majority, derived from its alleged or perceived lack of radicalism and sense of conviction. Rather like the Bennite Left in the Labour Party during the early 1980s, the Thatcherite Right in the Conservative Party during the early 1990s insisted that the loss of public or electoral support for the Conservatives could largely be explained in terms of the party's apparent betrayal of principles and its failure to continue providing strong, radical leadership. This perspective thus deemed it essential that the Conservative Party under John Major's leadership became more, not less, radical if it was to maintain and enhance its electoral support and political supremacy.

Such have been the conflicts and conundrums impinging upon John Major's premiership, particularly since 1992, and which have affected his ability to stamp his authority on the Government (and the country at large), as well as inhibiting the development of a clear unequivocal sense of his own policy objectives. In the 1980s everyone knew what Margaret Thatcher stood for and believed in; during the 1990s, few could say the same of John Major.

The 1992 General Election

As was noted in the previous chapter, a number of factors (economic mismanagement and recession, the community charge, the unpopularity of Margaret Thatcher and the more moderate policies and image presented by the Labour Party in the wake of the 'policy review') had, by 1990, provided Labour with a massive lead in repeated opinion polls – and thereby partly contributed to Thatcher's own downfall. When John Major replaced her in November 1990, the Conservative Party enjoyed a significant recovery in the opinion polls, partly because of John Major's more moderate, caring image and style, partly because this leadership change itself was perceived by some voters as tantamount to the election of a new government, and partly because of the pledge to replace the community charge. John Major's leadership during the Gulf War (which followed Iraq's invasion of Kuwait in August 1990, and which involved an international military campaign – including British troops – to liberate Kuwait) was also important in boosting his popularity in the country; indeed, by early 1991, Major's ratings in the opinion polls were higher than those for the Conservative Party itself.

However, after a brief 'honeymoon' period, Major found that the Labour Party was matching, and at times, leading, the Conservatives in the opinion polls, whilst the Liberal Democrats also increased their support – 19.4 per cent, for example, in May 1991. Economic recession was not only persistent (in spite of ministers repeatedly talking about the 'green shoots of recovery' which were ready to blossom) but affecting more than ever before the middle class Conservative heartland of the Home Counties and south-east England generally. It was no longer just coal miners and steel-workers being made redundant, but also chartered accountants and stockbrokers. As the next general election loomed, therefore, it looked highly probable that the Conservative Party would lose its parliamentary majority and be replaced by either a small Labour majority or a hung Parliament in which no party enjoyed an outright majority of seats. There was thus considerable surprise – not least amongst opinion pollsters – when the Conservatives actually won the 1992 general election, albeit with a (greatly reduced) majority of 21. Labour gained 42 more seats than in 1987, whilst the Liberal Democrats actually lost two seats.

The unexpected Conservative victory suggests that in spite of traditional claims to the contrary, election campaigns can – and in April 1992 did – make a decisive difference to the outcome. This in turn implies that in the 1992 general election, short-term factors were more important than long-term ones. Clearly, the Labour Party has been much more detrimentally affected by the dual phenomena of class and partisan dealignment, and the contraction of Britain's manufacturing heavy industries, and these obviously affected Labour's chances of winning in 1992. Yet the fact that Labour had been expected to obtain either a small parliamentary majority or the larger share of seats in a hung Parliament, tacitly indicated that the long-term socio-economic changes had not made the Labour Party unelectable; rather, they had made it more difficult for Labour to win – which is not quite the same thing, of course.

The 1992 general election result, therefore, and in particular the Conservative Party's surprise victory (or perhaps Labour's surprise defeat), can be best understood in terms of issues and events which manifested themselves during the four-week campaign itself. Indeed, one factor which has been seen as fundamental was the scale of the late swing to the Conservative Party amongst voters. Certainly the opinion pollsters themselves subsequently saw this as a major reason for their failure to predict the actual outcome accurately. A great many voters, it is argued, changed their minds at the last minute, so that rather than voting Liberal Democrat or Labour, they switched (back) to the Conservative Party. Certainly the Conservatives had expressly targeted wavering Tories contemplating the Liberal Democrats, warning them that to do so would allow Labour to 'get in through the back door'. This is likely to have weighed heavily on the minds of such 'waverers' when they were about to put pen to ballot paper inside the polling booth.

Another vital factor which might well have proved instrumental in ensuring a Conservative victory in 1992 was the issue of taxation, and if one accepts that there was a late swing to the Conservatives, then one is as likely to place great importance on their warnings – which were stepped up later in the campaign – of the increase in income tax which would result if Labour were elected. Conservative allegations that the election of a Labour Government would mean higher income tax being imposed on ordinary working people (rather than just the 'highest earners', as Labour claimed) were faithfully echoed and embellished by many tabloid newspapers: readers were regaled with dire warnings about what Labour's 'tax bombshell' would mean to them and their families.

However, a number of commentators have disputed whether there was really a large swing to the Conservatives at the end of the election campaign. Such sceptics of the late swing explanation suggest that, instead, opinion polls might not have accurately gauged the extent of Conservative support throughout the campaign, not least because the replies of the respondents were not always entirely honest. It has been claimed, for example, that some of those asked about their voting intentions feared that they might appear 'selfish' if they declared their intention to vote Conservative, and thus declared their support for the Liberal Democrats or Labour Party so as to seem more 'caring' or 'socially responsible'. Other voters may have used the opinion polls as a means of 'frightening' or 'chastising' the Conservative Government with regard to its performance in office (particularly *vis-à-vis* the economy and the community charge), whilst fully intending to vote for it on election day itself (Denver 1994: 163–4; Sanders 1993: 183–6).

One other group who may have been crucial in terms of the under-estimation of Conservative support in the 1992 election were the 'floating voters' or 'don't knows'. With the increase in dealignment has come an increase in 'uncommitted' voters, those who are not particularly aligned to any one political party, or who do not make a decision about who to cast their vote for until the last minute. Now it is reasonable to assume that such 'dealigned' or 'don't know' voters are those most likely to be influenced by the election campaign itself. In 1992, the Conservatives – and most of the tabloid press – launched a ferocious campaign against the Labour Party, not only regarding its tax plans, but more generally as well on its alleged lack of fitness and competence to govern Britain. In spite of the recession, high unemployment, high interest rates, etc. which Britain had experienced since 1979, the Conservative Party, and much of the press, still convinced many voters that the return to a Labour Government would spell economic disaster for the British people, due to higher taxes, increased interest rates, further unemployment, spiralling inflation and exorbitant wage demands as a consequence of 'restored' trade union power under a Labour administration. In other words, the Conservative Party managed to retain an image of greater economic competence than the Labour Party, to the extent that when asked by Gallup *immediately* after the 1992 election which party they thought was the most capable of handling Britain's economic problems, the response was 52–31 per cent in favour of the Conservatives. It is important to note, also, that many Conservative voters did not apportion too much blame on to John Major and his 1990–2 Government for Britain's economic recession, claiming instead that the responsibility lay either with the *world* recession, or with the policies pursued under Margaret Thatcher's premiership (in spite of the fact that, during the late 1980s, John Major had been Chancellor of the Exchequer!). Even when the Conservatives did apportion blame to the Major Government for Britain's economic problems in the early 1990s, they still maintained that his administration was best equipped to solve them, far more so than the Labour Party.

Other factors which also accounted for Labour's relatively poor performance included distrust of Neil Kinnock's suitability as a Prime Minister; compared to John Major's calm, reassuring 'bank manager' image, Kinnock was viewed with disdain by some voters for being too verbose and too volatile. This also fuelled doubts about his potential reliability and political judgement should he enter 10 Downing Street. Certainly the infamous Sheffield Rally held a week before the end of the campaign, when Kinnock appeared overly triumphant and confident due to a belief that Labour was about to return to office, alienated some voters and itself raised questions about Kinnock's political wisdom and judgement, and about whether he possessed the temperament for the post of Prime Minister.

To a considerable extent, the Conservative Party's victory in the 1992 general election, like its campaign in the preceding four weeks, was largely 'negative'. It was less an emphatic and resounding endorsement of a further five years of Conservatism than a dislike or distrust of the alternatives on offer. Certainly much of the tone of Conservative campaigning had been along the lines of 'things *are* bad under us, but they'd be a lot worse under Labour'. In other words the central message emitted by the Conservative Party throughout the run-up to the 1992 election, and one evidently endorsed by many voters, was 'better the devil you know . . . '

The Conservatives' victory in 1992 immediately raised questions about whether Labour could *ever* win a general election again, or whether Britain now had a system of one-party Government, instead of the pre-1974 two-party model entailing an alternation of power between Labour and the Conservative Party. If Labour could not win in 1992, it was wondered – when so many factors seemed to be in its favour and circumstances so propitious – then when, and in what sort of scenario, could it ever win?

Maastricht and Its Aftermath

The 1990s have not witnessed any diminution of the 'European issue' in British politics. Indeed, over 20 years after Britain's entry to the European Community, the country's relations with, and commitment to, the EC have continued to prove a source of heated debate and political division. As was noted in the previous chapter, it was 'the European issue' which played a significant part in bringing about Margaret Thatcher's downfall.

The issue of Britain's relationship with the EC (now the EU – European Union) has proved no less vexatious for John Major during his time as Conservative Party leader and Prime Minister, and his leadership also has occasionally looked precarious as a result. The 1990s have clearly illustrated the deep and damaging divisions which have riven the Conservative Party over the direction in which the EC/EU ought to move, and concomitantly, Britain's role within Europe.

Without doubt, the key issue concerning Britain's relationship with Europe in the 1990s has been – and remains – the Maastricht Treaty, formally signed in December 1991, and then referred to the twelve member states to be ratified, either through a parliamentary vote or via a referendum. The Maastricht Treaty (officially entitled the Treaty on European Union) both reflected previous moves towards closer European 'union' and integration, and sought to provide those moves with added impetus by expressly widening or increasing the range of issues and policies over which the European Union (as the EC was to be known) exercised jurisdiction. The Maastricht Treaty also increased further the policy areas which could be determined by qualified majority voting in the Council of Ministers, whilst also empowering the European Parliament to veto certain categories of proposed legislation. Of particular importance were the Maastricht Treaty's provisions on Economic and Monetary Union (EMU), for these stipulated a timetable, entailing three stages, for the creation – by 1999 at the latest – of a single currency, and the establishment of a European Central Bank.

It was these provisions which Britain – or more accurately, the Major Government – found so objectionable, and thus negotiated for Britain the right to opt out of the commitment to joining a single European currency in, or by, 1999; Britain would only join such a currency if Parliament voted in favour of doing so nearer the time. The objection to Britain joining a single European currency, and being bound by a Central European Bank, was that sovereignty would be fundamentally eroded, because economic decisions concerning interest rates, taxation and the like would be determined at supra-national level, rather than by the domestic Government. Given the crucial importance of economic policy to *any* Government, it was felt that committing Britain to stage three of EMU would constitute a major surrender of sovereignty and leave ministers bereft of much of their political power and authority. If politicians could no longer determine economic policies and strategies at domestic level, then what exactly could they do?

The other aspect of the Maastricht Treaty for which the Major Government negotiated an opt-out was the 'Social Chapter' which sought, among other things, to provide a minimum wage and a framework of employment rights for workers in the member states. Such provisions were deemed by the Major Government to be sharply at odds with the Conservatives' programme of deregulating the labour market, increasing flexibility and restoring 'management's right to manage'. The Social Chapter, the Major Government insisted, would increase labour costs to employers, making firms uncompetitive and thereby increasing unemployment. The proposals on greater consultation and partnership between employers and employees, meanwhile, were denounced not only for constituting an impediment to managerial authority, but also for enhancing the power and role of trade unions in the workplace. With regard to the Social Chapter's proposal for a minimum wage, this was clearly at odds with the Conservatives' insistence that wages should not (and could not) be determined politically or by legislation, but only through the unfettered operation of market forces, whereby the price of labour, like the price of any other commodity, would be determined by the economic laws of supply and demand.

One other very significant concession which John Major negotiated prior to signing the Maastricht Treaty concerned a key objective stipulated in a draft version, namely that: 'This Treaty marks a new stage in a process leading gradually to a Union with a federal goal.' In view of the Conservative Government's vehement opposition to the creation of a *federal* Europe, John Major was involved in protracted negotiations to have the shocking 'F-word' removed from the final draft of the Maastricht Treaty. Consequently the version finally signed by John Major in December 1991 proclaimed that: 'This Treaty marks a new stage in the process of creating an ever closer union among the peoples of Europe, in which decisions are taken as closely as possible to the citizen.'

For many, if not most, Conservatives, *federalism* is perceived or portrayed as a political system or institutional structure in which power is concentrated and decisions taken at the centre, whereupon they are imposed on the constituent regions or, in this case, member states. As such, a federal Europe would, in the eyes of many Conservatives, result in a further, and fatal, loss of British sovereignty, as ever more decisions and policies were determined in Brussels. Yet for most other member states of the European Union, this is not what federalism means. On the contrary, they – like any decent student of politics – would point out that federalism is concerned with decentralizing political power and decision-making, and empowering the regions, with the centre merely establishing a general framework, and retaining responsibility for policies in certain spheres. Hence Germany, Switzerland and the United States of America all have federal political systems, and are acclaimed precisely for the extent to which power and decision-making are decentralized to the Länder, cantons and individual states respectively. Thus the dispute between Britain and its European partners over the issue of federalism partly reflects different political cultures and traditions, and maybe even a different political vocabulary.

In spite of negotiating opt-outs for Britain over the third stage of EMU and the Social Chapter, as well as getting the word 'federal' removed from the final draft, John Major still experienced considerable difficulty in getting the Maastricht Treaty ratified in Parliament, due to the vehement and vocal opposition emanating from numerous Conservatives – widely dubbed 'Euro-sceptics'. Many such Conservatives were – and still are – to be found on the Thatcherite wing of the Conservative Party, and like their departed idol, they are in favour of the creation of a free trade area in Europe entailing the removal of legislative and institutional impediments to the free movement of goods, services and capital between member states, but are bitterly opposed to political or institutional integration, and to the imposition of a European social policy (of which the Social Chapter would be an integral component). Such Conservatives believe that in spite of the rewording negotiated by John Major, the Maastricht Treaty still heralds the development of a federal Europe, in which policies binding on member states will increasingly be formulated in Brussels, whilst a number of economic issues will eventually be determined by a European Central Bank. Such developments would, it is argued, result in a further, and fatal, loss of sovereignty, and render the British Parliament impotent. The British people would no longer be masters of their own destiny, the 'Euro-sceptics' warn, but instead, be bound by Brussels.

Of course, the Maastricht Treaty did not create the divisions in the Conservative Party over Europe, instead, it served to exacerbate and intensify those divisions which already existed. It served to confirm the fears and suspicions of the 'Euro-sceptics' about the drift of the European Community/Union and the direction in which it would inevitably lead, dragging Britain along with it, whilst also providing Conservative critics with a specific, more tangible, focus or target for their anti-Europeanism. All the fears and phobias which tormented the 'Euro-sceptics' were embodied in the Maastricht Treaty.

These divisions over the Maastricht Treaty became starkly apparent when the European Communities (Amendment) Bill, to ratify the Treaty, was debated and voted upon in Parliament after the Conservatives' 1992 election victory. Initially, it seemed as if John Major would not have too much trouble getting the Bill through, for it received its second reading by 336 votes to 92, with the Labour Opposition abstaining primarily because of the 'opt-out' over the Social Chapter. At this stage, only 22 Conservatives voted against their Government.

However, a referendum on the Maastricht Treaty was held in Denmark on 2 June, and yielded a narrow majority *against* acceptance. The consequences for the Major Government of the Danish 'No' vote were twofold. Firstly, it served to delay further consideration of the Bill until the autumn. Secondly, it both emboldened and swelled the ranks of the 'Euro-sceptics' wishing to defeat the Bill. The position of the 'Euro-sceptics' was subsequently strengthened by Britain's humiliating withdrawal from the Exchange Rate Mechanism on 16 September 1992.

By the time that the committee stage of the Bill commenced, over 400 amendments had been tabled by MPs opposed to the Maastricht Treaty. In view of the Conservatives' narrow parliamentary majority, and the opposition to the Maastricht Treaty of a significant minority of Conservative back-benchers, the committee stage (taken on the Floor of the House of Commons, involving all MPs, due to its constitutional importance) was a lengthy and fraught one for the Major Government.

At one point, the Government felt obliged – in order to avoid a defeat in the lobbies – to accept an amendment demanding that Parliament debate a resolution concerning the Social Chapter, before the Maastricht Treaty could finally be ratified. A motion endorsing the Government's stance *vis-à-vis* the Social Chapter was held on 22 July, whereupon the Labour Party tabled an amendment, demanding that ratification of the Maastricht Treaty should only take place after the Government had agreed to accept the Social Chapter. The vote on Labour's amendment resulted in a tied vote, 317 votes to 317, although in accordance with parliamentary precedent, the Speaker cast her vote in favour of the status quo, thus voting against the amendment, and thereby ensuring its defeat. Significantly, 15 Conservative MPs had voted in support of Labour's amendment, whilst at least seven abstained.

In the subsequent vote on the motion itself, the Government was defeated by 324 votes to 316, with 22 Conservative back-benchers voting against, and at least two abstaining. As things now stood, the Maastricht Treaty could not now be ratified, to the delight of the 'Euro-sceptics'. However, John Major then made the issue a vote of confidence: 'That this House has confidence in the policy of Her Majesty's Government on the adoption of the Protocol on Social Policy'. The significance of making it a vote of confidence was the constitutional convention that a government defeated in such a vote would resign, and call a general election. In adopting such a tactic, Major was effectively daring the 'Euro-sceptics' to bring down their own Government, and in so doing, pave the way for a Labour Government which would commit Britain to adoption of the Social Chapter. As Major calculated, the 'Euro-sceptics' were not willing to bear such a responsibility and the condemnation which they would attract, so that Major's motion was supported by 339 votes to 299. It had thus taken, in effect, a threatened dissolution of Parliament to ensure the ratification of the Maastricht Treaty.

Of course, the ratification of the Maastricht Treaty by no means meant an end to Conservative divisions over Europe. Indeed, ratification served to exacerbate the hostility of the 'Euro-sceptics', who subsequently posed a constant challenge to John Major's authority as Conservative leader and Prime Minister, not least by repeatedly seeking to mobilize public opinion – aided by the jingoism of most of the tabloid press – through speeches railing against federalism, the loss of sovereignty and alleged interference in domestic affairs by Brussels. Such speeches were clearly calculated to appeal to the xenophobia of the British people, painting a picture of Britain *versus* Europe, of a small, independent and democratic nation valiantly seeking to defend itself against absorption into Europe, and hence domination by 'foreigners'.

During 1994, there were a number of disagreements between Britain and its European partners, such as the issue of enlargement of the Union (through granting membership to more countries) and the implications this would have on Qualified Majority Voting in the Council of Ministers. The Major Government also vetoed, in June, the selection of Jean-Luc Dehaene (the Belgian Prime Minister) as the new President of the European Commission, arguing that he was a 'federalist', and represented 'a tradition of interventionism'. Consequently, another candidate had to be found, namely Jacques Santer, the Prime Minister of Luxembourg, who was unanimously endorsed by all twelve member states in mid-July. A further divergence between Britain and its European Union partners occurred in September when the recently appointed Employment Secretary, Michael Portillo, exercised Britain's opt-out from an EU initiative to extend paternity provision, claiming that it would impose intolerable costs on employers – particularly small businesses – and undermine the competitiveness of British industry.

With Portillo as Employment Secretary and John Major needing to continue assuaging the 'Euro-sceptics' on the Right of the Conservative

Party, it is apparent that Britain will remain an 'awkward partner' for some time to come. Indeed, as other member states seek to give effect to proposals for greater European integration and monetary union, as enshrined in the Maastricht Treaty, it is likely that Britain will find itself even more at odds with its European partners, and thus risk being left behind. At the same time, the 'European issue' is likely to maintain, and possibly deepen, the divisions in the Conservative Party, particularly in the run up to the 1996 Inter-Governmental Conference, at which the Maastricht Treaty will be subject to revision and amendments.

Civil Service Reform

Although the 'Next Steps' programme of Civil Service reform was unveiled in 1988, it is considered in this chapter because it is during the 1990s that it has been most extensively implemented, and its significance become even more apparent. Yet the 'Next Steps' represents the culmination of a series of Civil Service reforms pursued by the Conservative Governments since 1979. In accordance with 'New Right' principles generally, and the so-called 'public choice' school in particular, bureaucrats such as civil servants are seen as inherently inefficient, profligate and self-serving. With their salaries and other resources financed mainly from taxation, civil servants are then perceived as parasitic on ordinary taxpayers and a burden on the wealth-creating activities of private enterprise. At the same time, they are deemed to be immunized against the competitive ethos prevailing elsewhere, and this, coupled with a 'job-for-life' culture, militates against the need to become more efficient or productive. Finally, this 'New Right/public choice' perspective charged bureaucrats and civil servants with being 'resource maximizers' and 'empire builders', constantly seeking to expand their budgets and power yet claiming that the extra funding and facilities were for the benefit of the public they were serving.

For all these reasons (along with the fact that 'bashing bureaucrats' is always good for populist politicians pandering to public prejudice), the Conservative Governments since 1979 have sought to reform the British Civil Service in a number of ways, and through a variety of initiatives. Of course, it is evident that if the state is being 'rolled back', with nationalized industries being privatized and welfare provision curbed, then the diminution of the public sector ought to yield a concomitant reduction in the number of bureaucrats employed by Government.

The key initiatives and reforms which preceded the 'Next Steps' programme of Civil Service reform were as follows.

1   The abolition, in 1981, of the Civil Service Department, which had been established in 1968 in accordance with the proposals of the Fulton Report. The first Thatcher Government, however, suspected that the Civil Service Department – which had formally been responsible for supervising the management of the Civil Service – had come to see itself as a kind of pressure group serving the interests of the Civil Service itself, rather than simply managing it on behalf of the Government. In abolishing the Civil Service Department, the Thatcher Government transferred its managerial responsibilities to the Cabinet Office and the Treasury, thus enabling the Prime Minister to take a closer and more direct interest in the management of the Civil Service.

2   Reducing costs and increasing efficiency. When the first Thatcher Government entered office in 1979, the Civil Service comprised a staff of 732,000. By the end of 1991, the number of civil servants had been reduced to 554,000. Obviously, reducing the size of the Civil Service was a major means of cutting costs. Also concerned with seeking financial savings was the Efficiency Unit established in 1979, and located within the Cabinet Office. Initially headed by Sir Derek Rayner (a successful businessman and chairman of Marks and Spencer), the Efficiency Unit was charged with responsibility for examining specific aspects of the work carried out by Government departments to see whether they could be performed more effectively, and at less cost, or whether particular tasks were necessary in the first place. By early 1993, over 350 of these so-called 'Rayner scrutinies' had been carried out, yielding savings of £1.5 billion in administration costs (Burch 1993: 167).

3   Introducing the Financial Management Initiative (FMI), which itself was partly based on a Management and Information System for Ministers (MINIS) set up in the Department of the Environment by its then Minister, Michael Heseltine.

Established in 1982, the FMI sought to introduce links between departmental budgets for those managing Government departments. The intention was both to instil a greater managerial ethos into Government departments, and to expose the Civil Service to some of the market criteria hitherto associated with the private sector and the business community. This latter objective has been enhanced by the increased secondment of civil servants to (temporary) posts in business, commerce and industry.

The Next Steps

Significant though the above initiatives and reforms undoubtedly were, it is the 'Next Steps' programme embarked upon in 1988 which has proved to be most radical: 'the most far-reaching since the Northcote–Trevelyan reforms in the nineteenth century' (HMSO 1988: paragraph 1). These reforms were not only intended to change the organization and structure of the British·Civil Service, but also its whole culture, so as 'to establish a quite different way of conducting the business of government' (Efficiency Unit 1988: paragraph 44).

The 'Next Steps' programme was the outcome of a study of the functioning of the Civil Service, conducted by the Efficiency Unit under the leadership of Sir Robin Ibbs during the mid-1980s. Although a preliminary report was presented to Margaret Thatcher shortly before the 1987 general election, the whole matter was suppressed as far as possible at the time, due, it seems, to the controversial character of the recommendations contained therein. However, following the Conservatives' election victory, there was less need for reticence, and so in February 1988 a final draft of the report was published entitled *Improving Management in Government: The Next Steps.*

'The Next Steps' deemed that the existing organization and operation of the Civil Service was too much geared towards policy advice for ministers, with insufficient attention being paid to the management and delivery of services. The Civil Service was considered too big, and suffered from too much centralization. It was therefore recommended that: 'The Central Civil Service should consist of a relatively small core engaged in the function of servicing Ministers and managing departments . . . ' (Efficiency Unit 1988: paragraph 44). The remainder of the Civil Service, by contrast, was to be transformed into a series of 'agencies' which would be exclusively concerned with the delivery of services, albeit within a framework set by the appropriate Government department. These agencies were to be headed by 'chief executives' who would enjoy considerable autonomy regarding the day-to-day running of their agency, thereby enabling them significant discretion over such matters as staff recruitment and deployment.

By 1992, no fewer than 72 agencies had been created, employing almost 300,000 – over half of the Civil Service. This was well on the way to the Government's target of having 70–75 per cent of civil servants working in/for agencies by 1998. The largest agency to date has been the Benefits Agency, whose 63,000 staff are responsible for the administration and payment of social security, whilst the most controversial has been the Child Support Agency, established in April 1993 to collect child maintenance payments from 'absent fathers'.

The implementation of the 'Next Steps' has raised important constitutional questions about the relationship between ministers and the work of the agencies, particularly with regard to the traditional doctrine of 'individual ministerial responsibility'. This doctrine stipulates that Government ministers are ultimately responsible for the policies and practices of their departments, and of the staff employed therein. Admittedly, whilst no-one seriously expects a minister personally to take the blame for the mistake of a local clerical officer, for example, the doctrine has none the less long been deemed a cardinal principle of responsible and accountable government, with ministers required to defend and explain the activities of their department on the Floor of the House of Commons, and in the case of major mistakes, tender their resignation.

Yet with the 'chief executives' of the agencies being granted greater autonomy and authority for the day-to-day administration of activities of their agencies, the question is raised as to how far ministers can – or will – be held responsible for major errors or policy failures. Admittedly, the 'Next Steps' insisted that ministers were to be responsible for establishing the overall framework and policy objectives by which 'chief executives' and their agencies were to be bound. As such, 'chief executives' were to remain personally responsible to the minister of the appropriate Government department, who in turn would remain answerable to Parliament. Yet it is not too difficult to imagine instances where the 'chief executive' of an agency blames a failure on the inadequate or incompatible objectives laid down by the minister, whilst the minister insists that the objectives were clear and coherent, but not efficiently or effectively pursued by the 'chief executive'. With the implementation of the 'Next Steps' programme, it is not just the Civil Service which is in a state of flux, but a long-standing constitutional convention of British politics as well.

Economic Competence Challenged

The Conservative Party had won the 1992 election partly because of its reputation or image as *the* party of economic competence and financial rectitude. Whilst the Labour Party was widely seen (as it had been in the 1987 election also) as having the best policies on issues such as education, health and tackling unemployment, the Conservatives successfully convinced many voters that they alone could create or sustain the right conditions for economic growth, renewed prosperity, low interest rates and lower taxation. By the same token, the Conservative Party predicted dire economic consequences should a Labour Government be elected: panic in the city and a massive flight of capital out of the country, higher interest rates, profligate public spending, tax increases, and spiralling inflation fuelled by a return to trade union militancy and excessive wage demands. Meanwhile, the Conservatives warned, Labour's pledge to adopt the Social Chapter and its provisions for a statutory minimum wage would push up employers' labour costs, and thus result in higher unemployment. The Conservatives were emphatic: 'You can't trust Labour', they repeatedly told the British electorate. And as opinion polls and surveys invariably indicated, many voters did not trust Labour economically, even though they might have preferred Labour's social policies.

Yet since being re-elected in April 1992, the Major Government has found itself compelled to pursue and take decisions which have served to undermine its former reputation for economic competence. Trust in the Conservative Party's ability to manage the economy effectively has been seriously damaged, although this is not to say that at the next general election, the Conservatives will not have regained some of that trust, or at least be able to convince enough voters that they are still *more* trustworthy than the Labour Party on economic affairs. Three main events or factors have combined to tarnish the mantle of economic competence which the Conservative Party successfully donned in April 1992.

Firstly, and most generally, the economic recession has continued for much longer than Ministers suggested. Throughout the 1992 election campaign, the voters were told that 'green shoots of recovery' were clearly visible, and that provided the Conservative Government was re-elected, Britain would emerge from recession and enjoy renewed prosperity. Yet the promised recovery proved weaker and slower than expected, a patchy, fragile affair.

The second event or factor which tarnished the Major Government's mantle of economic competence was the enforced withdrawal from the Exchange Rate Mechanism (ERM) on 16 September 1992, particularly as it seemed to vindicate the strong scepticism which Margaret Thatcher and Sir Alan Walters had originally felt about Britain's membership of the ERM. Furthermore, it was John Major, whilst Chancellor of the Exchequer, who took Britain into the ERM in 1990. At this time, the value of the pound (sterling) was to be maintained *vis-à-vis* the German Deutschmark, within a band ranging from DM 2.78 to DM 3.13, although many commentators at the time insisted that the value of the pound was too high, thus casting immediate doubts on the Chancellor's approach.

Towards the end of August 1992, the pound had fallen to DM 2.79, almost at the bottom of its ERM band, a downward trend in the pound's value having occurred throughout the two years since Britain joined the ERM. Financial instability spread through Europe during early September, placing further pressure on the pound, resulting in Germany agreeing with Italy to reduce interest rates in return for Italy's devaluation of the lira by 7 per cent. The next two days placed intolerable pressure on the pound in the European currency markets, with the Government spending up to £10 billion of Britain's currency reserves in a desperate attempt at maintaining the value of the pound. At the same time, on 16 September, interest rates were raised twice in the same day, initially from 10 to 12 per cent, and then to 15 per cent. Yet neither of these measures was successful, and so in the evening of 16 September, the Chancellor, Norman Lamont, ruefully announced that Britain had suspended its membership of the ERM, and would allow the pound to 'float', whereupon it subsequently fell to DM 2.65, before recovering slightly. In effect, the pound had been devalued by

13 per cent, even though the Government had repeatedly insisted that devaluation was not an option (Jones 1993).

It has been suggested that 'Black Wednesday' – as 16 September 1992 became known – 'was a catastrophe' entailing 'tactical ineptitude of the highest order', and 'a rout which ended with the Treasury scrabbling around for an alternative anchor for its economic strategy' (Elliot 1994). The Government understandably sought to put on a brave face, suggesting that Britain had been 'betrayed' by Bonn and the Bundesbank, whilst pointing out that entry into the ERM had been supported by the Labour Party itself. In addition, the Major Government has variously sought to claim that since leaving the ERM, Britain has experienced falling unemployment and an overall reduction in interest rates. In other words, Britain's enforced withdrawal from the ERM has been presented as a blessing in disguise.

Yet the British public seem rather sceptical. The whole episode of 'Black Wednesday' dealt a deeply damaging blow to the mantle of economic competence which had played such an important role in securing victory for the Major Government in the 1992 election. The economic problems and policies experienced since – such as continued high unemployment, a Public Sector Borrowing Requirement of £50 billion in 1993, public expenditure curbs, pay freezes or only marginal increases for many workers, white collar redundancies, increases in indirect taxation, etc. – have greatly compounded the damage which 'Black Wednesday' did to the Conservatives' reputation for economic competence.

Thirdly, by late 1993, the Major Government found itself presiding over a Public Sector Borrowing Requirement (PSBR) of nearly £50 billion. This clearly conflicted with the Government's claim to be an administration of economic competence and lower public expenditure. The size of this 'public debt' also greatly impinged upon the Chancellor's ability to deliver income tax cuts. Such an economic situation led to an unpopular Budget in December 1993 (the decision having been previously taken that the Budget would forthwith be announced in November or December rather than April, so as to tie in with the usual November publication of government expenditure plans for the years ahead) in which indirect taxes were increased, and plans announced to cut public spending significantly over the next three years.

Indirect tax increases had already been prepared by Kenneth Clarke's predecessor Norman Lamont, when he had announced rises of £6.7 billion for 1994/5 and £10.3 billion in 1995/6. Kenneth Clarke added a further £1.68 billion to the former figure and £4.9 billion to the latter. He also proposed an increase in indirect taxation of over £6 billion for 1996/7. This 'indirect taxation' was to be accrued mainly through higher national insurance contributions and the imposition of VAT on domestic fuel (gas and electricity). A 'duty' of 3 per cent was also imposed on household and car insurance premiums.

At the same time, the Budget made clear the extent of the Government's commitment to reducing public expenditure by announcing cuts of £10 billion over the next three years, with at least some of this reduction to be achieved through cutting 'capital' spending. The biggest cuts were to be in the policy areas of environment, defence and transport, but savings were also sought in other areas, such as by cutting mortgage tax relief or reducing student grants – both of which would most directly affect the traditionally Conservative middle class. As such, there were suggestions from some commentators about whether the Conservative Party would further alienate its own supporters, many of whom were already experiencing 'white collar' unemployment, repossessed homes due to mortgage arrears (caused by either unemployment or previously high interest rates), negative equity, and so on.

Kenneth Clarke's Budget also served to heighten speculation about the future of the welfare state, for on both ideological and economic grounds, many Conservatives saw social security as a prime source of savings in public expenditure, as well as a means of eradicating the 'dependency culture'. The Budget announced a further tightening-up of eligibility rules for entitlement to welfare payments, and a reduction from one year to six months in the payment of unemployment benefit, which was to be renamed 'job-seekers' allowance'. Yet Clarke insisted that he was not seeking to dismantle the welfare state; indeed, he emphasized that he did not believe in a 'minimalist' state, as sought by neo-liberals in the Conservative Party. Yet concern remained amongst some Conservatives on the left of the party that the Thatcherite wing (such as Michael Portillo, Peter Lilley and John Redwood) was seeking to set the agenda, one which would entail a fundamental contraction of the welfare state, involving such measures as allowing people aged under 40 to opt out of the state retirement pension. According to one senior Conservative back-bencher: 'Portillo's words are too frightening and Lilley should not talk about the "welfare society". Let's hope there is no more talk about lone parents. We need to constrain state spending, but not blame those who are on it' (*The Times*, 2 December 1993).

The Major Government's attempt at curbing public expenditure thus had serious political implications, greatly compounding its electoral unpopularity, and, more generally, undermining further its reputation for economic competence. The introduction of VAT on the domestic use of gas and electricity proved particularly unpopular, not least amongst elderly voters, who were traditionally the staunchest of Conservative supporters. Some Conservative back-benchers, particularly on the right of the Party, constantly demanded income tax cuts, partly as a matter of principle, but also as a means of countering the unpopularity which the Major Government was experiencing over the VAT increases and public expenditure curbs. Throughout 1994, many Conservatives and political commentators expected the Chancellor, Kenneth Clarke, to introduce income tax cuts during 1995, in order to restore the Conservative Party's popularity in readiness for a general election in 1996.

Back to Basics

Eighteen months after the euphoria of the surprise of the 1992 election victory, John Major felt compelled to use the platform of the Conservatives' 1993 annual conference to restore the Government's flagging popularity by launching a new policy initiative, one that called for a return to 'traditional' values and standards – 'back to basics'. It was envisaged that 'back to basics' would win John Major greater respect from the right of the Conservative Party and thereby re-establish his authority as leader and Prime Minister. It was also intended to seize back the political initiative from the Opposition.

Guaranteed to appeal to the instincts of the party's grass-roots activists, 'back to basics' reiterated traditional Conservative principles and objectives, such as tougher action against criminals and pornography, restoring standards and discipline in education and promoting the values and institution of the family. There was also a reaffirmation of the avowed commitment to lower taxes and public expenditure. In calling for a return to traditional values, Major delighted Conference delegates by attacking 'trendy theories' and 'progressive ideas', claiming that 'We have listened too often and for too long to people whose ideas are light years away from common sense.' The 'back to basics' speech earned John Major an eleven-minute standing ovation, whilst ministers on the right of the Conservative Party – often seen as critics of Major's style and policies – added their endorsement, with Michael Portillo claiming that Major's speech was a 'brilliant, brilliant performance' which identified with the instincts of the British people (*The Times*, 9 October 1993).

Within weeks of its rapturous reception at the Conservatives' annual conference, however, John Major's 'back to basics' initiative was engulfed in controversy and confusion. Its emphasis on family values was widely perceived as part of a wider campaign against single parents, not least because of autumn speeches by various right-wing ministers condemning lone parent families as both a burden on the welfare state and a symptom of moral decay in post-war Britain. Indeed, there had been suggestions that plans were afoot to cut social security benefits to lone parents. Many Conservatives were concerned that an attack on single parents either would backfire by creating a wave of sympathy for lone parents, or would detract from other aspects of the 'back to basics' initiative, John Major therefore used the occasion of his speech at the Lord Mayor's Banquet in mid-November to resuscitate the 'back to basics' programme, deliberately omitting reference to the family and concentrating instead on education and law and order.

Yet this provided 'back to basics' with only a temporary reprieve. Before the end of the year, a Conservative minister, Tim Yeo, was obliged to resign following the revelation that he was the father of a 'love child' born in July following an affair with a Conservative councillor. The disclosure about Yeo's affair and 'love child' itself followed earlier revelations, in October, about the amorous activities of another minister, Steven Norris. In the context of John Major's 'back to basics' campaign, and its call for a return to traditional family values, such ministerial indiscretions were clearly a serious embarrassment, and left the Government vulnerable to accusations of hypocrisy and double standards. Therefore, whilst some Conservatives believed that these were private matters and did not impinge upon a minister's public responsibilities, others were of the opinion that the Conservative Party could not be taken seriously in espousing family values and traditional morality if it was seen to be lenient when its own ministers were found to be guilty of infidelity or indiscretions.

In this context, the 'back to basics' drive received another setback in February 1994, when Hartley Booth, a Parliamentary Private Secretary to Foreign Office Minister Douglas Hogg, resigned in the wake of disclosures about an affair with his former Parliamentary Research Assistant. By this time, some Conservatives were convinced that 'back to basics' was so tarnished that it ought to be abandoned, although ministers were emphatic that this was out of the question, and insisted that the whole strategy was about much more than just personal morality and family values, important though these were. None the less, an opinion poll in the *Sunday Telegraph* (13 February 1994) indicated that 64 per cent of people believed the Conservatives to appear 'very sleazy and disreputable', whilst 39 per cent claimed that the recent scandals would affect how they voted at the next general election. Furthermore, over half of those polled believed that 'back to basics' ought to be abandoned, whilst less than a third felt it ought to be maintained.

In the event, the Government did formally maintain 'back to basics' – abandoning it would have been too humiliating – but it subsequently received less prominence than previously. However, by this time, the damage had been done, for the type of events just referred to, occurring as they did against the back-drop of 'back to basics', merely added to the growing public perception of an incompetent, accident-prone Government which could get nothing right. This in turn, led to the Conservatives falling further behind in the opinion polls, whilst fuelling the doubts of an increasing number of Conservative MPs that John Major had been the right man for the exalted posts of Party Leader and Prime Minister after all.

Another Tranche of Trade Union Legislation

The 1990 Employment Act had seemed like the final move in the Conservative Government's offensive against the trade unions since 1979. By finally outlawing the closed shop, it appeared that all of the Conservatives' objectives concerning the decimation of trade unionism had been achieved. Surely there was nothing left to be done, nothing more that *could* be done against the trade unions?

Such an assumption clearly underestimated the continuing antipathy towards trade unionism rife in the Conservative Party, and its inventiveness in discovering further aspects against which to legislate. Thus it was that 1993 witnessed the arrival of the Trade Union Reform and Employment Rights Act. This legislation had been presaged by a White Paper, published in August 1991, entitled *Industrial Relations in the 1990s*. The then Employment secretary, Michael Howard, suggested that further reforms were intended to 'consolidate and build on the improvement in the country's industrial relations over the last 13 years' and thereby provide 'an effective and up-to-date framework of law in order to maintain that progress through the 1990s'. Proposals mooted in *Industrial Relations in the 1990s* were then pledged in the Conservatives' 1992 election manifesto, before finally being enacted in the 1993 legislation. Among the provisions included in the 1993 Trade Union Reform and Employment Rights Act were:

- The right of employers to offer financial incentives or rewards to employees if they gave up their union membership.
- The automatic deduction of trade union membership subscriptions (the check-off system) by employers from wages / salaries only to be lawful if employees give written approval, every three years.
- Wages Councils to be abolished; no more fixing of a minimum wage.
- All pre-strike ballots to be postal, and subject to independent scrutiny.
- Trade union ballots to give employees at least seven days' notice (after the result of the ballot) of impending strike action.
- Customers of 'public services' entitled to seek injunctions to prevent or to terminate unlawful industrial action by public service employees.
- The conciliation service ACAS given new terms of reference, so that it is no longer required to promote *collective* bargaining.

This last provision tied in with a more general objective espoused by a number of Conservative ministers and intellectual supporters, namely to replace, as far as possible, *collective* bargaining by *individual* bargaining. Instead of the terms and conditions of employment (including pay awards) being negotiated by and between trade unions and employers, it became evident in the early 1990s that the Conservatives were seeking a fundamental shift to a system whereby more and more workers had individual contracts, which they themselves would 'negotiate' with management. This, of course, perfectly accorded with the Conservative emphasis on *individualism* (as opposed to *collectivism*). It also, very importantly, provided much greater scope for performance-related pay, productivity bonuses and the like, so that employers could reward their hardest working employees individually. As a Department of Employment White Paper, published in 1988, had declared:

> Many existing approaches to pay bargaining, beloved of trade unions and employers alike, will need to change if we are to secure the flexibility essential to employment growth. In particular, 'the going rate', comparability and 'cost of living increases' are all outmoded concepts – they take no account of differences in performance, ability to pay or difficulties in recruitment, retention or motivation . . . National agreements . . . all too often give scant regard to differences in individual circumstances or performance.

This perspective was reiterated in a 1992 White Paper, *People, Jobs and Opportunity*, which proclaimed:

> There is a new recognition of the role and importance of the individual employee. Traditional patterns of industrial relations, based on collective bargaining and collective agreements, seem increasingly inappropriate and are in decline. Many employers are replacing outdated personnel practices with new policies for human resource management which put the emphasis on developing the talents and capacities of each individual employee. Many are looking to communicate directly with their employees rather than through the medium of a trade union or formal works council. There is a growing trend to individually negotiated reward packages which reflect the individuals skills, experience, efforts and performance.

It was apparent, therefore, that by the early 1990s – if not before – the Conservatives were concerned not merely to limit the power of the trade unions through legislation, but also to bypass them as far as, and whenever, possible. Indeed, on this point, it is worth noting that in June 1992, just weeks after its fourth consecutive election victory, the Conservative Government announced the imminent (from 1 January 1993) abolition of the NEDC, although the real surprise was that this key symbol of corporatism and trade union 'partnership' with the Government had not already been abolished in the 1980s by Margaret Thatcher.

One measure that had not been included in any of the trade union laws introduced between 1980 and 1993 was the prohibition of strikes in 'essential services'. Although a number of Conservative back-benchers on the right of the Party had constantly sought such a measure, successive Employment secretaries had omitted it from their trade union legislation, partly because of the 'technical' questions such a provision would raise over what services would be deemed 'essential' (some, such as the fire, police and ambulance services, would obviously be categorized as such, but what about education, for example? Would that be deemed an 'essential' service?). There were also the questions of enforcing such legislation in practice, and of what sort of 'compensation' might be offered to employees in 'essential' services in return for being denied the right to take strike action.

However, the series of 24- and 48-hour stoppages carried out by railway signal workers during the summer of 1994, and the inconvenience thereby caused to Railtrack customers (formerly known as passengers), pushed the issue of legislation concerning industrial action by employees in 'essential' or 'public' services back onto the political agenda with the Government making it known that the issue was being considered, along with the notion of 'refresher' ballots to gauge support among trade union members for the *continuation* of industrial action once begun.

Trade Unions and the Labour Party – A Loosening of the Links

The links between the Labour Party and the trade unions – links which are both organizational and financial – have always been an obvious target for Conservatives and much of the press. Voters too, according to various opinion polls over a great many years, disapproved or were suspicious of such a close, symbiotic relationship between a major – sometimes governing – political party and a sectional interest. As concern developed from about 1960 onwards about trade union power and 'irresponsibility', so too did the view that the Labour Party was too closely bound, and therefore beholden, to the trade unions. The unpopularity of the trade unions in the context of the 'winter of discontent' was profoundly damaging electorally to the Labour Party, and remained so throughout the 1980s and into the 1990s. Certainly the Conservative Party and much of the press were able to frighten voters with dire warnings of how a Labour Government would be dominated, and dictated to, by the trade unions, to the extent that the unions themselves would effectively be running the country, just as they allegedly had done during the 1970s, with all that implied regarding 'excessive' wage demands and constant strike activity making life a misery for ordinary people.

It was the 1992 general election defeat, however, which finally served to convince the Labour leadership that the party's relationship with the trade unions needed to be reconsidered. A report was presented to Labour's National Executive Committee (NEC) in June 1992, distilled from a number of surveys conducted by the party's Shadow Communications Agency, which indicated that 'many people were deterred from voting Labour because of its outdated, strike-prone, cloth-cap image; and that the Party's union links present the biggest single obstacle to reforming that image' (Kellner 1992). Since then, the Labour leadership has sought to revise the party's relationship with the trade unions, seeking a 'more open marriage', rather than 'total divorce' as urged by some commentators (Lloyd 1989: 54; Macshane 1993: vii; Walsh and Tindale 1992: 10).

Reform has been pursued in two main areas, namely the size of the trade unions' block vote at Labour's annual conference (where the party's policy commitments are *formally* determined – although not necessarily acted upon by the parliamentary leadership) and the operation of the electoral college for selecting the leader (and deputy leader) of the Labour Party.

With regard to the block vote, Labour's 1993 annual conference voted – narrowly – to implement a reform whereby the unions' share of votes at Labour Party conferences would be reduced to 70 per cent, with the other 30 per cent held by Constituency Labour Party delegates (a reform which had originally been approved in principle at Labour's 1990 annual conference). Furthermore, whilst a union's vote has hitherto been cast *en bloc* for or against a policy proposal, and thus not reflected differences of opinion or preference within the union (i.e. if a union had been 60:40 in favour of unilateral nuclear disarmament, *all* of its votes would have been cast in support of the policy), under the reform package endorsed at the 1993 Labour conference, trade union votes will reflect the division or balance of views amongst union delegates, so that a trade union might, in future, cast 60 per cent of its votes in favour of a policy, and 40 per cent against. A further proposal endorsed at this conference was that the trade unions' 70 per cent share of the vote would be reduced further if the party managed to increase its individual membership to a total beyond 300,000 (it stood at about 260,000 during 1993) whereupon the balance between trade union votes and those of Constituency Labour Parties might eventually be altered to 50:50.

Meanwhile, Labour's 1993 annual conference also endorsed the implementation of changes to the party's electoral college, used to select the party leader and deputy leader. As a result of the 1993 conference vote, the trade unions' 40 per cent of the electoral college vote was reduced to 33 ⅓ per cent, with Labour MPs and Constituency Labour Parties also allocated one-third each. Once again, the *en bloc* aspect of the trade union vote was scrapped, so that the way in which a trade union voted in a leadership election reflected the preferences *within* the union; hence a union might cast 40 per cent of its vote for one leadership contender, and 30 per cent each for two others.

One other change endorsed at the 1993 Labour conference concerned the selection of parliamentary candidates, which had also been determined via an electoral college at constituency level, in which the unions enjoyed up to 40 per cent of the vote. Henceforth, the principle of One Member One Vote (OMOV) was to be applied to the selection of Labour's parliamentary candidates. OMOV means that votes will be cast individually by members of Constituency Labour Parties. Trade union members will only be eligible to participate if they have acquired affiliated Labour membership status, by paying a small levy to the Labour Party separate from the political levy (the 'levy-plus' scheme).

Such reforms *vis-à-vis* the organizational links between the Labour Party and the trade unions have been prompted by two, not unrelated, objectives: firstly, to 'democratize' the internal structure of the Labour Party, and accord a greater role to individual members; secondly, but following on from this, to 'modernize' the image of the Labour Party in the eyes of the British electorate, and thereby convince voters that it is no longer (entirely) dominated by the trade unions. Indeed, this is itself an integral part of Labour's more general attempt at broadening its electoral appeal, and of presenting itself as a 'catch-all' party appealing to many sections of British society, rather than representing, and being beholden to, just one particular vested interest.

There is a clear recognition that 'the old male-dominated industrial image presented by many unions and their leaders does not always fit easily with the image of a modern broad based Party we are seeking to project' (Sawyer 1992: 3). With both the 'old' working class and trade union membership continuing to decline, the Labour Party has been compelled to woo other sections of the electorate in its efforts to prevent further general election defeats. The 1992 defeat indicated that the more moderate policies presented as a consequence of Neil Kinnock's policy review were not quite sufficient; the internal structure of the Labour Party, particularly with regard to the trade unions' input, also needed modernizing.

It is not only the Labour Party which has recognized the need to tone down its links with the trade unions, however. Many union leaders have themselves acknowledged the desirability of a looser relationship with Labour – after all, many unions clearly do not want Labour consigned to permanent Opposition. In any case, some trade union leaders have envisaged that a loosening of their links with the Labour Party might enable them to recruit new members among the white-collar service sector and part-time workers. It might also enable them to *increase* their political links by liaising with other organizations, a prospect alluded to by the TUC General Secretary, John Monks, when he declared that:

> For the past fourteen years or so, most of our eggs have been in the basket of a Labour victory . . . we have been constrained from building influence in other political groupings . . . giving the impression that all we can do is to wait and hope for a Labour victory . . . there is now a chance for us to break free from some of these constraints. (Monks 1993: 4)

The election of Tony Blair as Labour Party leader (see next section) seemed to herald a further loosening of the links with the trade unions. Even more than Kinnock and Smith before him, Blair seemed determined to broaden the Labour Party's electoral appeal by making it attractive to middle-class voters, including disillusioned Conservatives. This required convincing such voters that the Labour Party was not beholden to the trade unions, but able to serve the interests and aspirations of all sections of British society. Hence Blair's assertion, on his first full day as party leader, that under a Labour Government, the trade unions would be treated with 'fairness not favours'. He emphasized that:

> Trade unions will have no special and privileged place. They will have the same access as the other side of industry. In other words, they will be listened to . . . They are an important part of the democratic process.

But we are not running the next Labour government for anything other than the people of this country. (*The Guardian*, 23 July 1994)

Not surprisingly, this stance caused unease in certain quarters of the trade union movement and the Labour Party, where there was concern over the scale of the 'loosening of the links' between Labour and the unions. The then Labour Party chairman, David Blunkett, was among those who believed that the 'modernizers' were in danger of going too far, and as such, he called for a halt to any further weakening of the constitutional relationship between Labour and the trade unions (*The Guardian*, 3 September 1994).

There was also tension between Tony Blair and some trade unions during the early autumn of 1994, following the Labour leader's scaling down of the target for Labour's proposed statutory minimum wage. The party's official policy had been for the introduction of a minimum wage initially set at half of male median earnings, and subsequently to be raised to two thirds of average earnings. Tony Blair and some other senior Labour figures supported the *principle* of a statutory minimum wage, but believed that the level at which it was to be set was too high. Hence they sought to reduce it from approximately £4.05 per hour to £3–3.50 per hour. Tony Blair – and his Shadow Chancellor Gordon Brown – also intimated that a statutory minimum wage might be phased in, rather than introduced immediately, emphasizing the need for such a policy to be introduced with 'flexibility' and 'sensibility'. Such changes were opposed by Bill Morris, leader of the largest trade union affiliated to the Labour Party, the TGWU. Other union leaders, however, such as John Edmonds, of the GMB general union, suggested that a full employment policy ought to take precedence over the policy on a minimum wage, for 'without full employment the national minimum wage would mean very little' (*The Independent*, 3 October 1994). It became clear, therefore, that Blair's commitment to Labour Party 'modernization' provided scope not only for tension between the party and the trade unions, but also between trade unions themselves.

Labour's Unwanted Leadership Contest

John Smith, who had succeeded Neil Kinnock as Labour Party leader in 1992, died suddenly from a heart attack on 12 May 1994. The political impact of John Smith's death reverberated far beyond the Labour Party itself. For example, doubts were raised in the Conservative Party about the future leadership prospects of Michael Heseltine, who had himself suffered a heart attack back in 1993. As such, some Conservative and political commentators suggested that John Smith's death served to strengthen slightly John Major's position as Conservative leader, because Heseltine had widely been seen as his main rival in any leadership contest.

The Labour Party found itself facing the prospect of a potentially damaging leadership contest at a time when it was enjoying record leads in numerous opinion polls. It also meant that the Labour Party would be campaigning in the European Parliament elections without an established leader (Margaret Beckett, deputy leader under John Smith, became *de facto* leader following his death, pending the leadership election). Indeed, it was agreed that the leadership contest would be deferred until after the Euro-election, possibly until the Labour Party's annual conference in October.

In the event, Labour's leadership election was held in July, with three contenders taking part: Margaret Beckett, Tony Blair and John Prescott. The leadership contest entailed the contenders seeking to set out their objectives and goals for the Labour Party, whilst simultaneously seeking to avoid giving the impression that they personified sharp divisions within the Party. Of course, Labour's opponents could ask why, if there was little substantive disagreement between the leadership contenders, were they putting themselves forward in the first place?

Right from the outset – even before he had formally declared himself a candidate – Tony Blair was widely portrayed and perceived to be the 'favourite' to succeed John Smith as Labour Party leader. Consequently, it came as little surprise when the result was announced, on 21 July 1994, that Tony Blair had won, with 57 per cent of the electoral college vote, with John Prescott obtaining 24.1 per cent, and Margaret Beckett in third place on 18.9 per cent. When Blair's vote was broken down into the constituent parts of the electoral college, it was shown that he had been supported by 169 MPs and 29 MEPs (60.5 per cent), 58.2 per cent of individual Labour Party members, and 52.3 per cent of the trade union levy payers' vote (although only 779,426 out of 4 million bothered to take part).

Amongst the trade union levy payers, Tony Blair enjoyed a clear majority of support amongst members of NCU (60 per cent), GMB (56 per cent), MSF (56 per cent) and UNISON (53 per cent). Blair was also the single most popular leadership candidate amongst TGWU voters, from whom he received 44 per cent of the vote, compared to 33 per cent for Margaret Beckett, and 22 per cent for John Prescott. However, both the RMT and the GPMU preferred John Prescott to Tony Blair by 45 per cent to 43 per cent.

Not surprisingly, Blair's convincing victory was widely perceived as an endorsement from all sections of the Labour movement for the 'modernizing' strategy instigated by Neil Kinnock, and subsequently pursued by John Smith. Blair himself had become widely perceived as an enthusiast of Labour 'modernizing', compared to Prescott and Beckett who tended to be seen as more 'traditional' in their left-inclined views and allegiance to the trade unions. Just how much of a 'modernizer' Tony Blair was would become clear at Labour's annual conference in October 1994.

As the previous section indicated, Blair soon became subject to the suspicion of some trade union leaders and members of the Labour Party over his attempts at distancing Labour from the unions, his refusal to express his support for striking signal workers during the summer of 1994, and his apparent watering-down of the party's commitment to a minimum wage. There was also concern on the left of the Labour Party over Blair's opposition to higher taxes to increase public expenditure. Blair was anxious to shake off Labour's image as *the* party of high taxation and profligate spending, thereby reassuring middle-income, middle-class voters that they would not be taxed more heavily if they voted Labour. Suspicions or fears that Tony Blair was turning the Labour Party merely into a gentler or softer version of the Conservative Party were not dispelled by his claim that: 'We are the party that understands and can run a dynamic market economy' (*The Independent*, 3 October 1994).

Most controversial, however, was Blair's surprise declaration at Labour's 1994 annual conference that he wanted the party to rewrite its constitution, with the notorious Clause IV to be eliminated. Arguing that: 'If the world changes and we don't, then we become no use to the world. Our principles cease being principles and just ossify into dogma.' Blair evidently hoped to succeed where Gaitskell failed 35 years previously. Like Gaitskell, though, Blair immediately aroused the ire of some figures on the left of the Labour movement, for whom

Clause IV was an article of faith; to remove it was treachery in their eyes. Indeed, a couple of days later, after his speech, Blair suffered a setback when delegates at the conference voted 50.9 per cent to 49.1 per cent in favour of retaining the commitment to public ownership enshrined in Clause IV, although within the 70 per cent share of the vote enjoyed by the trade unions, 36.6 per cent supported the rewriting of Clause IV, and 33.3 per cent wished to retain it in its present form. Blair thus seemed to enjoy a majority amongst trade union delegates in favour of rewriting Clause IV and redefining the Labour Party's principles and objectives. Shrugging off the narrow conference defeat, one Labour Party official suggested that: 'If he [Blair] can achieve such a close result after 48 hours, imagine what he can do in 48 weeks' (referring to Blair's hope that Clause IV would be revised in readiness for Labour's 1995 annual conference). Blair was clearly taking a gamble, because in spite of confidence that he would emerge victorious on the issue, it none the less presaged twelve months of potentially damaging debate and disagreement within the Labour Party, something which would be eagerly seized upon by Conservatives eager to divert attention away from their own divisions and disunity.

Yet Blair and his supporters in the Labour movement could respond to their critics by pointing out that since his election 40,000 new members had joined the Labour Party. More importantly, they could point to the continuation of Labour's large opinion poll lead over the Conservatives, and also to Blair's own high ratings in the polls compared to both John Major and Paddy Ashdown, leader of the Liberal Democrats. Yet these high ratings in the opinion polls would be certain to diminish in the run-up to the next general election (to be held in or before the spring of 1997), particularly if the Conservatives should have engineered a short-term economic recovery and/or cut income tax in the preceding Budget. That would be the true test of Tony Blair's popularity. A Labour victory would be widely seen as vindication of the 'modernizers' strategy, and tribute to the work initiated by Neil Kinnock and John Smith. But should Labour be defeated, Blair and his fellow 'modernizers' would be blamed by many in the Labour movement for having ditched Labour's principles, and thus creating the impression that the party stood for very little at all – and thus was not worth voting for.

Local Elections, By-Elections and a Euro-Election – Defeats and Disasters Abound for the Major Government

Governments are used to mid-term unpopularity and the concomitant loss of support which they often experience in local by-elections during their term of office. It is taken for granted that disillusioned voters will use such elections as an opportunity to register protest against the Government, whilst 'returning to the fold' by voting for it at the next general election. As such, ministers and Governments generally tend to dismiss by-election and local election defeats as par for the course in politics. Such defeats are doubtless inconvenient and often embarrassing, but rarely seen as a source of fundamental concern or danger. Or so it seemed prior to 1990. For as we noted in the previous chapter, one of the many factors which convinced many Conservative MPs and ministers that Margaret Thatcher had become an electoral liability to the party was the by-election defeat in Eastbourne in October 1990.

In the late spring and early summer of 1994, John Major's own leadership was also being seriously questioned in the context of disastrous performances by the Conservative Party in the May local elections, five by-elections in June, and also, in the same month, a Euro-election. So bad were some of these results for the Major Government that many believed they constituted rather more than 'mid-term blues'. Not only did these results further fuel speculation about a challenge to Major's leadership before the end of the year, they also exacerbated the ideological debates and divisions within the Conservative Party over the type of Conservatism needed in the 1990s – a continuation of Thatcherite radicalism or an emphasis on 'consolidation' and consensus?

What proved particularly alarming for the Conservative Party in the May 1994 local elections was not solely the scale of their defeat – dramatic though that was – but the extent to which they lost their seats in their hitherto traditional Tory heartlands in much of the south of England and the Home Counties. Overall, the Conservatives lost over 400 seats, while losing control of 18 councils. Their share of the vote was 27 per cent – the same as the Liberal Democrats – whilst Labour secured 42 per cent. The Conservative Party won a total of 888 seats compared to the Liberal Democrats' 1,098 and Labour's 2,769. In Basildon, Basingstoke and Deane, Epping Forest,

North Hertfordshire, Southend, Stratford-on-Avon, Tunbridge Wells and Woking, for example, the Conservatives lost control of the councils, whilst in Eastleigh, St Albans and Winchester, Conservative losses enabled the Liberal Democrats to gain overall control of previously 'hung councils'. In London meanwhile, the Conservatives lost control of Barnet, Bexley, Croydon, Enfield, Harrow and Redbridge, whilst in Scotland, the Conservative Party was relegated to fourth place in terms of the seats held, with the Scottish National Party polling more than twice as many votes as the Conservatives. As one analysis of the results noted; 'For the Conservatives the local elections were quite simply the worst that they have ever had' (Curtice and Linton 1994: 5)

Barely one month later, the Conservative Party was again seeking to come to terms with electoral calamity, this time in five by-elections held on 9 June. Admittedly, four of the by-elections were in safe Labour seats, yet in all of them, Labour increased its vote; in both Barking and Dagenham, Labour's vote was 20 per cent up on the 1992 general election result, whilst in Newham North-East, it was up by 17 per cent. Given that the turn-out was in the 35–38.5 per cent range, and the fact that in safe seats, by-elections usually yield a lower vote for the incumbent party compared to a general election, Labour's increased vote was seen as a further manifestation of the strength of anti-Conservative feeling in the country.

The most important by-election, however, was that held in the traditionally rock-solid safe Conservative seat of Eastleigh, in Hampshire. Opinion polls had been predicting a Liberal Democrat victory throughout the campaign, the main question being not *whether* the Liberal Democrats would win but by what margin. There was also considerable interest in how well Labour would perform in such a constituency in view of the Government's unpopularity, coupled with the fact that the Labour Party would need to be capable of securing support – and seats – in the south if it was to have any chance of winning the next general election.

In the event, the Eastleigh by-election yielded a 21.5 per cent swing to the Liberal Democrats, who polled 24,473 votes (44.3 per cent of votes cast). Labour received 15,234 votes (27.6 per cent), putting it in second place, ahead of the Conservatives who polled 13,675 votes (24.7 per cent). However, the Conservatives were able to derive some comfort from the fact that the Liberal Democrat vote was only up on its

1992 performance by little over 3,000 votes whilst Labour received 564 votes less than in the general election. This indicated that the Liberal Democrat victory, and Labour's pushing the Conservative Party into third place, owed less to a massive switch by former Conservatives than to the tendency for unhappy Conservative supporters to abstain, and remain at home on polling day. Conservative Party spokespersons were quick to point out that such abstainers would more readily be wooed back to voting Conservative in the next general election than if they had actually voted Labour or Liberal Democrat in the Eastleigh by-election.

Yet such a gloss did not prevent a further bout of internecine squabbling in the Conservative Party, as scapegoats were sought for the Government's dismal display at the polls, and John Major's leadership was yet again made a matter of criticism, doubt and speculation. Anxiety in the Conservative Party was heightened because of the European Parliament elections which were held on the same day as the by-elections, although the results would not be known until the following Sunday night. Once again the opinion polls suggested that the issue was not merely how many seats the Conservatives would lose, but whether they would be reduced to single figures, as some pundits were predicting. With Britain electing a total of 87 seats (compared to 81 in 1989), and the Conservatives having returned 32 MEPs in 1989 – itself considered a poor result at the time – there were 'doomsday' scenarios prophesied in which the Conservative Party would be reduced to 10 MEPs or less, in which case John Major's premiership would almost certainly be challenged.

Consequently, the fact that the Conservative Party managed to return 18 MEPs was almost something of a success, although this still constituted a thoroughly disappointing result when compared to Labour's 62 MEPs, representing 42.67 per cent of the vote compared to the Conservatives' 26.88 per cent. Meanwhile the Liberal Democrats won their first ever two seats in the European Parliament, although this, along with their 16.13 per cent share of the vote, was less than they had been hoping for.

One particular feature of the Euro-election results which caused further consternation in the Conservative Party were the victories secured by Labour in London and southern England, areas which had, during the 1980s and in the 1992 general election, seemed solidly Conservative. Yet in June 1994, Labour MEPs were elected in the 'Euro-constituencies' of Bedfordshire & Milton Keynes, Essex South, Essex West & Hertfordshire East, Hertfordshire, Kent East, Kent West, Norfolk, Northamptonshire & Blaby and Suffolk & South-West Norfolk. Labour also won all but one of the 'Euro-seats' in London with a swing of 15 per cent. Meanwhile, in 'Euro-constituencies' such as Sussex-South & Crawley and Thames Valley, Labour lost to the Conservatives by fewer than 1,000 votes. While Conservative spokespersons insisted that the results reflected the traditional mid-term loss of support which would start to return once the next general election was imminent, a jubilant Labour Party was claiming that it was now a serious challenger to the Conservatives in the south of England, and was now poised to defeat them in a general election. Although the eighteen seats won by the Conservatives was sufficient temporarily to dampen down much of the speculation about an imminent leadership challenge against John Major, the result was accompanied by further internecine squabbling in the party, with the acrimony and accusations visible for all to see. The 'Euro-sceptics' insisted that the results proved the need for John Major to adopt an even more critical stance towards Europe, thereby showing the electorate that he was resolutely defending Britain's interests and sovereignty. According to Bill Cash, a prominent 'Euro-sceptic' on the Conservative back-benches, the caution displayed by John Major during the Euro-election campaign – such as his talk of a multi-speed, multi-track Europe – was welcome but 'could have gone further' (*The Times*, 13 June 1994).

However, the Euro-election results also prompted a counter-attack by pro-European Conservatives, who claimed that too much attention and credence had been lent, by both the media and John Major himself, to the 'Euro-sceptics'. According to Sir David Knox MP: 'The trouble is that the Prime Minister and other Ministers have bent over backwards to meet the views expressed by the people who call themselves Euro-sceptics. Unfortunately every concession that is made to them they are demanding more . . . It is a comparatively small tail which has been wagging the dog for too long' (*The Times*, 13 June 1994). Another Conservative 'Euro-enthusiast', Andrew Rowe MP, echoed this view, claiming that it was a mistake for the party leadership continually to make concessions to the Euro-sceptics, whilst David Nicholson MP suggested that such concessions did not provide the image of strong leadership which the electorate were looking for. A number of Conservative candidates in the Euro-elections were also critical of the party leadership's constant concessions to the Euro-sceptics, pointing out that their campaigning on the doorstep and in the streets had been more difficult as a consequence (*The Times*, 13 June 1994). Needless to say, the fact that John Major was now being criticized by Conservative 'Euro-enthusiasts' as well as 'Euro-sceptics' compounded his image as a weak leader, lacking authority in his own party.

Yet some Conservatives drew at least a little comfort from the Euro-election results, emphasizing that not only had they been better for the party than everyone was expecting, but that, as in the Eastleigh by-election, many Conservative supporters had remained at home in protest, rather than actually voting for one of the other parties. Abstainers were more readily wooed back than the 'switchers' once a general election loomed, it was argued. It was also suggested by a number of Conservatives that although the economy was now coming out of recession, the benefits had not yet been experienced by the voters 'in their pockets'. Once the electorate did begin enjoying the fruits of economic recovery, then they would once more return to the Conservative camp, particularly if the Government delivered income tax cuts before the next general election, due in 1997 at the latest. One other crumb of comfort providing some succour for the Conservative Party was the failure of the Liberal Democrats to perform as well as expected in the south of England. The significance of this was that the Conservatives could enter the general election presenting it as a straight fight between them and Labour, in which case, it was reasoned, their wavering supporters were far more likely to turn out and actually vote for the Conservative Party. Drawing upon such analyses, many Conservatives sought to present the Euro-election results not as a disaster but as the start of the Conservative recovery on the road to the next general election.

The 'Downing Street Declaration'

During November 1993, the vexatious 'Irish Question' once again moved towards the top of the political agenda, with John Major declaring that 'there may now be a better opportunity for peace in Northern Ireland than for many years' (*The Times*, 16 November 1993). This optimistic assessment followed a series of talks between Major and the leaders of Northern Ireland's 'constitutional' political parties, and also with Albert Reynolds, the Prime Minister of the Republic of Ireland. There were also claims, initially denied but subsequently confirmed, that officials acting on behalf of John Major had been in contact with members of the IRA and its political wing, Sinn Fein (*The Times*, 16 November and 1 December 1993).

The outcome of such talks was the 'Downing Street Declaration', signed by John Major and Albert Reynolds on 15 December. The declaration expressly acknowledged that 'the ending of divisions can come about only through the agreement and co-operation of the people, North–South, representing both traditions in Ireland'. One of the key passages declared that:

> The Prime Minister, on behalf of the British Government, reaffirms that they will uphold the democratic wish of a greater number of the people of Northern Ireland on the issue of whether they prefer to support the Union or a sovereign united Ireland. On this basis, he reiterates, on behalf of the British Government, that they have no selfish strategic or economic interest in Northern Ireland. Their primary interest is to see peace, stability and reconciliation established by agreement among all of the people who inhabit the island and they will work together with the Irish Government to achieve such an agreement . . .

The 'declaration' stated that the role of the British Government was 'to encourage, facilitate and enable the achievement of such an agreement over a period, through a process of dialogue and co-operation based on full respect for the rights and identities of both traditions in Ireland'. A pledge was given that if and when 'the people of the island of Ireland' wished to create a United Ireland, the British Government would readily introduce the appropriate legislation to fulfil this wish. Meanwhile, Albert Reynolds, on behalf of the Irish Government, declared that 'it would be wrong to attempt to impose a united Ireland, in the absence of the freely given consent of a majority of the people of Northern Ireland'. (For a fuller, yet succinct, summary of the main proposals enshrined in the Downing Street Declaration, see Aughey 1994: 61–2.)

One particularly controversial aspect of the Downing Street Declaration was the 'olive branch' offered to Sinn Fein and the IRA, whereby they would be permitted 'to join in dialogue in due course between the governments and the political parties on the way ahead', provided that they abandoned terrorism and renounced violence.

This element aside, some commentators viewed the Downing Street Declaration as a bland, anodyne document, attempting to offer something to everyone, and thereby ending up offering very little at all. It was suggested that the Downing Street Declaration was 'a confusing collection of gestures to both sides of Northern Ireland's sectarian divide . . . a mish-mash of seemingly contradictory statements meant to woo everyone . . . ' (*The Economist*, 18 December 1993: 15, 25).

Yet the overall response was generally favourable, with the predictable exception of the Democratic Unionist Party, particularly its leader Ian Paisley, who accused John Major of having 'sold Ulster to buy off the fiendish republican scum', and warned him that: 'You will learn in a bitter school that all appeasement of these monsters is self-destructive' (*The Independent*, 16 December 1993).

The response of the Official Unionist Party was guarded, its leader James Molyneaux neither condemning nor congratulating the Downing Street Declaration, but apparently reserving judgement. Similarly, another OUP MP, David Trimble, declared that: 'We are suspending judgement today on this statement in the hope that it will lead to a way out of the cul-de-sac' (*The Independent*, 16 December 1993). Yet even this cautious and non-committal response was perceived positively by many commentators, on the grounds that at least the main Unionist party in Northern Ireland was not actually rejecting the Downing Street Declaration.

On the nationalist side, the SDLP was extremely enthusiastic, its leader, John Hume, expressing his hope that the Declaration would constitute 'the first major step on a road that will remove forever the gun and the bomb from our small island' (*The Independent*, 16 December 1993).

However, it was the response of Sinn Fein which was most eagerly awaited by many. By addressing certain nationalist concerns, and offering Sinn Fein the possibility of inclusion in political talks on the future of Northern Ireland provided that they renounced violence, the Downing Street Declaration placed the ball firmly in the Republicans' court. In the event, Sinn Fein was also non-committal, insisting that it needed time to gauge opinion within the Republican movement, whilst also demanding 'clarification' of the Downing Street Declaration from the British Government. In particular, Sinn Fein argued that the Unionists in Northern Ireland should not be allowed to exercise a 'veto' over any move towards Irish unification. Sinn Fein also sought a more active role from the British Government in 'persuading' Unionists of the case for a united Ireland. There was also a call by Sinn Fein for a time span to be constructed so as to indicate when Irish unification might be achieved (Aughey, 1994: 63).

By the summer of 1994, Sinn Fein had still not formally accepted or rejected the Downing Street Declaration. Indeed, there were contradictory signs as to the direction in which they were moving. On the one hand, IRA bomb attacks, both in Northern Ireland itself and on mainland Britain, continued unabated. Furthermore, a special one-day conference of 800 Sinn Fein delegates held in County Donegal towards the end of July was broadly critical of the Downing Street Declaration, with the alleged Unionist 'veto' continuing to be cited as an obstacle to progress (*The Guardian*, 25 July 1994). Yet on the other hand, there were hints and rumours that the IRA was preparing an imminent ceasefire, some of these hints emanating from individuals closely involved with Sinn Fein, such as Danny Morrison, their former publicity director, who, in August, suggested that the Republican movement's 'ballot box and bullet' approach had run its course and would be replaced by a non-violent strategy (*The Guardian*, 13 August 1994).

Morrison's prediction was borne out a couple of weeks later when, on 31 August, the IRA announced a 'complete cessation of military operations' to take effect from midnight; no conditions were attached. In its ceasefire statement, the IRA acknowledged that 'an opportunity to secure a just and lasting settlement has been created'. This time, it was the British Government which displayed caution, pointing out that the IRA had not made it clear whether their cessation of terrorism was permanent. Until they did so, John Major insisted, the Government would not actually begin the three-month 'count-down' which was required before Sinn Fein could be directly included in talks over the future of Northern Ireland: 'I hope they will make it clear that it is permanent and then we can look at the elapse of that three-month period. The moment I am clear in my mind that this is a permanent end to violence, then the clock starts ticking' (*The Guardian*, 1 September 1994).

However, three weeks after the announcement of the ceasefire, John

Major and the Northern Ireland Secretary, Sir Patrick Mayhew, indicated that they were less concerned about the actual inclusion or use of the word 'permanent' with regard to the IRA's cessation of violence than with the IRA making clear 'that what they have said is meant to convey that they have given up violence for good' (*The Guardian*, 24 September 1994).

British Politics in the 1990s – A New Consensus?

In the wake of Labour's policy review in the late 1980s, and Margaret Thatcher's resignation in 1990, it has become commonplace for commentators to suggest that the 1990s have witnessed the forging of a new consensus in British politics. Indeed, such a view gained greater credence in the wake of Tony Blair's election to the leadership of the Labour Party in July 1994. Blair, even more than his predecessors, seemed intent on taking Labour onto the centre ground of British politics, from where it could attract support from all sections of society. This itself entailed discarding ideological baggage, so that whilst Blair made no secret of his Christian or Ethical Socialism, the emphasis was on principles such as 'opportunity' and 'justice' which could appeal equally to non-socialists. At the same time, the rejection of anything which could be construed or characterized as 'left-wing ideology' suggested a return to the policies of pragmatism (a feature of much of the 1945–79 period), when governance was more to do with a 'technocratic managerialism', running the existing system efficiently and competently, rather than being rigidly bound by adherence to doctrine.

Certainly since Kinnock's policy review, the Labour Party has declared its general acceptance of a number of key policies or reforms introduced by the Thatcher–Major Governments, even though it has sought to qualify some of them or add caveats. For example, the Labour Party of the 1990s broadly accepts the market economy as the most effective and efficient mechanism for generating wealth and allocating resources, but still believes that some government regulation or intervention is necessary or justified in order to alleviate defects in 'the market', and to ensure a degree of social responsibility and justice. However, a return to state ownership and nationalization associated with previous Labour Governments is not envisaged (hence Tony Blair's intention to get rid of Clause IV of Labour's constitution). Just as the original post-war consensus had derived in part from Conservative acceptance of the public ownership and Government-regulated economy introduced by wartime coalition and subsequent Attlee Governments, so the apparent consensus emerging in the 1990s derives in part from Labour's broad acceptance of privatization and the market economy introduced by the Conservative Governments since 1979.

A similar broad acceptance of Conservative reforms is also evident with regard to Labour's proposals on industrial relations, for as the policy review made clear, a Labour Government would retain the use of ballots for trade union leadership elections and prior to strike action. The prohibition of the closed shop would also remain. Only on the issue of secondary or sympathy action have there been indications that a Labour Government might amend Conservative trade union legislation in the unions' favour. Of course, the fundamental distinction between the two political parties concerns Labour's pledge to incorporate the Social Chapter into domestic law, whereas the Conservatives have resisted it to the point of negotiating Britain's 'opt-out' of implementing it. Meanwhile, shortly after his election a Labour leader, Tony Blair announced that the trade unions would not enjoy privileged access or special treatment under a Labour Government, but would, instead, be consulted or listened to in the same manner as any other interest group or professional body.

Since Tony Blair became Labour leader in July 1994, he has sought to divest the party of its 'tax and spend' image, by insisting that Labour would not seek to 'soak the rich', nor would it increase public expenditure unless it was necessary and could be afforded. To this extent, it was suggested that the money needed to improve public services could be found from cutting waste and inefficiency generally, and from ensuring economic growth. In other words, Labour was attempting to challenge the Conservatives' image as *the* party of economic competence and fiscal prudence. To the extent that a new consensus has emerged, it entails both main parties seeking to convince the electorate that they alone can manage the existing market economy more effectively and efficiently than any other party. The debate has become increasingly 'technocratic', about who would best govern a market economy, rather than an ideological divide over which sort of economy ought to be created or developed.

One reason, however, why it is difficult to ascertain the degree to which a new consensus has emerged in the 1990s is the division within the Conservative Party over the direction in which it ought to be moving in the post-Thatcher era. In many respects, Margaret Thatcher's downfall served to fuel further the debates within the Conservative Party concerning the purpose and the future of British Conservatism. Of course, a number of MPs and ministers equated Thatcherism with Conservatism, and thus insisted that the Conservative Party's task under John Major (or anyone else for that matter) was to continue the 'Thatcher Revolution'. Indeed according to this perspective, if the Labour Party is seeking to occupy the centre ground of British politics, then it becomes even more important for the Conservative Party not to lose its nerve by also seeking to return to the (non)ideological centre, but instead to maintain the radicalism and conviction evinced under Margaret Thatcher's premiership. If the Conservative Party was returned in 1992 with a reduced majority and has since trailed Labour in the opinion polls – not to mention enduring humiliating by-election and Euro-election defeats – then this is deemed to signify, not the electorate's disillusionment or disenchantment with 'Thatcherite Conservatism', but its disappointment and despair at the apparent lack of strong leadership and clear conviction under John Major. For the Thatcherite wing of the Conservative Party, the key to restoring electoral popularity lies in much greater commitment to, and emphasis on, themes such as standing up for Britain against the European Union and Brussels, law and order, and cutting public expenditure further rather than increasing taxation.

Such a progress fills the non-Thatcherites on the left of the Conservative Party with considerable alarm and anxiety. Whilst acknowledging that Thatcherism did indeed secure some laudable achievements and changes during the 1980s, there is an equally strong belief that a continuation of Thatcherism is not what the 1990s need, nor what most of the British electorate want. Indeed, Lord (Geoffrey) Howe, who had been a senior minister throughout the 1980s, was suggesting by the mid-1990s that 'We have been reducing the role of Government for 15 years so there is little fat left . . . There is not much point pushing a good case too far' (*The Guardian*, 2 August 1994). Meanwhile, as was noted near the beginning of this chapter, Douglas Hurd's speech to a fringe meeting at the Conservatives' 1993 annual conference crisply enunciated the view that the party ought not to preoccupy itself with pursuing a 'permanent' or 'cultural' revolution. Hurd was by no means alone in subscribing to this essentially 'consolidationist' approach. One of his former ministerial colleagues has noted that:

> Many of the 1992 intake of Conservative MPs were formed politically in the heyday of Thatcherism. It appears to have escaped some of them that the world has moved on. The permanent contribution of Thatcherism must be maintained and renewed. But the unmet needs in our politics are now to redress the balance with individualism, for the renewal of our civic institutions and democratic accountability, and for fairness and opportunity for all. (Howarth 1994: 18)

With regard to specific policy issues, for example, Howarth warned that the tax cuts deemed an article of faith by Thatcherite Conservatives 'could only be financed through cuts in public expenditure. But such cuts in public expenditure would devastate the social fabric.' Meanwhile, he argued that: 'In social security there is a strong case for spending more, and no case for spending less . . . It would be repellent to decent opinion if any further attempt were made . . . to make the poor and disadvantaged pay the price for the problems of the economy.' In any case, Howarth claimed that 'there is deep unease that the poorest have not shared in the growth in the nation's wealth', and hence: 'poverty and jobs should be at the heart of the Government's concerns'.

Here was the voice of authentic 'one nation', paternalistic Conservatism, engaged in battle with the Thatcheristic Right in seeking to determine the style and direction of the Conservative Party in the 1990s. And it is precisely because of this battle that John Major has so often been preoccupied primarily with holding the Conservative Party together, and maintaining any sense of unity. Repeatedly, public speeches by Conservative politicians, and 'confidential' papers and memos leaked to the quality press, have highlighted the ideological gulf dividing the Conservative Party of the 1990s. A good example of the latter was the publication of a letter sent by Michael Portillo, whilst he was Chief Secretary to the Treasury, to the Trade and Industry Secretary, Michael Heseltine, in which the former – widely seen as *the* potential leadership contender from the Thatcherite wing of the party – strongly rebuked the latter for failing to introduce sufficient public expenditure cutbacks and free-market policies in his Department. As one Editorial was moved to comment:

> The Portillo letter is not just about particular spending battles. It goes

to the heart of the great divide in the Conservative Party and in modern Conservatism . . . It raises, in as stark a way as it has yet been raised, whether the Conservative Party can for long contain the conflicting impulses of free-market fundamentalism and one nation social solidarity. (*The Guardian*, 2 August 1994)

Yet the apparent emergence of a new consensus in British politics also posed problems for the Liberal Democrats, widely seen as occupying the centre ground. Indeed, the Liberal Democrat leader had long sought to maintain an 'equidistance' between the Conservative and Labour Parties, so as to confirm the Liberal Democrats' image as a truly independent party, linked neither to the Labour Party and the trade unions nor to the Conservative Party and big business.

However, the election of Tony Blair as Labour leader significantly fuelled debate amongst Liberal Democrats about whether they ought to establish closer links with the Labour Party (as was already the case in some parts of the country at local government level), or resolutely retain their independence and 'equidistance' between Labour and the Conservatives. For those adhering to the latter option, the problem was that the more Labour itself moved towards the centre ground, the more it seemed to encroach upon traditional Liberal Democrat 'territory' and make 'equidistance' ever more difficult to maintain.

None the less, it was the independence or 'equidistance' strategy which prevailed at the Liberal Democrats' 1994 annual conference, where many delegates were angered at calls by Shirley Williams and other former SDP luminaries for the Liberal Democrats to develop closer, more formal links with the Labour Party, including a commitment to the formation of a Labour–Liberal Democrat Coalition Government in the event of a hung Parliament.

Perhaps the most that can be said is that British politics in the 1990s is in a state of considerable flux. Whilst, compared to the 1980s, 'the guns of think tanks and the pens of intellectuals have largely fallen silent. The radical right has lost much of its self-confidence' (Seldon 1994: 57), there are a number of Conservatives who remain passionate adherents and advocates of Thatcherism, with one of them, Michael Portillo, being mooted as a future challenger to John Major for the Conservative Party leadership.

Meanwhile, it is important to emphasize that 'until Labour forms a government, and having done so decides to continue with the Conservatives' policies, talk of a new consensus is premature'. This is because: 'It is continuity of government policies between both parties *in office* which defines consensus' (Seldon 1994: 57). This scepticism over the extent, or even existence, of a new consensus is shared by Riddell, who insists that although 'the parties have moved towards the centre since the mid-1980s, . . . movement does not mean identity. While . . . Tory and Labour are in the same playing field, they are still at opposite ends. . . . The scope of argument has been narrowed, but not eliminated' (Riddell 1993). Yet maybe commentators such as Riddell overstate the case against the emergence of a new consensus. After all, during the previous consensus from 1945 to the 1970s, the two parties were not 'identical' in their policies or approach, nor had the 'scope of argument' been 'eliminated'. Differences remained, but manifested themselves within certain widely recognized and respected parameters. Policies were pursued within a general framework, one largely accepted by both main political parties, particularly at senior levels. To deny the emergence of a new consensus on the grounds that Riddell puts forward is to adopt an unreasonably narrow definition of consensus.

None the less, Seldon is right; proof that a new consensus has been established would require the election of a Labour Government, whereupon the degree of policy continuity and similarity could be empirically gauged. Until or unless the Labour Party does win a general election, we will be compelled to remain a while longer in the realm of speculation and conjecture.

7 Perspectives on British Politics since 1945

> England had done one thing; it has invented and established Public Opinion, which is an attempt to organize the ignorance of the community, and to elevate it to the dignity of physical force. But Wisdom has always been hidden from it. Considered as an instrument of thought, the English mind is coarse and undeveloped. The only thing that can purify it is the growth of the critical instinct.
>
> Oscar Wilde, *The Critic as Artist*

One of the commonplace assumptions or assertions of everyday life is the claim that 'facts speak for themselves'. They do not. Not only do historians and political scientists have to determine what the facts are in many cases, but having done so, they then have to interpret and explain them. A single fact can be subject to a number of different approaches and accounts.

What follows is a brief overview of three particular approaches to, or accounts of, British politics since 1945. Each provides a markedly different interpretation or explanation of the events and developments delineated in the previous six chapters. It is not, however, this author's task or intention to discuss the merits or otherwise of these three perspectives: merely to adumbrate the main attributes and arguments of each. The terms used to categorize the three perspectives, though – namely the Right, the Centre and the Left – do warrant a brief word of caution or clarification. In the discussion which follows, 'the Right' is used mainly to denote the critique put forward by the New Right (also widely termed 'neo-conservatives') from the 1970s onwards. The prefix 'New' is not used, however, partly for the sake of simplicity, and partly because it is questionable whether it can any longer be considered 'new' in the 1990s.

Meanwhile, 'the Centre' denotes an ideological or intellectual position which is widely seen as neither Left nor Right, but is deemed to occupy a middle position between the two 'extremes'. Indeed, it sometimes holds that the very terms 'Left' and 'Right' are either meaningless or misleading, and that a new vocabulary or discourse is required in modern politics. Thus, for example, the Liberal Democrats argue that the choice is not between Left or Right, but between parties who wish to centralize power in the hands of Government and the state, and those who are committed to decentralizing it to local and regional level. Indeed, much of the 'Centrist' viewpoint delineated in this chapter is subscribed to by Liberal Democrats, and was equally proclaimed by their predecessors, the Social Democratic Party – for example, former SDP leader David Owen opened his 1981 book *Face the Future* with the assertion that: 'The centralist–decentralist argument and the complex issues it raises have little relevance to the rather facile press-labelling of Left and Right which has always dominated public comment about British politics. It is the question of decentralisation which now forms the real divide in British politics' (Owen 1981: 3). However, it is not merely a party political perspective; during the 1970s and 1980s, it was also articulated by a number of distinguished academics and political commentators.

The Left perspective deals with an interpretation subscribed to mainly – but not solely – by Marxist writers. It should be borne in mind, however, that whilst Marxists and non-Marxists on the Left may well agree on certain points, Marxists often disagree amongst themselves to a surprising extent. Indeed, in the absence of any 'proletarian revolution', many Marxists have kept themselves occupied by engaging in academic hair-splitting and semantic nit-picking with each other, and competing to see who can use the most abstruse terminology and jargon. In any case, there are various 'schools' of Marxism, and numerous far-Left political parties each claiming to be 'true Marxists', and criticizing the others for 'revisionism' or 'betrayal'. If there is one thing which many Marxists hate more than capitalism, it is each other! As such, any text which presents a 'Left' or 'Marxist' critique must of necessity offer a somewhat simplistic outline, highlighting the main features whilst avoiding getting bogged down in some of the turgid and tiresome in-house debates and semantic squabbles.

The View from the Right

It is the perspective from the (New) Right which has become most important and influential in Britain since the 1960s, with their prescriptions and policies being widely applied by the Thatcher Governments, and maintained, to a considerable extent, by the Conservative administrations headed by John Major. Not only did the neo-conservative characterization of post-war British politics enjoy considerable intellectual support – sometimes from commenators previously on the Left (see, for example, P. Johnson 1980) – it also struck a chord with many British people generally, although the breadth and depth of this support ought not be exaggerated, because throughout the 1980s and into the 1990s, attitude surveys and opinion polls have revealed extensive support for what might be termed 'social democratic values', such as comprehensive welfare provision, the belief that governments ought to pursue full employment as far as possible, introduce measures to eradicate poverty and reduce inequality, and so on.

None the less, in many intellectual and political circles throughout the 1970s and 1980s, this social democratic approach was thoroughly discredited. Indeed, it was apportioned much of the blame for the economic, political and social problems which Britain has increasingly experienced since 1945, and which became particularly pronounced during the 1970s – the decade when the 'post-war social democratic consensus' was finally seen to be collapsing. This 'collapse' provided neo-conservatism with both the intellectual authority and the political space with which to launch a counter-attack against the social democratic values and policies which had guided post-war Governments – Labour and Conservative – hitherto. As such, this new critique deemed post-war Conservative Governments to be as culpable as Labour Governments in pursuing policies which had allegedly led to the crises of the 1970s. Not only were post-war Conservative administrations and leaders condemned for apparently accepting the premises and principles of Keynesian economics and social democratic politics, but also, and as a consequence, for not seeking to reverse the 'collectivist tide' when in Office.

According to this aspect of the neo-conservative analysis, British politics since 1945 had steadily moved to the left, not just because of the policies pursued by Labour Governments, but equally because Conservative Governments themselves had failed to repeal such policies.

Instead, Conservatives had taken their name too literally; they had merely sought to conserve, to maintain the status quo. Yet, as Sir Keith Joseph (1976) argued, if Labour Governments introduced policies which pulled Britain leftwards politically, and then the next Conservative Government merely conserved the system which existed when it entered office, then Conservatives were guilty of aiding and abetting the drift towards the left. This 'ratchet effect' was deemed by Sir Keith to mean that the Labour Party was pulling both the Conservative Party and Britain towards socialism.

Up until the 1970s, therefore, the Conservative Party was charged with 'a failure of leadership'. Instead of exercising authority and taking the initiative, Conservative leaders had

> only repeated the shibboleths of the hour, condemning what it is fashionable to condemn and praising what it is fashionable to praise. They have accepted, almost without question, the idea of the omnicompetent state . . . In particular they have been obsessed with the fiction of the middle ground . . . (Coleraine 1970: 153)

The term 'neo-conservatism' therefore signifies a qualitatively different mode of Conservative politics from that which prevailed from 1945 through to the 1970s. The essentially 'consolidationist' approach adopted by Conservative Governments during this time was to be replaced by a much more confident, combative style, whereby Conservatism and the Conservative Party were expected to go on the offensive, and consciously embark on a mission to reverse the principles and policies of post-war British politics, with a view to restoring a status quo-ante, namely Victorian Britain.

Central to the neo-conservative critique of British politics since 1945 was the role of the state. This, it was argued, had become far too extensive and intrusive, and thus threatened to destroy – if it had not done so already – economic efficiency and individual liberty. Whereas Keynesianism and social democracy had urged state intervention in order to ameliorate and temper the inherent imperfections and inadequacies of the market economy, neo-conservatives discounted these alleged defects, insisting that not only was 'the market' the most effective and efficient economic system ever known, but also that it was innately self-regulating, operating as it did through the immutable, natural laws of supply and demand.

What was a major impediment to the effective functioning of 'the market', neo-conservatives insisted, was precisely the scale and scope of state intervention which had developed in Britain since 1945. In other words, state intervention was deemed to be the cause of, rather than the cure for, most economic problems. It was state intervention which prevented the smooth operation of 'the market', and which 'politicized' what were originally purely economic decisions and processes. Furthermore, neo-conservatives pointed out, the disruptive effects of state intervention in the economy then resulted in yet more intervention to rectify the problems which the state itself had caused in the first place. The overall result was that economic activity was subject to ever greater state intervention, to the extent that eventually nothing would remain of 'the market'. Instead, the state would control and determine all previously economic variables: what was produced, in what quantity, at what price, who was employed, at what wages, etc. This nightmare vision led neo-conservatives to endorse Hayek's warning that once governments sought to regulate economic activity, society was on 'the road to serfdom' (Hayek 1944). Sooner or later, the state would decide and determine everything. This was the route which post-war Britain was deemed to be following, according to neo-conservatives, and as such, it was considered absolutely crucial that the Conservative Party was alerted to this fact, so that it could immediately begin the task of 'reversing the trend' (Joseph 1975).

There was also the argument, increasingly fashionable in neo-conservative circles during the 1970s and early 1980s, that the public sector of the economy was not only inherently inefficient, but was also 'crowding out' the wealth-creating private sector. Furthermore, only the private or 'market' sector was deemed economically 'productive', in so far as it entailed the sale of goods or services on a commercial basis, thereby yielding a profit. By contrast, the public or 'non-market' sector tended to provide goods or services free at the point of delivery or use. They were thus funded by the Government out of revenue, that is, finance raised through taxes and national insurance contributions. Put simply, according to this critique, the public or 'non-market' sector is parasitic on the wealth generated by the private 'market' sector of the economy. Furthermore, as the public or 'non-market' sector increases in size, it effectively squeezes out the very private, 'market' sector on which it ultimately depends for its funding. To compound the problem, governments needed to increase the amount of taxes and other revenues raised from the private, 'market' sector, which both reduced demand in the economy – and thus further damaged the 'market' sector because fewer goods were being sold – whilst also fuelling wage inflation as workers sought pay increases to offset their tax and national insurance deductions (Bacon and Eltis 1976: 93–116).

Bacon and Eltis's analysis thus provided neo-conservatives and the (New) Right with further intellectual justification for reducing the size and scope of the public sector and nationalized industries – 'rolling back the state' – which would then enable the private, 'market' sector to flourish, whilst also paving the way for cuts in taxes on earnings and profits.

A further aspect of state intervention which formed an integral part of the neo-conservative perspective of British politics since 1945 concerned the notion of 'governmental overload'. This concept, originally articulated by Anthony King (1975), maintained that as the state had intervened more and more in the social and economic life of the nation, and accepted ever greater responsibility for a whole range of issues, so it rendered itself the target of an ever increasing number of pressure groups and organized interests, all of whom became accustomed to looking to Government to satisfy their demands or grievances. These pressures added to the responsibilities which Governments had assumed for managing the economy and maintaining an 'overload of government', with politicians and policy-makers over-burdened by the range of responsibilities and demands placed upon them.

Ultimately, Government would became less and less effective as it sought to do too much and keep everybody happy. King suggested that 'as the range of responsibilities of governments has increased, so their capacity to exercise their responsibilities has declined'. In other words, he claimed: 'The reach of British government exceeds its grasp . . .' (King 1975). If this trend was not checked, then eventually the very authority and legitimacy of Government and the political system would be undermined, and quite possibly destroyed. Although 'legitimation crisis' is a concept usually associated with the Left (of which we shall say more later), it does tie in very closely with much of this neo-conservative critique, for as the economist Samuel Brittan observes: 'If a succession of governments . . . stir up expectations only to disappoint them, there is a risk of the whole system snapping under the strain' (Brittan 1983: 17).

For many neo-conservatives, part of this problem derived from what Brittan terms the 'economic contradictions of democracy'. This concept held that in the competition for votes and electoral popularity, politicians and political parties in post-war Britain had made ever more extravagant promises and pledges to the electorate, constantly claiming that they would spend more on education, or health, or pensions, etc., than their opponents. This process had effectively turned general elections into auctions, in which the parties sought to outbid each other in order to obtain the largest vote.

Yet this was only part of the problem, according to commentators such as Brittan. What was also a major feature of the 'economic contradictions of democracy' was that the pledges made by the political parties in their attempt at winning votes invariably entailed further increases in public expenditure. However, the electorate were beguiled into believing that the provision of greater welfare services, for example, was free, so that any party which failed to commit itself to expanding social policy or improving welfare benefits was assumed to be mean or miserly (Brittan 1983: 3–21). Yet increased expenditure in any particular sphere of policy will invariably mean either less spent in another area, thereby creating conflict between different sections of the community and a sense of grievance against the state from the 'losers', or a further increase in taxation, with a corresponding decrease in the disposable income of ordinary people. It would also entail a further increase in the size and scope of the public sector at the expense of the private sector upon which wealth creation is deemed to depend. The consequence would be that whilst Governments were committing themselves for electoral purposes to spending ever greater sums of money on welfare services and 'public goods', the processes by which wealth was created would be undermined, leaving less money available in the economy. A vicious circle would be set in motion, leading to what Marxists have termed a 'fiscal crisis of the state' (discussed more fully later).

According to Brittan's critique, therefore, British politics since 1945 had been characterized, to some extent, by an excess of democracy. Electoral considerations and voters' wishes had led successive Governments to pursue policies which were politically popular but economically damaging, if not downright dangerous. For ultimately, the ballot box was yielding policies which were destructive of the private sector and the market economy upon which not only wealth creation, but freedom, depended. In essence, democracy was destroying liberty.

However, whilst the neo-conservative perspective of British politics since 1945 was highly critical of the extent to which the state sought to regulate the economy and assume responsibility for the provision of welfare, it simultaneously criticized the weakness of the state in maintaining social discipline. Indeed, the state's increased acceptance of responsibility for the provision of welfare is itself deemed by the Right to have undermined social discipline. This is because an 'over generous' welfare state encouraged an abdication of individual responsibility on the part of an increasing number of citizens. To give but two examples, it has often been claimed that welfare provision has undermined the work ethic (by making unemployment a less unattractive option than it was prior to the availability of social security), and has undermined the traditional nuclear family (by making it viable, even appealing, for young women to become single parents).

However, many on the Right have viewed the welfare state as part of a wider breakdown in social discipline, order and morality, both reflected and greatly reinforced – if not actually prompted – by the so-called 'permissive society' which is alleged to have emerged in the 1960s. Certainly for many commentators and politicians on the Right, the 1960s have been damned as the decade which sowed the seeds of many of the social problems which erupted during the 1970s and 1980s. As we noted in chapter 3, it was during the 1960s that Britain apparently underwent a sexual revolution, with the liberalization or legalization of abortion, divorce and homosexuality. Meanwhile, the development of the contraceptive pill, coupled with an upsurge in feminism, provided many women with a new-found sexual freedom. Such developments have since been seen by many on the Right as a source or symbol of moral decline and decay, the consequences of which we are still deemed to be suffering from today, as evinced by the number of children raised in broken homes or one-parent households, the spread of AIDS, and the like.

At the same time, the 1960s have been 'demonized' by the Right as the decade in which 'trendy' theories on education and crime became prevalent amongst many professionals in the educational and social work 'establishments' respectively. The consequence is said to be a lowering of standards and lack of discipline in the classroom, and a massive increase in crime as individuals came to realize that they were less likely to go to prison due to the 'fashionable' theories which explained criminal behaviour in terms of social deprivation and a disadvantaged upbringing, and thus urged alternatives to custody.

In view of these trends, and the Right's interpretation of their underlying causes, the demand was made for a restoration of discipline and order, to be secured in large part through a greater assertion of state authority. Thus, whilst the Right was calling for a 'rolling back' of the state in the economic sphere, and also a contraction of the welfare state, it was simultaneously demanding that the state become more active and interventionist in certain social spheres, not least that of law and order.

Indeed, during the late 1970s, when Conservative politicians such as Margaret Thatcher were claiming that Britain under a Labour Government would suffer increasing state control until the country resembled a (former) Eastern European regime, Peregrine Worsthorne was gently chiding her, claiming instead that:

> The spectre haunting most ordinary people in Britain is neither of a Totalitarian State nor of Big Brother, but of other ordinary people being allowed to run wild. What they are worried about is crime, violence, disorder in the schools, promiscuity, idleness, pornography, football hooliganism, vandalism and urban terrorism . . . Lack of supervision, lack of interference, excessive tolerance, excessive compassion – these are the causes of popular bitterness. (Worsthorne 1978: 150–1)

Consequently, Worsthorne warned that it would be 'an error for the Conservative Party to seem obsessed with nineteenth-century ideas of individual freedom which cannot fail to strike the mass of people as absurdly irrelevant to their deepest concerns', and as such, he suggested that 'social discipline' was 'surely . . . a more fruitful and rewarding theme for contemporary conservatism than individual freedom' (*ibid.*: 150–1).

The various views delineated above became more widely respected and accepted in many Conservative and intellectual circles from the 1960s onwards, as the apparent failures of Keynesian economics and social democratic politics became more serious, and visible. A counter-attack was mobilized against Keynesianism and social democracy, with the various ideas, individuals and institutions of the New Right developing not merely greater coherency in their critique of post-war Britain, but also more confidence as they sensed the intellectual tide turning in their favour. Having been forced onto the defensive since 1945, and perceived or portrayed as political mavericks out of touch with the modern world, the New Right and their ideas and arguments seemed to be in the ascendant by the 1970s, apparently vindicating those in their ranks – such as Enoch Powell – who had consistently warned of the likely consequences of government control of the economy, incomes policies, a comprehensive welfare state, and so on.

The dissemination of the New Right's ideas and arguments was greatly assisted by the plethora of intellectuals and 'think-tanks' that emerged from the late 1950s onwards, and who assiduously published books, newspaper articles and pamphlets attacking the role of the state in post-war Britain, whilst simultaneously presenting the case for a restoration of the free market. Given the Conservatives had often suspected or accused intellectuals of being predominantly left-wing or Marxist, it was rather ironic that some of the most enthusiastic and prolific proponents of the New Right critique themselves emanated from academic disciplines such as political science, history, economics and philosophy. Furthermore, some of those who were to become key figures espousing New Right principles and policies – such as Sir Alfred Sherman and Paul Johnson – had themselves once been firmly on the Left, but had subsequently 'seen the light' and apparently learnt the error of their ways. Meanwhile, the promulgation of these New Right ideas and arguments was greatly assisted by the development of a number of 'think-tanks' and pressure groups, such as the Institute of Economic Affairs and the Adam Smith Institute, which added to the articulation and dissemination of New Right principles and policies. In the context of the mounting economic problems besetting Britain throughout the 1960s and 1970s, and the apparent breakdown of social order during the same period, the New Right's critique of British politics since 1945 attracted considerable credence and credibility.

The View from the Centre

This perspective demurs from the widely held view that British politics from 1945 until the 1970s was characterized by a 'social democratic' consensus entailing broad agreement between the Labour and Conservative

Parties over policies and objectives, coupled with a remarkable degree of policy continuity irrespective of which party was in office. Instead, the 'Centrist' perspective argues that British politics since 1945 – but more especially from the 1960s – increasingly became dominated by an adversarial pattern, in which changes of government up until (and including) 1979 entailed a marked change in ideology and policies, and thus swings from Left to Right and vice versa.

This mode of 'adversarial politics' is deemed to have had two particular damaging consequences. Firstly, ideology and dogma are alleged to have prevailed over the real needs of the country and its people, as Governments sought to impose a rigid set of principles and policies drawn up in Opposition. A major reason for the degree of ideological content and rigidity ascribed to a party's programme upon first entering office is the tendency – until recently – for an Opposition party to go back to 'first principles'. It was usually the case that a Conservative Government which was defeated in a general election would swing sharply to the right in Opposition, claiming that in office, it had lost sight of its principles, or had lost touch with the views of its supporters. Similarly, defeat for a Labour Government used to result in a lurch to the left by the Labour Party in Opposition, as its activists and certain back-benchers insisted that it had not pursued sufficiently socialist policies in office.

The second damaging consequence of this adversarial politics is the lack of continuity in policy since 1945, but more particularly from the early 1960s onwards, since when 'a rapid alternation of government . . . produced a customary disorder' whereby 'Policies have usually been disowned by incoming administrations . . . ' (Walkland 1984: 93). It is argued that the swings from left to right and vice versa which have resulted from changes in Government have meant repeated reversals of policies, as one political party entered office and set about rejecting and repealing the policies of its predecessor. Sooner or later, this party too would be defeated in an election, whereupon its own policies would be reversed by its successor. The consequence is that since the early 1960s, Britain and its economy have suffered greatly from 'the number of reversals and re-reversals and in some cases, the re-re-reversals of policy which have occurred . . . ' (Finer 1975: 16–17).

Post-war Britain is thus deemed to have experienced 'too much short-lived legislation, measures put on the statute book by one party in the almost certain knowledge that they will be reversed by the other' (Jenkins 1982: 20). Consequently, there has been widespread uncertainty over longer term policy, so that neither bureaucrats nor businessmen enjoyed the confidence of making long-term plans or embarking on long-term projects. Fear of a change of Government, and hence a major change of policy and strategy after the next general election, served to encourage or reinforce a short-term approach to policy-making and investment, an approach which is deemed to have had a disastrous impact *vis-à-vis* British industry and the economy – after all, one of the major problems experienced by British industry in the post-war era has been a chronic lack of investment. Of course, there are a number of reasons for this – reasons which lie beyond the remit of this discussion – but the 'Centrist' critique does hold that the 'adversarial politics' which has predominated in Britain since 1945 is itself a major factor in encouraging this lack of long-term investment and strategic planning, with one commentator observing (in the 1970s) that 'the quick fire changes put across by successive governments of both parties are doing a great deal of damage. They are a major cause of uncertainty; it is difficult for anyone to make long-term plans when there is no telling whether it will be possible to carry them out after the next general election' (Rogaly 1976: 38–9). Furthermore, there were suggestions that: 'The resulting poor performance of the economy can itself become a potential threat to a democratic system og government' (Stewart 1977: 244).

The 'Centrist' perspective apportions much of the blame for the predominance of 'adversarial politics' in post-war Britain to the electoral system, namely the 'first-past-the-post' or plurality system as it is commonly known. This electoral system is charged with encouraging a divisive two-party system in Parliament which perpetuates ideological divisions and policy discontinuities, and which encourages a confrontational stance between the main political parties, all of which, in turn, exacerbates economic and social instability (Rogaly 1976: 22). According to Alderman: 'If it is true that since 1945 British society has been dogged by needless industrial strife, sterile political argument and absence of realistic economic and financial policies, it is equally true that the electoral system has contributed to all these shortcomings' (Alderman 1984: 19). Indeed, it is suggested that the electoral system fosters an irresponsible system of government, for the first-past-the-post method of election enables a political party to win a majority in the House of Commons with a minority of the votes cast. That Commons' majority, subsequently enforced by Government Whips and the powers of patronage which the Prime Minister can bestow upon – or withhold from – back-bench MPs, enables ministers to pass almost any legislation or policy they wish, secure in the knowledge that their parliamentary majority will push the measure through. This means that many damaging or unpopular measures have been introduced by Governments who were elected by a minority of the British people, thereby giving rise to what Lord Hailsham once termed 'elective dictatorship'. According to this 'Centrist' perspective of British politics since 1945, the two-party system, and the first-past-the-post system which underpins it, have not delivered 'representative and responsible government' (to borrow Anthony Birch's term), but, in fact, precisely the opposite.

This 'irresponsibility' is also said to have applied to the Opposition in Parliament, not least because it has tended to take its title too literally. As such, whichever party was in Opposition at any given time merely opposed, automatically and as a matter of course, anything which the Government proposed or introduced, irrespective of any merits in the Government's case (Stewart 1977: 243–4). Indeed, recognition that the Government was unlikely to be defeated in the Commons (due to its majority, as discussed above) merely added to the irresponsibility of the Opposition in seeking to oppose everything the Government did, knowing that it would not itself be required to implement an alternative policy or proposal.

In other words, the Opposition could be totally negative and irresponsible in its stance *vis-à-vis* the Government. This in turn served to ensure that Parliament rarely provided the arena for rational argument, reasoned discussion or intelligent debate, but instead was rendered a forum for simple, simplistic 'for or against' posturing and prattling; 'a shrill and unconvincing attempt to portray almost everyone on the other side as either a fool or a knave' (Jenkins 1982: 21). As Johnson has observed:

> The danger of adversary politics . . . is that it encourages persistent irresponsible competition and too much over-simplification . . . Where conflict does not exist, adversary politics manufactures it; where

genuine conflict is present, adversary politics exacerbates it. (N. Johnson 1980: 67)

Furthermore, it is argued that 'adversarial politics' both reflects and reinforces assumptions that there are merely 'two sides to every story', that there are only two alternatives on any policy or issue in British political life. This is condemned as 'an adversary conception of politics which is far too crude to cope with the complexities of modern industrial society' (Bogdanor 1984: 155), yet, as Johnson has noted, 'where there is a many-sided and complex pattern of interests involved in the political argument, adversary politics imposes on its own crudities and dogmatism' (N. Johnson 1980: 67). In turn, this whole adversarial approach, and the assumptions which underpin it, can be said to have had a deeply detrimental effect on the role and authority of Parliament itself. For if Governments know that they can push through virtually any measures or laws they wish, by virtue of their Commons' majority and party discipline, then Parliament ceases to fulfil effectively its constitutional role as a check on the executive. Parliament is reduced to little more than a 'rubber stamp'; MPs little more than 'lobby fodder'. British democracy, far from becoming more mature, has become more infantile. The whole currency of democratic politics has been debased.

There is one further reason, according to the 'Centrist' perspective, why Britain's two-party system and its adversarial politics have proved so damaging to Britain since 1945, and that concerns the extent to which the two main political parties, Conservative and Labour, are deemed to be tied to particular sectional interests, namely big business and the trade unions respectively. As Shirley Williams expressed it:

> Labour is the party of the trade unions, financed by them and expected to dance to their tune. The Conservative Party is the party of the Institute of Directors and the boardrooms, largely financed by private-sector companies, and expected to govern with their interests in mind. So the parties legislate each for its own, in an absurd ping-pong of laws passed and then repealed by the subsequent government, with no effort made to construct a lasting accord. (Williams 1982: 133)

Thus the Centrist view holds that the two main parties have been unable or unwilling to pursue consistently the policies needed by Britain as a whole, because of their close relationship with these sectional interests. By being so closely bound in this manner, neither Conservative nor Labour Governments in post-war Britain have enjoyed sufficient autonomy to take a broader or more dispassionate view of events and problems. Instead, it is alleged that 'in their search for ways of managing the economy governments headed by both major parties have mistaken the will of the Trades Union Congress or the Confederation of British Industries, or abstract groupings such as "labour" or "business" for the will of the people' (Rogaly 1976: 22). In view of this, the 'Centrist' perspective casts serious doubt on the extent to which post-war Governments can genuinely be said to have been acting in the interests of the British people as a whole.

Whilst this chapter is not primarily concerned to examine the proposals and policies which follow from the various perspectives, it cannot be overlooked that the 'Centrist' perspective clearly provides the rationale for major constitutional reform. Indeed, it is invariably advocates of such reform – particularly electoral reform – who subscribe most strongly to the 'adversarial politics' thesis. The constitutional framework of British politics is deemed to have sustained and even encouraged 'adversarial politics', it is argued, and hence the way to eradicate the divisive, class-based, ideologically driven, two-party system is to reform that constitutional framework. In particular, it is claimed, electoral reform is vital, whereby the first-past-the-post method of election would be replaced by some form of proportional representation (bearing in mind that 'PR' is a generic term denoting a number of electoral systems seeking greater proportionality between votes cast and seats won; it is not actually an electoral system in its own right).

Electoral reform – as part of a wider programme of constitutional reform – is urged on both political and economic grounds, although these are closely related. Politically, it is held that some form of proportional representation would enhance British democracy by ensuring that the allocation of seats in the House of Commons and the composition of the Government much more closely reflected the wishes of the electorate as expressed via the ballot box. No longer would one political party be able to get elected in its own right by virtue of winning a majority of seats in the Commons despite having received a minority of votes in the country at large. Instead it is assumed, either explicitly or implicitly, that electoral reform would yield some form of coalition government, in which the Liberal Democrats – as Britain's 'centre' party – would occupy a pivotal place and position. This in turn would result in greater moderation and consensus, as the other parties sought to work with their coalition partners, something which they would not be able to do if they continued to adhere rigidly to ideology. Electoral reform, it is assumed, 'would severely restrict the adversarial input into government and opposition', and this, in turn, would enable 'greater continuity of policy' to the extent that 'planning for the longer term might become more feasible' (Ingle 1987: 211).

At the same time, it is envisaged, the introduction of electoral reform would greatly hasten the process of class and partisan dealignment, because people could subsequently vote for parties such as the Liberal Democrats knowing that their vote would no longer be 'wasted'. The electoral map and political landscape of Britain would be completely transformed.

This 'Centrist' perspective also insists that electoral reform would serve to revitalize the role and authority of Parliament, for a coalition government would not only entail ministers from more than one party being involved in policy-making, it would also mean that the Government would have to be much more responsive to the views of ordinary MPs in order to obtain the parliamentary support necessary to get its measures approved. In other words, a coalition government could not take Parliament for granted in the way that single-party governments do. Hence a proper balance would be struck between executive and legislature, rather than the former dominating the latter.

However, the 'Centrist' perspective is also emphatic that the political changes engendered by electoral reform would have a major and beneficial impact on the British economy. This, it is argued, is because governmental policies would no longer be determined primarily on ideology, but instead on a more general and consensual appraisal of the country's actual economic needs. Furthermore, the eschewal of ideology – itself linked to the pivotal role of the Liberal Democrats in any coalition government – would result in greater continuity of policies, thereby affording them sufficient time in which to be fully implemented and yield success. This in turn would foster much greater confidence on the part of the business community, thereby encouraging greater, and longer-term, investment.

Thus we observe that whereas other perspectives often give prime importance to the economic sphere, and see social or political problems as a manifestation of underlying economic defects or difficulties, the

'Centrist' perspective turns this on its head, alleging that many of the economic and social problems which have emerged in Britain since 1945 – but particularly since the late 1960s – can be ascribed to an allegedly archaic political system. The key to Britain's economic recovery and revival is therefore thought to be located in the reform of political institutions. Indeed, according to this approach, democratization in the political sphere will itself provide the impetus for economic regeneration. A more democratic Britain will, *pari passu*, become a more prosperous Britain.

The View from the Left

Whilst one would obviously expect the Left's perspective to differ fundamentally from that of the Right, there are also, in some respects, certain similarities between them. Both perspectives, for example, are inclined to characterize the mounting problems facing Britain since the 1960s as a 'crisis of social democracy', a system which was doomed to fail due to the contradictions contained therein. However, whereas the Right viewed social democracy as a variant of socialism, albeit watered down, and thus a system which placed too many restrictions and restraints on the workings of the free market, the Left have tended to characterize post-war social democracy in Britain as merely a modified form of capitalism. The Left point out, for example, that even at the height of nationalization, 80 per cent of the economy still remained in private hands, with profit still the main motive or purpose of the majority of economic activity. In other words, the economy still retained its essentially capitalist character, and as such, was still susceptible to the same contradictions and crises that any capitalist system is prone to. As such, the Left would argue that the full employment and economic prosperity of the 1950s was never likely to last, and that the 1960s and 1970s served to reveal the fragility – and futility – of the attempt at managing capitalism, and of seeking to embellish it with a human face. Indeed, at this point, a second similarity emerges between the Left's perspective and that put forward by the Right, concerning the 'economic contradictions of democracy'.

The terms invoked by the Left, however, include 'fiscal crisis of the state' and 'legitimation crisis', but both seek to explain broadly the same phenomenon, namely the tension or contradiction between satisfying the wishes of the people for welfare provision on the one hand, and ensuring the conditions for profitable economic activity and production on the other. The provision of welfare benefits and services was deemed necessary to provide the capitalist system with 'legitimacy', not least by satisfying the demands and aspirations of the electorate, which in turn compelled political parties to compete by promising – and providing – greater social expenditure and services (precisely the point made by Samuel Brittan). At the same time, however, the state needs to ensure the continued, effective operation of the predominantly capitalist economy by facilitating the processes of (what Marxists term) 'capital accumulation'. Whilst there iss sufficient economic growth or stability, then the state is able to satisfy both economic and social objectives. A buoyant economy permits the funding of the welfare state. Capital accumulation and a contented citizenry co-exist side by side.

However, sooner or later, a situation will emerge in which the costs of maintaining existing, let alone higher, levels of welfare provision become too much for the state, and also come to constitute a burden on the private sector of the economy. This situation will be greatly compounded if the economy itself enters into recession; indeed, according to this perspective, the very cost of providing public and welfare services is itself a contributory factor to the decline of the economy, due to the obstacles it places on capital accumulation. A point is reached whereby the state can no longer provide simultaneously the conditions for capital accumulation and the level of welfare and public services which the populace have come to expect. As capital acccumulation and the maximization of profit are the very rationale of capitalism as an economic system, and also a prerequisite of creating the wealth necessary to provide welfare services, the state is compelled to curb, and often reduce, its provision of public services. This is liable to anger or alienate sections of the public who have come to expect, as of right, that the state will provide welfare services and other such social benefits. It is at this point, according to writers such as Habermas, that there will occur a 'legitimation crisis' (Habermas 1976). This, a number of Left writers contend, is ultimately what developed in Britain during the 1970s, and thereby paved the way for a radical Conservative Government explicitly committed to facilitating the conditions for renewed capital accumulation by cutting public expenditure, particularly welfare provision, whilst simultaneously curbing drastically the power of the trade unions.

Governments coming to power in such circumstances, and with such policy commitments, this perspective holds, will of necessity prove authoritarian, due to the need to overcome resistance from those sections of society whose expectations and living standards are being reduced. The 'firm smack of government' is also necessary ideologically to convince the electorate that the harsh measures are necessary and justified, thereby restoring legitimacy. It is in this context that many on the Left trace the trajectory of British politics from the 1960s through to the emergence of Thatcherism. The collapse of social democracy did not result in a surge of support for 'true socialism', but on the contrary, created the space in which a backlash against the Left could be mobilized. By convincing sufficient numbers of people that thed problems which had beset Britain during the 1960s and 1970s were largely a consequence of social democracy – defined in terms of over-generous welfare provision, inefficient state industries and public services, burgeoning bureaucracy, anti-enterprise attitudes, excessive trade union power, and social/sexual permissiveness bordering on rampant immorality – considerable intellectual and electoral support could be garnered for a 'return' to capitalism in the economic sphere, and discipline in the social sphere (Hall 1980: 19–39): in other words, what Gamble termed 'the free economy and the strong state' (Gamble 1988).

In fact, a number of Marxist writers discerned this trend towards authoritarianism – as part of the 'legitimation crisis' – before the election of Margaret Thatcher as Prime Minister. Such commentators would point to a number of trends and developments taking place in British politics during the 1970s which reflected the increasingly desperate attempts of Governments (Conservative and Labour) to grapple with the deepening problems of the British economy. Indeed, one group of writers published a detailed analysis of the trend towards right-wing authoritarianism in 1970s Britain the year before Margaret Thatcher first became Prime Minister (Hall *et al.* 1978; see also Hall 1980; Kettle 1983).

The Left's view that post-war Britain remained essentially capitalist has important implications for their characterization of power in British politics (and society generally) since 1945, and the consequences for the Labour Party, the trade unions and the working class. For if Britain did remain a predominantly capitalist society even prior to the election of the first Thatcher Government in 1979, then this raises questions about the nature and behaviour of the Labour Party, or more particularly, Labour Governments – from 1945 onwards. Here, a number of observations are advanced by commentators on the Left, even though there is often disagreement amongst them on specific points or over which factors are most important.

A common observation amongst many writers on the Left – more particularly on the Marxist Left – is that the Labour Party has never been committed to the goal of socialism, but, instead, has always been a broadly social democratic party satisfied with pursuing modest reforms and improvements within the existing, predominantly capitalist, system. According to this view, therefore, the failure of post-war Labour Governments to bring about a transition to socialism is not a case of 'betrayal', because the Labour Party, especially most of its leadership, had never intended to get rid of capitalism in the first place. Instead, Labour Governments have set themselves the much more limited objective of seeking to ameliorate the worst excesses of capitalism, and imbue it with a degree of fairness and social responsibility. Indeed, many such commentators would point to the policies of the Attlee Government, and the subsequent 'revisionist' critique articulated by Crosland, as evidence that the Labour Party, since 1945, has primarily sought to manage the capitalist system, rather than replace it with socialism.

Following on from this critique, some commentators point to Labour's historical relationship with the trade unions as a reason for its alleged lack of socialist commitment. According to this approach, the Labour Party was not established as, or to be, an explicitly socialist political party, even though it obviously contained many socialists amongst its membership. Instead, it was founded (as the Labour Representation Committee in 1900, before becoming the Labour Party in 1906) for the express purpose of securing representation in Parliament for working people and trade unionists, whereupon legislation could be pursued both to protect the legal and financial position of the trade unions themselves, and to defend or advance the material interests of ordinary working people. There was nothing inherently socialist in any of this. Indeed, as has often been noted, the very name 'Labour Party' was significant, signifying not a type of society being aspired to (i.e., socialist, social democratic, Communist), but merely the name of a particular socio-economic interest within the existing capitalist society. The Labour Party, in other words, committed itself to representing the organized working class within the existing capitalist framework (and primarily within Parliament), rather than leading the workers in a struggle to transcend capitalism (Coates 1975: 5–6; Dearlove and Saunders 1991: 289–90; Hindess 1983: 92; Miliband 1972: 13). Consequently, a number of writers have characterized the Labour Party's 'ideology' as one best termed 'labourism', rather than socialism, whereby 'workers have taken the wage relationship under capitalism as unalterable, and have concentrated their industrial and political efforts on improving their lot within it . . . within the existing system of wage labour' (Coates 1980: 271; see also Foote 1985: ch. 1; Saville 1988: 14).

Another critique from many on the Left argues that Labour Governments since 1945 have been prevented from pursuing more radical or socialist policies due to the power of key institutions, such as 'the City' and the Civil Service. These have had the ability to block or deter Labour proposals or policies which they deemed too radical and thus damaging to the overall status quo, so that Labour Governments have been compelled to pursue 'orthodox' economic policies (i.e. deflation, curbing public expenditure, holding down wages, etc.) because of the constraints imposed by the 'business community' and the Treasury. Indeed, such Governments are deemed to have faced the same dilemma that any left-of-centre Government faces; the desire to improve social and welfare benefits, improve public services and tackle poverty requires economic growth, which in turn requires massive investment. However, this will only be forthcoming if the confidence of the business community can be secured, which in turn requires that Labour Governments pursue policies favoured by financiers and industrialists, namely wage restraint, curbs on public expenditure, less 'generous' welfare provision, etc.

The Civil Service is also deemed to have been a major impediment to the ability of post-war Labour Governments to pursue radical policies. According to the Left, the Civil Service is an innately conservative institution, due in large part to the socio-economic background of the people who occupy posts in its higher echelons. These senior civil servants – the very people within the Civil Service who have traditionally played a considerable role in helping ministers to formulate and implement policies – have usually come from middle- or upper-middle class families, and been to a public school prior to attending Oxbridge (for example, it has long been the case that about 80 per cent of those in the highest three levels of the Civil Service had attended Oxford or Cambridge

University). This, according to commentators on the Left, renders such civil servants part of 'the establishment' and of the existing system of power and privilege in British society. As such, and in spite of constitutional conventions concerning the political neutrality and impartiality of the Civil Service and its staff, such civil servants are deemed by the Left to be inherently conservative, if not with a large 'C' then certainly with a small 'c', and therefore hostile to any Labour Government seeking to pursue radical policies. Accordingly, it is alleged, post-war Labour Governments have either been pressured into watering down or even abandoning various policies, or had them impeded through the obstruction or obfuscation of senior civil servants. Ralph Miliband neatly encapsulated this approach, arguing that:

> Top civil servants are generally people with conventional views . . . The majority of them are the products of middle- and upper-class homes, with a public-school and Oxford or Cambridge education . . . Such a background does not automatically and inevitably produce conformity; but it mainly does . . . there is at the heart of British government a very powerful braking mechanism against radical change. (Miliband 1982: 101–8; see also Sedgemore 1980: 26)

On the issue of powerful groups and vested interests, the Left perspective rejects the widespread view that the trade unions acquired immense – too much – power in post-war British politics. On the contrary, many commentators and scholars on the Left, particularly those writing from a Marxist perspective, insist that as Britain remained a predominantly capitalist society after the end of the war, then the power and interests of trade unions and their members were invariably subordinated to those of the business community (for examples of the Marxist view on the 'weakness' of trade unions under capitalism, see Anderson 1977: 333–50, and Coates 1983: 55–82). Economically, it is argued, trade unions are simply unable to match the financial resources, organizational skills and instant mobility enjoyed by financiers and industrialists. For all the allegations and accusations about 'trade union power' and trade unions 'running the country' in post-war Britain, the Left insist that the unions enjoyed very little say in day-to-day economic and industrial decisions. On the contrary, it is claimed that:

> labour has nothing of the power of capital in the day-to-day economic decision-making of capitalist enterprise. What a firm produces;

whether it exports or does not export; whether it invests, and in what, and for what purpose; whether it absorbs or is absorbed by other firms – these and many other such decisions are matters over which labour has . . . generally no influence at all . . . labour lacks a firm basis of economic power, and has consequently that much less pressure potential *vis-à-vis* the state . . . governments are much less concerned to obtain the 'confidence' of labour than of business. (Miliband 1973: 139–40)

Indeed, many on the Left would point out that although the business community is itself subject to internal divisions and disagreements over particular policies or strategies from time to time, these are as nothing compared to the divisions which characterize the working class and their trade unions, for whom demarcations along lines of gender, race and occupation are ever-present obstacles to greater unity (Westergaard and Resler 1976: 343–80).

Thus labour in post-war Britain, it is suggested, has not enjoyed anything like the degree of cohesion and consciousness of common interest which usually characterizes the business community, and which tend to be reinforced – as with senior civil servants – by similar socio-economic backgrounds, connections, etc. Furthermore, Miliband points out:

labour does not have anything, by way of exercising pressure, which corresponds to the foreign influences which are readily marshalled on behalf of capital. There are no labour 'gnomes' of Zurich, no labour equivalent of the World Bank, the International Monetary Fund, or the OECD, to ensure that governments desist from taking measures detrimental to wage-earners . . . or to press for policies which are of advantage to 'lower income groups'. (Miliband 1973: 140)

Nor was this fundamental inequality and imbalance of economic power ameliorated by the apparent equal status and influence accorde to trade unions by virtue of corporatist trends during the 1960s and 1970s. The formal involvement of trade unions in economic policy-making during these decades may have given the impression that they were participating on an equal footing with the business community, but the reality, according to writers such as Miliband, was that trade union leaders became 'junior partners of capitalist enterprise', whereupon 'their incorporation . . . served to saddle them with responsibilities which have further weakened their bargaining position . . . and helped to reduce their effectiveness' (Miliband 1973: 144; see also Panitch 1986: chs 5 and 7).

The Left was equally sceptical about the widely held assumption that the welfare state had served to make Britain a more equal society since 1945. On the contrary, the Left was inclined to argue, the welfare state had merely served to legitimize capitalism, thereby providing a fundamentally exploitative and unequal socio-economic system with an aura of compassion and egalitarianism. The welfare state was thus deemed by the Left to provide a facade behind which the fundamental inequalities intrinsic to capitalism could continue largely unabated, yet without the legitimacy of the system being called into question by the British people. The welfare state allegedly encouraged the view that poverty had been abolished, that wealth was being redistributed from the rich to the poor, and that equality of opportunity had been enhanced, thereby permitting the social advancement of individuals from working-class backgrounds. Yet the extent to which any of these policies were actually achieved by virtue of the welfare state in post-war Britain has been hotly contested by many commentators on the Left. At the most, such commentators might acknowledge that the worst or most glaring excesses of poverty and inequality had been tempered by the welfare state, but that, ultimately, widespread inequalities remained. Indeed, it has been suggested that instead of entailing a transfer of wealth from rich to poor, the welfare state has generally involved a horizontal distribution of wealth within social classes (Field 1981: 92–116; Westergaard 1983: 160–1). In any case, the Left point out, the better-off have tended to enjoy other 'benefits' or 'perks' – such as mortgage tax relief, tax relief on private insurance schemes, greater job security and promotion prospects, occupational pensions, and possibly the ability to hire an accountant to advise on other means of avoiding certain tax payments – which served to mitigate the effects of higher income tax imposed on them by a progressive, 'redistributive' taxation system.

Furthermore, a number of Left commentators argue that whilst the initial establishment of the welfare state may have yielded a small degree of wealth redistribution from the richest to the poorest in British society, this process soon dissipated, and even reversed by the 1970s; in other words, it is suggested that thirty or so years after the implementation of the Beveridge reforms by the Attlee Government, the gap between the richest and the poorest in Britain was actually becoming wider (Westergaard 1983: 149–52; Westergaard and Resler 1976: 38–51). Furthermore, to the extent that wealth redistribution did take place in post-war Britain, it was overwhelmingly from the wealthiest to the middle, rather than the working, class. Certainly, various studies suggest that the middle classes have been the main beneficiaries of the welfare state in post-war Britain (see, for example, Le Grand 1982) – even though they will often be the first to complain that too much welfare is allocated to those who least need or deserve it, and hence that social security expenditure and provision needs to be pruned (Galbraith 1992).

In all these ways, therefore, the Left are inclined to emphasize just how limited have been the changes in British politics since 1945, and the extent to which fundamental inequalities of wealth, economic power and social privilege have remained largely intact, in spite of the apparent or alleged trends towards a more egalitarian, meritocratic society (see, for example, Urry and Wakeford 1973; Westergaard and Resler 1976; Miliband 1982; Coates 1984; Panitch 1986). Not only are post-war reforms deemed to have been extremely modest, in both design and effect, they are also considered to have proved very fragile, as evinced by their inability to withstand the Conservative assault on them since 1979.

8 Concluding Considerations

No, no; it must not be so:
They are the ways we do not go . . .
Had you been sharer of that scene,
you would not ask while it bites in keen,
why it is so, we can no more go,
by the summer paths we used to know.

Thomas Hardy, 'Paths of Former Time'

One particular aspect of British politics since 1945 which has become apparent in the preceding text is the extent to which pragmatism and empiricism, rather than ideology and doctrines, have shaped the policies of successive Governments for most of the post-war era. British people and their politicians have long considered themselves to be guided by common sense and experience, and are thus suspicious of abstract theories advocated by philosophers and political scientists. Indeed, the British are proudly 'anti-intellectual', and seem to treat with a mixture of suspicion and derision those who are deemed to be 'ivory-tower academics', rather than inhabitants of the 'real world'.

This empiricist tradition has been reflected and reinforced to a large extent by Britain's politicians since 1945 (and long before, as a matter of fact). The Conservative Party has elevated to the status of virtue its alleged lack of ideology, insisting that Conservatism owes far more to intuition and instinct than doctrine or dogma. It is perhaps not surprising, therefore, that many of those texts which do purport to provide a framework or outline of Conservative philosophy have actually been written by Conservative politicians themselves, the precedent being set, it seems, by Edmund Burke, whose *Reflections on the French Revolution* has been widely claimed as a statement of Conservative philosophy which simultaneously eschews the pursuit of political activity which is based on abstract goals or philosophical blueprints for creating a new society. From Burke through to the present day, Conservatives have thus tended to insist on the importance of pragmatism and practicability in governing the country.

The Labour Party has also exhibited considerable pragmatism in British politics since 1945. Whilst its Conservative opponents have always accused Labour of representing and pursuing 'doctrinaire socialism', the fact is that the Labour Party, particularly when in office, was notable for the extent to which its leadership eschewed ideology, and proceeded pragmatically in the implementation of policies. Even the apparent doctrinal core of the Labour Party, Clause IV, has largely received lip-service from Labour leaders. On the occasions when they have expressed their support for the objectives enshrined in Clause IV, Labour leaders have invariably emphasized the extent to which these are open to differing interpretations and emphases, as well as different means of achieving them. In short, Labour Prime Ministers have refused to be bound by a strict or single interpretation of Clause IV.

Neither have Labour leaders, particularly when in office, necessarily considered themselves beholden to decisions taken at the party's annual conference. According to Labour's constitution, its annual conference is the supreme decision-making body of the party, and a policy which is supported by a two-thirds majority amongst the delegates formally becomes official Labour policy. Yet Labour leaders have tended to be selective about which conference decisions they will actually implement when Labour is in power, insisting on the need for a degree of autonomy, and the ability to exercise their own judgement and discretion according to circumstances at any given juncture.

In so doing, Labour leaders have tended to point to the impossible position which they and their ministers would be placed in if they were rigidly bound by the decisions and demands of delegates at the party's annual conference. Quite apart from the fact that a particular conference decision might not be practicable or feasible from the party leadership's point of view or perspective, it is also emphasized that literal adherence to conference decisions would place ministers in an untenable position, for if annual conference voted for the abandonment of a specific policy or programme and sought to replace it by a new one, then ministers would find themselves espousing views and arguments entirely different from, and at odds with, those they had been articulating a few weeks or months previously. Furthermore, conference decisions might be incompatible with the known preference or position of a particular minister in any given sphere of policy. For example, when Labour's annual conference formally committed the party to unilateral disarmament in the early 1980s, it was universally known that the party's defence spokesperson, Denis Healey, was a committed multilateralist.

This would render Labour leaders bereft of credibilty in the eyes of the electorate, making them appear as little more than puppets or mouthpieces of Labour's grass-roots activists and delegates attending the party's annual conference. Labour leaders have thus always insisted that they and the party's MPs are first and foremost representatives, not delegates who can simply be instructed or mandated by annual conference as to what policies and laws they adopt. In emphasizing their role as 'representatives', rather than delegates of annual conference, Labour leaders an MPs have frequently sought to remind the party's rank-and-file activists that a Labour Government would be concerned to represent all of those who voted for it, whilst simultaneously taking into account the perceived national interest at any given moment. These considerations are therefore deemed totally incompatible with an interpretation that sees Labour MPs and ministers as the mere servants of the party's annual conference. Indeed, such an interpretation is also deemed to be incompatible with the very character of parliamentary democracy and sovereignty themselves.

Another reason why the Labour Party has tended to eschew a doctrinaire approach to politics and governance derives from its intimate links with the trade unions. The vast majority of Britain's trade unions have themselves eschewed abstract theories in favour of pragmatism and piecemeal improvements in their members' terms and conditions of employment. Whatever their avowed objectives may be in terms of replacing capitalism and ushering in socialism, trade unions in Britain have tended to be far more modest and pragmatic in their immediate objectives than their fiery conference speeches and declarations seem to suggest.

After all, the trade unions were originally established in order to defend and promote the interests of groups of workers *vis-à-vis* their employers, with their attention invariably focused on improving wages, working conditions, etc. When and where trade unions did espouse socialism, it was often rhetorical in nature, and where it was genuine, the attainment of socialism was usually seen as a long-term objective, to be achieved somewhere in the future. Thus, although many trade unionists throughout the nineteenth and twentieth centuries have been socialists, it by no means follows that the trade unions *qua* institutions have been socialist, at least not in anything more than a vague or rhetorical sense.

It is also important to remember that the trade unions actually formed the Labour Party, in 1906, in order to ensure that their interests, and those of their members, were represented and articulated within Parliament. Whilst there were those in the labour movement who envisaged that the Labour Party would indeed be a vehicle for socialism, this was not the primary purpose ascribed to it by its founders in the trade unions. Instead, there concern was that trade unionists and ordinary working people in general were not being adequately represented by the Conservative and Liberal Parties at Westminster. Thus the trade union movement envisaged that the Labour Party would articulate in Parliament the interests of ordinary working people, just as the Conservative Party was deemed to advance the interests of employers and the business community. In establishing the Labour Party, therefore, the trade unions were not so much seeking the transcendence of the capitalist system as securing fairer representation and treatment of working people within it.

This emphasis on achieving more immediate and tangible improvements for working people itself both reflected and reinforced the trade unions' eschewal of doctrine and ideology in favour of empiricism and pragmatism. The trade unions 'are for the most part sceptical, even resentful, of intellectuals with highbrow ideas', a scepticism which 'is reinforced by the average Labour voter, who wants a better deal for workers and their families, but is easily frightened by grandiose projects that seem impracticable' (Smith and Polsby 1981: 102).

This scepticism, as we have already intimated, has largely been shared by the Labour Party itself, particularly its parliamentary leaders, most of whom have been positively Burkean in their rejection of abstract theories and philosophical genuflection. As Attlee himself acknowledged in recalling the work of the 1945 Labour Government:

> It had always been our practice, in accord with the natural genius of the
> British people, to work empirically. We were not afraid of compromises
> and partial solutions. We knew that mistakes would be made, and that
> advance would often be by trial and error. We realised that the application
> of socialist principles in a country such as Britain . . . required great
> flexibilty. (Attlee 1954: 163)

It is not difficult to imagine virtually any subsequent Labour leader
making exactly the same declaration. Harold Wilson, for example,
emphasized that the Labour Party owed more to Methodism than
Marxism, and elevated to the status of virtue the fact that he had
never advanced beyond the third page of the first volume of Karl
Marx's *Capital*!

A further factor which has underpinned the essentially pragmatic,
empirical approach of British politics since 1945, at least up until 1979,
has been the tendency for the Prime Ministers during this period to
have emanated from, or identified with, the moderate wing of their
respective political parties. In other words, prior to Margaret Thatcher,
Conservative leaders and Prime Ministers tended to be on the left of
the party, thereby representing the 'one nation' tradition of British
Conservatism. This was certainly the case with Conservative leaders
such as Anthony Eden, Harold Macmillan and Alec Douglas-Home.
Meanwhile, the post-war Winston Churchill proved a much more
emollient figure than had been the case in the 1920s and 1930s, and
as such, he too broadly adopted a policy stance from 1951 to 1955 which
was more warmly welcomed on the left of the party than on the right.

The one exception up until 1979 might be Edward Heath, whose
'Selsdon Man' incarnation was widely seen as constituting a marked
shift to the right. Compared to the approach of previous post-war
leaders, there is undoubtedly considerable truth in this interpretation,
but it is easy to overstate the case. Heath was, during the 'Selsdon
Man' phase, more in tune with the managerialist and technocratic ethos
which pervaded Britain's political elites during the 1960s, whereby the
reversal of Britain's relative economic decline was to derive from greater
competition and efficiency. To this extent, it has been suggested that
whilst he appeared to personify a marked shift to the right by the
Conservative Party after its 1964 election defeat, Heath's 'Selsdon Man'
was actually concerned primarily to salvage the post-war settlement,
rather than destroy it. In any case, shortly after coming to power, as we

saw in chapter 4, 'Selsdon Man' was slain by Heath in favour of a return to a consensual, neo-corporatist mode of politics which delighted the left of the Conservative Party and disgusted the right. As one commentary on post-war British politics has noted with regard to Heath's adoption of a more ideological stance, 'he never really adopted it wholeheartedly and has since been considered one of the most conspicuous of the pragmatists' (Smith and Polsby 1981: 109).

Meanwhile, the Labour Party since 1945 has predominantly been led by figures from the centre-right of the party, certainly whilst in office. Whilst he undoubtedly presided over the most radical Labour Government ever, Attlee was no ideologue. On the contrary, the quote from Attlee cited earlier in this chapter illustrated the extent to which he himself eschewed a doctrinaire, ideological approach in favour of pragmatism and empiricism. As such, he was susceptible to the charge from the left of the Labour Party that he was not sufficiently committed to the goal of socialism, but instead, far too willing to accept compromise and exude caution.

Attlee's successor, Hugh Gaitskell, incurred even more displeasure from Labour's left, for he was undoubtedly on the right of the party, and firmly in the revisionist school personified by Anthony Crosland. Hence Gaitskell's attempt at ridding the Labour Party's constitution of Clause IV in order to modernize the party and extend its appeal to the expanding middle classes.

Modernization was also a key theme of Harold Wilson, who succeeded Gaitskell as Labour leader in 1963, before becoming Prime Minister in 1964. At the time, Wilson had a reputation for being on the left of the party, but much of this was due to his resignation alongside Bevan over the imposition of NHS charges in 1951. By the time he became Labour leader, there was little which could seriously be considered left-wing about Wilson, and he too seemed more concerned about the modernization of Britain – through the application of science, technology and rationalism – than adherence to any socialist doctrine, beyond the risible rhetoric about harnessing socialism to science and vice versa.

When Wilson stood down as Labour Prime Minister in 1976, having led the party to victory in 1974 (after having lost in 1970), he was succeeded by the avuncular James Callaghan who was himself firmly on the right of the party, and whose talk of socialism appeared symbolic rather than substantive.

Up until 1979, therefore, it can be seen that a major reason for the essentially pragmatic, empirical character of British politics since 1945 was derived from the tendency of successive party leaders and Prime Ministers to emanate from, or incline towards, the moderate, non-ideological wings of their respective parties. Ideology and idealism were largely subordinated to an approach which emphasized pragmatism and practicability. The key criterion for Conservative and Labour leaders when in office appeared to be the resolution of immediate or short-term problems, rather than the pursuit of specific long-term ideological goals or creation of a new social order. If politics was the art of the possible, then what was deemed possible by successive party leaders and Prime Ministers was often narrowly defined.

If there was a consensus in British politics from 1945 to the 1970s, whereby successive Governments were inclined to pursue broadly similar policies in a wide range of areas, then it surely owed much to this tendency for the leaders of both main political parties to emanate from the moderate or non-ideological wings of their particular party. This meant that whichever party was in office at any given juncture, it largely accepted the framework and parameters inherited from its predecessor. Governance was primarily about administration of the existing system, and of pursuing pragmatic, piecemeal reforms as and when these were deemed desirable or necessary in order to ameliorate particular problems or make the system function more effectively. The day-to-day concerns and considerations of politicians were technocratic rather than theoretical. The approach to problem-solving was invariably incremental rather than ideological.

Indeed, the concept of incrementalism as applied to British politics since 1945 warrants further consideration. Incrementalism is a model of, or approach to, policy-making which emphasizes the importance of gradual, step-by-step reforms to the status quo, whereby change occurs only slowly over a period of time, and with the minimum of disruption. Politicians and other policy-makers, such as civil servants, deal with problems and issues as and when they arise, so that governance is largely about short-term adjustments to the status quo.

Now whilst it is possible to pursue radical objectives and ideological goals in such an incremental manner, so that minor changes in the short term amount to a significant change in the longer term, incrementalism usually implies that politicians and policy-makers are not motivated to any great extent by ideological objectives, but are primarily concerned to manage and administer the existing system as effectively as possible. Rather than planning ahead or explicating particular partisan objectives, therefore, political leaders and civil servants *react* to problems and issues as and when they arise. When such problems and issues arise, the emphasis is then on immediate and practicable solutions rather than considerations of ideology or long-term strategy. Politics becomes, in the words of Charles Lindblom, 'the science of muddling through' (Lindblom 1959).

The essentially *reactive* character of much of British politics since 1945 was clearly noted by Jack Hayward when – writing during the mid-1970s – he noted that:

> Firstly, there are no explicit, over-riding medium or long-term objectives. Secondly, unplanned decision-making is incremental. Thirdly, humdrum or unplanned decisions are arrived at by a continuous process of mutual adjustment between a plurality of autonomous policy-makers operating in the context of a highly fragmented multiple flow of influence. Not only is plenty of scope offered to interest groups' spokesmen to shape the outcome by participation in the advisory process. The aim is to secure through bargaining at least passive acceptance of the decision by the interests affected. (Hayward 1974: 398–9)

If this is indeed the case, then successive British Governments since 1945 would appear to have been seasoned practitioners of this art. This is partly because of the degree of broad agreement between the two main political parties over the general framework and parameters of politics in post-war Britain, and an overall acceptance concerning the role and purpose of Government and the state, coupled with a widespread belief in the legitimacy of Britain's political institutions and policy-making procedures. As Jordan and Richardson expressed it (writing in 1982):

> Britain is best characterised as emphasising consensus and a desire to avoid the imposition of solutions on sections of society. In that there is no particular priority accorded to anticipatory solutions – and the stress on negotiation itself inhibits radical change – the British style is also 'reactive'. (Jordan and Richardson 1982: 81)

Another feature of incrementalism, particularly as it applies to British politics from 1945 to 1979, is the emphasis placed on consultation with affected groups and 'interested parties'. The 'post-war consensus' entailed not only general agreement on the actual policies and objectives pursued, but on the desirability or necessity of obtaining the 'consent of the governed' in the pursuit of these policies and objectives. There were two particular reasons why consultation with certain groups and organized interests became an established feature of British politics in this period.

Firstly, it was recognized by political leaders and policy-makers that governmental objectives and decisions would acquire greater *legitimacy* (moral authority and acceptability) if those affected by them had been consulted, and believed that their views and concerns had been taken into account by political leaders. This in turn, Governments believed, would increase the likelihood of their policies proving successful, for potential opposition would have been pre-empted.

Secondly, greater Government intervention in, and responsibility for, an unprecedented range of economic and social affairs rendered politicians and civil servants dependent upon certain key groups for advice in formulating policies, and assistance (or at least acquiescence) in implementing them. The greater the degree of Government intervention, the greater becomes the Government's need for the specialist knowledge and expertise which organized interests possess, along with their co-operation in enabling policies to be put into practice. Or as Jordan and Richardson express it: 'An interventionist state tends towards a functionally differentiated and fragmented bureaucracy and the relations between department and sectoral interests tend to become closer' (Jordan and Richardson 1982: 86; see also Beer 1967: 85). Thus did Jean Blondel once remark that if pressure groups withheld information and co-operation from policy-makers, then the governance of the country would come to a halt (Blondel 1963: 225).

Thirdly, there was concern that if certain pressure groups were not consulted by politicians and civil servants, they might respond by exercising a veto power over Government policies, using their professional or socio-economic position to block or undermine those policies with which they disapproved or deemed inimical to their interests. Thus did Governments frequently consider it sensible to consult with the representatives of key pressure groups, thereby increasing the likelihood that policies would be more acceptable to organized interests, and consequently less likely to suffer from active opposition or obstruction. As Richardson emphasizes:

whatever governments wish to achieve in the National Health Service or in education, it cannot be delivered without the co-operation of doctors and teachers. In the end, everyone realizes that the system cannot work if it is based on continuous conflict. Compromise is, therefore, institutionalized and regularized in, literally, hundreds of advisory committees (some permanent, some *ad hoc*) surrounding government departments. (Richardson 1993: 94–5)

It was characteristics such as those outlined above which, to a considerable extent, convinced Richard Rose that in post-war British politics, political parties did not make that much difference to governmental policies (Rose 1984). Whichever political party was in office, the same sort of problems would manifest themselves, and broadly similar policies would be pursued. Credence to this view was provided by Lord Croham, a former Head of the Civil Service when, in 1978, he gave a talk to new civil servants in which he pointed out that:

... the more central government seeks to intervene in the economy, the less powerful it will become, because it will have to rely on an ever-increasing number of bodies and individuals to do what it wants. Those people in this situation will bargain and make terms. If you believe that elections should determine policies, that policy choices should be clear cut alternatives, and that there is, or should be a wide range of possible alternatives, you will not enjoy the general situation I have forecast, because it is one which creates the need for consensus politics, interparty deals, and bargains with pressure groups. Without such arrangement, it will be difficult to put central government majorities together, or get the various levels of government to function. (quoted in Richardson 1993)

In similar vein, Dennis Kavanagh has suggested that 'parties and general elections do not make much difference'. Even the 'landmark' elections of 1945 and 1979, he points out, reflected and reinforced trends which were already taking place (Kavanagh 1991). Further endorsement of this perspective is provided by Jordan and Richardson when they assert that: 'The need to consult with a specific set of groups concerned with each policy problem . . . normally leads to incremental policy change, irrespective of the party forming the government at any one time' (Jordan and Richardson 1982: 92).

However, the preceding analysis might be deemed grossly inappropriate or inapplicable to British politics since 1979. To what extent is it plausible or meaningful to invoke concepts such as incrementalism or consultation to the years of Margaret Thatcher's premiership from 1979 to 1990? Surely this was a period of conviction politics during which the Government actively pursued specific, clearly defined or discernible objectives, rather than reacting to events as and when they occurred? After all, was not Margaret Thatcher's avowed objective – or one of them – to break with the post-war social democratic consensus?

Now, there is certainly some truth in all of these observations. Yet it may well be that the extent to which 1979 heralded a sharp break with the preceding period from 1945 has been exaggerated or overstated by both critics and sycophants of Thatcherism alike. Writing in 1988, Andrew Gamble claimed that: 'The gulf between the achievements and the rhetoric of Thatcherism still looked very wide' (Gamble 1988: 210; see also Jordan and Richardson 1982: 107–8).

In support of this more sober assessment of the Thatcher years, five particular factors can be cited, each suggesting that the changes wrought by the Thatcher Governments were perhaps not as profound as has hitherto been widely alleged or assumed.

Firstly, a number of policies which became associated with Thatcherism during the 1980s had already been initiated by the Callaghan Government during 1976–9. Most notable of these were monetarism, cutbacks in public expenditure (including curbs on public sector pay), tax cuts, the selling off of shares in certain state industries, and the selling of council houses. Obviously the Thatcher Governments pursued such policies with rather greater commitment and conviction, but the fact remains that the change lay more in the manner in which these policies were implemented after 1979, and the extent to which they were presented as part of an ideological project rather than a pragmatic response to unfavourable economic circumstances and constraints.

Secondly, but following on from this last point, it is worth noting that many of the policies associated with Thatcherism were themselves *incremental* and *reactive*, but were often furnished with an ideological gloss through the process of *post hoc* rationalization.

Thirdly, the extent to which a number of policies and objectives pursued by the Thatcher Governments can be said to have proved successful is questionable. For example, admirers of Thatcherism might point with pride to the fact that one million council houses were sold during the 1980s, but this only represented 20 per cent of local authority housing stock. When the Thatcher Governments then sought to reduce further the number of council houses by offering tenants the opportunity to opt out of local authority control in favour of being managed by a housing association or private landlord, tenants frequently voted to remain under the control of their local authority.

The privatization policy might also be cited as a policy whose success was less marked than Thatcherites would like to believe. As was noted in chapter 5, whilst share ownership may indeed have been extended, so that more people than ever before acquired shares during the 1980s through the Thatcher Governments' privatization programme, many of these first-time share owners quickly sold their shares in order to obtain a quick profit. In other words, the bulk of shares in former nationalized industries remained concentrated in the hands of a small number of share-holders and City institutions, irrespective of how many ordinary people may have purchased shares initially.

If privatization was intended to provide for a dispersal of wealth amongst ordinary people, then its success is highly questionable. Indeed, privatization may have served to make the rich richer in two ways: firstly, as has just been noted, because of the extent to which 'small investors' soon sold their shares, thereby reversing any initial, short-term transfer of capital to ordinary people. Secondly, the proceeds of privatization (coupled with the sums of money saved by the Government by virtue of no longer having to subsidize former nationalized industries) enabled the Thatcher Governments to finance significant income tax cuts, and these were of particular benefit to those on the highest incomes. To this extent, far from spreading wealth and capital more widely, privatization could be said to have contributed significantly towards its concentration at the top of Britain's socio-economic hierarchy, thereby reversing the modest trend towards a reduction in socio-economic inequality which many discerned in Britain from 1945 to 1979.

One other example of what might be deemed a policy failure of the Thatcher Governments is that of public expenditure. As we again observed in chapter 5, the 1980s witnessed an overall increase in public expenditure, particularly during the early part of the decade. Yet this was precisely when Thatcherites were proclaiming their goal of reducing public expenditure as part of the wider strategy of 'rolling back the state'. The Thatcher Governments were faced with the problem that their anti-inflationary strategy, entailing the toleration of high levels of unemployment, greatly increased the amount of revenue which had to be paid out in the form of social security benefits.

Similarly, the Thatcher Governments' commitment to nuclear defence, and the greater priority accorded to law-and-order, both served to boost overall levels of public expenditure further. The Thatcher Governments therefore found themselves redefining the meaning of 'cutting' public expenditure; instead of seeking absolute reductions, the goal was redefined as that of reducing the proportion of the nation's wealth devoted to public expenditure. This revised objective meant that public expenditure could be increased provided that it was at a slower rate than that of the increase in national wealth and economic growth, in which case it would represent a *proportional* reduction. This represented a subtle, yet important shift in the Thatcher Governments' objective of curbing public expenditure.

Fourthly, whilst the Thatcher Governments proudly proclaimed their eschewal of 'pandering' to vested or sectional interests, and thereby indicated a reduced role for pressure groups, the extent of exclusion is too often exaggerated. Certain groups which had formerly enjoyed 'insider' status, such as the TUC and the CBI, were undoubtedly marginalized, but this did not mean that groups in general became less important. The Thatcher Governments' image of pursuing 'high politics' above and beyond consultation with organized interests is far too simplistic and misleading.

What did take place under Thatcherism was a re-ordering of the pressure groups system, so that a few groups were excluded or downgraded whilst others gained access in their place. At the same time, the marginalization of certain groups in terms of consultation over the formulation of policy did not alter their importance at the *implementation* stage. Ultimately, the Thatcher Governments recognized that even if certain organized interests could be ignored during the making of policy, their acquiescence or assistance was often necessary in order that policy could be successfully put into practice. Furthermore, Richardson has suggested that even when and where certain groups did experience hostility from the Thatcher Governments, this was often temporary, so that a return to some kind of rapport and working relationship developed eventually. In other words, he explains:

> This destabilisation of policy communities – evident in such areas as health, education, law reform and the structure of the legal profession, and water policy – was almost invariably followed, however, by a return to the accepted values and norms of the policy process . . . once a sector had been 'shaken and stirred', the affected interests were then soothed by being invited back into the inner circle of negotiations with government. (Richardson 1993: 97)

Even when the Thatcher Governments declined to consult with certain pressure groups during the policy formulation phase, Richardson adds, it none the less tended 'to negotiate the implementation phase with the affected interests and to make significant concessions on the process' (*ibid.*: 98). Indeed Marsh and Rhodes suggest that it was at the implementation stage that a number of the Thatcher Governments' policies failed, or at the most, enjoyed only limited success. This was in large part due to the behaviour of certain organized interests, for as Marsh and Rhodes explain:

> the Thatcher Governments' . . . rejection of consultation and negotiation almost inevitably led to implementation problems, because those groups/interests affected by the policy, and who were not consulted, failed to co-operate, or comply, with the administration of policy . . . it is the continued existence and power of policy networks which has acted as the greatest constraint on the development and implementation of radical policy. (Marsh and Rhodes 1992: 181, 185)

The fifth and final factor which might be cited as evidence that the changes ascribed to Thatcherism were not as radical as often assumed concerns that of public opinion. Thatcherites would doubtless claim that the election of four successive Conservative Governments (three under Margaret Thatcher's leadership and one under the leadership of John Major) serves as testimony to the extent to which the British electorate embraced Thatcherite values, and thus ushered in a new culture based around the values of individualism, self-help, anti-statism, entrepreneurialism, cuts in welfare provision, and so on.

Such a perspective, however, does not stand up particularly well to closer scrutiny. Admittedly, on certain issues, such as immigration, law and order, and trade union reform, the Thatcher Governments drew from a deep well of public support for a much more authoritarian approach than had been pursued hitherto (although towards the end of the 1980s and into the 1990s, public support for trade union reform diminished, and if anything, seemed to become much more sympathetic to the severely weakened trade unions).

Overall, however, the most surprising feature of Thatcherism's impact on public opinion during the 1980s is the extent to which it failed to eradicate what might be termed 'social democratic' values amongst much of the British public. Indeed, as the decade progressed, support for such values actually seemed to increase. Opinion polls and attitude surveys conducted throughout the 1980s revealed continued (and ever growing) widespread public support for social democratic positions on a range of policies. For example, when asked in November 1980 (by Gallup) whether the Government ought to give more priority to curbing inflation or reducing unemployment, 30 per cent of respondents cited inflation whilst 62 per cent specified unemployment. When the same question was asked in May 1986, the response had changed to 13 per cent to 81 per cent respectively.

On the question of tax cuts versus increasing public expenditure, Gallup found that in March 1980, 25 per cent voters favoured tax cuts compared to 47 per cent who believed that extending public services was more important, even if this entailed increasing taxes. By June 1986, the respective figures were 17 and 64 per cent. Meanwhile, in 1979, Gallup discovered that 50 per cent of British people thought that the scope and scale of welfare provision had 'gone too far'; by 1987, only 17 per cent of people held this view. Other examples of the extent to which various policies pursued by the Thatcher Governments were at odds with public opinion are illustrated in table 8.1.

Furthermore, on a number of issues throughout the 1980s, the Labour Party enjoyed a consistent lead over the Conservative Party. For example, in countless opinion polls – both between and during general elections – Labour was adjudged by most voters to have 'better' policies on, for example, education, the NHS, and tackling unemployment. However, as the 1987 election clearly illustrated, the Conservatives did enjoy considerable public support or trust in the crucial sphere of economic competence, meaning that many voters had more faith in the Conservative Party's ability to deliver economic growth and increased prosperity. In other words, Labour enjoyed significant popularity on broad social issues, but trailed behind the Conservatives on the issue of economic competence, which served ultimately to ensure Conservative victories in the 1987 and 1992 general elections (see, for example, Crewe 1987; Sanders 1993: 194–213).

Table 8.1 Thatcherism and public opinion

Policy/Issue	Approve/Agree (%)	Disapprove/Disagree (%)
Abolition of the GLC	21	79
Banning trade unions at GCHQ	31	69
Privatization of British Gas	43	57
Privatization of British Telecom	44	56
Community charge/poll tax	29	71
Cutting top rate of income tax from 60% to 40%	35	65

(Source: Gallup; Crewe 1988)

What all of this seems to suggest is that whilst the Conservative Party enjoyed remarkable electoral success since 1979, this success has to a large extent been in spite of, rather than because of, public opinion on a range of issues and policies. Margaret Thatcher may have perceived and presented herself as a leader with a proselytizing mission to spread the gospel of rugged individualism and Smilesian self-help, but the British electorate still adhered – increasingly so – to social democratic values. She did not, after all, win their 'hearts and minds', even though she did lead the Conservative Party to three consecutive election victories. Indeed, it ought to be remembered that whilst the Conservative Party has been winning general elections since 1979 with 42–43 per cent of the vote (an impressive tally, admittedly, and one which the Labour Party and Liberal Democrats would dearly love to achieve!), this still means that 57–58 per cent of voters have *not* been voting Conservative. This also indicates that a majority of the electorate *do* vote for political parties which actually promise to increase income tax in order to fund improved public services, contrary to received wisdom about 'the majority' voting for tax cuts once they enter the privacy of the polling booth.

What the preceding overview suggests is that one of the most notable features of British politics since 1945 is just how little, and how slowly, things have changed in many areas. Politicians and Governments have been beset by similar problems throughout, namely securing economic growth, controlling inflation, reducing unemployment, persuading trade unions and their members to restrain wage demands, improving Britain's balance of payments problems, satisfying public demands for investment in areas such as education and health care, and so on.

At the same time, all Governments have frequently found their room for manoeuvre limited by a variety of factors and forces which have placed considerable constraints on their autonomy. In an increasingly complex and interdependent world, one characterized by a truly international global economy, post-war British Governments have found that more and more of their time and energy has been devoted to events and crises over which they have had little, if any, control.

This last point reinforces our earlier observation about the extent to which British politics since 1945 has been characterized by considerable incrementalism, with Governments responding to problems as and when they have arisen. The Thatcher Governments were undoubtedly more ideological in their objectives and approach than previous post-war governments, but even they were repeatedly compelled to *react to* problems and events as and when they emerged, whilst simultaneously having to acknowledge the practical problems of pursuing certain policies in view of the economic, international and political constraints impinging upon them (not the least of these being the European Union, of course).

Of course, it would absurd to claim that *nothing* has changed in British politics since 1945. Clearly Britain in the mid-1990s is not the same as Britain in 1945. What we would insist upon, however, is that many of the changes which have occurred have not only been gradual and incremental, but have also been, in many respects, relatively independent of the will or wishes of the Government. Policies have often been adopted in response to extraneous pressures and circumstances, even though Governments will usually attempt to present their responses as part of their ideological repertoire or long-term strategy anyway. Writing during Margaret Thatcher's first term of office, Richard Rose prophesied that:

> Post-1984 general elections will not mark an Orwellian end of time. They will be but one more step in the endless journey of representative government. The party that wins control of the next Parliament will differ in some of its intentions and policies from its opponents. But the differences in practice may be less than some voters (and MPs) expect. Moreover, in management of the economy changes may be less

(or different) than many voters would wish. Neither the Labour Party, the Conservative Party, nor the Alliance can expect to make all the difference to British society by winning a general election. (Rose 1984: 162)

Similarly, in their 'audit of an era', examining the extent to which the Thatcher Governments had successfully implemented their policies and achieved their avowed objectives, Marsh and Rhodes argue that whilst there were undoubtedly some significant changes to pre-1979 policies and practices, the overall scope and scale of change or success should not be exaggerated. Instead, they suggest that 'as far as outcomes are concerned much less has changed. The Thatcher Government may have had far more radical objectives than previous governments, but they were probably no better at achieving those objectives' (Marsh and Rhodes 1992: 170).

In view of the preceding analysis, therefore, maybe we should heed the wisdom of an old Chinese proverb which declares: 'Only fools exult when governments change.'

Appendix 1: Glossary

Act of Parliament: Item of legislation once it has received the Royal Assent.

Adversary politics: Characterization of British politics which deems it to be dominated by two ideologically motivated parties, so that changes of Government result in damaging left–right swings and changes of policy.

Bill: Item of legislation which has not yet been approved by Parliament and received the Royal Assent.

Block vote: Casting of trade union votes *en masse* according to the number of members (i.e., one million members could mean that one million votes will be cast for or against a policy by a handful of delegates at a conference).

Butskellism: Term coined in the early 1950s to denote the broadly similar policies pursued by Winston Churchill's Conservative Government after it had replaced Attlee's Labour Government in the 1951 general election. Derived from amalgamating the surnames of Rab Butler, the Conservative Chancellor after 1951, and Hugh Gaitskell, Labour's Chancellor prior to 1951.

Cabinet committees: Partial Cabinets mainly comprising the ministers whose departments are most closely concerned with a particular policy or piece of legislation. Their decisions have the same authority as those of the full Cabinet.

Class dealignment: The weakening of prevailing links between social class and political allegiance. Denotes declining working-class support for the Labour Party and a diminution of middle-class support for the Conservative Party.

Collective ministerial responsibility: All ministers must publicly support government policies, even if they personally were not involved in the decisions, or even if they personally disagree with them. If they cannot give their public support, they are expected to resign and return to the back-benches.

Consensus politics: Characterization of British politics from 1945 to the 1970s which perceives little fundamental difference between the Labour and Conservative Parties during this time, and insists that whichever party was in government, there was general agreement and continuity concerning policies.

Corporatism: The incorporation of key pressure groups (particularly trade unions and employers' associations) into economic policy-making. In return for their involvement in policy formulation, the relevant groups are expected to assist government by implementing the decisions reached, and to ensure the compliance of their members.

Embourgeoisement: Sociological term denoting the adoption and acquisition of middle-class lifestyles and values by sections of the working class due to increased affluence and prosperity, and greater social mobility.

Floating voters: Voters who are not committed to any particular political party, and thus vote pragmatically in general elections.

Green Paper: Consultative paper issued by the Government outlining a proposed policy and inviting responses from 'interested parties' or seeking to prompt a public debate. Usually a cosmetic exercise, as the Government is likely to have a fairly firm idea by this stage of what it intends to do. As such, the 'consultation' involved will often be a 'softening-up' exercise preparing the public for the imminent policy, or an attempt to imbue it with greater legitimacy.

Incrementalism: Whereby policies and changes occur gradually on a pragmatic, piecemeal basis. New policies seek to adapt or build upon existing policies. Policy-making is often *reactive*, responding to problems as and when they arise, and concerned primarily with practical remedies rather than ideological principles.

Individual ministerial responsibility: Entails two features. Firstly, that ministers are answerable and accountable to Parliament for their (and their departments') policies and actions: hence their attendance at Question Time, in front of Select Committees, etc. Secondly, that ministers are constitutionally expected to resign in cases of major policy failure or maladministration. Whether they actually do so, however, depends on a number of factors, most notably the nature of the mistake, and the degree of support for the minister amongst Cabinet colleagues and / or MPs on the Government's back-benches.

Keynesianism: Economic doctrine which holds that the unfettered free market is economically inefficient and socially unjust, and requires Government regulation through fiscal and monetary policies to ensure high and stable levels of employment and growth.

Legitimacy / legitimation: Whereby a policy is imbued with moral legitimacy by virtue of having been introduced through established procedures by accountable individuals such as elected politicians and ministers answerable to Parliament.

Mandate: The authority which Governments claim to have for their policies by virtue of having won a general election in which those policies were pledged in their manifesto. Election victory is deemed to constitute popular endorsement of the policies.

New Right: A combative, ideological strand of Conservatism which emerged in Britain (along with parts of Europe, and the USA) during the 1970s, and became dominant in the Conservative Party during the 1980s. Aggressively in favour of the free market, but equally fervent in supporting tougher law and order measures and traditional (Victorian) morality. Proclaimed its belief in individual liberty and choice, but intolerant of anyone who did not 'conform' (such as single parents, homosexuals, ethnic minorities, New Age travellers, etc.). In its own way, as dogmatic and fanatical as the very Marxists the New Right would claim to despise.

Parliamentary sovereignty: The cherished notion that Parliament is the highest law-making body in the country, and that the British people cannot – or should not – be subject to the jurisdiction of any institution higher than Parliament. Membership of the European

Community / Union has significantly compromised Britain's parliamentary sovereignty, for European Community / Union law takes precedence over domestic law.

Partisan dealignment: The weakening of voters' identification with, or allegiance to, a particular political party. Closely linked to *class dealignment*. The result is greater electoral volatility and more *floating voters*.

Private Member's Bill: Legislation introduced by back-bench MPs rather than by the Government or its ministers. At the beginning of each parliamentary session, in November, the names of twenty MPs are drawn in a ballot, entitling them to introduce a Bill on a topic or issue of their choice, provided that it does not entail an increase in public expenditure (unless approved by the Treasury beforehand). However, few Private Members' Bills reach the Statute Book, due to insufficient time being available in the House of Commons and the Government's control of the parliamentary timetable.

Quango (Quasi Autonomous Non-Governmental Organization): Term used to denote public organizations such as advisory bodies or regulatory agencies which carry out functions on behalf of the Government, whilst formally enjoying considerable independence. Examples include the Arts Council, Countryside Commission, Oftel, Ofwat, Urban Development Corporations, Welsh Development Agency, White Fish Authority, etc.

Select Committee: A parliamentary committee established to monitor the activities, administration and expenditure of government departments. Most Government departments are *shadowed* by a particular Select Committee, with the ministers and civil servants routinely required to present themselves for cross-examination about their (and the department's) work. Most Select Committees comprise 11 back-bench MPs, six from the Government back-benches, and five from the Opposition parties.

Shadow Cabinet: The Opposition front-bench.

Whip: Those MPs in each party appointed to keep back-bench colleagues informed of policy initiatives and parliamentary business. Their role involves communication as well as seeking to maintain party discipline.

White Paper: A publication delineating the Government's legislative proposals or imminent reforms *vis-à-vis* a particular policy. It is a statement of intent, not a consultative document.

Appendix 2: Chronology of British Politics since 1945

1945

8 May	VE (Victory in Europe) Day; War in Europe officially over.
5 July	General election held.
26 July	Election results announced. Labour returned with 393 MPs, the Conservatives 210, and the Liberals 12. Clement Attlee becomes Prime Minister.
15 August	Japan surrenders; end of Second World War.
6 December	Britain signs an agreement with the USA to secure a loan of $3,750 to assist in post-war reconstruction.

1946

1 March	Bank of England nationalized.
22 May	Repeal of the 1927 Trades Disputes Act.
12 July	Coal Nationalization Bill enacted.
1 August	National Insurance Bill enacted.
6 November	National Health Service Bill, and the Cable & Wireless Bill, enacted.

1947

1 January	Inauguration of National Coal Board. Cable and Wireless nationalized.
11 May	The Conservative Party publishes the *Industrial Charter*, indicating its acceptance of a mixed economy, workers' rights, industrial partnership, and a constructive approach towards the trade unions.
5 June	General Marshall's speech on (Marshall) aid to Europe.

15 July	The pound (sterling) made convertible into dollars on the foreign exchanges.
20 August	Convertibility of sterling suspended.

1948

1 January	Nationalization of the railways.
1 April	Nationalization of the electricity industry comes into effect.
11 May	Transport nationalized.
5 July	Inauguration of the NHS.
30 July	The Gas Bill is enacted, nationalizing the gas industry.

1949

4 April	Britain signs the North Atlantic Treaty, establishing NATO.
18 September	Devaluation of the pound from $4.03 to $2.80.
24 November	Iron and Steel Bill enacted, although actual nationalization deferred until after the next general election.
16 December	Parliament (No. 2) Bill enacted, reducing the delaying power of the House of Lords from two years to one.

1950

23 February	General election. Labour returned with a majority of just 5 seats, winning 315 seats compared to 298 for the Conservatives, 9 for the Liberals, and 3 for other parties.

1951

15 February	Iron and Steel nationalization takes effect.
19 March	European Coal and Steel Community formed, although Britain declines membership.
10 April	Hugh Gaitskell, the Labour Chancellor, presents a Budget which includes the introduction of prescription charges for false teeth and spectacles.
21 April	Aneurin Bevan resigns from the Cabinet in protest at the imposition of prescription charges.
23 April	Harold Wilson resigns from the Cabinet in protest at the scale of defence expenditure.
25 October	General election. The Conservatives are victorious, winning 321 seats, compared to 295 for Labour, 6 for the

Liberals, and 3 for other parties. Labour actually won more votes than the Conservatives, however, obtaining 48.8% of votes cast compared to the Conservatives' 48%.

1952

6 *February*   King George VI dies, and is succeeded by Queen Elizabeth II.

1953

6 *May*   Transport Act enacted, denationalizing road haulage.

14 *May*   Iron and Steel Bill enacted, denationalizing the industry.

1954

13 *February*   An article in *The Economist* introduces the term 'Butskellism'.

1955

5 *April*   Winston Churchill resigns as Prime Minister. He is succeeded by Anthony Eden.

26 *May*   General election. Conservatives returned with 345 MPs, Labour 277, and the Liberals 6. The Conservatives have an overall majority of 60 seats.

7 *December*   Clement Attlee announces his resignation as Labour Party leader. He is succeeded, on 14 December, by Hugh Gaitskell.

1956

22 *March*   Publication of White Paper on *The Economic Implications of Full Employment*.

13 *June*   Last British troops leave Suez Canal zone.

26 *June*   The Chancellor, Harold Macmillan, announces large savings in defence expenditure.

26 *July*   President Nasser of Egypt nationalizes the Suez Canal.

5 *November*   British (and French) troops land in Egypt.

7 *November*   Ceasefire in Egypt accepted by Britain (and France).

22 *December*   British (and French) troops withdraw from Egypt.

1957

9 *January*   Anthony Eden resigns as Prime Minister.

10 January	Harold Macmillan becomes Prime Minister.
25 March	European Economic Community formed, although Britain declines membership.
25 June	Harold Macmillan's famous 'you've never had it so good' speech.
12 August	Council on Prices, Productivity and Incomes established.

1958

6 January	Peter Thorneycroft, Enoch Powell and Nigel Birch resign as Treasury ministers over Cabinet refusal to endorse their demands for reductions in public expenditure.
30 April	Life Peerages Bill enacted, permitting the creation of non-hereditary peers. Women also permitted to sit in the House of Lords.

1959

8 October	General election. Conservatives returned with 365 MPs, Labour 258 and the Liberals 6. The Conservatives' overall majority is increased to 100 seats.
28–29 October	Hugh Gaitskell informs delegates at Labour's annual conference that the party ought to abandon Clause IV of its constitution.

1960

3 February	Harold Macmillan makes his 'winds of change' speech in Cape Town, South Africa.
13 July	Labour's NEC decides to retain Clause IV in the wake of widespread opposition within the labour movement to Gaitskell's call for it to be abandoned.
5 October	Labour's annual conference supports a motion formally committing the party leadership to a unilateralist nuclear defence policy, against the wishes of Gaitskell who consequently vows to 'fight and fight again' to save the Labour Party.

1961

25 July	The Chancellor, Selwyn Lloyd, announces a 'pay pause' as part of the Government's drive against rising inflation.

10 August	Britain makes first formal application for membership of the European Economic Community. This is subsequently opposed by the French President General De Gaulle.
2–6 October	Gaitskell secures the reversal of the unilateralist nuclear defence policy adopted at Labour's annual conference the previous year.

1962

8 February	The National Economic Development Council (NEDC) established, providing a forum for discussion between ministers, employers' representatives and trade union leaders on economic policy and planning.
14 March	Orpington by-election, in which the Conservatives' majority of 14,760 is transformed into a 7,855 majority for the Liberal Party.
31 March	End of the 'pay pause', which is now succeeded by a 2.5% 'guiding light' for wage increases.
13 July	The so-called 'night of the long knives', in which Harold Macmillan sacks seven of his Cabinet ministers in an attempt at reviving the Government's flagging popularity following a number of local government and by-election defeats.
26 July	Government announces creation of a National Incomes Commission.

1963

18 January	Death of Labour leader, Hugh Gaitskell.
14 February	Harold Wilson is elected Labour leader.
10 October	Harold Macmillan's resignation as Prime Minister is announced to delegates at the Conservative Party's annual conference. Macmillan is unable to inform delegates himself because he is in hospital recovering from an operation.
19 October	Lord Home becomes Conservative leader and Prime Minister, having 'emerged' through the party's consultative process conducted by senior figures, the so-called 'men in grey suits'. Home's appointment, and the manner of it, cause considerable disquiet within the Conservative party.

1964

15 October   General election. Labour returned with a narrow majority of 4 seats, having secured the election of 317 MPs, compared to 304 for the Conservative Party and 9 for the Liberals.

1965

2 February   Government appoints a Royal Commission on Trade Union Reform and Employers' Associations, chaired by Lord Donovan.

11 February   Prices and Incomes Board established.

25 February   Conservative Party announces new method of selecting future party leaders, entailing a ballot of its MPs.

12 July   Government launches programme to reform secondary education by introducing comprehensive schools.

22 July   Sir Alec Douglas-Home (formerly Lord Home) resigns as Conservative leader.

28 July   Edward Heath elected leader of the Conservative Party.

8 November   Abolition of death penalty.

1966

31 March   General election. Labour returned with a greatly increased majority of 97, winning 363 seats compared to 253 for the Conservatives and 12 for the Liberals.

14 July   Plaid Cymru victory in Carmarthen by-election.

1967

7 February   National Front formed from the amalgamation of three far-right organizations.

22 March   Iron and Steel Bill enacted, renationalizing the industry.

2 May   Britain makes second application for membership of the EEC.

27 October   Abortion Bill enacted.

18 November   Devaluation of the pound from $2.80 to $2.40.

27 November   General de Gaulle opposes Britain's second application to join the European Economic Community.

1968

20 April	Enoch Powell's 'rivers of blood' speech.
21 April	Powell sacked from Shadow Cabinet, although he attracts widespread public support.
13 June	Donovan Report published, highlighting the development of a 'two tier' industrial relations system in British industry, one of which is formal and recognized, whilst the other is informal yet widespread, and often underpins unofficial strike action.
26 June	Fulton Report on the Civil Service published.
25 October	Transport Bill enacted, renationalizing road transport.

1969

17 January	White Paper entitled *In Place of Strife* published, outlining legislation for the reform of industrial relations in the wake of the Donovan Report.
17 April	Voting age reduced to 18.
18 June	Harold Wilson abandons *In Place of Strife* following strong opposition from the trade unions, many Labour MPs and several Cabinet colleagues.
14 August	British troops sent to Northern Ireland to restore order following escalating conflict between Catholics and Protestants in the wake of the former's demands for civil rights and an end to descrimination against them.
22 October	Divorce Reform Bill enacted.

1970

30–31 Jan.	Conservative Party's pre-election conference at the Selsdon Park Hotel in Surrey, at which the right-wing 'Selsdon Man' programme is finalized.
29 May	Equal Pay Bill enacted.
18 June	General election. Conservative Party elected to office with 330 seats, compared to 287 for Labour and 6 for the Liberal Party.
3 December	Publication of the Industrial Relations Bill.
8 December	Over a quarter of a million workers strike in protest against the Industrial Relations Bill.

1971

25 February	Heath Government nationalizes Rolls Royce following its bankruptcy.
1 March	Over 1.5 million workers strike against the Industrial Relations Bill.
6 August	Industrial Relations Bill enacted.
29 September	Democratic Unionist Party formed in Northern Ireland, led by Ian Paisley, in response to the alleged conciliatory stance towards Catholics evinced by the (Official) Unionist Party.

1972

9 January	Strike by National Union of Mineworkers begins in support of pay claim.
30 January	'Bloody Sunday' in Derry, Northern Ireland, when 13 demonstrators are shot dead by British troops.
10 February	Mass picketing by miners (and supporters) leads to the closure of the Saltley Coke Depot in the West Midlands.
28 February	Miners return to work after pay claim is granted.
30 March	Suspension of the Northern Ireland Parliament (Stormont) announced. Direct rule from London to be imposed via a Northern Ireland Office.
26 July	Solicitor-General intervenes to secure release of 5 dockers imprisoned under the Industrial Relations Act, following the threat of a one-day general strike organized by the TUC.
17 October	European Communities Bill enacted, ratifying Britain's membership of the EC.
6 November	Heath announces 90-day pay and prices freeze, following the failure to secure trade union agreement on a voluntary incomes policy.

1973

1 January	Britain joins the EEC.
28 February	Labour Party and the TUC launch their 'Social Contract'.
1 April	Heath introduces new prices and incomes policy to succeed the statutory freeze.
12 November	Miners start overtime ban in support of pay claim which exceeds Government limit.

1974

5 February	NUM announces all-out strike.
28 February	General election. Labour wins 301 seats, the Conservatives 297, and the Liberals 14. Other parties, including Scottish and Welsh nationalists, win 23 seats.
4 March	Harold Wilson forms minority Labour Government after Edward Heath fails to create a Coalition Government with the Liberals.
6 March	Miners' strike resolved.
15 May	Ulster Workers' Council strike begins against Power-sharing Executive in Northern Ireland.
28 May	Power-sharing Executive dissolved. Ulster Workers' Council calls off strike, victorious.
10 October	General election. Labour obtains a small majority by winning 319 seats, compared to 277 for the Conservatives, 13 for the Liberals and 26 for other parties.

1975

11 February	Margaret Thatcher elected leader of the Conservative Party.
5 June	Referendum on continued membership of the EEC following renegotiation of terms and conditions. 'Yes' vote obtained by 2:1 majority.
11 July	Voluntary pay policy announced by Government and TUC. Wage increases limited to £6 per week for those earning less than £8,500 per annum.
14 July	Unemployment rises above 1 million.

1976

16 March	Harold Wilson resigns as Labour Party leader and Prime Minister.
5 April	James Callaghan elected Labour leader, and thus becomes Prime Minister.
5 May	Government secures TUC agreement for a further 12 months of pay restraint. Wage increases to be limited to 4%.
2 July	David Steel elected leader of the Liberal Party.
9 September	Unemployment exceeds 1.5 million.
28 September	Callaghan warns delegates at Labour's annual conference

that problems such as unemployment and recession can no longer be solved by increasing government expenditure.

29 September Government turns to International Monetary Fund for a loan of £2,300 million. The loan is conditional on massive cuts in public expenditure.

4 November Two by-election defeats finally eradicate Labour's parliamentary majority.

1977

17 March Aircraft and Shipbuilding Bill enacted, nationalizing these two industries.

23 March Labour Government enters into a pact with the Liberal Party to ensure a working majority in the House of Commons.

15 July Denis Healey announces the Government's intention of maintaining a pay policy for a third successive year, with wage increases to be limited to a maximum of 10%, and sanctions applied to firms who breach this figure.

9 October Reg Prentice leaves the Labour Party to join the Conservatives, claiming that Labour is taking Britain 'down the Marxist road'.

1978

30 January Margaret Thatcher talks on television of 'swamping' by immigrants.

21 July Government announces its intention of pursuing a fourth year of incomes policy, during which wage increases will be limited to 5%. Many trade unions have already expressed their opposition to continuation of pay restraint, calling instead for a return to free collective bargaining.

1979

3 January Lorry drivers begin strike in support of a 25% pay claim.

22 January Public sector workers engage in a 24-hour strike which heralds 6 weeks of strike activity against the Government's pay policy.

1 March Referendum on devolution in Scotland yields majority

	support, but fails to secure the 40% threshold required. In Wales, devolution is decisively rejected by 4:1.
28 March	Government defeated in vote of confidence by 311 votes to 310. It therefore announces its resignation.
3 May	General election. Conservatives victorious, winning 339 seats, compared to Labour's 269 and the Liberals' 11. With other parties obtaining 16 seats between them, the Conservatives have a majority of 43.
12 June	Geoffrey Howe's first Budget cuts income tax by 3p in the pound, but increases VAT to 15%. Meanwhile, public expenditure is cut by nearly £4 billion.
22 November	Roy Jenkins's Dimbleby Lecture, in which he calls for a realignment of the 'radical centre' in British politics to counter the trend towards ideological extremes evinced by the two main parties. Speculation immediately increases that the formation of a new 'centre' party is imminent.

1980

1 May	British Aerospace Bill enacted, privatizing the industry.
1 August	Employment Bill enacted, curbing the closed shop and secondary picketing.
8 August	Housing Bill enacted, giving council tenants the right to buy their homes.
15 October	James Callaghan resigns as Labour leader.
10 November	Michael Foot is elected Labour leader, defeating Denis Healey by 10 votes.
13 November	Civil Aviation Bill enacted.

1981

5 January	Unemployment exceeds 2.25 million.
24 January	Labour holds a special conference at Wembley, where an electoral college is adopted for the election of future party leaders and deputy leaders. The trade unions are allocated 40% of the vote in this new college, whilst Labour MPs and constituency parties are awarded 30% each.
26 March	Social Democratic Party launched.
11–13 April	Riots by youth in Brixton.
7 May	Ken Livingstone becomes leader of the Greater

London Council (GLC) in the wake of local government elections.

16 June   Social Democratic Party and the Liberal Party launch their electoral and political 'Alliance'.

4–8 July   Riots in the Toxteth district of Liverpool and Moss Side in Manchester.

8 December   Arthur Scargill elected as President of the National Union of Mineworkers.

1982

2 April   Argentina invades the Falkland Islands.

5 April   Lord Carrington resigns (as Foreign Secretary), as do his two ministerial colleagues at the Foreign Office. Meanwhile, a Royal Navy Task Force sets sail to recapture the Falklands.

14 June   British troops recapture the Falklands' capital, Port Stanley, from the Argentinians, thereby signifying Britain's victory.

2 July   Roy Jenkins defeats David Owen in the election for leadership of the SDP.

1983

9 June   General election. Conservatives re-elected with a massive majority of 144 seats, having returned 397 MPs, compared to Labour's 209 and the SDP/Liberal Alliance's 23.

13 June   Roy Jenkins resigns as leader of the SDP.

15 June   Michael Foot announces that he will be resigning as Labour leader at the party's annual conference.

21 June   David Owen is elected (unopposed) leader of the SDP.

2 October   Neil Kinnock elected leader of the Labour Party, with Roy Hattersley as deputy leader.

1984

25 January   Government announces ban on trade union membership at its Communication Headquarters (GCHQ) in Cheltenham.

5 March   Start of year-long miners' strike begins following NCB's announcement that Cortonwood colliery in South Yorkshire is to close.

12 April	Telecommunications Bill enacted, heralding the privatization of British Telecom.
12 October	IRA bomb blast at Grand Hotel, Brighton, where many Conservative ministers are staying during the party's annual conference. Margaret Thatcher is unscathed, but others, such as Norman Tebbit and his wife, are seriously injured.
28 Nov.	Sale of British Telecom yields £8 billion for the Treasury, with one million 'ordinary' people buying shares.

·1985

5 March	Return to work by miners still on strike.
14 May	Francis Pym launches Centre Forward, a 'one nation' group in the Conservative Party which is highly critical of Thatcherism. However, it proves totally ineffective.
3 June	Norman Fowler announces a fundamental review of the Welfare State.
16 July	Local Government Bill enacted, heralding the imminent abolition of the GLC and 6 metropolitan authorities.
9–10 Sept.	Rioting in the Handsworth district of Birmingham.
6–7 October	Rioting at the Broadwater Farm Estate in Tottenham, London, following the death of a black woman during a police search of her home. A policeman is killed by a gang of youths wielding machetes.
30 October	Transport Bill enacted, privatizing the National Bus Company.
15 November	Margaret Thatcher and the Irish Prime Minister, Garret Fitzgerald, sign the Anglo-Irish Agreement at Hillsborough Castle, near Belfast. Unionists are outraged.

1986

9 January	Michael Heseltine resigns as Defence Secretary in the wake of disagreements with Cabinet colleagues, and particularly Margaret Thatcher, over the future of the Westland helicopter company.
24 January	Leon Brittan resigns as Trade and Industry Secretary, accepting ministerial responsibility for the leaking of a confidential letter in order to discredit Michael Heseltine.

17 February	Margaret Thatcher signs the Single European Act.
1 April	Abolition of the GLC and 6 metropolitan authorities.
15 April	Government defeated on 2nd Reading of Shops Bill, which sought to legalize Sunday trading. 68 Conservative MPs vote against the Bill.
2 December	British Gas privatized, with millions of shares bought by members of the public following a massive advertising campaign by the Government.

1987

27 January	Privatization of British Airways.
17 March	Budget cuts income tax by 2p in the pound.
11 June	General election. Conservatives returned with a majority of 101, winning 376 seats, compared to 229 for Labour, 22 for the Alliance, and 23 others.
14 June	David Steel calls for 'democratic fusion' between the SDP and the Liberal Party.
6 August	David Owen resigns as leader of the SDP.

1988

25 July	Announcement that the Department of Health and Social Security will be broken up into two distinct departments.

1989

13 May	SDP decides that it is no longer viable to operate as a national political party.
18 May	Labour publishes outcome of its 18-month policy review in a document entitled *Meet the Challenge, Make the Change*.
15 June	Labour wins 13 seats from the Conservatives in the election for the European Parliament, whilst the Green Party secures 15% of the vote, but no seats.
24 July	Cabinet reshuffle, in which Sir Geoffrey Howe is given the 'non-post' of Deputy Prime Minister.
26 October	Nigel Lawson resigns as Chancellor, claiming that his position and authority were being undermined by Margaret Thatcher's insistence on retaining Sir Alan Walters as her personal economic adviser.

5 December   Conservative Party leadership contest after Margaret Thatcher is challenged by 'stalking horse' candidate Sir Anthony Meyer. Although she wins comfortably, the the fact that 60 Conservative MPs either voted in favour of Sir Anthony, spoilt their ballot papers or abstained is seen by many as a warning to Thatcher.

1990

1 April   Introduction of the poll tax in England and Wales.

3 June   SDP disbanded by David Owen.

8 October   Britain joins the European Exchange Rate Mechanism.

18 October   By-election in Eastbourne, in which a Conservative majority of over 17,000 is turned into a 4,550 majority for the Liberal Democrats.

1 November   Sir Geoffrey Howe resigns as Deputy Prime Minister.

13 November   Sir Geoffrey Howe delivers resignation speech in House of Commons, in which he bitterly attacks Margaret Thatcher's stance towards Europe.

14 November   Michael Heseltine announces that he will challenge Margaret Thatcher for the leadership of the Conservative Party.

20 November   First ballot of Conservative Party leadership contest. Margaret Thatcher defeats Michael Heseltine by 204 votes to 152, but is 4 votes short of the required 15% majority.

22 November   Margaret Thatcher announces her resignation.

27 November   John Major wins 185 votes in the second ballot of the Conservative Party leadership contest, and whilst this left him 2 votes short of the required overall majority, the other two contenders, Michael Heseltine and Douglas Hurd, stand down to allow Major to become Conservative leader and Prime Minister.

1991

17 January   Gulf War begins following Iraq's invasion of Kuwait the previous August.

28 February   Ceasefire in Gulf War.

14 March   'Birmingham Six' freed by Court of Appeal.

1 April   Major reform of the NHS; general practitioners can

	become fundholders, hospitals and health authorities will operate an internal market, and hospitals can become self-governing NHS Trusts.
9–11 Dec.	Meeting in Maastricht of political leaders of European Community member states. Treaty produced outlining programmes for economic, monetary and political union, although Britain secures the removal of the Social Chapter.

1992

7 January	Britain signs the Maastricht Treaty.
9 April	General election. Conservative Party returned with a reduced majority of 21 seats, with 336 MPs, compared to 271 for Labour and 20 for the Liberal Democrats.
18 July	John Smith elected leader of the Labour Party, with Margaret Beckett elected Deputy leader.
16 September	Britain withdraws from the European Exchange Rate Mechanism.
13 October	Michael Heseltine announces the imminent closure of a further 31 pits, entailing the loss of 30,000 jobs in the mining industry, although following a public outcry, the plan is hastily modified.

1993

8 March	Maastricht Treaty Bill defeated in the House of Commons by 314 votes to 292.
1 April	Care in the Community programme instigated.
6 May	Liberal Democrats win the Newbury by-election from the Conservatives with a swing of 28.4%.
22 July	Government defeated by 324 votes to 316 in House of Commons on its motion concerning the Social Chapter. John Major immediately announces that the Government's stance on the Social Chapter would be presented to the House as a vote of confidence the following evening.
23 July	Government wins vote of confidence by 339 votes to 299.
29 July	Liberal Democrats win the Christchurch by-election from the Conservatives with a swing of 35%.

2 August	Britain ratifies the Maastricht Treaty.
17 September	British National Party wins a local council seat in the Isle of Dogs, East London.
7 November	John Major's speech to the Conservative Party's annual conference calls for a return to traditional values, 'back to basics'.
15 December	The 'Downing Street Declaration' signed by John Major and the Irish Prime Minister Albert Reynolds, heralding a major new peace initiative for Northern Ireland.

1994

21 February	House of Commons votes to reduce the age of homosexual consent to 18, rather than 16 as a number of MPs had demanded.
12 May	John Smith, leader of the Labour Party, dies from a heart attack.
9 June	Elections to the European Parliament witness Labour winning 62 seats compared to the Conservatives' 18. The Liberal Democrats win 2 seats.
	Five by-elections also take place, 4 in safe Labour seats, and one in the traditionally safe Conservative seat of Eastleigh, Hampshire, which is won by the Liberal Democrats.
15 June	Signal workers begin a series of 24- and 48-hour strikes in support of a pay claim. In spite of the disruption to train services, they enjoy considerable public support.
21 July	Tony Blair is elected leader of the Labour Party, with John Prescott elected deputy leader.
31 August	IRA announces a ceasefire in order to assist the peace process in Northern Ireland, and in response to John Major's insistence that this would be a prerequisite of Sinn Fein's admittance into negotiations over the future of Northern Ireland.
4 October	Tony Blair announces at Labour's annual conference that the party must modernize its constitution, the clear implication being that Clause IV needed to be amended or abandoned.
3 November	Cabinet decides to postpone plans to privatize the Post

Office, due to opposition from many Conservative MPs and amongst the Tory shires, where village post offices would be seriously endangered.

28 November   8 Conservative MPs abstain in a Commons vote on the European Communities (Finance) Bill, even though John Major had effectively made it a vote of confidence. As a result, although the Government won the vote, the 8 MPs had the Conservative whip withdrawn. Another Conservative MP resigned the whip. The Government was thus in an extremely vulnerable position, dependent upon the support of Ulster Unionist MPs in order to continue governing.

7 December   Government defeated in Commons vote on Budget measure to increase VAT on gas and electricity to 17.5%, with 15 Conservative back-benchers refusing to support the Government.

15 December   Labour wins the Dudley West by-election, polling 68.7% of the vote, compared to the Conservatives' 18.6%. This turned a Conservative majority of 5,789 in 1992 into a Labour majority of 20,694.

Appendix 3: General Election Results 1945–92

Party	Total votes	% of vote	Seats/MPs
5 July 1945			
Conservative	9,988,306	39.8	213
Labour	11,995,152	47.8	393
Liberal	2,248,226	9.0	12
Commonwealth	110,634	0.4	1
Communist	102,780	0.4	2
Others	640,880	2.0	19
23 February 1950			
Conservative	12,502,567	43.5	298
Labour	13,266,592	46.1	315
Liberal	2,621,548	9.1	9
Communist	91,746	0.3	0
Others	290,218	1.0	3
25 October 1951			
Conservative	13,717,538	48.0	321
Labour	13,948,605	48.8	295
Liberal	730,556	2.5	6
Others	177,329	0.6	3

Party	Total votes	% of vote	Seats/MPs
26 May 1955			
Conservative	13,286,569	49.7	345
Labour	12,404,970	46.4	277
Liberal	722,405	2.7	6
Others	313,410	1.1	3
8 October 1959			
Conservative	13,749,830	49.4	365
Labour	12,215,538	43.8	258
Liberal	1,638,571	5.9	6
Plaid Cymru	77,571	0.3	0
Scot. Nats	21,738	0.1	0
Others	175,987	0.4	1
15 October 1964			
Conservative	12,001,396	43.4	304
Labour	12,205,814	44.1	317
Liberal	3,092,878	11.2	9
Plaid Cymru	69,507	0.3	0
Scot. Nats	64,044	0.2	0
Others	168,422	0.6	0
31 March 1966			
Conservative	11,418,433	41.9	253
Labour	13,064,951	47.9	363
Liberal	2,327,533	8.5	12
Plaid Cymru	61,071	0.2	0
Scot. Nats	128,474	0.4	0
Others	201,302	0.6	2
18 June 1970			
Conservative	13,145,123	46.4	330
Labour	12,179,341	43.0	287

Party	Total votes	% of vote	Seats/MPs
Liberal	2,117,035	7.5	6
Plaid Cymru	175,016	0.6	0
Scot. Nats	306,802	1.1	1
Others	383,511	1.4	6

28 February 1974

Conservative	11,872,180	37.9	297
Labour	11,646,391	37.1	301
Liberal	6,058,744	19.3	14
Plaid Cymru	171,364	0.6	2
Scot. Nats	633,180	2.0	7
National Front	76,865	0.3	0
N.I. Parties	717,986	2.3	12
Others	131,059	0.4	2

10 October 1974

Conservative	10,464,817	35.8	277
Labour	11,457,079	39.2	319
Liberal	5,346,754	18.3	13
Plaid Cymru	166,321	0.6	3
Scot. Nats	839,628	2.9	11
National Front	113,843	0.4	0
N.I. Parties	702,094	2.4	12
Others	81,227	0.3	0

3 May 1979

Conservative	13,697,923	43.9	339
Labour	11,532,218	36.9	269
Liberal	4,313,804	13.8	11
Plaid Cymru	132,544	0.4	2
Scot. Nats	504,259	1.6	2
National Front	190,747	0.6	0
N.I. Parties	695,889	2.2	12
Others	85,338	0.3	0

Party	Total votes	% of vote	Seats/MPs
9 June 1983			
Conservative	13,012,315	42.4	397
Labour	8,456,934	27.6	209
Liberal	4,210,115	13.7	17
Social Democrats	3,570,834	11.6	6
(Alliance)	(7,780,949)	(25.3)	(23)
Plaid Cymru	125,309	0.4	2
Scot. Nats	331,975	1.1	2
N.I. Parties	764,925	3.1	17
Others	193,383	0.6	0
11 June 1987			
Conservative	13,763,066	42.3	376
Labour	10,029,778	31.7	229
Liberal	4,173,450	12.8	17
Social Democrats	3,168,183	9.7	5
(Alliance)	(7,341,633)	(22.5)	(22)
Plaid Cymru	123,599	0.3	3
Scot. Nats	416,473	1.3	3
N.I. Parties	730,152	2.2	17
Others	151,519	0.5	0
9 April 1992			
Conservative	14,092,891	42.3	336
Labour	11,559,735	35.2	271
Lib. Dems	5,999,384	18.3	20
Plaid Cymru	154,439	0.5	4
Scot. Nats	629,552	1.9	3
N.I. Parties	740,485	2.2	17
Others	436,207	1.0	0

Appendix 4: Ministers since 1945

Prime Minister	Party	Date of appointment
Clement Attlee	Labour	26 July 1945
Winston Churchill	Conservative	27 October 1951
Anthony Eden	Conservative	5 April 1955
Harold Macmillan	Conservative	10 January 1957
Alec Douglas-Home	Conservative	19 October 1963
Harold Wilson	Labour	15 October 1964
Edward Heath	Conservative	18 June 1970
Harold Wilson	Labour	4 March 1974
James Callaghan	Labour	5 April 1976
Margaret Thatcher	Conservative	3 May 1979
John Major	Conservative	28 November 1990

Chancellor of the Exchequer	Party	Date of appointment
Hugh Dalton	Labour	27 July 1945
Stafford Cripps	Labour	13 November 1947
Hugh Gaitskell	Labour	19 October 1950
Rab Butler	Conservative	28 October 1951
Harold Macmillan	Conservative	20 December 1955
Peter Thorneycroft	Conservative	13 January 1957

David Heathcoat Amory	Conservative	6 January 1958
Selwyn Lloyd	Conservative	27 July 1960
Reginald Maudling	Conservative	13 July 1962
James Callaghan	Labour	16 October 1964
Roy Jenkins	Labour	30 November 1967
Ian Macleod	Conservative	20 June 1970
Anthony Barber	Conservative	25 July 1970
Denis Healey	Labour	5 March 1974
Geoffrey Howe	Conservative	5 May 1979
Nigel Lawson	Conservative	11 June 1983
John Major	Conservative	26 October 1989
Norman Lamont	Conservative	28 November 1990
Kenneth Clarke	Conservative	27 May 1993

Foreign Secretary	*Party*	*Date of appointment*
Ernest Bevin	Labour	27 July 1945
Herbert Morrison	Labour	9 March 1951
Anthony Eden	Conservative	28 October 1951
Harold Macmillan	Conservative	7 April 1955
Selwyn Lloyd	Conservative	20 December 1955
Lord Home	Conservative	27 July 1960
Rab Butler	Conservative	20 October 1963
Patrick Gordon Walker	Labour	16 October 1964
Michael Stewart	Labour	22 January 1966
George Brown	Labour	11 August 1966
Michael Stewart	Labour	16 March 1968
Alec Douglas-Home	Conservative	20 June 1970
James Callaghan	Labour	5 March 1974
Anthony Crosland	Labour	8 April 1976
David Owen	Labour	21 February 1977
Lord Carrington	Conservative	5 May 1979
Francis Pym	Conservative	6 April 1982
Geoffrey Howe	Conservative	11 June 1983
John Major	Conservative	24 July 1989
Douglas Hurd	Conservative	26 October 1989

Home Secretary	Party	Date of appointment
Chuter Ede	Labour	3 August 1945
David Maxwell-Fyfe	Conservative	28 October 1951
Gwilym Lloyd George	Conservative	18 October 1954
Rab Butler	Conservative	13 January 1957
Henry Brooke	Conservative	13 July 1962
Frank Soskice	Labour	18 October 1964
Roy Jenkins	Labour	23 December 1965
James Callaghan	Labour	30 November 1967
Reginald Maudling	Conservative	20 June 1970
Robert Carr	Conservative	18 July 1972
Roy Jenkins	Labour	5 March 1974
Merlyn Rees	Labour	10 September 1976
William Whitelaw	Conservative	5 May 1979
Leon Brittan	Conservative	11 June 1983
Douglas Hurd	Conservative	3 September 1985
David Waddington	Conservative	26 October 1989
Kenneth Baker	Conservative	28 November 1990
Kenneth Clarke	Conservative	10 April 1992
Michael Howard	Conservative	27 May 1993

Employment Secretary *	Party	Date of appointment
George Isaacs	Labour	3 August 1945
Aneurin Bevan	Labour	17 January 1951
Alfred Robens	Labour	24 April 1951
Walter Monckton	Conservative	28 October 1951
Ian Macleod	Conservative	20 December 1955
Edward Heath	Conservative	14 October 1959
John Hare	Conservative	27 July 1960
Joseph Godber	Conservative	20 October 1963
Ray Gunter	Labour	18 October 1964
Barbara Castle	Labour	6 April 1968
Robert Carr	Conservative	20 June 1970

Maurice Macmillan	Conservative	7 February 1972
William Whitelaw	Conservative	2 December 1973
Michael Foot	Labour	5 March 1974
Albert Booth	Labour	8 April 1976
James Prior	Conservative	5 May 1979
Norman Tebbit	Conservative	14 September 1981
Tom King	Conservative	16 October 1983
Lord Young	Conservative	2 September 1985
Norman Fowler	Conservative	13 September 1987
Michael Howard	Conservative	3 January 1990
Gillian Shephard	Conservative	11 April 1992
David Hunt	Conservative	27 May 1993
Michael Portillo	Conservative	20 July 1994

*Until April 1968, Secretary of State for Labour.

Education Secretary	Party	Date of appointment
Ellen Wilkinson	Labour	3 August 1945
George Tomlinson	Labour	10 February 1947
Florence Horsbrugh	Conservative	2 November 1951
David Eccles	Conservative	18 October 1954
Viscount Hailsham	Conservative	13 January 1957
Geoffrey Lloyd	Conservative	17 September 1957
David Eccles	Conservative	14 October 1959
Edward Boyle	Conservative	13 July 1962
Quintin Hogg*	Conservative	1 April 1964
Michael Stewart	Labour	18 October 1964
Anthony Crosland	Labour	22 January 1965
Patrick Gordon Walker	Labour	29 August 1967
Edward Short	Labour	6 April 1968
Margaret Thatcher	Conservative	20 June 1970
Reginald Prentice	Labour	5 March 1974
Fred Mulley	Labour	10 June 1975
Shirley Williams	Labour	10 September 1976
Mark Carlisle	Conservative	5 May 1979
Keith Joseph	Conservative	14 September 1981

Kenneth Baker	Conservative	21 May 1986
John MacGregor	Conservative	24 July 1989
Kenneth Clarke	Conservative	2 November 1990
John Patten	Conservative	10 April 1992
Gillian Shephard	Conservative	20 July 1994

* Formerly Viscount Hailsham

Defence Secretary	Party	Date of appointment
Clement Atlee	Labour	27 July 1945
Albert V. Alexander	Labour	20 December 1946
Emanuel Shinwell	Labour	28 February 1950
Winston Churchill	Conservative	28 October 1951
Earl Alexander	Conservative	1 March 1952
Harold Macmillan	Conservative	18 October 1954
Selwyn Lloyd	Conservative	7 April 1955
Walter Monckton	Conservative	20 December 1955
Antony Head	Conservative	18 October 1956
Duncan Sandys	Conservative	13 January 1957
Harold Watkinson	Conservative	14 October 1959
Peter Thorneycroft	Conservative	13 July 1962
Denis Healey	Labour	16 October 1964
Lord Carrington	Conservative	20 June 1970
Ian Gilmour	Conservative	8 January 1974
Roy Mason	Labour	5 MArch 1974
Fred Mulley	Labour	10 September 1976
Francis Pym	Conservative	5 May 1979
John Nott	Conservative	5 January 1981
Michael Heseltine	Conservative	6 January 1983
George Younger	Conservative	9 January 1986
Tom King	Conservative	24 July 1989
Malcolm Rifkind	Conservative	10 April 1992

Health Secretary	Party	Date of appointment
Aneurin Bevan	Labour	3 August 1945
Hilary Marquand	Labour	17 January 1951
Harry Crookshank	Conservative	30 October 1951
Ian Macleod	Conservative	7 May 1952
Robert Turton	Conservative	20 December 1955
Dennis Vosper	Conservative	16 January 1957
Derek Walker-Smith	Conservative	17 September 1957
Enoch Powell	Conservative	13 July 1962
Anthony Barber	Conservative	18 October 1963
Kenneth Robinson	Labour	20 October 1963
Richard Crossman	* Labour	1 November 1968
Keith Joseph	Conservative	20 June 1970
Barbara Castle	Labour	5 March 1974
David Ennals	Labour	8 April 1976
Patrick Jenkin	Conservative	5 May 1979
Norman Fowler	Conservative	14 September 1981
John Moore	Conservative	13 June 1987
William Waldegrave	Conservative	28 November 1990
Virginia Bottomley	Conservative	10 April 1992

*From November 1968 to July 1988, Secretary for Health & Social Security.

Transport Secretary	Party	Date of appointment
Alfred Barnes	Labour	3 August 1945
John Maclay	Conservative	31 October 1951
Alan Lennox-Boyd	Conservative	7 May 1952
John Boyd-Carpenter	Conservative	28 July 1954
Harold Watkinson	Conservative	20 July 1955
Ernest Marples	Conservative	14 October 1959
Thomas Fraser	Labour	18 October 1964
Barbara Castle	Labour	23 December 1965
Richard Marsh	Labour	6 April 1968
John Peyton	Conservative	20 June 1970

Fred Mulley	Labour	7 March 1974
John Gilbert	Labour	12 June 1975
William Rogers	Labour	10 September 1976
Norman Fowler	Conservative	11 May 1979
David Howell	Conservative	14 September 1981
Tom King	Conservative	11 June 1983
Nicholas Ridley	Conservative	16 October 1983
John Moore	Conservative	21 May 1986
Paul Channon	Conservative	13 June 1987
Cecil Parkinson	Conservative	24 July 1989
Malcolm Rifkind	Conservative	28 November 1990
John MacGregor	Conservative	10 April 1992
Brian Mawhinney	Conservative	20 July 1994

Agriculture Secretary	*Party*	*Date of appointment*
Tom Williams	Labour	3 August 1945
Thomas Dugdale	Conservative	31 October 1951
Derek Heathcoat-Amory	Conservative	28 July 1954
John Hare	Conservative	6 January 1958
Christopher Soames	Conservative	27 July 1960
Fred Peart	Labour	18 October 1964
Cledwyn Hughes	Labour	6 April 1968
James Prior	Conservative	20 June 1907
Joseph Godber	Conservative	5 November 1972
Fred Peart	Labour	5 March 1974
John Silkin	Labour	10 September 1976
Peter Walker	Conservative	5 May 1979
Michael Jopling	Conservative	11 June 1983
John MacGregor	Conservative	13 June 1987
John Selwyn Gummer	Conservative	24 July 1989
Gillian Shephard	Conservative	27 May 1993
William Waldegrave	Conservative	20 July 1994

Trade & Industry Secretary/Board of Trade	Party	Date of appointment
Stafford Cripps	Labour	27 July 1945
Harold Wilson	Labour	29 September 1947
Hartley Shawcross	Labour	24 April 1951
Peter Thorneycroft	Conservative	30 October 1951
Derek Heathcoat-Amory	Conservative	3 September 1953
Austin Low	Conservative	28 July 1954
David Eccles	Conservative	13 January 1957
Reginald Maudling	Conservative	14 October 1959
Frederick Erroll	Conservative	9 October 1961
Edward Heath	Conservative	20 October 1963
Douglas Jay	Labour	18 October 1964
Anthony Crosland	Labour	29 August 1967
Roy Mason	Labour	6 October 1969
Michael Noble	Conservative	20 June 1970
John Davies	Conservative	15 October 1970
Peter Walker	Conservative	5 November 1972
Peter Shore	Labour	5 March 1974
Edmund Dell	Labour	8 April 1976
John Smith	Labour	11 November 1978
Keith Joseph (Industry)	Conservative	7 May 1979
John Nott (Trade)	Conservative	5 May 1979
Patrick Jenkin (Industry)	Conservative	14 September 1981
John Biffen (Trade)	Conservative	5 January 1981
Lord Cockfield	Conservative	6 April 1982
Cecil Parkinson	Conservative	12 June 1983
Norman Tebbit	Conservative	15 October 1983
Leon Brittan	Conservative	2 September 1985
Paul Channon	Conservative	24 January 1986
Lord Young	Conservative	13 June 1987
Nicholas Ridley	Conservative	24 July 1989
Peter Lilley	Conservative	14 July 1990
Michael Heseltine	Conservative	10 April 1992

Housing & Local Government Secretary (Environment Secretary from October 1970)	Party	Date of appointment
Lewis Silkin	Labour	4 August 1945
Hugh Dalton	Labour	28 February 1950
Harold Macmillan	Conservative	30 October 1951
Duncan Sandys	Conservative	18 October 1954
Henry Brooke	Conservative	13 January 1957
Charles Hill	Conservative	9 October 1961
Keith Joseph	Conservative	13 July 1962
Richard Crossman	Labour	18 October 1964
Arthur Greenwood	Labour	11 August 1966
Peter Walker	Conservative	20 June 1970
Geoffrey Rippon	Conservative	5 November 1972
Anthony Crosland	Labour	5 March 1974
Peter Shore	Labour	8 April 1976
Michael Heseltine	Conservative	5 May 1979
Tom King	Conservative	6 January 1983
Patrick Jenkin	Conservative	11 June 1983
Kenneth Baker	Conservative	2 September 1985
Nicholas Ridley	Conservative	21 May 1986
Chris Patten	Conservative	24 July 1989
Michael Heseltine	Conservative	28 November 1990
Michael Howard	Conservative	11 April 1992
John Selwyn Gummer	Conservative	27 May 1993

Northern Ireland Secretary *	Party	Date of appointment
William Whitelaw	Conservative	24 March 1972
Francis Pym	Conservative	2 December 1973

Merlyn Rees	Labour	5 March 1974
Roy Mason	Labour	10 September 1976
Humphrey Atkins	Conservative	5 May 1979
James Prior	Conservative	14 September 1981
Douglas Hurd	Conservative	11 September 1984
Tom King	Conservative	3 September 1985
Peter Brooke	Conservative	24 July 1989
Patrick Mayhew	Conservative	10 April 1992

* Post established in March 1972.

Scottish Secretary	Party	Date of appointment
Joseph Westwood	Labour	3 August 1945
Arthur Woodburn	Labour	7 October 1947
Hector McNeil	Labour	28 February 1950
James Stuart	Conservative	30 October 1951
John Maclay	Conservative	13 January 1957
Michael Noble	Conservative	13 July 1962
William Rose	Labour	18 October 1964
Gordon Campbell	Conservative	20 June 1970
William Ross	Labour	5 March 1974
Bruce Millan	Labour	8 April 1976
George Younger	Conservative	5 May 1979
Malcolm Rifkind	Conservative	11 January 1986
Ian Lang	Conservative	28 November 1990

Welsh Secretary *	Party	Date of appointment
James Griffiths	Labour	18 October 1964
Cledwyn Hughes	Labour	6 April 1966
George Thomas	Labour	6 April 1968
Peter Thomas	Conservative	20 June 1970
John Morris	Labour	5 March 1974

Nicholas Edwards	Conservative	5 May 1979
Peter Walker	Conservative	13 June 1987
David Hunt	Conservative	4 May 1990
John Redwood	Conservative	27 May 1993

*Post established in October 1964.

Bibliography

Abrams, Mark (1960) *Must Labour Lose?* Harmondsworth: Penguin.

Abromeit, Heidrun (1988) 'British privatisation policy'. *Parliamentary Affairs*, vol. 41, no. 1.

Addison, Paul (1977) *The Road to 1945*. London, Quartet.

Alderman, Geoffrey (1984) 'The electoral system'. In R. L. Borthwick and J. E. Spence (eds) *British Politics in Perspective*. Leicester: Leicester University Press.

Alderman, R. K. and Carter, Neil (1991) 'A very Tory coup: the ousting of Mrs Thatcher'. *Parliamentary Affairs*, vol. 44, no. 2, pp. 125–39.

Allen, V. L. (1960) *Trade Unions and the Government*. London: Longman.

Almond, Gabriel and Verba, Sidney (1965) *Civic Culture*. Boston: Little, Brown & Co.

Alport, C. J. (1946) *About Conservative Principles*. London: publisher unknown.

Anderson, Perry (1977) 'The limits and possibilities of trade union action'. In Tom Clarke and Laurie Clements (eds) *Trade Unions under Capitalism*. London: Fontana.

Arthur, Paul and Jeffery, Keith (1988) *Northern Ireland Since 1968*. Oxford: Blackwell.

Attlee, Clement (1937) *The Labour Party in Perspective*. London: Gollancz.

Attlee, Clement (1954) *As It Happened*. London: Heinemann.

Aughey, Arthur (1994) 'The Downing Street Declaration: a clarification'. *Talking Politics* (Autumn), vol. 7, no. 1, pp. 59–63.

Bacon, Roger and Eltis, Walter (1976) *Britain's Economic Problem: Too Few Producers*. Basingstoke: Macmillan.

Balfour, Arthur (1927) 'Introduction' to W. Bagehot, *The English Constitution*. London: Oxford University Press.

Balsom, Dennis (1979) 'Plaid Cymru; the Welsh Nationalist Party'. In H. M. Drucker (ed.) *Multi Party Britain*. Basingstoke: Macmillan.

Barker, Elisabeth (1976) *The Common Market*. Publisher unknown.

Barnett, Anthony (1982) *Iron Britannia*. London: Allison & Busby.

Bartlett, Christopher (1977) *A History of Post-War Britain 1945–1974*. London: Longman.

Beer, Samuel (1967) *Modern British Politics*. London: Faber & Faber.

Beer, Samuel (1982) *Britain Against Itself*. London: Faber & Faber.

Behrens, Robert (1980) *The Conservative Party from Heath to Thatcher*. London: Saxon House.

Bell, Daniel (1960) *The End of Ideology*. New York: The Free Press.

Bevan, Aneurin (1978) *In Place of Fear*. London: Quartet.

Birch, Anthony (1977) *Political Integration and Disintegration in the British Isles*. London: George Allen & Unwin.

Birch, Anthony (1993) *The British System of Government* (9th edn). London: Routledge.

Birkenhead, Lord (1969) *Walter Monckton*. London: Weidenfeld & Nicolson.

Blake, Robert (1985) *The Conservative Party from Peel to Thatcher*. London: Methuen.

Blondel, Jean (1963) *Voters, Parties and Leaders*. Harmondsworth: Penguin.

Bogdanor, Vernon (1984) *What is Proportional Representation?* Oxford: Martin Robertson.

Brittan, Samuel (1983) *The Role and Limits of Government*. London: Temple Smith.

Burch, Martin (1993) 'The Nest Steps for Britain's Civil Service'. *Talking Politics* (Summer), vol. 5, no. 3.

Butler, David (1989) *British General Elections since 1945*. Oxford: Blackwell.

Butler, David and Kavanagh, Dennis (1974) *The British General Election of February 1974*. Basingstoke: Macmillan.

Butler, David and Kavanagh, Dennis (1975) *The British General Election of October 1974*. Basingstoke: Macmillan.

Butler, David and King, Anthony (1965) *The British General Election of 1964*. Basingstoke: Macmillan.

Butler, David and Kitzinger, Uwe (1976) *The 1975 Referendum*. Basingstoke: Macmillan.

Butler, David and Pinto-Duschinsky, Michael (1971) *The British General Election of 1970*. Basingstoke: Macmillan.

Butler, Lord (Rab) (1971) *The Art of the Possible*. London: Hamish Hamilton.

Callaghan, James (1987) *Time and Chance*. London: Collins.

Calvocoressi, Peter (1978) *The British Experience 1945–75*. London: Bodley Head.

Carlton, David (1981) *Anthony Eden*. London: Allen Lane.

Castle, Barbara (1984) *The Castle Diaries 1964–70*. London: Weidenfeld & Nicolson.

Chandler, J. A. (1991) *Local Government Today*. Manchester: Manchester University Press.

Clarke, Peter (1991) *A Question of Leadership*. London: Hamish Hamilton.

Clutterbuck, Richard (1978) *Britain in Agony*. London: Faber & Faber.

Coates, David (1975) *The Labour Party and the Struggle for Socialism*. London: Cambridge University Press.

Coates, David (1980) *Labour in Power?*. London: Longman.

Coates, David (1983) 'The question of trade union power'. In David Coates and Gordon Johnston (eds) *Socialist Arguments*. Oxford: Martin Robertson.

Coates, David (1984) *The Context of British Politics*. London: Hutchinson.

Coleraine, Lord (1970) *For Conservatives Only*. London: Tom Stacey.

Collins, Larry and Lapierre, Dominique (1975) *Freedom at Midnight*. Publisher unknown.

Connolly, Michael (1990) *Politics and Policy Making in Northern Ireland*. Hemel Hempstead: Philip Allan.

Conservative & Unionist Central Office (1947) *The Industrial Charter*. London.

Conservative & Unionist Central Office (1949) *The Right Road for Britain*. London.

Conservative Political Centre (1963) *Change or Decay?* London.

Craig, F. W. S (1975) *British General Election Manifestos 1900–74*. Basingstoke: Macmillan.

Crewe, Ivor (1987) 'Tories prosper from a paradox'. *The Guardian*, 16 June.

Crewe, Ivor (1988) 'Has the electorate become Thatcherite?' In Robert Skidelsky (ed.) *Thatcherism*. Oxford: Blackwell.

Crewe, Ivor, Sarlvik, Bo and Alt, James (1977) 'Partisan dealignment in Britain 1964–1974'. *British Journal of Political Science 7*.

Crick, Bernard (1964) *The Reform of Parliament*. London: Weidenfeld & Nicolson.

Criddle, Brian (1994) 'Members of Parliament'. In Anthony Seldon and Stuart Ball (eds) *Conservative Century*. Oxford: Oxford University Press.

Crosland, Anthony (1956) *The Future of Socialism*. London: Jonathan Cape.

Crosland, Anthony (1960) *Can Labour Win?* London: Fabian Society.

Crosland, Susan (1982) *Tony Crosland*. London: Jonathan Cape.

Crossman, Richard (1979) *The Crossman Diaries*. London: Book Club Associates.

Curtice, John and Linton, Martin (1994) 'Major escaped meltdown by a Lib–Dem whisker'. *The Guardian*, 14 June.

Dalton, Hugh (1962) *High Tide and After*. London: Muller.

Dearlove, John and Saunders, Peter (1991) *Introduction to British Politics* (2nd edn). Cambridge: Polity.

Denver, David (1989) *Elections and Voting Behaviour in Britain*. Hemel Hempstead: Philip Allan.

Denver, David (1994) *Elections and Voting Behaviour in Britain* (2nd edn). Hemel Hempstead: Philip Allan.

Dickie, John (1992) *Inside the Foreign Office*. London: Chapmans.

Dorey, Peter (1993) 'One step at a time: the Conservative Government's reform of industrial relations since 1979'. *Political Quarterly* (January–March), vol. 64, no. 1, pp. 24–36.

Dorfman, Gerald (1979) *Government Versus Trade Unionism in British Politics since 1968*. Basingstoke: Macmillan.

Drewry, Gavin and Butcher, Tony (1991) *The Civil Service Today* (2nd edn). Oxford: Blackwell.

Eatwell, Roger (1979) *The 1945–51 Labour Governments*. London: Batsford.

Eden, Anthony (1960) *Full Circle*. London: Cassell.

Efficency Unit (1988) *Improving Management in Government: The Next Steps*. London: HMSO.

Elliot, Larry (1994) 'Day of disaster Tories insist did not happen'. *The Guardian*, 16 September.

Field, Frank (1981) *Inequality in Britain: Freedom, Welfare and the State*. London: Fontana.

Finer, S. E. (1975) 'Adversary politics and electoral reform'. In S. E. Finer (ed.) *Adversary Politics and Electoral Reform*. London: Anthony Wigram.

Fisher, Nigel (1977) *The Tory Leaders*. London: Weidenfeld & Nicolson.

Foote, Geoffrey (1985) *The Labour Party's Political Thought*. Beckenham: Croom Helm.

Galbraith, John Kenneth (1992) *The Culture of Contentment*. Harmondsworth: Penguin.

Gamble, Andrew (1974) *The Conservative Nation*. London: Routledge & Kegan Paul.

Gamble, Andrew (1981) *Britain in Decline*. Basingstoke: Macmillan.

Gamble, Andrew (1988) *The Free Economy and the Strong State*. Basingstoke: Macmillan.

Gardner, Nick (1987) *Decade of Discontent: The Changing British Economy since 1973*. Oxford: Blackwell.

Garner, Robert (1990) 'Labour and the Policy Review: a party fit to govern?' *Talking Politics* (Autumn), vol. 3, no. 1, pp. 31–6.

George, Stephen (1990) *An Awkward Partner*. Oxford: Oxford University Press.

Gilbert, B. (1970) *British Social Policy 1914–1939*. London: Batsford.

Gilmour, Ian (1992) *Dancing with Dogma*. Hemel Hempstead: Simon & Schuster.

Goodman, Geoffrey (1985) *The Miners' Strike*. London: Pluto Press.

Gourvish, Terry (1991) 'The rise (and fall?) of state-owned enterprise'. In Terry Gourvish and Alan O'Day (eds) *Britain since 1945*. Basingstoke: Macmillan.

Greenleaf, W. H. (1983) *The British Political Tradition: Volume Two; The Ideological Heritage*. London: Routledge.

Grigg, John (1963) 'The Commons in eclipse'. *The Observer*, 10 March.

Habermas, Jurgen (1976) *Legitimation Crisis*. London: Heinemann.

Hailsham, Lord (1990) *A Sparrow's Flight*. London: Collins.

Hall, Stuart (1980) *Drifting into a Law and Order Society*. London: Cobden Trust.

Hall, Stuart et al. (1978) *Policing the Crisis: Mugging, the State, and Law and Order*. Basingstoke: Macmillan.

Harrop, Martin (1982) 'Labour-voting conservatives: policy differences between the Labour Party and Labour voters'. In Robert Worcester and Martin Harrop (eds) *Political Communications: The General Election Campaign of 1979*. London: Allen & Unwin.

Hayek, Friedrich (1944) *The Road to Serfdom*. London: Routledge & Kegan Paul.

Hayward, Jack (1974) 'National aptitudes for planning in Britain, France and Italy'. *Government and Opposition*, vol. 9, no. 4.

Hennessy, Peter (1987) 'The Attlee Governments'. In Peter Hennessy and Anthony Seldon (eds) *Ruling Performance: British Governments from Attlee to Thatcher*. Oxford: Basil Blackwell.

Hennessy, Peter (1990) *Whitehall*. London: Fontana.

Hinchingbrooke, Lord (1944) *Full Speed Ahead: Essays in Tory Reform*. London: Simpkin.

Hindess, Barry (1983) *Parliamentary Democracy and Socialist Politics*. London: Routledge & Kegan Paul.

HMSO (1988) Eighth Report from the Treasury & Civil Service Committee, 1987–88: *Civil Service Management Reform: The Next Steps* (HC 494 1–11). London.

Hoffman, John (1964) *The Conservative Party in Opposition*. London: Macgibbon & Kee.

Hogg, Quintin (1947) *The Case for Conservatism*. Harmondsworth: Penguin.

Hollis, Christopher (1960) *Has Parliament a Future?* London: Liberal Publications Department.

Holmes, Martin (1985) *The First Thatcher Government 1979–1983*. Brighton: Harvester Wheatsheaf.

Horne, Alistair (1989) *Macmillan 1957–1986*. Basingstoke: Macmillan.

Howarth, Alan (1994) 'No exit to the right'. *The Guardian*, 25 July.

Howell, David (1976) *British Social Democracy*. London: Croom Helm.

Hurd, Douglas (1979) *An End to Promises*. London: Collins.

Husbands, Christopher (1988) 'Extreme right-wing politics in Great Britain: the recent marginalisation of the National Front'. *West European Politics*, vol. 11, no. 2.

Hutber, Patrick (ed.) (1978) *What's Wrong With Britain?* London: Sphere.

Ingle, Stephen (1987) *The British Party System*. Oxford: Blackwell.

James, Robert Rhodes (1986) *Anthony Eden*. London: Weidenfeld & Nicolson.

Jenkins, Roy (1982) 'Home thoughts from abroad'. In Wayland Kennet (ed.) *The Rebirth of Britain*. London: Weidenfeld & Nicolson.

Jenkins, Peter (1970) *The Battle of Downing Street*. London: Charles Knight.

Johnson, Nevil (1980) *In Search of the Constitution*. London: Methuen.

Johnson, Paul (1980) *The Recovery of Freedom*. Oxford: Basil Blackwell.

Jones, Bernard (1993) '"Black Wednesday": the political and economic significance of Wednesday 16 September 1992'. *Talking Politics* (Summer), vol. 5, no. 3, pp. 172–4.

Jones, Russell (1987) *Wages and Employment Policy 1936–1985*. London: Allen & Unwin.

Jones, Tudor (1991) 'Labour revisionism and public ownership'. *Contemporary Record*, vol. 5, no. 3.

Jordan, Grant and Richardson, Jeremy (1982) 'The British policy style or the logic of negotiation?' In Jeremy Richardson (ed.) *Policy Styles in Western Europe*. London: George Allen & Unwin.

Joseph, Sir Keith (1975) *Reversing the Trend*. Chichester: Barry Rose.

Joseph, Sir Keith (1976) *Stranded on the Middle Ground*. London: Centre for Policy Studies.

Joseph, Sir Keith (1978) 'Proclaim the message: Keynes is dead'. In Patrick Hutber (ed.) *What's Wrong With Britain?* London: Sphere.

Judge, David (1983) 'Why reform?: Parliamentary reform since 1832; an interpretation'. In David Judge (ed.) *The Politics of Parliamentary Reform*. London: Heinemann.

Kavanagh, Dennis (1980) 'Political culture in Great Britain: the decline of the civic culture'. In Gabriel Almond and Sidney Verba (eds) *The Civic Culture Revisited*. Boston: Little, Brown & Company.

Kavanagh, Dennis (1987) *Thatcherism and British Politics*. Oxford: Oxford University Press.

Kavanagh, Dennis (1991) 'The phoney wars'. *The Guardian*, 17 December.

Kavanagh, Dennis and Morris, Peter (1989) *Consensus Politics: From Attlee to Thatcher*. Oxford: Blackwell.

Keegan, William (1984) *Mrs Thatcher's Economic Experiment*. Harmondsworth: Penguin.

Kellas, James (1975) *The Scottish Political System*. Cambridge: Cambridge University Press.

Kellas, James (1990) 'Scottish and Welsh Nationalist parties since 1945'. In Anthony Seldon (ed.) *UK Political Parties since 1945*. Hemel Hempstead: Philip Allan.

Kellner, Peter (1992) 'Time for Labour to bid goodbye to the unions'. *The*

Independent, 12 June.

Kellner, Peter and Crowther-Hunt, Lord (1980) *The Civil Servants: An Inquiry into Britain's Ruling Class*. London: Macdonald & Jane's.

Kettle, Martin (1983) 'The drift to law and order'. In Stuart Hall and Martin Jacques (eds) *The Politics of Thatcherism*. London: Lawrence & Wishart/Marxism Today.

Kilmuir, Lord (1964) *Political Adventure*. London: Weidenfeld & Nicolson.

King, Anthony (1975) 'The problem of overload'. *British Journal of Political Science*, 5.

King, Anthony (ed.) (1976) *Why Is Britain Becoming Harder to Govern?* London: BBC.

King, Anthony (1985) 'Margaret Thatcher: the style of a Prime Minister'. In Anthony King (ed.) *The British Prime Minister*. Basingstoke: Macmillan.

King, Anthony (1993) 'The Thatcher legacy'. In Anthony King *et al.* (eds) *Britain at the Polls 1992*. New Jersey: Chatham House.

Kingdom, John (1991) *Local Government and Politics in Britain*. Hemel Hempstead: Philip Allen.

Lawson, Nigel (1992) *The View From No. 11*. London: Bantam.

Layton-Henry, Zig (1980) 'Immigration'. In Zig Layton-Henry (ed.) *Conservative Party Politics*. Basingstoke: Macmillan.

Le Grand, Julian (1982) *The Strategy of Equality*. London: George Allen & Unwin.

Lindblom, Charles (1959) 'The science of muddling through'. *Public Administration Review*, 19.

Lloyd, John (1989) *A Rational Advance for the Labour Party*. London: Chatto & Windus.

Lyons, Frank (1990) 'Beyond political stalemate: new thinking on Northern Ireland'. In Stephen Savage and Lynton Robins (eds) *Public Policy under Thatcher*. Basingstoke: Macmillan.

Macmillan, Harold (1966) *Winds of Change*. London: Macmillan.

Macmillan, Harold (1972) *Pointing the Way*. London: Macmillan.

Macmillan, Harold (1973) *At the End of the Day*. London: Macmillan.

Macshane, Denis (1993) 'State of the unions'. *New Statesman & Society* (September).

Marsh, Alan (1977) *Protest and Political Consciousness*. London: Sage.

Marsh, David (1992) *The New Politics of British Trade Unionism*. Basingstoke: Macmillan.

Marsh, David & Rhodes, R. A. W. (1992) 'The implementation gap: explaining policy change and continuity'. In David Marsh and R. A. W. Rhodes (eds) *Implementing Thatcherite Policies: Audit of an Era*. Buckingham: Open University Press.

Maude, Angus (1969) *The Common Problem: A Policy for the Future*. London: Conservative Political Centre.

Maudling, Reginald (1978) *Memoirs*. London: André Deutsch.

McKenzie, Robert and Silver, A. (1968) *Angels in Marble*. London: Heinemann.

Middlemas, Keith (1979) *Politics in Industrial Society*. London: André Deutsch.

Miliband, Ralph (1972) *Parliamentary Socialism*. London: Merlin Press.

Miliband, Ralph (1973) *The State in Capitalist Society*. London: Quartet.

Miliband, Ralph (1982) *Capitalist Democracy in Britain*. Oxford: Oxford University Press.

Monks, John (1993) 'A change of mood is in the air'. *New Statesman & Society Guide to the Trade Unions and the Labour Movement 1994* (September).

Moran, Michael (1977) *The Politics of Industrial Relations*. Basingstoke: Macmillan.

Moran, Michael (1985) *Politics and Society in Britain*. Basingstoke: Macmillan.

Morgan, Kenneth O. (1984) *Labour in Power 1945–51*. Oxford: Oxford University Press.

Moss, Robert (1977) *The Collapse of Democracy*. London: Sphere.

Nairn, Tom (1977) *The Break-Up of Britain*. London: Verso.

Nicoll, William and Salmon, Trevor (1990) *Understanding the European Communities*. Hemel Hempstead: Philip Allan.

Norton, Philip (1975) *Dissension in the House of Commons 1945–74*. Basingstoke: Macmillan.

Norton, Philip (1978) *Conservative Dissidents*. London: Temple Smith.

Norton, Philip (1981) *The Commons in Perspective*. Oxford: Martin Robertson.

Norton, Philip (1984) *The British Polity*. London: Longman.

Norton, Philip (1990) 'The Lady's not for turning: but what about the rest? Margaret Thatcher and the Conservative Party 1979–89'. *Parliamentary Affairs*, vol. 43, no. 1, pp. 41–58.

Orwell, George (1982) *The Lion and the Unicorn*. Harmondsworth: Penguin.

Owen, David (1981) *Face the Future*. Oxford: Oxford University Press.

Owen, David (1991) *Time to Declare*. London: Michael Joseph.

Panitch, Leo (1986) *Working Class Politics in Crisis*. London: Verso.

Pearce, Malcolm and Stewart, Geoffrey (1992) *British Political History 1867–1990*. London: Routledge.

Pelling, Henry (1961) *A Short History of the Labour Party*. Basingstoke: Macmillan.

Pelling, Henry (1963) *A History of British Trade Unionism*. Harmondsworth: Penguin.

Pelling, Henry (1983) 'The Labour Party of 1945–51: the determinants of policy'. In Michael Bentley and John Stevenson (eds) *High and Low Politics in Modern Britain*. Oxford: Clarendon Press.

Pimlott, Ben (1988) 'The myth of consensus'. In Lesley M. Smith (ed.) *The Making of Britain: Echoes of Greatness*. Basingstoke: Macmillan.

Ponting, Clive (1989) *Breach of Promise: Labour in Power 1964–70*. London: Hamish Hamilton.

Powell, Enoch (1968) *Conference on Economic Policy for the 1970s*. London: Monday Club.

Prior, Jim (1986) *A Balance of Power*. London: Hamish Hamilton.

Pulzer, Peter (1967) *Political Representation and Elections in Britain*. London: George Allen & Unwin.

Pyper, Robert (1984) 'The Foreign Office resignations: individual ministerial responsibility revived?' In Lynton Robins (ed.) *Updating British Politics*. London: The Politics Association.

Raison, Timothy (1965) *Conflict and Conservatism*. London: Conservative Political Centre.

Raison, Timothy (1979) *Parliament and Power*. Oxford: Blackwell.

Ramsden, John (1980) *The Making of Conservative Party Policy*. London: Longman.

Richards, Peter G. (1970) *Parliament and Conscience*. London: George Allen & Unwin.

Richardson, Jeremy (1993) 'Interest group behaviour in Britain: continuity and change'. In Jeremy Richardson (ed.) *Pressure Groups*. Oxford: Oxford University Press.

Richardson, Jeremy (1994) 'The politics and practice of privatisation in Britain'. In Vincent Wright (ed.) *Privatization in Western Europe*. London: Pinter.

Riddell, Peter (1983) *Mrs Thatcher's Economic Experiment*. Harmondsworth: Penguin.

Riddell, Peter (1993) 'Consensus, what consensus?' *The Times*, 12 April.

Rogaly, Joe (1976) *Parliament for the People*. London: Temple Smith.

Rose, Richard (1984) *Do Parties Make a Difference?* (2nd edn). Basingstoke: Macmillan.

Runciman, Walter (1966) *Relative Deprivation and Social Justice*. Harmondsworth: Penguin.

Russel, Trevor (1978) *The Tory Party*. Harmondsworth: Penguin.

Ryle, Michael (1965) 'Committees of the House of Commons'. *Political Quarterly*, 36.

Sanders, David (1993) 'Why the Conservative Party won – again'. In Anthony King *et al.* (eds) *Britain at the Polls 1992*. New Jersey: Chatham House.

Saville, John (1988) *The Labour Movement in Britain*. London: Faber & Faber.

Sawyer, Tom (1992) 'Roots and resources'. *Fabian Review* (July).

Sedgemore, Brian (1980) *The Secret Constitution*. London: Hodder & Stoughton.

Seldon, Anthony (1981) *Churchill's Indian Summer*. London: Hodder & Stoughton.

Seldon, Anthony (1994) 'The rise and fall (and rise again?) of the post-War consensus'. In Bill Jones *et al.* (eds) *Politics UK* (2nd edn). Hemel Hempstead: Harvester Wheatsheaf.

Seyd, Patrick (1987) *The Rise and Fall of the Labour Left*. Basingstoke: Macmillan.

Shell, Donald (1992) *The House of Lords* (2nd edn). Hemel Hempstead: Harvester Wheatsheaf.

Smith, Geoffrey and Polsby, Nelson (1981) *British Government and its Discontents*. New York: Basic Books.

Smith, Martin (1992a) 'The Labour Party in Opposition'. In Martin Smith and Joanna Speer (eds) *The Changing Labour Party*. London: Routledge.

Smith, Martin (1992b) 'A return to revisionism: the Labour Party Policy Review'. In Martin Smith and Joanna Speer (eds) *The Changing Labour Party*. London: Routledge.

Smith, Trevor (1986) 'The British Constitution: unwritten and unravelled'. In Jack Hayward and Philip Norton (eds) *The Political Science of British Politics*. Hemel Hempstead: Wheatsheaf.

Stephenson, Hugh (1982) *Claret and Chips*. London: Michael Joseph.

Stevenson, John (1993) *Third Party Politics since 1945*. Oxford: Blackwell.

Stewart, Michael (1977) *The Jekyll and Hyde Years*. London: J. M. Dent.

Stoker, Gerry (1991) *The Politics of Local Government* (2nd edn). Basingstoke: Macmillan.

Study of Parliament Group (1965) *Reforming the Commons*. London: PEP.

Taylor, Andrew J. (1987) *The Trade Unions and the Labour Party*. London: Croom Helm.

Taylor, Robert (1993) *The Trade Union Question in British Politics*. Oxford: Blackwell.

Tebbit, Norman (1988) *Upwardly Mobile*. London: Weidenfeld & Nicolson.

The Treasury (1990) *Privatisations in the United Kingdom: Background Briefing*. London: HM Treasury.

TUC (1978) *Annual Report*.

Urry, John and Wakeford, John (eds) (1973) *Power in Britain*. London: Heinemann.

Walker, Martin (1977) *The National Front*. London: Fontana/Collins.

Walkland, Stuart (1984) 'Economic planning and dysfunctional politics in Britain 1945–1983'. In Andrew Gamble and Stuart Walkland *The British Party System and and Economic Policy 1945–1983*. Oxford: Clarendon Press.

Walsh, Tim and Tindale, Stephen (1992) 'Time for divorce'. *Fabian Review* (July).

Werth, Alexander (1965) *De Gaulle: A Political Biography.* Harmondsworth: Penguin.

Westergaard, John (1983) 'Income, wealth and the welfare state'. In David Coates and Gordon Johnston (eds) *Socialist Arguments.* Oxford: Martin Robertson.

Westergaard, John and Resler, Henrietta (1976) *Class in a Capitalist Society.* Harmondsworth: Pelican.

Whitelaw, William (1989) *The Whitelaw Memoirs.* London: Aurum Press.

Wickham-Jones, Mark and Shell, Donald (1991) 'What went wrong? The fall of Mrs Thatcher'. *Contemporary Record* (Autumn).

Williams, F. (1952) *Ernest Bevin.* Publisher unknown.

Williams, Shirley (1982) 'On modernising Britain'. In Wayland Kennet (ed.) *The Rebirth of Britain.* London: Weidenfeld & Nicolson.

Wilson, Harold (1971) *The Labour Government 1964–1970.* London: Weidenfeld & Nicolson.

Woolton, Lord (1959) *Memoirs.* London: Cassell.

Worsthorne, Peregrine (1978) 'Too much freedom'. In Maurice Cowling (ed.) *Conservative Essays.* London: Cassell.

Wright, Esmond (1970) 'Parliament and Government'. In Michael Ivens and Clive Bradley (eds) *Which Way?* London: Michael Joseph.

Index